Semantic Web

Edited by

Gang Wu

Semantic Web

Edited by Gang Wu

Republished by InTech

Janeza Trdine 9, 51000 Rijeka, Croatia

Technical Editor Sonja Mujacic

Cover Designer Dino Smrekar

Additional hard copies can be obtained from orders@intechopen.com

Semantic Web,
Edited by Gang Wu
p. cm.
ISBN 978-953-7619-54-1

For EU product safety concerns:
IN TECH d.o.o., Prolaz Marije Krucifikse Kozulić 3, 51000 Rijeka, Croatia,
info@intechopen.com or visit our website at intechopen.com.

Preface

Having lived with the World Wide Web for twenty years, surfing the Web becomes a way of our life that cannot be separated. From latest news, photos sharing, social activities, to research collaborations, and even commercial activities and government affairs, almost all kinds of information are available and processible via the Web. When people are appreciating the great invention, the father of the Web, Sir Tim Berners-Lee, has started the plan of next generation of the Web, the Semantic Web.

Unlike the Web that originally designed for reading by people, the Semantic Web aims at a more intelligent Web severing machines as well as people. The idea behind it is simple: machines can automatically process or "understand" the information, if explicit meanings are given to it. In this way, it facilitates the sharing and reuse of data across applications, enterprises, and communities. Although, great efforts from industries and researchers have been made, there are still fundamental problems confront the community of the Semantic Web, such as: the availability of semantic content, the scalability of semantic search and reasoning, and the mapping of heterogeneous ontologies. At the same time, the community needs to find more appropriate application domains and scenarios to demonstrate the abilities of the Semantic Web. This book is an effort to showcase the latest achievements in Semantic Web research and application.

The book comprises 16 chapters covering two kinds of contributions from researchers and industrial partners.

Contributions related to the Semantic Web technology itself are organised into the first seven chapters where readers can find topics including: probabilistic ontology modelling; distributed registry-directory infrastructure for the Semantic Web; (arbitrary domains, multilingual) semantic content generation based on NLP technologies; ontology-driven semantic information extraction; survey of mainstream data description, querying, and semantic service infrastructures; index structure for Semantic Web data management; and automatic semantic data integration based on multi-agent ontology mapping framework.

From Chapter 8 to Chapter 15, contributions related to the following Semantic Web application domains are presented: behavioural coordination of heterogeneous systems; context-aware software engineering environment; viewpoint representation and reasoning in e-learning and cognitive process; knowledge management for EHR (Electronic Healthcare Records); quality management and validation of e-business process models; Semantic Web service for e-government; content-aware Web Service composition; and modelling linguistical metaphor relationship. In the last chapter, authors try to solve the problem of software source code clones by borrowing methodologies from the research of ontology mapping.

According to the organisation of the book, the intended readers may come from two groups, i.e. those whose interests include Semantic Web and want to catch on the state-of-the-art research progress in this field; and those who urgently need or just intend to seek the help from the Semantic Web. In this sense, readers are not limited to the computer science. Everyone is welcome to find their possible intersection of the Semantic Web.

Finally, we would like to thank all authors of the chapters for their great work, and hope the readers will enjoy its reading and be harvested in the field of the Semantic Web.

Editor

Gang Wu

Contents

UnBBayes: Modeling Uncertainty for Plausible Reasoning in the Semantic Web

Rommel Carvalho[1], Kathryn Laskey[1], Paulo Costa[1], Marcelo Ladeira[2], Laécio Santos[2] and Shou Matsumoto[2]
[1]*George Mason University*
USA
[2]*University of Brasilia*
Brazil

1. Introduction

The Semantic Web (SW), like the document web that preceded it, is based on radical notions of information sharing. These ideas [Allemang & Hendler, 2008] include: (*i*) the Anyone can say Anything about Any topic (AAA) slogan; (*ii*) the open world assumption, in which we assume there is always more information that could be known, and (*iii*) nonunique naming, which appreciates the reality that different speakers on the Web might use different names to define the same entity. In a fundamental departure from assumptions of traditional information systems architectures, the Semantic Web is intended to provide an environment in which information sharing can thrive and a network effect of knowledge synergy is possible. But this style of information gathering can generate a chaotic landscape rife with confusion, disagreement and conflict.

We call an environment characterized by the above assumptions a Radical Information Sharing (RIS) environment. The challenge facing SW architects is therefore to avoid the natural chaos to which RIS environments are prone, and move to a state characterized by information sharing, cooperation and collaboration. According to [Allemang & Hendler, 2008], one solution to this challenge lies in modeling. Modeling is the process of organizing information for community use. Modeling supports information sharing in three ways: It provides a framework for human communication, it provides a means for explaining conclusions, and it provides a structure for managing varying viewpoints.

There is an immense variety of modeling approaches. In this chapter we will go over a few of these approaches, showing how they can be used and their main limitations related to achieving the full potential of the Semantic Web.

First we will show how to apply Unified Modeling Language (UML) [Rumbaugh et al., 1998] and Entity/Relationship (ER) [Chen, 1976] diagrams for modeling. Then we will present Knowledge Representation and Reasoning (KR&R) [Brachman & Levesque, 2004] and describe how KR&R overcomes some of the limitations of UML and ER. Finally, we present Ontology and the Semantic Web [Berners-Lee, 1999] and discuss how it differs from and moves beyond the previous approaches.

In the past few years, as the Semantic Web community has developed standards and more complex use cases, the need for principled approaches for representing and reasoning under uncertainty has received increasing appreciation. As a consequence, the World Wide Web Consortium (W3C) created the Uncertainty Reasoning for the World Wide Web Incubator Group (URW3-XG) in 2007 to better define the challenge of reasoning with and representing uncertain information available through the World Wide Web and related WWW technologies. The work of the URW3-XG provided an important beginning for characterizing the range of uncertainty that affects reasoning on the scale of the World Wide Web, and the issues to be considered in designing a standard representation of that uncertainty. However, the work to date likely falls short of what would be needed to charter an effort to develop that representation. A possible representation for uncertainty reasoning in the semantic web is Probabilistic OWL (PR-OWL), an extension of the OWL language used for building probabilistic ontologies based on Multi-Entity Bayesian Networks (MEBN).

We will describe PR-OWL and MEBN and show how they contribute to the Semantic Web. Once we have an understanding of the role each modeling approach plays in the Semantic Web we will discuss UnBBayes, an open source, Java-based application based on the PR-OWL/MEBN framework. UnBBayes provides a natural, modeler friendly interface for building probabilistic ontologies and performing reasoning.

This Chapter has three main objectives. First, as described above, we highlight some differences between well-known and used modeling approaches and new ones involving the Semantic Web. Second, we present the main modules of UnBBayes and how to use them to build a probabilistic ontology. Finally, our third objective is to illustrate our approach to model a probabilistic ontology by going through a use case from the Brazilian General Comptroller Office (CGU). This probabilistic ontology was developed using UnBBayes. The objective of constructing the ontology is to support fusion of information to detect possible frauds in procurements involving Federal money.

CGU is the Brazilian central body of the internal control system of the federal executive branch. It has, among its responsibilities, the task of inspecting and auditing the Brazilian Government projects and programs with respect to their legality, results, efficacy and efficiency. In Brazil, all contracts with the private sector must be in accordance with the Law N° 8,666/93, also known as the national Procurement Law.

According to [Meirelles, 1996] procurement is the administrative procedure by which the Public Administration selects the most advantageous proposal for a contract in its interest. From the former definition, the conclusion is that the public interest must always be the objective of the procedure. In terms of purchasing with the use of public money, this means that not only must the winner of the procurement process be the best supplier in terms of the price of the good or service supplied, but also in terms of other objectives of the procurement process.

Corruption can happen in many ways in Public Procurements [Mueller, 1998]. The Public Agent may favor a specific supplier that he happens to know. He may receive, from the bidder, a financial compensation for awarding a contract to his firm. Bidders may collude as to set the results of the procurement. The whole process is susceptible to many forms of corruption, from within and outside the public administration.

The government purchases large quantities of goods and services. It is also the sole purchaser for some goods, such as hydraulic turbines for large damns. The government spends large quantities of money in the market and is a guaranteed payer. Hence, the many firms have a strong interest in negotiating with the public administration. There is a temptation for many suppliers to cheat in the procurement process to find means of being awarded a lucrative government contract.

The Brazilian Procurement Law has as one of its main objectives the curbing of corruption in public purchasing and contracting. Concern over corruption is evident in Brazil's daily press. There are frequent accusations of public administrators who did not abide by the procurement rules, and are accused of favoring a certain supplier or worse, receiving a payment for their favor.

When writing the law, legislators included many articles that established penalties for firms or/and public legislators caught in corruption activities. There are two types of penalties stated in Law N° 8,666/93 dealing with this subject. They are administrative actions and penal actions.

Since enforcing the law is difficult [Mueller, 1998], legislators will have to find another manner to prevent corruption in public procurement. The question is one of preventing corruption practices, against one of punishing ones that have already happened.

This is exactly what we are modeling in the use case presented in this Chapter. We try to prevent and detect corruption by analyzing data from the various databases collected by different agencies. It is worth noting that this is still a work in progress. Its use in this Chapter is intended to show the benefits of dealing with uncertainty in the Semantic Web as well as to show how to model this kind of problem. It is not our intention to claim this model as a solution to corruption in Brazilian public procurements.

This Chapter is structured as follows. Section 2 introduces UML and ER. Section 3 presents KR&R and describes how it overcomes some of the limitations of UML and ER. Section 4 describes Ontology and the Semantic Web, and discusses how they differ from the modeling approaches presented in the previous sections. Section 5 summarizes PR-OWL and MEBN as a way to model uncertainty in the Semantic Web. Finally, Section 6 describes UnBBayes main modules by going through a use case being developed at CGU for identifying and preventing fraud in public procurements.

2. UML and ER

Before analyzing what we can model in UML and ER, we will define some terms that will be used from now on:

- **Classes** represent concepts, which are understood in a broad sense. For instance, in the procurement domain, the *Goal* class represents a specific objective that needs to be achieved.
- **Instances** are used to represent elements or individuals. For instance, *build a bridge* and *buy 500 chairs* might be specific individuals of the class *Goal*.
- **Relations** represent a type of association between concepts of the domain. Although it is possible to represent a relation of higher arity, the most common is a binary relation, where the first argument is known as the domain of the relation, and the second argument is the range. For instance, classes are usually organized in taxonomies through which inheritance mechanisms can be applied. The binary relation *subclassOf* is used to construct this taxonomy (e.g.

PublicServant – someone who works for the Government – might be modeled as a subclass of *Person*).

- **Functions** are a special case of relations in which the *n-th* element of the relation is unique for the *n-l* preceding elements. For instance, a function *EvaluateEnterprise* applies a set of score rules to compute the final score an enterprise receives when participating in a specific procurement.
- **Formal axioms** [Gómez-Pérez et al., 2005] serve to model sentences that are always true. They are normally used to represent knowledge that cannot be formally defined by the other components. In addition, formal axioms are used to verify the consistency of the model. They are also very useful for inferring new knowledge.

Unified Modeling Language (UML) [Rumbaugh et al., 1998] and Entity/Relationship (ER) [Chen, 1976] diagrams are often used to organize information for community use. Some of the reasons to use these tools are: (*i*) UML and ER are easy to understand and use even for people outside the Artificial Intelligence (AI) community; (*ii*) there are standard graphical representations for UML and ER diagrams; and (*iii*) many CASE tools are available to support development of UML and ER representations.

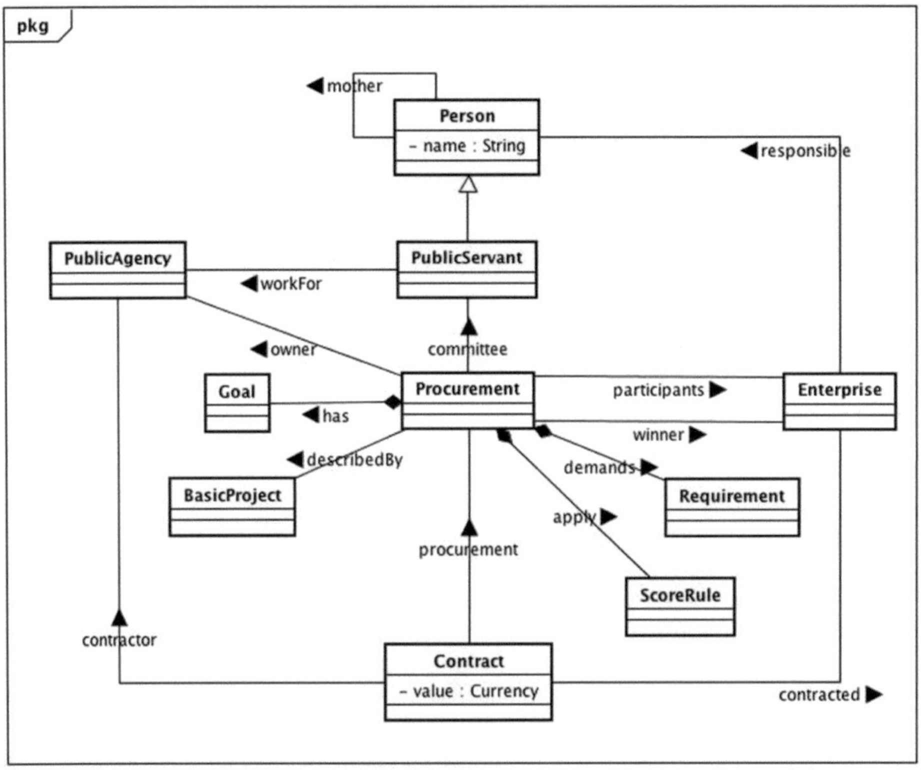

Fig. 1. A class diagram for the procurement domain

UML models can be enriched by adding Object Constraint Language (OCL) [OMG, 1997; Warner & Kleppe, 1998] expressions. OCL is a declarative language for describing rules that

apply to UML by providing expressions that do not have the ambiguities of natural language, and avoid the inherent difficulty of using complex mathematics.
In UML, classes are represented with rectangles divided into three parts: the name (top), the attributes (middle), and the operations (bottom). Since operations are not used in the context of the Semantic Web [Gómez-Pérez et al., 2005], we will not deal with them here. The attribute types, possible attribute values, and default values are included in their description. For instance, in Figure 1 *Person* is a class with attributes *name* and *ID* of types *String* and *int*[1] respectively.
Class instances are represented as rectangles divided into two parts. The first part is the name of the instance, followed by ":" and the name of the class it represents. The second part is the attributes of the instance and their respective values. For example, Figure 2 shows four instances, *winner1, participant2, participant3,* and *participant4,* of the class *Enterprise.*
Concept taxonomies are created through generalization relationships between classes. These are shown on a UML diagram by a solid line extending from the more specific to the more generic class, and ending with a large hollow triangle. In Figure 1, *Person* is a generalization of *PublicServant,* thus it inherits its attributes *name* and *ID.*
Binary relations are expressed as associations (solid arrows) between classes. In Figure 1 a *PublicServant* works for a *PublicAgency.* However, higher arity relations cannot be represented directly in UML, though we can represent them by creating a class. This class is associated with other classes that represent the relation arguments, as shown in the ternary relation *Contract* in Figure 1.

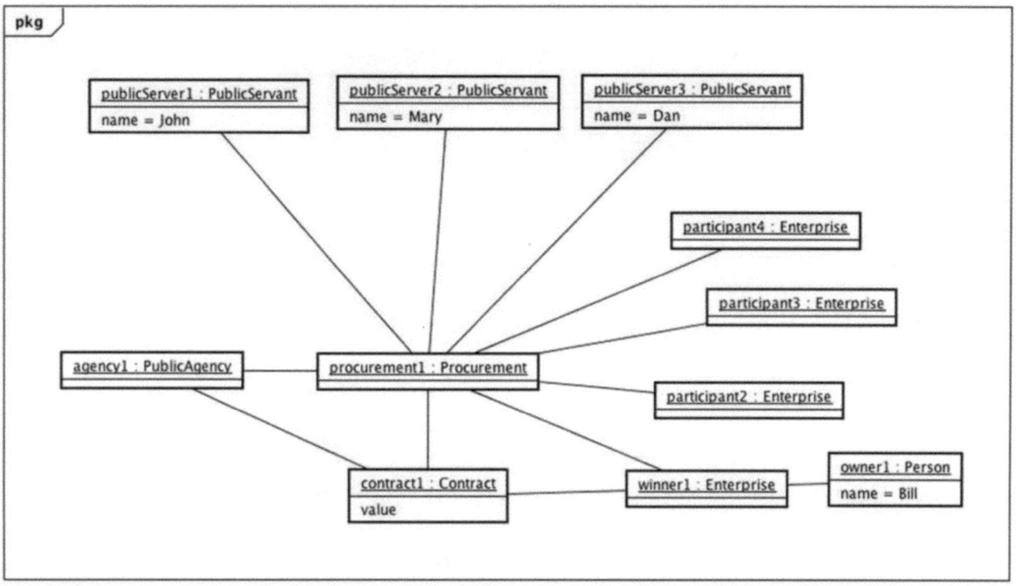

Fig. 2. A class diagram with instances of classes from the procurement domain

[1] In UML it is common to use uppercase for classes (e.g., String) and lowercase for primitive types (e.g., int).

More complex modeling such as cardinalities of the attributes, disjoint and exhaustive knowledge, and formal axioms can be represented in UML only with the use of OCL. However, according to [Gómez-Pérez et al., 2005], there is no standard support for this language in common CASE tools. Because of this, and because UML models lack formal semantics, expressions in OCL cannot be evaluated by many CASE tools, and cannot be shared among developers.

In ER, with the common extension of generalization relationships between entities, it is possible to represent classes through the use of ER-entities. Furthermore, classes can be organized in taxonomies with the generalization relationship between ER-entities. For example, Figure 3 shows the class *PublicServant,* which is a subclass of the class *Person.*

It is also possible to represent attributes and their types through ER-attributes. In Figure 3 the class *Person* has the attributes *name* and *ID* with types *VARCHAR(255)* and *INTEGER*[2] respectively.

Ad hoc relations can be represented through ER-relations between ER-entities. These relations can have any arity and can have specified cardinalities. Figure 3 presents several relations. One of these is *Apply,* which relates one or more *ScoreRule* to just one *Procurement.* Although a ternary relation can be easily represented, none were included in Figure 3for reasons of clarity.

Instances can be created through the use of the *insert* sentence from the Structured Query Language (SQL), which essentially becomes a filled row in its respective table.

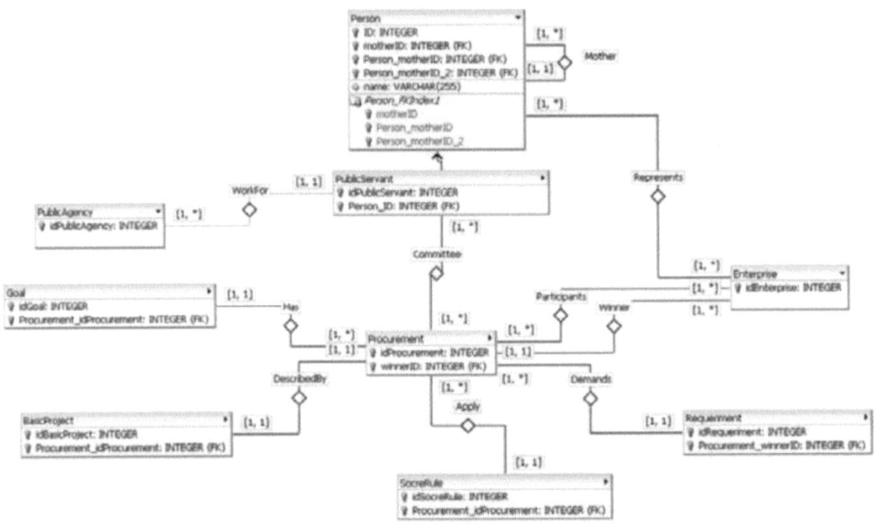

Fig. 3. An extended entity-relationship diagram for the procurement domain

According to [Gómez-Pérez et al., 2005], representing formal axioms in ER requires either extending the language, or using complementary notations, such as first-order logic or production rules.

---

[2] In E/R, instead of using String and int, the types used are VARCHAR(size) and INTEGER, respectively.

3. Knowledge Representation and Reasoning

We have seen in Section 2 that UML and ER are able to represent classes, attributes, relations, and instances. However, they fall short when dealing with formal axioms. Knowledge representation systems, on the other hand, can naturally represent formal axioms. Furthermore, there are standard and readily available formal systems for reasoning with axioms.

Knowledge Representation [Levesque & Lakemeyer, 2000] is the field of study within AI concerned with using formal symbols to represent a collection of propositions believed by some putative agent. It is not necessary that there be symbols to represent each of the propositions believed by the agent. There may very well be an infinite number of propositions believed, only a finite number of which are ever represented. It will be the role of reasoning to bridge the gap between what is represented and the full set of propositions believed. For our purposes, what makes a system knowledge-based is the presence of a Knowledge Base (KB): a collection of symbolic structures representing what the agent believes and reasons with during the operation of the system.

To see the benefits of using KR&R, we will augment the models presented in Section 2 by introducing axioms related to the domain. Based on Law Nº 8,666/93, a member of a procurement committee must not be related to the enterprises that are participating in the procurement. For the sake of simplicity we will only deal with the relation that a public servant cannot be a brother, son/daughter, or mother of someone who is responsible for that enterprise. Consider the following simple representation:

```
01.∀x PublicServant(x) => Person(x)
02.∀x,y,z Mother(x,y)^Mother(z,y) => Sibling(x,z)
03.∀x,y Mother(x,y) => Related(x,y)
04.∀x,y Sibling(x,y) => Related(x,y)
05.∀x,y,z,r Committee(x,y)^Participant(z,y)^Responsible(r,z)
            => ¬Related(x,r)
06.PublicServant(John)
07.PublicServant(Mary)
08.PublicServer(Dan)
09.Person(Bill)
10.Person(Rebecca)
11.Mother(John,Rebecca)
12.Mother(Bill,Rebecca)
13.Procurement(Procurement1)
14.Committee(John,Procurement1)
15.Committee(Mary,Procurement1)
16.Committee(Dan,Procurement1)
17.Enterprise(Winner1)
18.Responsible(Bill,Winner1)
19.Participant(Winner1,Procurement1)
...
```

To be concise, we will not define the entire model. We assume the definitions are set up to reproduce the models from Section 2. Nevertheless, with the information presented above, we can identify an inconsistency. By combining lines 11, 12, 02, and 04, we can infer

Related(John,Bill). However, if we combine lines 14, 19, 18, and 05, we can infer that *Related(John,Bill)*. Therefore, we have encountered an inconsistency in our KB. Fortunately, this representation allows us to debug, and to discover that this procurement is actually violating the law. We can then fix the inconsistency by modifying Rule 05 to say that if a member of a procurement committee is related to the enterprises that are participating in the procurement, then there is a violation of the law.

One could argue that this restriction can be easily implemented by adding an operation *isCommitteeRelatedToParticipants()* to the class *Procurement* from our UML model in Section 2, for instance. This operation would return true if there is a relation, as defined above, between one of the members of the committee and one of the responsible persons of the enterprises that participates in the procurement. However, UML lacks a formal way to define such an operation in detail, leaving its implementation open to the implementer. This has at least two main disadvantages. First, every system that uses this model has to implement its own interpretation of the operation. In addition to creating duplication of effort, this could easily lead to differing interpretations and inconsistent implementations. Second, if for some reason the rule changes (e.g., we realize we need to include father in our relation), then every interpretation of the model, i.e. every system that uses this model, would have to change its implementation, instead of just changing the model as we would do in a knowledge-based system.

This simple example illustrates several advantages of using KR&R in modeling.

From a system design point of view, the knowledge-based approach seems to have a number of desirable features [Levesque & Lakemeyer, 2000; Brachman & Levesque, 2004]:

- We can add new tasks and easily make them depend on previous knowledge.
- We can extend the existing behavior by adding new beliefs.
- We can debug faulty behavior by locating erroneous beliefs of the system.
- We can concisely explain and justify the behavior of the system.

To see the motivation behind reasoning with a knowledge-based system, it suffices to observe that we would like action to depend on what the system believes about the world, as opposed to just what the system has explicitly represented. We could easily see that in the example given above where the information inferred by the system was crucial in finding an infringement of the law.

In fact, the inference process described above is entailment [Levesque & Lakemeyer, 2000; Brachman & Levesque, 2004]. We say that the propositions represented by a set of sentences S entail the proposition represented by a sentence p when the truth of p is implicit in the truth of the sentences in S. In other words, entailment means that if the world is such that every element of S comes out true, then p does as well. That is exactly what makes logic relevant to knowledge representation and reasoning, since logic is the study of entailment relations - languages, truth conditions, and rules of inference.

A knowledge-based system can be seen as a system that performs some problem-solving activity such as verifying whether there is a member of the committee who is related to one of the responsible persons of an enterprise that participates in a specific procurement. It does so intelligently by appealing at various points to what it knows: Is a member mother of a responsible person of a participant enterprise? Does a member have the same mother as a responsible person of a participant enterprise? The mechanism used by the system to answer such questions involves reasoning from a stored KB of facts about the world. It makes sense in this scenario to separate the management of the KB from the rest of the system. The data structures within a KB and the reasoning algorithms used are not really of concern to the problem-solving system.

It is the role of a knowledge representation system [Levesque & Lakemeyer, 2000; Brachman & Levesque, 2004] to manage the KB within a larger knowledge-based system. Its job is to make various sorts of information about the world available to the rest of the system based on the information it has obtained, perhaps from other parts of the system, and by using whatever reasoning it can perform. Therefore, the job of the KR system is smaller than that of a full knowledge-based problem solver, but larger than that of a database management system, which would merely retrieve the contents of the KB.

4. Ontology and the Semantic Web

According to [Berners-Lee, 1999] the Semantic Web is a web of data that can be processed directly or indirectly by machines. This technology will drive us to a new phase where the arduous and manual task of identifying, accessing and utilizing information was successfully assigned to computers, allowing human beings to change their focus from data driven to knowledge driven activities.

The W3C [Heflin, 2004] states that ontologies are envisioned as the technology providing the cement for building the SW. Ontology was taken from Philosophy, where it means a systematic explanation of being. It contains a common set of terms for describing and representing a domain in a way that allows automated tools to use stored data in a wiser, context-aware fashion, intelligent software agents to a afford better knowledge management, and many other possibilities brought by a standardized, more intensive use of metadata. [Studer et al., 1998] defines ontology as:

> **Definition 1.** *An ontology is a formal, explicit specification of a shared conceptualization. Conceptualization refers to an abstract model of some phenomenon in the world by having identified the relevant concepts of that phenomenon. Explicit means that the type of concepts used, and the constraints on their use are explicitly defined. Formal refers to the fact that the ontology should be machine-readable. Shared reflects the notion that an ontology captures consensual knowledge, that is, it is not private of some individual, but accepted by a group.*

Since ontologies are widely used for different purposes and in different communities, [Uschold & Jasper, 1999] provided a new definition of the word ontology to popularize it in other disciplines:

> **Definition 2.** *An ontology may take a variety of forms, but it will necessarily include a vocabulary of terms and some specification of their meaning. This includes definitions and an indication of how concepts are inter-related which collectively impose a structure on the domain and constrain the possible interpretation of terms.*

The ontology community distinguishes [Gómez-Pérez et al., 2005] ontologies that are mainly taxonomies from ontologies that model the domain in a deeper way and provide more restrictions on domain semantics. The community calls them lightweight and heavyweight ontologies respectively. On the one hand, lightweight ontologies include concepts, concept

taxonomies, relationships between concepts, and properties that describe concepts. On the other hand, heavyweight ontologies add axioms and constraints to lightweight ontologies. Axioms and constraints clarify the intended meaning of the terms gathered on the ontology.
How do Ontology and the SW differ from what we have seen that UML, ER, and knowledge-based KR&R systems can model? Well, as seen before, the SW is designed for RIS environments, which are characterized by the AAA slogan, the open world assumption, and nonunique naming. But this style of information gathering can create a chaotic landscape rife with confusion, disagreement and conflict. UML, ER, and knowledge-based KR&R systems were developed under a more constrained paradigm for information sharing, and lack some important features needed to contain the chaos to which RIS environments are prone. A number of SW modeling languages have been developed expressly for the RIS environments. These languages differ in their capabilities and their level of expressivity, but all incorporate features necessary to foster cooperative and collaborative information sharing in RIS environments.
It is easy to see that our domain of fraud detection/prevention is a RIS environment. The data CGU has available does not come only from its audits and inspections. In fact, much complementary information can be retrieved from other Federal Agencies, including Federal Revenue Agency, Federal Police, and others. Imagine we have information about the enterprise that won the procurement, and we want to know information about its owners, such as their personal data and annual income. This type of information is not available at CGU's Data Base (DB), but must be retrieved from the Federal Revenue Agency's DB. Once the information about the owners is available, it might be useful to check their criminal history. For that (see Figure 4), information from the Federal Police must be used. In this example, we have different sources saying different things about the same person: thus, the AAA slogan applies. Moreover, there might be other Agencies with crucial information related to our person of interest; in other words, we are operating in an open world. Finally, to make this sharing and integration process possible, we have to make sure we are talking about the same person, who may (especially in case of fraud) be known by different names in different contexts.

Fig. 4. Retrieving information through the SW for the procurement domain

According to [Allemang & Hendler, 2008] Resource Description Framework (RDF) is the basic framework on which the rest of the SW is based. RDF is a Web language, and as such, it addresses the distribution of information from multiple sources, supporting the AAA slogan, by allowing any data source to refer to resources in any namespace. Even a single triple can refer to resources in multiple namespaces. Moreover, it also addresses the nonunique naming by borrowing a standard solution from the infrastructure of the Web itself: URI. Finally, RDF gives up in compactness what it gains in flexibility. Every relationship between any two data elements is explicitly represented, allowing for a very simple model of merging data. There is no need to arrange the columns of tables so that they "match up" or to worry about data "missing" from a particular column. A relationship (expressed in a familiar form of subject/predicate/object) is either present or it is not. Merging data is thus reduced to a simple matter of considering all such statements from all sources, together in a single place. Therefore, as a data model, RDF provides a clear specification of what has to happen to merge information from multiple sources, supporting the open world assumption.

5. Uncertainty in the Semantic Web

Consider our example from Section 3, in which we stipulate that a member of the procurement must not be related to a person responsible for an enterprise that is participating in the same procurement. Current SW deterministic reasoning algorithms will either consider this relation to be true, false, or unknown, with no way of expressing gradations of plausibility.

This is acceptable in situations where complete information is available. However, in open world environments such as the Web, partial (not complete) or approximate (not exact)

information is more the rule than the exception. For example, we may not have the information from lines 11 and 12 from Section 3 stating that John and Bill have the same mother, Rebecca. However, we do have information about John and Bill stating that they have a common last name and live at the same address. Although we are uncertain about whether or how they are related, there is evidence suggesting they are. It is important to consider that information when reasoning about possible violations of procurement regulations.

Although the above and similar examples imply the need for principled representation and reasoning with uncertainty within the SW, current SW applications (including current automated reasoning methods) are primarily based on classical logic. This includes OWL, the W3C standard web ontology language, which has its logical basis in classical description logic, and therefore lacks built-in support for uncertainty. This is a major shortcoming for a technology intended to operate in RIS environments. The W3C responded to this limitation by initiating the Uncertainty Reasoning for the World Wide Web Incubator group (URW3-XG), created in 2007 and concluded a year later. The group's mission was to better define the challenge of representing and reasoning with uncertain information within the World Wide Web and its related technologies. The use of probabilistic reasoning enables information systems to derive benefit from uncertain, incomplete information, instead of being restricted to complete knowledge alone. This seems to be a promising prospect for the SW.

Uncertainty is especially important to applications such as corruption prevention, in which perpetrators seek to conceal illicit intentions and activities. To address the SW lack of support to uncertainty, [Costa, 2005] proposed a Bayesian framework for probabilistic ontologies. Probabilistic ontologies have the expressiveness required for SW applications, and yet provide a principled logical basis for representing and reasoning under uncertainty. The probabilistic ontology language PR-OWL [Costa et al., 2005; Costa & Laskey, 2006] is based on Multi-Entity Bayesian Networks (MEBN) [Laskey, 2007; Laskey & Costa 2005] a probabilistic logic that combines the expressive power of First-Order Logic (FOL) with Bayesian networks' ability to perform plausible reasoning.

5.1 MEBN

Multi-Entity Bayesian Networks (MEBN) extend Bayesian Networks (BN) to achieve first-order expressive power. MEBN represents knowledge as a collection of MEBN Fragments (MFrags), which are organized into MEBN Theories (MTheories).

An MFrag contains random variables (RVs) and a fragment graph representing dependencies among these RVs. It represents a repeatable pattern of knowledge that can be instantiated many times as needed to form a BN addressing a specific situation, and thus can be seen as a template for building fragments of a Bayesian network. It is instantiated by binding its arguments to domain entity identifiers to create instances of its RVs. There are three kinds of RV: context, resident and input. Context RVs represent conditions that must be satisfied for the distributions represented in the MFrag to apply. Input RVs may influence the distributions of other RVs in an MFrag, but their distributions are defined in their home MFrags. Distributions for resident RV instances are defined within the MFrag by specifying local distributions conditioned on the values of the instances of their parents in the fragment graph.

A set of MFrags represents a joint distribution over instances of its random variables. MEBN provides a compact way to represent repeated structures in a BN. An important advantage of MEBN is that there is no fixed limit on the number of RV instances, and the random variable instances are dynamically instantiated as needed.

An MTheory is a set of MFrags that collectively satisfy conditions of consistency ensuring the existence of a unique joint probability distribution over its random variable instances.

To apply an MTheory to reason about particular scenarios, one needs to provide the system with specific information about the individual entity instances involved in the scenario. Upon receipt of this information, Bayesian inference can be used both to answer specific questions of interest (e.g., how likely is it that a particular procurement is being directed to a specific enterprise?) and to refine the MTheory (e.g., each new situation includes additional data about the likelihood of fraud for that set of circumstances). Bayesian inference is used to perform both problem specific inference and learning from data in a sound, logically coherent manner.

5.2 PR-OWL

The usual workaround for representing uncertainty in languages lacking inbuilt support for it is to use custom-designed XML tags to annotate statements with numerical probabilities. This is a palliative solution that cannot represent how uncertainties depend on structural features of the domain. This is a major shortcoming that makes this simple approach unsuitable for all but the simplest real world problems involving uncertainty representation and reasoning. Researchers have consistently stressed the importance of structural information in probabilistic models (see [Schum, 1994]). For instance, [Shafer, 1986] stated that probability is more about structure than it is about numbers.

PR-OWL is a language for representing probabilistic ontologies. Probabilistic ontologies go beyond simply annotating ontologies with probabilities to provide a means of expressing subtle features required to express a first-order Bayesian theory. Because PR-OWL is based on MEBN logic, it not only provides a consistent representation of uncertain knowledge that can be reused by different probabilistic systems, but also allows applications to perform plausible reasoning with that knowledge, in an efficient way. Work on PR-OWL is based on the following definition of a probabilistic ontology [Costa, 2005]:

> **Definition 3.** *A probabilistic ontology is an explicit, formal knowledge representation that expresses knowledge about a domain of application. This includes:*
>
> *a. Types of entities existing in the domain;*
> *b. Properties of those entities;*
> *c. Relationships among entities;*
> *d. Processes and events that happen with those entities;*
> *e. Statistical regularities that characterize the domain;*
> *f. Inconclusive, ambiguous, incomplete, unreliable, and dissonant knowledge;*
> *g. Uncertainty about all the above forms of knowledge;*
>
> *where the term entity refers to any concept (real or factitious, concrete or abstract) that can be described and reasoned about within the domain of application.*

Probabilistic ontologies are used for the purpose of comprehensively describing knowledge about a domain and the uncertainty associated with that knowledge in a principled, structured, and sharable way. PR-OWL was developed as an extension enabling OWL ontologies to represent complex Bayesian probabilistic models in a way that is flexible enough to be used by diverse Bayesian probabilistic tools based on different probabilistic technologies (e.g. PRMs, BNs, etc). More specifically, PR-OWL is an upper ontology (i.e. an ontology that represents fundamental concepts that cross disciplines and applications) for probabilistic systems. PR-OWL is expressive enough to represent even the most complex probabilistic models. It consists of a set of classes, subclasses and properties that collectively form a framework for building probabilistic ontologies.

OWL has three different versions with increasing expressive power designed for specific communities of developers and users. The least expressive version is OWL Lite, which has a limited set of simple restrictions. The next step in expressiveness in the OWL family is OWL DL, which is based on Descriptive Logic and aims to maximize expressiveness while maintaining completeness (all logical consequences are provable) and decidability (all proofs terminate in finite time). OWL-DL has all OWL constructions, but there are certain restrictions on use. The most expressive version, OWL Full, was built for users who want the strongest representational power possible in OWL format. As a consequence, there are no guaranties of computability. Following the same reasoning, a PR-OWL Lite version could be created as suggested in [Costa, 2005] with some restrictions.

PR-OWL was proposed as an extension to the OWL language based on MEBN, which can express a probability distribution on interpretations of any first-order theory. As a consequence, there are no guaranties that reasoning with PR-OWL ontology will be efficient or even decidable [Costa, 2005]. For problems in which computational efficiency is a concern, well-known classes of computationally efficient Bayesian theories can be represented in PR-OWL. PR-OWL was built to be interoperable with non-probabilistic ontologies. Since PR-OWL adds new definitions to OWL while retaining backward compatibility with its base language, OWL-built legacy ontologies will be able to interoperate with newly developed probabilistic ontologies. However, the ontology's probabilistic definitions have to form a valid complete or partial MTheory. Figure 5 shows the main concepts involved in defining an MTheory in PR-OWL.

In the diagram, ellipses represent general classes while arrows represent the main relationships between these classes. A probabilistic ontology (PO) has to have at least one individual of class MTheory, which is basically a label linking a group of MFrags that collectively form a valid MTheory. In actual PR-OWL syntax, that link is expressed via the object property *hasMFrag* (which is the inverse of object property *isMFragIn*). Individuals of class *MFrag* are comprised of nodes (not shown in the picture). Each individual of class *Node* is a random variable (RV) and thus has a mutually exclusive, collectively exhaustive set of possible states. In PR-OWL, the object property *hasPossibleValues* links each node with its possible states, which are individuals of class *Entity*. Finally, random variables (represented by the class *Node* in PR-OWL) have unconditional or conditional probability distributions, which are represented by class *ProbabilityDistribution* and linked to their respective nodes via the object property *hasProbDist*.

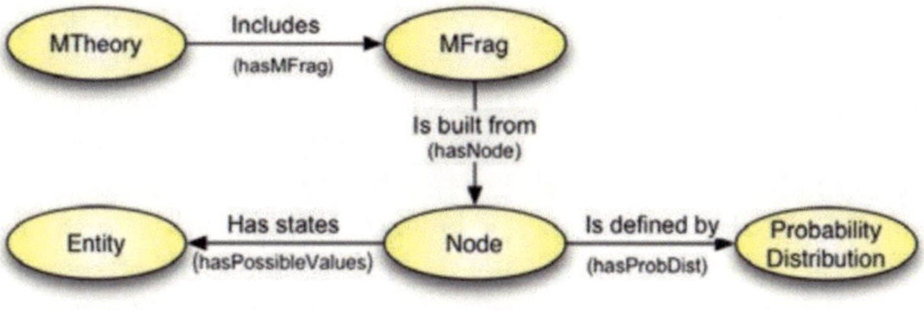

Fig. 5. PR-OWL simple model

Figure 6 depicts the main elements of the PR-OWL language, its subclasses, and the secondary elements necessary for representing an MTheory. The relations necessary to express the complex structure of MEBN probabilistic models using the OWL syntax are also depicted.

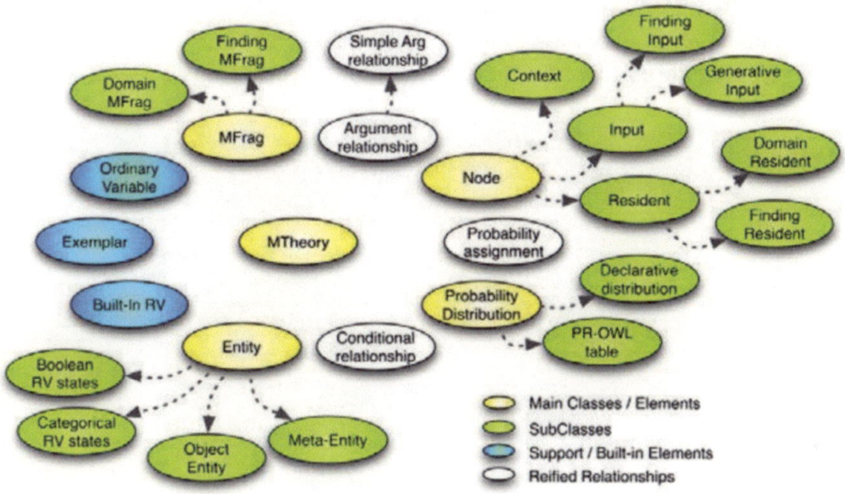

Fig. 6. PR-OWL detailed model

Previously, the first step towards building a probabilistic ontology as defined above is to import the PR-OWL ontology into an ontology editor (e.g. OntoEdit, Protégé, Swoop, etc.) and start constructing the domain-specific concepts using the PR-OWL definitions to represent uncertainty about their attributes and relationships. Using this procedure, a knowledge engineer is not only able to build a coherent generative MTheory and other probabilistic ontology elements, but also make it compatible with other ontologies that use PR-OWL concepts. However, building MFrags this way is a manual, error prone, and tedious process that requires deep knowledge of the logic and of the data structures of PR-OWL in order to avoid errors or inconsistencies. UnBBayes changes all that by providing a GUI-based editing process for building probabilistic ontologies based on the PR-OWL upper ontology for probabilistic theories [Carvalho et al., 2007a]. Another important feature is the ability to save and open models created by the UnBBayes GUI in PR-OWL format, with backwards compatibility to OWL through the use of the Protégé API. Protégé is an ontology editor and a flexible and configurable framework for building knowledge-based tools and

applications. Protégé was developed by the Stanford Center for Biomedical Medical Informatics Research.
The major advantages of using PR-OWL are its flexibility and representational power, both inherited from the fact that the language is based on MEBN, a full integration of First-Order Logic (FOL) and probability theory that merges the expressiveness of the former with the inferential power of the latter. UnBBayes leverages this power with a built-in MEBN reasoner. The next section provides an overall view of the current state of that tool. The prospective reader can find additional details on PR-OWL at http://www.pr-owl.org.

6. Modeling a Probabilistic Ontology in UnBBayes

PR-OWL has been proposed as a language for representing uncertainty in the SW. Although there is now substantial literature about what PR-OWL is [Costa, 2005; Costa et al., 2005; Costa et al., 2008b], how to implement it [Carvalho et al., 2007; Carvalho et al., 2008a; Carvalho et al., 2008b; Costa et al., 2008a], and where it can be used [Costa et al., 2006; Costa et al., 2009a; Costa et al., 2009b; Laskey et al., 2007; Laskey et al., 2008a; Laskey et al., 2008b;], little has been written about how to model a probabilistic ontology.

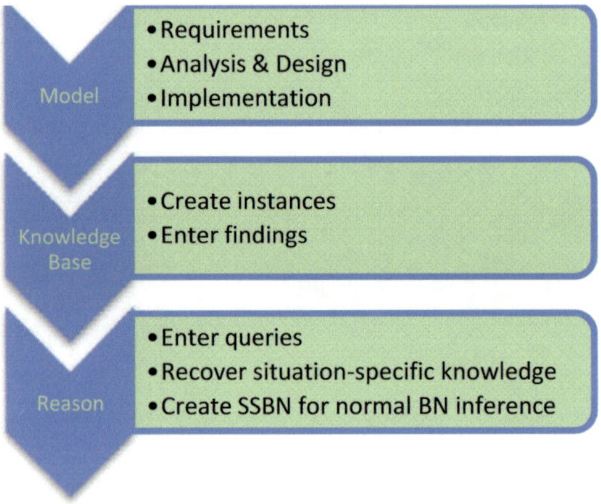

Fig. 7. Uncertainty Modeling Process for the SW (UMP-SW) using MEBN

Therefore, in this Section we will describe an approach for modeling a probabilistic ontology and how to use it for plausible reasoning in the SW. The Uncertainty Modeling Process for the SW (UMP-SW) presented in Figure 7 is divided into three steps: First we have to model the domain, then we need to populate the KB, and finally we can use the model and KB for reasoning.

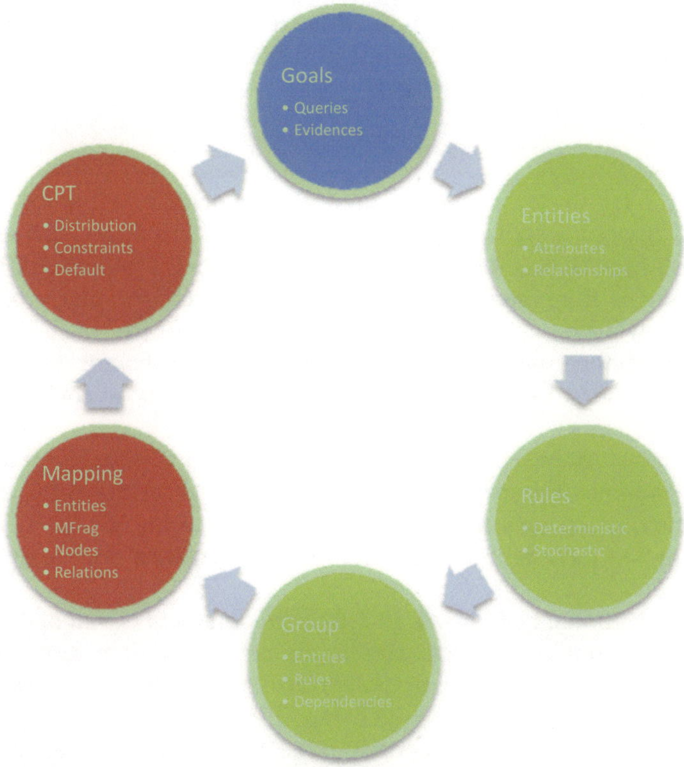

Fig. 8. Probabilistic Ontology Modeling Cycle (POMC) - Requirements in blue, Analysis & Design in green, and Implementation in red

The modeling step consists of three major stages: Requirements, Analysis & Design, and Implementation. These terms are borrowed from the Unified Process (UP) [Jacobson et al., 1999] with some modifications to reflect our domain of ontology modeling instead of development process. The methodology described here is also consistent with the Bayesian network modeling methodology described by [Laskey & Mahoney, 2000] and [Korb & Nicholson, 2003]. Figure 8 depicts these three stages of the Probabilistic Ontology Modeling Cycle (POMC). Like the UP, POMC is iterative and incremental. The basic idea behind iterative enhancement is to model our domain incrementally, allowing the modeler to take advantage of what was being learned during the modeling of earlier, incremental, deliverable versions of the model. Learning comes from discovering new rules, entities, and relations that were not obvious previously, which can give rise to new questions and evidence that might help us achieve our previously defined goal as well as give rise to new goals.

In the POMC (Figure 8) the Requirements stage (blue circle) defines the goals that must be achieved by reasoning with the semantics provided by our model. The Analysis and Design stage describes classes of entities, their attributes, how they relate, and what rules apply to them in our domain (green circles). This definition is independent of the language used to implement the model. Finally, the Implementation stage maps our design to a specific language that allows uncertainty in the SW, which in this case is PR-OWL (red circles).

We will now illustrate the POMC through a case study in procurement fraud detection and prevention. We also demonstrate the use of UnBBayes to implement the model, to populate the KB, and to perform plausible reasoning.

6.1 Requirements

The objective of the requirements stage is to define the objectives that must be achieved by representing and reasoning with a computable representation of domain semantics. At this stage, it is important to define the questions that the model is expected to answer (i.e., the queries to be posed to the system being designed). For each question, a set of information that might help answer such question (evidence) must be defined.

In order to understand the requirements for the procurement fraud detection and prevention model, we first have to explain some of the problems encountered when dealing with public procurements.

One of the principles established by the Law Nº 8,666/93 is equality among the bidders. This principle prohibits the procurement agent from discriminating among potential suppliers. However, if the procurement agent is related to the bidder, he/she might feed information or define new requirements for the procurement in a way that favors the bidder.

Another principle that must be followed in public procurement is that of competition. Every public procurement should establish minimum requisites necessary to guarantee the execution of the contract in order to maximize the number of participating bidders. Nevertheless, it is common to have a fake competition when different bidders are, in fact, owned by the same person. This is usually done by having someone as a front for the enterprise, which is often someone with little or no education. Another common tactic is to set up front enterprises owned by relatives of the enterprise committing fraud.

According to [Mueller, 1998] participating in a public procurement can be very expensive and time consuming. Thus, some firms are unwilling to take part in a process that may yield favorable results. Since the process narrows down the number of firms who are willing to bid, it makes it much easier for collusion to take place among the bidders. What happens in Brazil is that a small group of firms regularly participate in procurements of certain goods and services. When this happens, the competitors in a public procurement take turns winning the contracts. They stipulate the winning bid, and all other firms bid below that price. There is no competition, and the government pays a higher price for the contract. Although collusion is not an easy thing to prove, it is reasonable to assume that collusion is enabled by some kind of relationship between the enterprises.

All firms in Brazil have a registration number, called CGC, which stands for General List of Contributors. When a firm is suspended from procuring with the public administration, its CGC number is passed to all public procuring agencies, so that all will know of the penalty being applied. But the problem is that the firm, if it wishes to continue to do business with the government, can close down, and register again, receiving a new number. Then it will continue to participate in procurements, as a new firm. The Commercial Code permits this change of CGC number.

One other problem is that public procurement is quite complex and may involve large sums of money. Therefore, the members that form the committee of the procurement must not only be prepared, but also have a clean history (no criminal nor administrative conviction) in order to maximize morality, one of the ethical principles that federal, state, municipal and district government should all adopt.

Having explained that, in our fraud detection and prevention in the procurements domain we have the following set of goals/queries/evidences:

1. Identify if a given procurement should be inspected and/or audited (i.e. evidence suggests further analysis is needed);
    a. Is there any relation between the committee and the enterprises that participated in the procurement?
        i. Look for member and responsible person of an enterprise who are related (mother, father, brother, or sister);
        ii. Look for member and responsible person of an enterprise who live at the same address.
    b. Is the responsible person of the winner enterprise of the procurement a front?
        i. Look for value of the contract related to this procurement;
        ii. Look for his education degree;
        iii. Look for annual income.
    c. Was the responsible person of the winner enterprise of the procurement responsible for an enterprise that has been suspended from procuring with the public administration?
        i. Look for this information in the General List of Contributors (CGC) database.
    d. Was competition compromised?
        i. Look for bidders related as defined above (1a).
2. Identify whether the committee of a given procurement should be changed.
    a. Is there any member of committee who does not have a clean history?
        i. Look for criminal history;
        ii. Look for administrative investigations.
    b. Is there any relation between members of the committee and the enterprises that participated in previous procurements?
        i. Look for member and responsible person of an enterprise who are relatives (mother, father, brother, or sister);
        ii. Look for member and responsible person of an enterprise who live at the same address.

6.2 Analysis & Design

Once we have defined our goals and described how to achieve them, it is time to start modeling the entities, their attributes, relationships, and rules to make that happen. This is the purpose of the Analysis and Design stage.

The major objective of this stage is to define the semantics of our model. In fact, most of our semantics can be defined in normal ontologies, including the deterministic rules that the concepts described in our model must obey. Since there are whole books describing how to design such ontologies, and our main concern is on the uncertain part of the ontology, we will not cover these methods in this Section. For more information see [Allemang & Hendler, 2008; Gómez-Pérez et al., 2005].

Nevertheless, we do need a starting point in order to design our probabilistic ontology. As a matter of fact, one good way to start modeling these properties is to use UML as described in Section 2. However, as we have seen, UML does not support complex rule definitions. So we will just document them separately to remind us of the rules that must be described when implementing our model in PR-OWL.

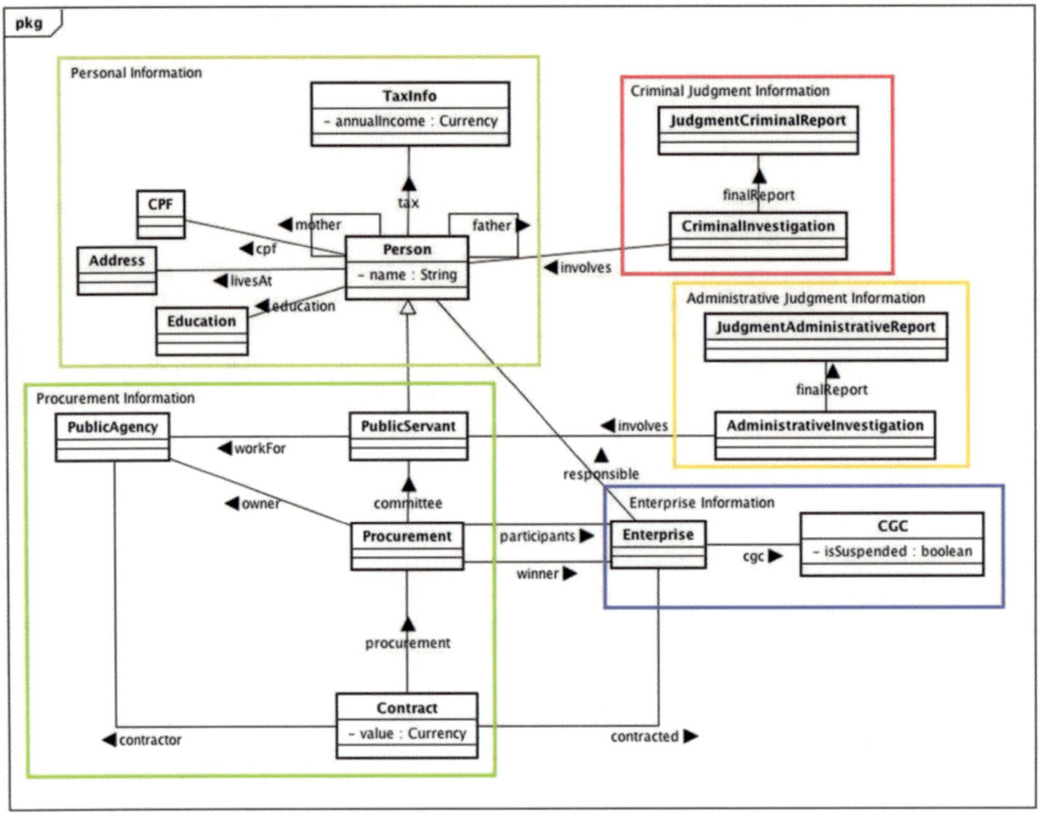

Fig. 9. Entities, their attributes, and relations for the procurement model

Figure 9 depicts a simplified design of our domain requirements. A *Person* has a *name*, a *mother* and a *father*[3] (also *Person*). Every *Person* has a unique identification that in Brazil is called *CPF*. A *Person* also has an *Education* and lives at a certain *Address*. In addition, everyone is obliged to file his/her *TaxInfo* every year, including his/her *annualIncome*. These entities can be grouped as *Personal Information*. A *PublicServant* is a *Person* who works for a *PublicAgency*, which is a Government Agency. Every public *Procurement* is owed by a *PublicAgency*, has a *committee* formed by a group of *PublicServants*, and has a group of *participants*, which are *Enterprises*. One of these will be the *winner* of the *Procurement*. Eventually, the *winner* of the *Procurement* will receive a *Contract* of some *value* with the *PublicAgency owner* of the *Procurement*. The entities just described can be grouped as

[3] When modeling in UML we will use the first letter uppercase for classes (e.g., Person) and lowercase for attributes (e.g., name).

Procurement Information. Every *Enterprise* has at least one *Person* that is *responsible* for its legal acts. An *Enterprise* also has an identification number, the General List of Contributors *CGC*, which can be used to inform that this *Enterprise* is suspended from procuring with the public administration, *isSuspended*. These are grouped as the *Enterprise Information*. We also have *AdminstrativeInvestigation*, which has information about investigations that *involves* one or more *PublicServer*.

Its *finalReport*, the *JudgmentAdministrativeReport*, contains information about the penalty applied, if any. These entities form the *Administrative Judgment Information*. Finally we have the *Criminal Judgment Information* group that describes the *CriminalInvestigation* that *involves* a *Person*, with its *finalReport*, the *JudgmentCriminalReport*, which has information about the verdict.

Besides the cardinality and uniqueness rules defined in the explanation above about the entities depicted in Figure 9, the probabilistic rules for our model include:

1. If a member of the committee has a relative (mother, father, brother, or sister) responsible for a bidder in the procurement, then it is more likely to exist a relation between the committee and the enterprises, which lowers competition.
2. If a member of the committee lives at the same address as a person responsible for a bidder in the procurement, then it is more likely to exist a relation between the committee and the enterprises, which lowers competition.
3. If a contract of high value related to a procurement has a responsible person of the winner enterprise with low education or low annual income, then this person is likely to be a front for the firm, which lowers competition.
4. If the responsible person of the winner enterprise is also responsible for another enterprise that has its CGC suspended for procuring with the public administration, then this procurement is more likely to need further investigation.
5. If the responsible people for the bidders in the procurement are related to each other, then a competition is more likely to have been compromised.
6. If 1, 2, 3, or 5, then the procurement is more likely to require further investigation.
7. If a member of the committee has been convicted of criminal crime or has been penalized administratively, then he/she does not have a clean history. If he/she was recently investigated, then it is likely that he/she does not have a clean history.
8. If the relation defined in 1 and 2 is found in previous procurements, then it is more likely that there will be a relation between this committee and future bidders.
9. If 7 or 8, then it is more likely that the committee needs to be changed.

6.3 Implementation

Once we have finished our Analysis and Design, it is time to start implementing our model in a specific language. This Chapter describes how to model procurement fraud detection and prevention in PR-OWL using UnBBayes. The first thing to do is to start mapping the entities, their attributes, and relations to PR-OWL, which uses essentially MEBN terms. It is often a good idea to start mapping the entities. There is no need to map all entities in our model to an entity in PR-OWL. In fact, in our model we will make many simplifications.

One of them is due to a limitation in UnBBayes' current version, which is the lack of support for a type hierarchy. Therefore, we will not have the *PublicServant* entity and we will assume that a *Person* might work for a *PublicAgency*. We will also assume that every *Person* and *Enterprise* in our KB is uniquely identified by its name, so we will not consider, in this simplified example, the *CPF* and *CGC* entities. Figure 10 presents the entities implemented in our PR-OWL ontology using UnBBayes. For more details about defining entities in UnBBayes see [Carvalho et al., 2009].

Fig. 10. Entities implemented in PR-OWL using UnBBayes

Once we have our entities defined, we consider characteristics that may be uncertain. Uncertainty is represented in MEBN by defining random variables (RVs). To define a RV in UnBBayes, we first define its Home MFrag. Grouping the RVs into MFrags is done by examining the grouping created during the Analysis and Design stage.

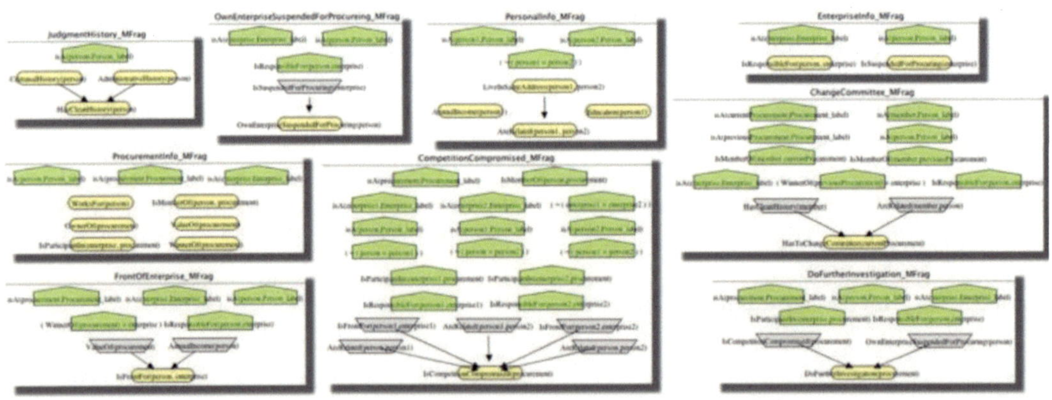

Fig. 11. Probabilistic ontology for fraud detection and prevention in the procurements

Typically, a RV represents an attribute or a relation from our designed model. For instance, the RV *LivesAt(Person)* maps the relation *livesAt* in our designed model. As it is a functional relation, *livesAt* relates a *Person* to an *Address*. Hence, the possible values (or states) of this RV are instances of *Address*. We can also avoid explicitly representing some entities, by simply defining discrete outputs. In our implementation, we only need to know if a *Person* has no education, just high school, an undergraduate degree, or a graduate degree. These are the states of the RV *Education(Person)*, therefore, there is no need to define the entity *Education*. Each of these RVs is represented in UnBBayes as a resident node in its home MFrag.

Because the current version of UnBBayes does not support continuous RVs, we must define a discretization for numerical attributes. For example, the attribute *value* of the *Contract* entity from our designed model is continuous, since it represents a *Currency*. However, we can discretize it by defining common intervals, as lower than 10,000.00, between 10,000.01 and 100,000.00, between 100,000.01 and 500,000.00, between 500,000.01 and 1,000,000.00, and greater than 1,000,000.01, which will be the sates of the resident node *ValueOf(Procurement)*. Future versions of UnBBayes will support continuous RVs.

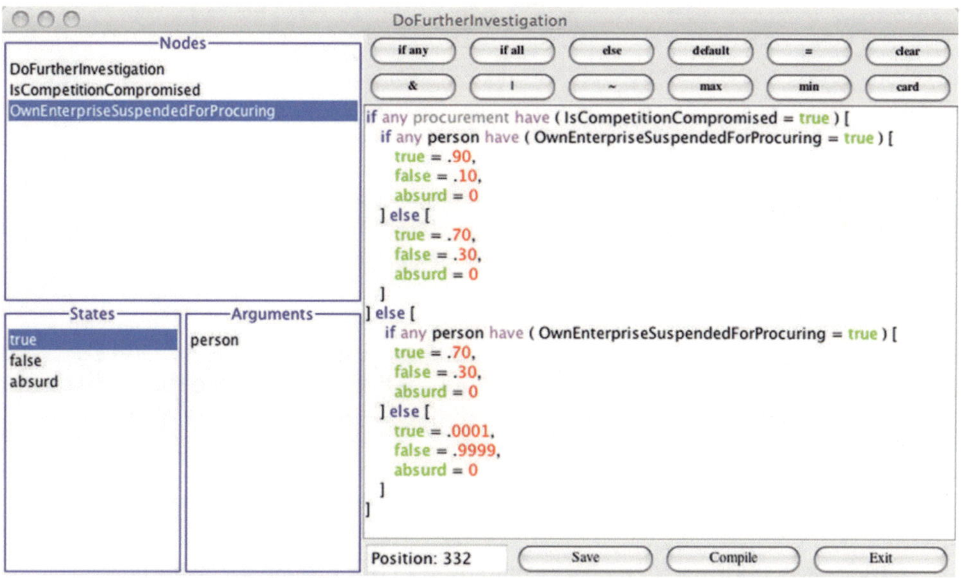

Fig. 12. Local probability distribution for node *DoFurtherInvestigation(Procurement)*

Once all resident RVs are created, their relations can be defined by analyzing dependence between nodes. One good way to look for dependence is by looking at the rules defined in our model. For instance, rule 3 indicates that there is a dependence between *ValueOf(Procurement)*, *Education(Person)*, and *IsFront(Person,Enterprise)*.

Figure 11 presents an MTheory that represents the final probabilistic ontology for the procurement fraud detection and prevention model. This MTheory is composed of nine MFrags. In each MFrag, the resident RVs are shown as yellow ovals; the input RVs are shown as gray trapezoids; the context RVs are shown as green pentagons. The two main goals described in our requirements are defined in the *DoFurtherInvestigation_MFrag* and *ChangeCommittee_MFrag*. A more sophisticated design to model whether to change the committee would define a utility function and use expected utility to make the decision. Future versions of UnBBayes will support Multi-Entity Influence Diagrams [Costa, 2005].

The final step in constructing a probabilistic ontology in UnBBayes is to define the local probability distribution (LPD) for all resident nodes. Figure 12 presents a LPD for the resident node *DoFurtherInvestigation(Procurement)*, which represents one of the main goals we want to achieve in our model. This LPD follows a grammar defined to allow declaring a more robust distribution. For more information see [Carvalho et al., 2008b].

6.4 Knowledge Base

After defining a probabilistic ontology, we can populate the KB by adding instances and findings. These can be added manually through or retrieved from a database (DB). Figure 13 shows how to add entities and findings manually using UnBBayes' GUI.

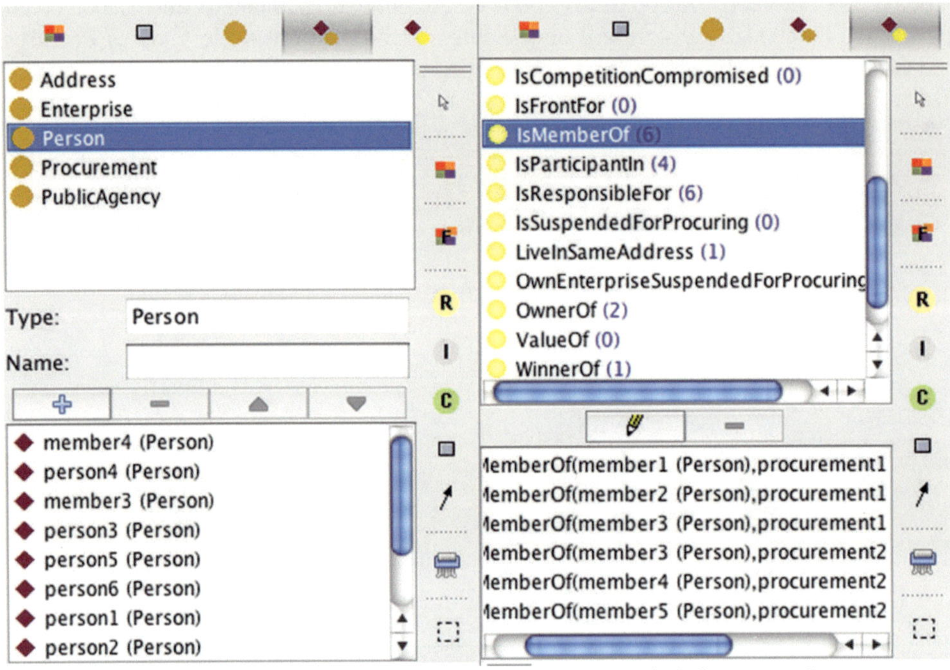

Fig. 13. Entities and findings for a specific situation in our probabilistic ontology

This specific situation has two procurements. The first, *procurement1*, had *member1*, *member2*, and *member3* forming its committee. This procurement was realized in the past and had *enterprise3* as its winner. Today, *procurement2* is still in progress and it has *member3*, *member4*, and *member5* forming its committee. It is also known that *member3* lives at the same address as *person3*, who is responsible for *enteprise3*, and that *member5* has been convicted by an administrative judgment.

6.5 Reasoning

Once we have a probabilistic ontology implemented in PR-OWL and we have a KB populated, it is possible to realize plausible reasoning through the process of creating a Situation-Specific Bayesian Network (SSBN) [Laskey, 2008]. UnBBayes has implemented an algorithm that creates a SSBN for a particular query (see [Carvalho et al., 2008a; Carvalho et al., 2008b; Costa et al., 2008a] for more details). In this specific situation we want to know if the current *procurement2* should change its committee, query *HasToChangeCommittee(procurement2)*. Figure 14 shows the generated SSBN.

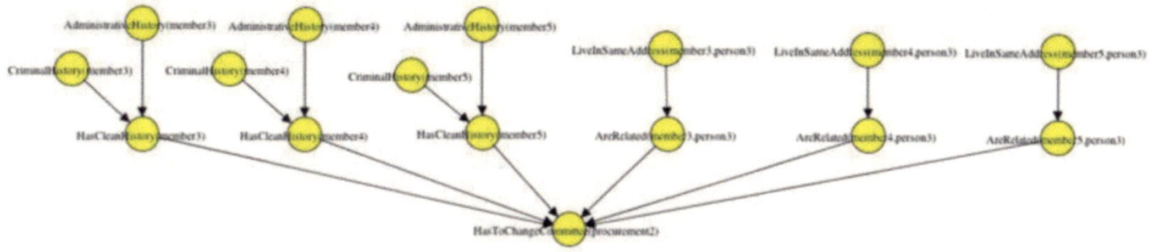

Fig. 14. SSBN for the query *HasToChangeCommittee(procurement2)*

With the current KB, the probability that *HasToChangeCommittee(procurement2)* is 87.76%. If we did not know that *member3* lives at the same address as *person3*, the probability would be 69.38%. On the other hand, if we did not know that *member5* has been convicted by an administrative judgment, the probability would be 63.84%. Finally, if we had no knowledge about neither of the information stated above, the probability would be only 2.6%.

7. Conclusion

Ontologies provide the "semantic glue" to enable knowledge sharing among systems collaborating in radical information sharing domains: open world domains in which Anyone can say Anything about Any topic (AAA), and entities may not have unique names. Traditional ontologies fail to provide adequate support for uncertainty, a ubiquitous characteristic of RIS environments. This paper presents a framework for modeling RIS domains using probabilistic ontologies. The case study presented in this work has shown that such research, albeit in its infancy, can help to support interoperability among systems in an open environment, fusing multiple sources of noisy information to perform reasoning and problem solving in an open world.

8. References

Allemang, Dean & Hendler, James A. (2008) *Semantic web for the working ontologist modeling in RDF, RDFS and OWL*. Elsevier, ISBN 978-0-12-373556-0, United States.

Berners-Lee, Tim (1999) *Weaving the Web: The Original Design and Ultimate Destiny of the World Wide Web*. Collins Business, ISBN 978- 0062515872.

Brachman, Ronald J. & Levesque, Hector J. (2004) *Knowledge representation and reasoning*. Elsevier, ISBN 978-1-55860-932-7, United States.

Carvalho, Rommel N.; Santos, Laécio L.; Ladeira, Marcelo & Costa, Paulo C. G. (2007) A GUI Tool for Plausible Reasoning in the Semantic Web using MEBN. *In Proceedings of the Seventh International Conference on Intelligent Systems Design and Applications (ISDA 2007)*. Mourele, L.; Nedjah, N.; Kacprzyk, J.; and Abraham, A. (eds.); pp. 381-386. October 22-24, 2007, Rio de Janeiro, Brazil.

Carvalho, Rommel N.; Ladeira, Marcelo; Santos, Laécio L.; Matsumoto, Shou & Costa, Paulo C. G. (2008a) A GUI Tool for Plausible Reasoning in the Semantic Web Using

MEBN. *Chapter in Innovative Applications in Data Mining*. Studies in Computational Science, Vol. 169/2009, pp. 17-45. Springer-Verlag: Berlin/Heidelberg.

Carvalho, Rommel N.; Ladeira, Marcelo; Santos, Laécio L.; Matsumoto, Shou & Costa, Paulo C. G. (2008b) UnBBayes-MEBN: Comments on Implementing a Probabilistic Ontology Tool. *In Proceedings of the IADIS International Conference - Applied Computing 2008*. N. Guimarães and P. Isaías (eds.), Algarve, Portugal, April 10-13, 2008, pp. 211-218.

Chen, Peter PS. (1976) The Entity-Relationship Model: Toward a Unified View of Data. *In ACM Transactions on Database Systems (TODS)*, Volume 1, Issue 1, Framingham, MA, pp. 9-36.

Costa, Paulo C. G. (2005) Bayesian Semantics for the Semantic Web. Doctoral Dissertation. Department of Systems Engineering and Operations Research, George Mason University: Fairfax, VA, USA. p. 312.

Costa, Paulo C. G.; Laskey, Kathryn B. & Laskey, Kenneth J. (2005) PR-OWL: A Bayesian Framework for the Semantic Web. *In Proceedings of the first workshop on Uncertainty Reasoning for the Semantic Web (URSW 2005), held at the Fourth International Semantic Web Conference (ISWC 2005)*. November 6-10, 2005, Galway, Ireland.

Costa, Paulo C. G.; Laskey, Kathryn B. & Laskey, Kenneth J. (2006) Probabilistic Ontologies for Efficient Resource Sharing in Semantic Web Services. *In Proceedings of the second workshop on Uncertainty Reasoning for the Semantic Web (URSW 2006), held at the Fifth International Semantic Web Conference (ISWC 2006)*. November 5-9, 2006, Athens, GA, USA.

Costa, Paulo C. G.; Ladeira, Marcelo; Carvalho, Rommel N.; Laskey, Kathryn B.; Santos, Laécio L. & Matsumoto, Shou (2008a) A First-Order Bayesian Tool for Probabilistic Ontologies. In Proceedings of the 21st International Florida Artificial Intelligence Research Society Conference (FLAIRS-21), Palo Alto: AAAI Press, 2008.

Costa, Paulo C. G.; Laskey, Kathryn B. & Laskey, Kenneth J. (2008b) PR-OWL: a Bayesian Language for the Semantic Web. *Chapter in Uncertainty Reasoning for the Semantic Web I*. LNAI 5327, pp. 88-107. Springer-Verlag: Berlin/Heidelberg.

Costa, Paulo C. G.; Laskey, Kathryn B. & Chang, KC (2009a) PROGNOS: Applying Probabilistic Ontologies to Distributed Predictive Situation Assessment in Naval Operations. *Accepted to the Fourteenth International Command and Control Research and Technology Conference (ICCRTS 2009)*. June, 15-17. Washington, D.C., USA.

Costa, Paulo C. G.; Chang, KC; Laskey, Kathryn B. & Carvalho, Rommel N. (2009b) A Multi-Disciplinary Approach to High Level Fusion in Predictive Situational Awareness. *Accepted to the Eleventh International Conference of the Society of Information Fusion (FUSION 2009)*. July 6-9. Seattle, WA, USA.

Creveld, Martin V. *Command in War*. 1987 reprint edition. Harvard University Press Cambridge, ISBN 978-0674144415, MA, USA.

Gómez-Pérez, Asunción; Fernández-López, Mariano; Corcho, Oscar (2005) *Ontological engineering: with examples from the areas of knowledge management, e-commerce and the semantic web*. Spring-Verlag, ISBN 1-85233-551-3, London Berlin Heidelberg.

Heflin, Jeff (2004) OWL Web Ontology Language - Use Cases and Requirements (W3C Recommendation). www.w3.org/TR/2004/REC-webont-req-20040210.

Jacobson, Ivar; Booch, Grady & Rumbaugh, James (1999) *The Unified Software Development Process*. Addison-Wesley Professional, ISBN 978-0201571691.

Korb, Kevin B. & Nicholson, Ann E. (2003) Bayesian Artificial Intelligence. Chapman and Hall, Boca Raton.

Laskey, Kathryn B. & Mahoney, Suzanne M. (2000) Network Engineering for Agile Belief Network Models. *IEEE Transactions in Knowledge and Data Engineering* 12(4): 487-498.

Laskey, Kathryn B. & Costa, Paulo .C. G. (2005) Of Klingons and Starships: Bayesian Logic for the 23rd Century. *In Uncertainty in Artificial Intelligence: Proceedings of the Twenty-first Conference (UAI 2005)*. AUAI Press: Edinburgh, Scotland.

Laskey, Kathryn B.; Costa, Paulo C. G.; Wright, Edward J. & Laskey, Kenneth J. (2007) Probabilistic Ontology for Net-Centric Fusion. *In Proceedings of the Tenth International Conference of the Society of Information Fusion (FUSION 2007)*. July 9 - 12, 2007, Québec, Canada.

Laskey, Kathryn B. (2008) MEBN: A language for first-order Bayesian knowledge bases. *In Artificial Intelligence*, Volume 172, Issues 2-3, February 2008, Pages 140-178

Laskey, Kathryn B.; Costa, Paulo C. G. & Janssen, T. (2008a) Probabilistic Ontologies for Knowledge Fusion. *In Proceedings of the Eleventh International Conference of the Society of Information Fusion (FUSION 2008)*. July 1-3, 2008, Cologne, Germany.

Laskey, Kathryn B.; Costa, Paulo C. G. & Janssen, T. (2008b) Probabilistic Ontologies for Multi-INT Fusion. *In Proceedings of the AFCEA-GMU C4I Center Symposium (GMU-AFCEA 2008) - "Critical Issues in C4I"*. May 20-21, 2008, George Mason University, Fairfax, VA, USA.

Levesque, Hector J. & Lakemeyer, Gerhard (2000) *The Logic of Knowledge Bases*. The MIT Press, ISBN 0-262-12232-4, Cambridge, Massachusetts and London, England.

Meirelles, Hely L. (1996) *Licitação e Contrato Administrativo*. Malheiros Editores, Brazil.

Mueller, André P. M. (1998) A Critical Study of the Brazilian Procurement Law. *In Minerva Research Papers*. The Institute of Brazilian Issues - IBI, The George Washington University, Washington DC.

Object Management Group (1997) *Object Constraint Language Specification*. http://www.omg.org/docs/ad/97-08-08.pdf.

Patel-Schneider , Peter F.; Hayes, Patrick & Horrocks, Ian (2004) OWL Web Ontology Language - Semantics and Abstract Syntax (W3C Recommendation). www.w3.org/TR/owl-semantics/.

Pearl, Judea (1988) Probabilistic Reasoning in Intelligent Systems: Networks of Plausible Inference. Morgan Kaufmann Publishers, ISBN 978-1558604797, San Mateo, CA, USA.

Rumbaugh, James; Jacobson, Ivar & Booch, Grady (1998) *The Unified Modeling Language Reference Manual*. Addison-Wesley, ISBN 978-0201309980, Boston, Massachusetts.

Schum, David A. (1994) *Evidential Foundations of Probabilistic Reasoning*. Wiley- Interscience, ISBN 978-0471579366.

Shafer, Glenn (1986) The Construction of Probability Arguments. Boston University Law Review, 66(3-4):799-823.

Studer, Rudi; Benjamins, V. Richard & Fensel, Dieter (1998) Knowledge Engineering: Principles and Methods. *In IEEE Transactions on Data and Knowledge Engineering*, Volume 25, Numbers 1-2, pp. 161-197.

Uschold, Mike & Jasper, Robert (1999) A Framework for Understanding and Classifying Ontology Applications. *In Benjamins BR (ed) IJCAI'99 Workshop on Ontology and*

Problem Solving Methods: Lessons Learned and Future Trends. Stockholm, Sweden. CEUR Workshop Proceedings 18:11.1-11.12. Amsterdam, The Netherlands http://CEUR-WS.org/Vol-18/.

Warner, Jos B. & Kleppe, Anneke G. (1998) *The Object Constraint Language: Precise Modeling With UML*. Addison-Wesley, ISBN 978-0201379402, Boston, Massachusetts.

2

Alternative Bootstrapping Design for the PORTAL-DOORS Cyberinfrastructure with Self-Referencing and Self-Describing Features

Carl Taswell
Global TeleGenetics, Inc.
USA

1. Introduction

A distributed registry-directory system as a cyberinfrastructure in support of navigation, search, and queries of the semantic web has been designed using a paradigm built in analogy with the corresponding systems established for the original web. The Problem Oriented Registry of Tags And Labels (PORTAL) and the Domain Ontology Oriented Resource System (DOORS) for the semantic web (Taswell, 2008a) are intended to function as interacting systems of registries and directories for the semantic web in a manner analogous to those used for the original web, namely, the Internet Registry Information Service (IRIS) and Domain Name System (DNS).

These interacting network systems of PORTAL registries and DOORS directories, collectively called the PORTAL-DOORS System (PDS), have been designed as resource metadata registering and publishing systems to address three major problems: cybersilos, transition barriers, and search engine consolidation. In a comprehensive literature review, Taswell (2008a) discussed the current cybersilo problem and barriers to the transition from original web to semantic web. More recently, Mowshowitz and Kumar (2009) provided commentary with growing concerns about search engine consolidation.

Guided by design principles intended to address all three major problems, the PDS is architected to operate as a hybrid between and bridge from original to semantic web by bootstrapping itself in a manner in which both the infrastructure system and its data are distributed physically and virtually in terms of both content and control of content. As a consequence, the distributed design itself prevents the possibility of search engine consolidation in a manner entirely analogous to the success of IRIS-DNS in preventing the consolidation of internet domain name registries or directories.

Beyond the original published design (Taswell, 2008a) that serves as the abstract architectural blueprint for PDS, some concrete interface schemas with basic ontologies have been drafted for prototype registries in fields relevant to biomedical computing and radiological informatics. These draft prototypes include a formal semantic definition of pharmacogenomic molecular imaging which provides a use case that demonstrates search across multiple specialty domains (Taswell, 2008b).

However, such XML-based models represent only a piece of the puzzle. A full implementation requires many other software components especially back-end database servers and front-end clients for the PORTAL registries and DOORS directories. In order to gain practical experience testing development of alternative implementations, it is necessary to begin working with real data stored in actual database servers. Therefore, the roadmap for PDS development shifted from revision of XML schemas and OWL ontologies to construction of a prototype relational database model.

This database model has been purposefully chosen to be initially a traditional relational model rather than an RDF-based triple store. This decision was made not only because of the guiding principle that PDS must be capable of operating as a hybrid and a bridge but also because of the pervasive availability of relational databases in comparison with newer kinds of databases. Recent research (Zhuge et al., 2008) on the use of relational database models for semantic systems also suggests that relational databases may continue to play an important role rather than being completely displaced by RDF-based triple stores for semantic systems.

This report describes the relational database models now implemented for revisions of the PDS design including both the original design with PORTAL and DOORS servers and a new bootstrapping design with NEXUS servers. This new design more explicitly realizes the guiding principle for PDS that it should operate in a bootstrapping manner.

2. Methods

Altova XMLSpy (www.altova.com) and Microsoft Visual Studio 2008 with SQL Server 2008 (www.microsoft.com) were used as the integrated development environments for software development experiments with various partial implementations of the PDS designs. An iterative process of software development, debugging, testing, and analysis for re-design beginning from both the XML perspective and the SQL perspective resulted in SQL, XML, and ASP.net code for both the original separate PORTAL-DOORS design as well as a new alternative combined NEXUS design with distinct advantages. Analysis for re-design of the entire system also addressed the following concerns: (i) eliminating redundancies, (ii) improving the separation of functionalities between the various servers and services, and (iii) resolving any other issues that may arise.

3. Analysis

All essential design concepts initially proposed (Taswell, 2008a) have been successfully retained in the software implementations. However, on analysis for re-design, certain redundancies were noted that precluded an improved separation of functionality between PORTAL registries and DOORS directories. For example, in the architectural blueprint for PDS (Taswell, 2008a), *resource tags* were declared as permitted metadata maintained for a resource at both PORTAL registries and DOORS directories. Redundancies of this kind complicate maintenance in general as well as the intended use of the PORTAL and DOORS networks primarily as lexical and semantic systems, respectively.

For the purposes of use in PDS, lexical and semantic systems are defined here as follows: A lexical system (aka "dumb" system) is an information system in which words are processed as character strings that have no inherent meaning to the processing agent, and more specifically, character strings are processed without use of RDF, OWL, and related technologies. A semantic system (aka "smart" system) is one in which words have defined meaning to the agent processing them with logic-based reasoners, and more specifically, character strings are processed with use of RDF, OWL, and related technologies. Thus, PORTAL registries, as primarily a lexical system should register the *resource labels* and *resource tags*, while DOORS directories, as primarily a semantic system should publish the *resource locations* and *resource descriptions*. This re-design eliminates the unnecessary redundancies and complications of maintaining *resource tags* at both PORTAL registries and DOORS directories.

Moreover, on analysis for re-design, a circular reference was noted that required resolution for implementation. According to the original blueprint (Taswell, 2008a), PORTAL registries were designed to restrict registration of resource metadata at each domain-specific registry to those resources meeting the criteria required for the problem-oriented domain declared for that particular registry. For example, a person or organization interested in building and maintaining a problem-oriented registry for zoology (say "ZooPORT") most likely would not permit registration of resources related to stars unless the star is an animal such as a starfish. And vice versa, managers of a problem-oriented registry for astronomy (say "AstroPORT") most likely would not permit registration of resources related to animals unless the animal is the name of a star or constellation of which there are many such as Leo (Lion), Lepus (Hare) or Lupus (Wolf).

At the same time, DOORS directories were designed to publish the resource descriptions providing the RDF triples and thus the semantic information necessary to determine eligibility of the resource for registration in the particular PORTAL registry. However, directories in the DOORS server network were intended for use not only in a manner that would serve any PORTAL registry (whether AstroPORT, ZooPORT, or any of the four existing prototype registries BioPORT, GeneScene, ManRay, and BrainWatch) but also in a manner that would publish the resource descriptions with the RDF triples about the resource. This important semantic information necessarily determines eligibility of the resource for registration in the relevant governing PORTAL registry if that registry has elected to impose restrictions for definition of the problem-oriented domain. This situation constitutes a contradictory circular reference, because according to the original blueprint (Taswell, 2008a), a resource must be registered first at a PORTAL registry before it can be described at a DOORS directory, whereas in this scenario, it must be described before it can be registered. Both temporal sequences are not simultaneously possible.

Various solutions for implementations that resolve this circular reference problem include the following: (A) Splitting the resource description into a PORTAL required portion and a

DOORS permitted portion; (B) Using record status codes "Invalid", "Pending", and "Valid" exchanged between PORTAL and DOORS; (C) Using PORTAL resource tags instead of DOORS resource descriptions to determine eligibility; and (D) Building an alternative design that combines both PORTAL and DOORS services into a single NEXUS service. Although solution (A) would resolve the circular reference problem, it would also preclude implementation of PORTAL and DOORS systems as primarily lexical and semantic, respectively, because it would require semantic processing on PORTAL in addition to that on DOORS. However, solution (D) would not only resolve the circular reference problem, but would also enable a multiplicity of configurations according to varying composition of service operations in different components that can co-exist with each other on the same or different servers.

Finally, throughout the iterative development, analysis, and re-design process, it became apparent that the terminology used by the original blueprint (Taswell, 2008a) for PDS could be improved for better clarity. In particular, the original terminology did not adequately distinguish between the metadata about the *resource entity*, and the metadata about the *resource record*. As a consequence, PDS terminology has been revised and used throughout code development to represent this distinction between the primary metadata about the *resource entity* and the secondary metadata about the *resource record*.

Here the primary metadata is metadata about the thing of interest (the entity) whereas the secondary metadata is the metadata about the metadata (the record). Moreover, the term *resource representation* refers to all of the metadata, both primary and secondary, when considered together collectively. In general, however, any use of the term *resource* by itself should be construed (when not otherwise apparent from context) as referring to the *entity* rather than the *record* or *representation* so that the original definition remains valid: *a resource may be any entity whether abstract or concrete, whether online in the virtual world or offline in the physical world.*

4. Results

Software has been developed for the PORTAL-DOORS System that eliminates the redundancies, clarifies the terminology, and resolves the circular reference problem of the original blueprint (Taswell, 2008a). To implement the necessary revision of the original design, both solutions (B) and (C) were chosen. In addition, solution (D) has also been implemented for the alternative new design. This new scheme called the *combined design* can coexist together with the original scheme called the *separate design*. Thus, any node in the PDS network can be built as a separate PORTAL node, separate DOORS node, or a combined PORTAL-DOORS node also called a NEXUS node (see Fig. 1). The new combined design offers significant advantages in enabling an efficient self-referencing, self-describing, and bootstrapping process amongst the core system constituents (agents, registrants) and components (registrars, registries, and directories).

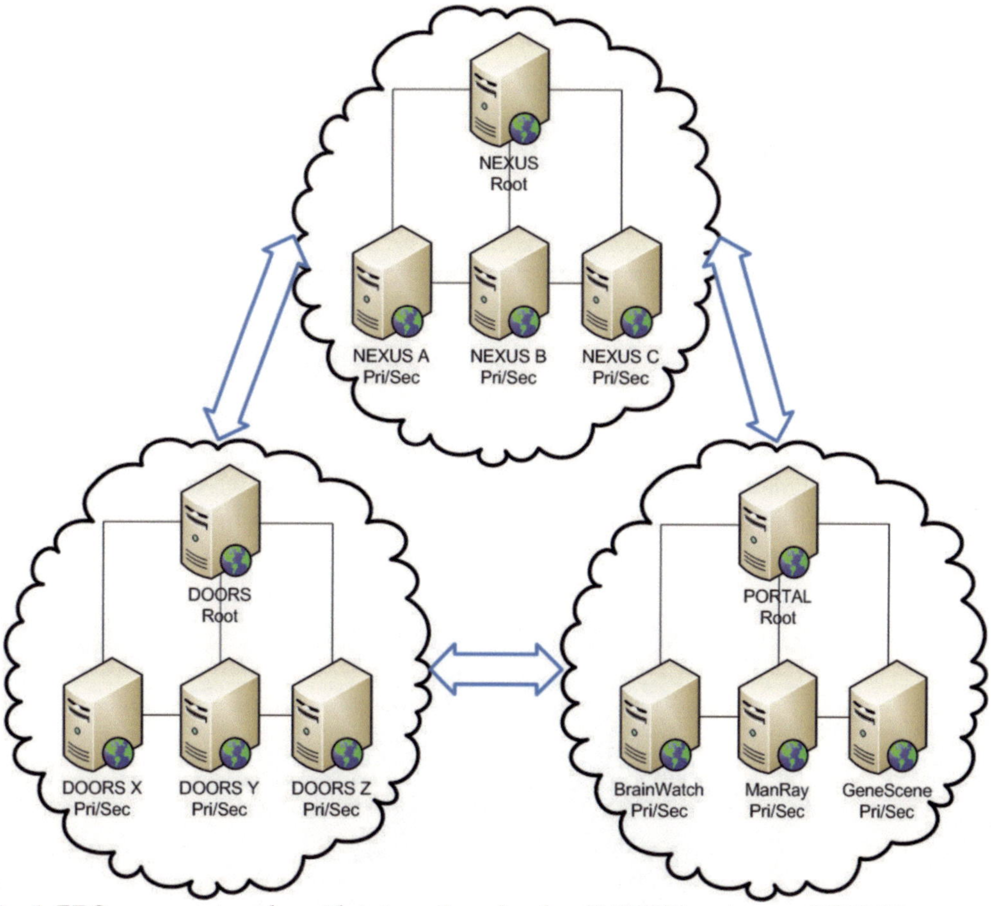

Fig. 1. PDS server networks with interacting clouds of NEXUS registrars, PORTAL registries, and DOORS directories. NEXUS servers may expose either the NEXUS registrar service for the separate design or the integrated set of NEXUS registrar, PORTAL registry, and DOORS directory services for the combined design.

Figure 2 displays a diagram summarizing the basic structure of data records with both *required* and *permitted* fields at both PORTAL registries and DOORS directories. When providing registrar services for separate PORTAL and DOORS nodes, NEXUS registrars operate in a manner consistent with the original separate design. However, when providing registrar services for a combined PORTAL-DOORS node, NEXUS registrars can also operate in a manner that enables integrated storage of both PORTAL and DOORS record data on the same server. Figure 3 displays a diagram depicting the relational database model for the current 0.5 draft version of the PDS schemas available at www.portaldoors.org. This data structure model shows the primary and foreign keys that provide referential integrity constraints for the relational database tables of a NEXUS server node in the network system.

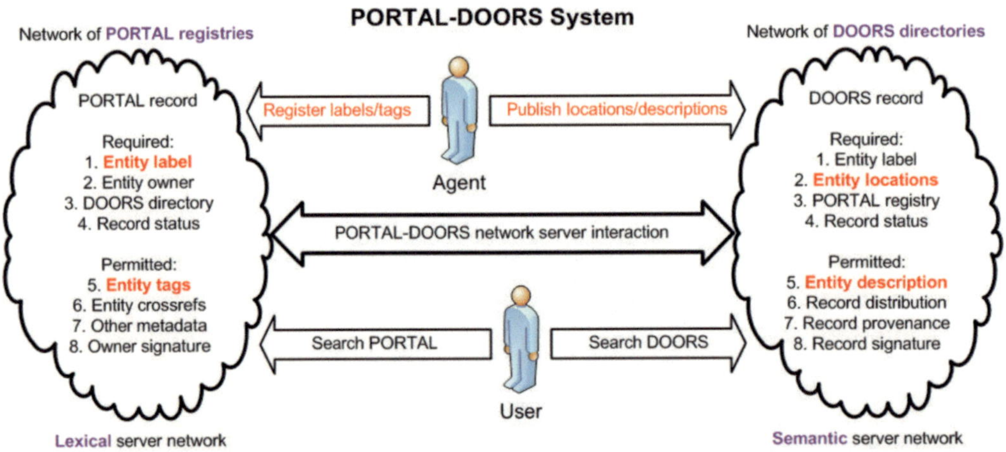

Fig. 2. Resource metadata registered and published by agents for search by users in the PDS networks. Fields within data records are considered *required* or *permitted* with respect to the schemas maintained by the root servers (see Fig. 1).

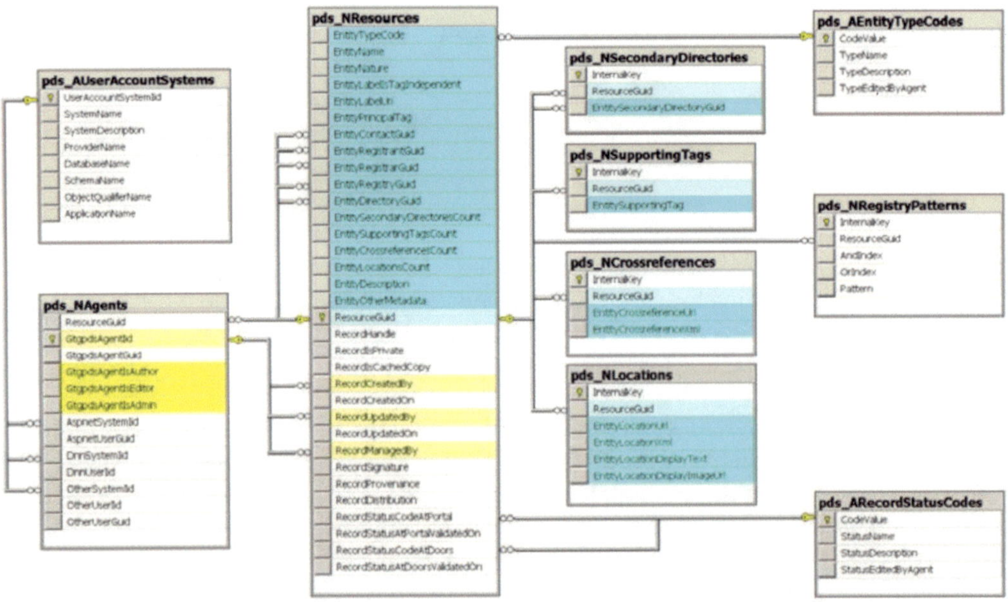

Fig. 3. Relational database model for NEXUS combined design server with integrated storage of both PORTAL and DOORS data record fields.

All PDS tables in the database are named with the prefix `pds_` to distinguish them from the tables of administrative providers such as Microsoft's ASP.Net authentication and authorization services and their database tables named with the prefix `aspnet_`. The table `pds_NResources` serves as the main NEXUS resources table with primary key

ResourceGuid for the related records connected via foreign keys ResourceGuid in each of the dependent tables pds_NSupportingTags, pds_NCrossReferences, pds_NSecondaryDirectories, and pds_NLocations. With the column ordering for the main table pds_NResources as displayed in Figure 3, note that the fields displayed above the primary key are *resource entity* metadata fields whereas those displayed below the primary key are *resource record* metadata fields. Because of the different ways that the metadata can be used, providing distinct keys for the different subsets of metadata offers greater convenience for various programming and interface contexts. Thus, RecordHandle, EntityLabelUri, and ResourceGuid serve as keys for the *resource entity, resource record,* and entire *resource representation*, respectively.

For the *resource entity* metadata within the main table pds_NResources, there are five directly self-referencing relations from fields with the suffix _Guid to five other resources for the EntityContact_, EntityRegistrant_, EntityRegistrar_, EntityRegistry_, and EntityDirectory_. There is no requirement that any of the necessary metadata for each of these five resources be stored at the same NEXUS server node. However, if so, then it can be referenced via the _Guid, and if not, then it can be referenced via the analogous _LabelUri fields (not shown in Figure 3). For example, the resource for the EntityContact_ can be referenced internally via EntityContactGuid or externally via EntityContactLabelUri. Check constraints can be used to prevent both the _Guid and the _LabelUri for the EntityContact_ from being simultaneously non-null. Alternatively, appropriate programming logic can be used to maintain precedence of the internal reference via the _Guid over the external reference via the _LabelUri, or vice versa, depending on the non-null values of these fields in the context of the status of the boolean field RecordIsCachedCopy.

For the *resource record* metadata within the main table pds_NResources, there are three indirectly self-referencing relations from fields with the suffix _By to three other potential resources for the RecordCreatedBy, RecordUpdatedBy, and RecordManagedBy agents. The indirect self-referencing via the auxiliary linking table pds_NAgents provides a simple permission management system implemented with the feature of sufficient flexibility to interface with various user account provider systems, and simultaneously, to render optional the publication of any information pertaining to agents as resources distinct from the contacts and registrants.

Thus, the linking table pds_NAgents mediates between the set of tables for PDS and another set of tables for the authentication and authorization system for managing agent access to inserting updating and deleting records in the NEXUS tables. The linking table has a primary key GtgpdsAgentIid and various alternative optional fields available for linking to user membership providers such as the field AspnetUserGuid for linking to Microsoft's ASP.Net membership provider, OtherUserGuid for linking to an alternate generic user membership provider, etc. In addition, the table pds_NAgents provides the foreign key ResourceGuid for linking back to a resource in the main table pds_NResources for use in a scenario where the persons with responsibility for managing resources in the database are themselves identified and described in the main table.

Regardless of whether an agent is published as a resource, and regardless of whether a resource is an agent, contact or registrant of type person or of any other type, any resource may be flagged as non-publishable by the boolean field `RecordIsPrivate` in the table `pds_NResources`. Also, regardless of code implementation with persistence of the value stored in the field `ResourceEntityLabelUri` or otherwise computed dynamically by concatenation of the `ResourceEntityPrincipalTag` with the label of the entity's registry, it should be emphasized that any PDS implementation must maintain the important requirement of uniquely identifying resources by the *resource entity label* which must be an IRI or URI. For PDS draft version 0.5, both SQL code for the relational database model and XML Schemas for data structure interfaces are available for download from www.portaldoors.org with an operational web site implemented at www.telegenetics.net now available for registration of resources relevant to the problem-oriented domains of the GeneScene, ManRay, BioPort, and BrainWatch registries.

5. Discussion

As a cyberinfrastructure, PDS can be considered an *information-seeking support system* (Marchionini and White, 2009). With an appropriately enhanced user interface, PDS can be considered a *facetted search tool* (Schraefel, 2009). Regardless of use as infrastructure system or application tool, PDS interlinks registries, directories, databases, and knowledgebases across domain-specific fields, disciplines, and specialties. It assures globally unique identification of resources while promoting interoperability and enabling cross registry and cross directory searches between different problem-oriented, not technology-restricted, domains because of the fundamental definition of a resource as any entity, abstract or concrete, online or offline.

PDS has been designed as a hybrid bootstrap and bridge to transition from the old lexical web to the new semantic web, and allows for all constructs from free tagging and folksonomies to microformats and ontologies. It supports mass participation and collaboration via its hierarchical and distributed but decentralized and localizable infrastructure, and as a consequence, provides a democratized solution to the problem of search engine consolidation. Mowshowitz and Kumar (2009) discuss both the realities and the risks of search engines that effectively restrict access to information, and argue that this problem represents a serious concern.

With its infrastructure designed in a distributed manner that permits localized control of policies and content and thereby prevents the possibility of search engine consolidation, the PORTAL-DOORS model is most similar in conceptual paradigm to the IRIS-DNS model that inspired it. In contrast, it can be compared to other familiar models for information management systems exemplified by the Google search engine (www.google.com) or the Wikipedia encyclopedia (www.wikipedia.org). In the case of Google, the server infrastructure is distributed (to some degree) but not the control of content (unless "paid placement" is considered). In the case of Wikipedia, the servers and content are centralized but the control of content is shared by all contributing anonymous authors and editors. However, in the case of PORTAL-DOORS, the server infrastructure, the content control, and the content itself are all shared and distributed. Moreover, the design of the PORTAL-

DOORS framework remains analogous to that of the IRIS-DNS framework with mechanisms that enable data records to be distributed and mobile with request forwarding and response caching.

Continuing progress on the development of PDS with its NEXUS registrars, PORTAL registries, and DOORS directories will focus on implementing all features of the design including both data structures and operational methods for both independent and interacting servers. Content for PORTAL-DOORS will be contributed manually by human agents as has been done for IRIS-DNS. Later, when software agents, webbots, and converters become available, content will be generated automatically or semi-automatically. For manually contributed content compared with automatically generated content, there may be a trade-off in the quality of content produced versus the rate of content production. This trade-off would not be applicable to those situations where existing databases only need an appropriate interface for inbound queries and wrappers for outbound responses.

6. Conclusion

A new bootstrapping combined design for PDS, together with the original separate design for PDS, has been implemented for NEXUS registrars, PORTAL registries, and DOORS directories and demonstrated with the problem-oriented domains declared for the GeneScene, ManRay, BioPORT, and BrainWatch prototype registries. The combined design has many important advantages during early stages of PDS adoption and use. However, the separate design will become useful when concerns about performance, efficiency, and scalability become more significant.

7. References

Marchionini, G. & White, R.W. (2009). Information-Seeking Support Systems (Guest Editors' Introduction to Beyond Search). *IEEE Computer*, Vol. 42, No. 3, pp. 30-32 (DOI 10.1109/MC.2009.88).

Mowshowitz, A. & Kumar, N. (2009). And Then There Were Three. *IEEE Computer*, Vol. 42, No. 2, pp. 108-107 (DOI 10.1109/MC.2009.36).

Schraefel, M.C. (2009). Building Knowledge: What's beyond Keyword Search? *IEEE Computer*, Vol. 42, No. 3, pp. 52-59 (DOI 10.1109/MC.2009.69).

Taswell, C. (2008a). DOORS to the semantic web and grid with a PORTAL for biomedical computing. IEEE *Transactions on Information Technology in Biomedicine*, Vol. 12, No. 2, pp. 191-204 in Special Section on Bio-Grid (DOI 10.1109/TITB.2008.905861).

Taswell, C. (2008b). PORTAL-DOORS Infrastructure System for Translational Biomedical Informatics on the Semantic Web and Grid. *Proceedings of American Medical Informatics Association Summit on Translational Bioinformatics*, poster 43, San Francisco, March 2008.

Zhuge, H.; Xing, Y. & Shi, P. (2008). Resource space model, OWL and database: Mapping and integration. *ACM Transactions on Internet Technology*, Vol. 8, No. 4, pp. 1-31 (DOI 10.1145/ 1391949.1391954).

3

Providing Semantic Content for the Next Generation Web

Irina Efimenko[1], Serge Minor[1], Anatoli Starostin[1],
Grigory Drobyazko[2] and Vladimir Khoroshevsky[3]
[1]*Avicomp Services,*
[2]*Ontos AG,*
[3]*Dorodnicyn Computing Centre, Russian Academy of Sciences,*
Russia

1. Introduction

Semantic Technologies and the Semantic Web (SW) as the embodiment of know-how for practical usage of these technologies are widely discussed, and it is already clear that semantic content available within knowledge portals shall lead us to a new generation of the Internet and knowledge intensive applications.

Some methods of knowledge extraction and processing for the Semantic Web have already been developed, and first applications are in use. But many pitfalls are still awaiting developers of such systems and consumers of solutions, since, in general, Tim Berners-Lee's idea that "The Semantic Web will globalize KR, just as the WWW globalized hypertext" at the technical level is still at an early stage. W3C recommendations exist for machine-readable semantics, appropriate markup and description languages, and sharable knowledge representation techniques, but implementation of the upper layers of the so-called Semantic Web tower (Berners-Lee et al., 2001) is still at R&D stage. So, we can say that the SW-era, in contrast to the Internet-age, is only just approaching, and there are many problems that still need to be solved on this path (Benjamins et al., 2002).

On the other hand, according to the Gartner Report (Cearley et al., 2007), during the next 10 years, Web-based technologies will improve the ability to embed semantic structures in documents, and create structured vocabularies and ontologies to define terms, concepts and relations. This will lead to extraordinary advances in the visibility and exploitation of information - especially in the ability of systems to interpret documents and infer meaning without human intervention. Moreover, by 2012, 80% of public Web sites will use some level of semantic hypertext to create Semantic Web documents and, by 2012, 15% of public Web sites will use more extensive Semantic Web-based ontologies to create semantic databases.

Today solutions aimed at overcoming information exposure are shifting from data gathering and processing to knowledge acquisition and usage. The aim of this chapter is to present one particular approach to this task – the Ontos Solution for the Semantic Web (OSSW). The chapter organization is as follows: in the next part we outline the main problems and tasks, and in part 3 present an overview of the state-of-art in this domain. The main part of this chapter is devoted to the description of the OSSW and to the discussion of some knowledge insensitive applications based on this solution. In particular, in part 4 we present the Ontos instrumental platform, ontology engineering based on this platform, information extraction with systems of the OntosMiner family and the Ontos knowledge store. In part 5 we describe several intelligent Web applications focusing on ontology-driven information extraction, knowledge-based analytics, and integration of extracted knowledge with semantic Wiki. In conclusion we briefly discuss the results presented in this chapter and possible lines of future research and development.

2. Core Issues

As it was mentioned above, one of the main goals of the Semantic Web is semantization of the content which already exists within the classic WWW, and of the new content created each day. Significantly, the semantic representation of processed content should be suitable for usage by program agents oriented at solving customers' tasks. This means that we should have the possibility to create semantic annotations of document collections and support appropriate knowledge bases.

Research and development in this domain started almost 50 years ago and has its roots in research on artificial intelligence (Khoroshevsky, 1998; Benjamins et al., 1999; Decker et al., 1999). The results achieved in these and many other projects set down the theoretical foundations of knowledge representation and manipulation on the Internet, and brought into practice several prototypes of instrumental tools for semantic annotation of documents. Later on, the focus of R&D projects in this domain shifted towards the Internet community and the Semantic Web (Maedche & Staab, 2001). Today the main efforts of the scientific community are aimed at the development of methods and tools for automatic and/or semiautomatic ontology-driven content annotation, both on the Internet and the Deep Web.

The main issues that will be discussed in this chapter are the following:

- Emergence of Semantic Content as a new kind of "raw material" for effective use in the framework of the Semantic Web.
- Need for a new kind of intelligent systems supporting customers' activities within the Semantic Web. Such systems can be characterized as common processing platforms with, at least, three key components:
  - Knowledge Extractor based on powerful information extraction methods and tools (multilingual, effective and easily scalable).
  - Knowledge Warehouse based on the RDF, OWL, SPARQL standards (effective and scalable).
  - Set of customer oriented Semantic Services (Semantic Navigation, Semantic Digesting and Summarization, Knowledge-Based Analytics, etc.).
- Presentation of the results achieved within the first stage of our project, which is oriented at the development and implementation of the OSSW.

3. State-of-Art in the NLP Domain

Several approaches to solving the content semantization problem have been proposed. Within one of them, actively promoted by W3C, it is proposed to use RDF(S) (Bray, 1998) and/or OWL (Heflin, 2004) for semantic annotation. According to Alex Iskold (Iskold, 2007; Iskold, 2008) this approach is powerful and promising but complex for understanding and usage by the bulk of specialists engaged in document annotation. Furthermore, this approach presupposes the availability of powerful and effective instrumental tools for converting existing HTML-content into RDF/OWL metadata. Another known approach,– Microformats (Çelik, 2008) ,–allows to add predefined semantic tags into existing HTML-pages with the use of simple instrumental tools. At the moment many popular sites (for example, Facebook, Yahoo! Local) use this approach to annotate events presented at their Web-pages. Significantly, appropriate instrumental tools within both of these approaches are based on Natural Language (NL) understanding.

Automatic natural language processing (NLP) has always been a major topic in the field of computational linguistics and artificial intelligence. But during the last 5-10 years a new surge of interest has occurred in this domain, not only among research teams but also within the IT industry. These R&D projects have special significance for the SW because NLP is the "bottle neck" within systems of semantic annotation.

A backward glance at R&D in the NLP domain shows (Khoroshevsky, 2002) that there have been several distinct periods of activity:

- *1960s - mid 1970s.* Development of formal models and methods, initial experience in NLP-systems prototyping.
- *Mid 1970s – 1980s.* Development of NLP methods and tools, first industry systems for NL-based communication with Data Bases.
- *Mid 1980s – mid 1990s.* Development of cognitive Natural Language Understanding (NLU) models, implementation of NLP-system prototypes driven by domain models.
- *Mid 1990s – 2000s.* Transition from linguistic analysis of individual sentence to the analysis of entire texts, development of methods and tools for NL-texts processing. First commercial systems for NL-text processing.

The main achievements of R&D during these periods include the following: the functionality of different classes of NLP-systems and their main components was specified (for the most part, these results have retained their importance to this day); theoretically and practically significant morphological models of analysis/synthesis of word forms were proposed; basic models of NL syntactic parsers were developed; a range of practical methods was proposed for the implementation of basic NL syntactic parsers; basic techniques were outlined for heuristic implementation of partial models of NL-statement interpretation; partial models of NL-text conceptual synthesis were developed; some models and methods of linguistic synthesis were suggested and tested within prototype implementations; multilevel (both, linguistic and cognitive) models of text understanding were developed; prototypes of intelligent NL-systems were implemented; several commercial implementations of NL-systems appeared that, for the most part, only mimic full-scale natural language understanding (NLU).

Key features of the modern (V) stage of R&D in this domain include the following: typically, automatic processing is aimed at real-life texts and Web-content, as opposed to artificially constructed (model) texts; multilingual document collections are processed instead of isolate (singular) texts; misprinting and\or misspelling, grammatical errors and other mistakes are present in the texts which undergo processing. Furthermore, today the goal of document processing is not simply representation of the text's meaning, but representation of this meaning in formats suitable for effective storage, acquisition, and further usage of knowledge.

Unfortunately, computational linguistics, artificial intelligence and information technologies haven't up to now come up with powerful and effective NLP-models, and no practically significant solution to the task of full automatic processing of arbitrary NL-texts (even monolingual) from arbitrary domains has yet been proposed. This is why R&D projects in this domain are primarily focused on Information Extraction (IE) systems, Text Mining, and on Semantic Clustering/Classification systems (TREC, 2003). One of the hot topics in this regard is the development and implementation of IE-systems that are oriented at processing multilingual document collections (Poibeau et al., 2003; LREC, 2004) obtained from Internet-pages, RSS feeds and blogs, as well as corporate data bases.

Retrospective literature overview and monitoring of the relevant Internet-resources shows that the leadership in this domain belongs to US, Germany, and Great Britain, followed by Italy, France, Spain, Portugal and Japan. Interesting teams and research centers also exist in Scandinavia and other countries. It should be noted that teams from different countries (and even within one country) differ significantly in the number of members, the level of their proficiency, and quality of results. For example, in the US there are several very large research centers and corporations working in the NLP domain (for instance, Thomas J. Watson Research Center of IBM Research (TALENT, 2009), Intelligent Systems Laboratory and its Natural Language Theory and Technology group from Palo Alto Research Center (PARC, 2009) or Teragram, a division of SAS (TERAGRAM, 2009), and at the same time there exist comparatively small research teams and companies which nevertheless manage to develop very interesting solutions (for example, The Natural Language Processing Group at Stanford University (SNLP, 2009) or company ClearForest (CLEARFOREST, 2009)).

The situation in Europe is a little bit different. As a rule, R&D is represented here by university teams, and the results that these groups achieve are "transported" to the industry by appropriate startup companies. Well-known examples of this approach is the German Research Center for Artificial Intelligence (DFKI) and its Competence Center for Speech & language Technology (LT-CC, 2009), and the company ontoprise GmbH (ONTOPRISE, 2009) founded in 1999 as a spin-off from Karlsruhe University. Another example from Great Britain - The Natural Language Processing Research Group within the Department of Computer Science at the University of Sheffield (NLP-RG, 2009).

The situation in Russia differs both from the US and from Europe in the sense that the spectrum of teams and organizations working in the NLP domain is considerably different both qualitatively and quantitatively. First of all, in Russia most of R&D in the NLP domain is performed by numerous small and very small research teams (there are about 100 projects/teams/organizations with 3-5, rarely 10 members) and within a very restricted number of commercial organizations. Secondly, R&D teams in Russia are mostly theoretically oriented. There are very few examples of research teams implementing their ideas in (prototypes of) working systems. Active R&D teams in Russia are concentrated in such institutions of the Russian Academy of Sciences as the Computing Centre (Khoroshevsky, 2008), ISA (Osipov, 2006), IITP (Boguslavsky et al., 2000), PSI (Kormalev et al., 2002), Institute of Automation and Control Processes with the Computation Center of the Far Eastern Scientific Center (Kleschev & Shalfeeva, 2005), as well as in the Moscow State University (Bolshakova, 2001; Boldasov et al., 2002; Bolshakov & Bolshakova 2006), Kazan State University (Suleymanov, 1997) and several others. Beside this, interesting R&D

projects in the NLP domain have recently been initiated in several commercial organizations such as Yandex (Maslov et a., 2006) and RCO (Ermakov, 2007). The leader among these is the Russian IT-company Avicomp Services (Khoroshevsky, 2003; Efimenko et al., 2004; Khoroshevsky, 2005; Hladky & Khoroshevsky, 2007; Efimenko, 2007; Dudchuk & Minor, 2009; Efimenko et al. 2008; Malkovskij & Starostin 2009).

The scope of this chapter does not allow us to present a complete overview of the progress made by different researchers in the domain of NLP. Nevertheless, summarizing these achievements we can state that important results in the domain of information extraction from texts in different languages in restricted domains already exist today. At the same time, there are very few works concerned with NLP of texts from arbitrary domains, there are no recognizable results in the processing of multilingual document collections, and there are practically no systems that support the full technological cycle of generating semantic content from NL-texts and using it within intelligent applied systems for the Semantic Web.

In the next parts of this chapter we present and discuss in depth the OSSW, which addresses many of the problems mentioned above. This approach is the result of multiyear R&D carried out by the Russian IT-company Avicomp Services in collaboration with the Swiss IT-company Ontos AG, and the Computing Center, RAS.

4. Our Approach to Semantic Content Generation

4.1 Related work

Our activity in the domain of Semantic Technologies and the Semantic Web in context of semantic content generation is related to a number of recent research and development projects outlined below.

4.1.1 Multilingual Information Extraction

Literature on information extraction methods, techniques and systems is well known (Manning & Schütze, 1999; Engels & Bremdal, 2000; Xu et al., 2002; Ciravegna, 2003; LREC, 2004). However, most of R&D projects in this domain focus either on statistical approaches to natural language processing (Manning & Schütze, 1999) or on classic information extraction approaches with the following core limitations: monolingual text processing; a moderate number of named entity (NE) types and very few types of semantic relations which are extracted; processing without control from the domain model (TREC, 2000; Poibeau et al., 2003). In contrast to that, our approach (Khoroshevsky, 2003; Efimenko et al., 2004; Khoroshevsky, 2005) is oriented at ontology-driven multilingual information extraction of a sizeable number of NE types and semantic relations, and at the representation of results in RDF(S)/XML/OWL/N3 formats. At the instrumental level our NLP engine is partially grounded in the GATE software platform (Cunningham et al., 2002), extended within the Ontos project by a powerful knowledge representation language and other linguistic modules and technological components (Karasev et al., 2003). Another important part of our NLP instrumental platform is the OntosMiner Domains Description database combined with a user interface for managing complex ontological data (see section 4.4 below).

4.1.2 Knowledge Management

One of the key topics in the domain of knowledge management is development and implementation of effective and scalable knowledge warehouses. A host of materials related to various aspects of such storages has appeared as a result of work performed by European and international workgroups (Beckett et al., 2001; Berners-Lee, 2000), within the proceedings of different conferences (WWW, 2003), and in open source communities (Broekstra et al., 2002; Wood et al., 2005). Some related materials are distributed by turnkey DBMS vendors, such as Oracle, etc. (ORACLE, 2007a). Furthermore, a number of semantic storages has already been developed and implemented, for example the KIM platform (Popov et al., 2004).

Generally speaking, within the Ontos project we follow the mainstream tendencies in the development and implementation of knowledge warehouses. At the same time, our prime focus is on the development of methods for aggregating knowledge extracted from documents and/or document collections, and on effective implementation of an integrated semantic RDF-store based on open source software platforms and packages, and within a commercial RDBS (ORACLE, 2007b). The basic requirements for our knowledge storage are the following: full support of all the main operations related to aggregation of semantically meaningful entities and relations, efficient pattern-matching search, and exchange with external applications in XML and/or OWL format.

4.1.3 Semantic Services

The idea of "Semantic Services" is widely discussed, and is sometimes seen as the next logical step for the Service Oriented Architecture (Hinchcliffe, 2005). There are many ideas and approaches in this field (Alesso, 2004; Akkiraju et al., 2005) but the mainstream seems to be the development and implementation of useful sets of knowledge intensive applications based on widgets technology (Garrett, 2005). Our approach to Semantic Services is oriented at the development and implementation of several knowledge intensive applications, such as Semantic Navigation, Semantic Digesting and Summarization, Business Intelligence, etc. (Hladky et al., 2007; Efimenko et al., 2007; Hladky, 2009).

4.2 Ontos Solution: An Overview

Semantic Content within the Semantic Web framework can be viewed as a new kind of "raw material", which serves as input for Semantic Services that process it and present the results to customers. According to such an understanding, the Ontos solution is oriented at the following aspects of Semantic Technologies:

- Information-intensity, and particularly:
  - Semantic content as a product.
  - Semantic services based on semantic content.
  - Interfaces for third-party development of services based on semantic content.
- Semantic Infrastructure for A2Ai (Application-to-Application integration) and B2Bi (Business-to-Business integration) solutions, including:
  - Services pertaining to the integration of existing applications and data based on semantics.
  - Semantic content as an additional information resource.
  - Semantic data warehouses with services.

The Ontos Service Oriented Architecture (Ontos SOA) and an appropriate software platform were developed to support these aspects of Semantic Technologies within the Ontos solution. The general workflow within the Ontos Solution is illustrated below.

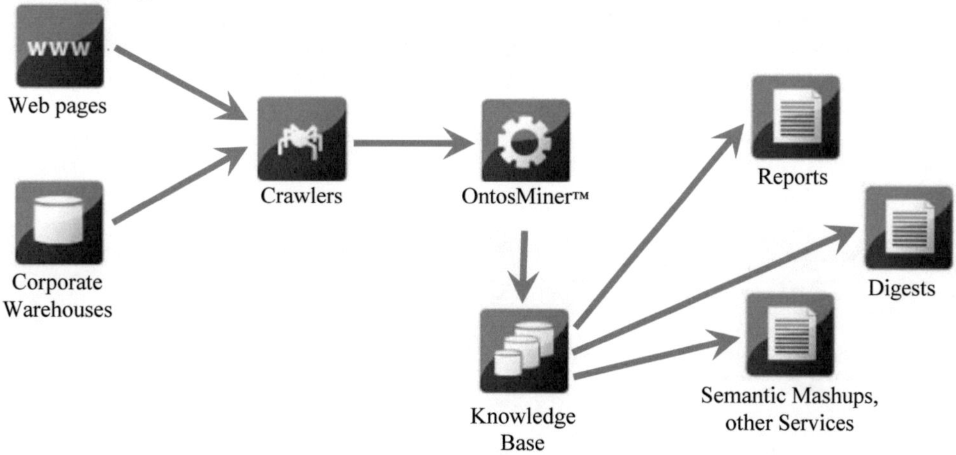

Fig 1. Workflow within the OSSW

This diagram consists of five basic components: input documents (from the WWW or corporate warehouses), crawlers, linguistic processors of the OntosMiner family, and semantic applications (reports, digests etc.).
The crawler component gathers web-pages from a pre-defined list of WWW-resources or documents from corporate warehouses, and transforms them into plain-text documents. These are then fed as input to the OntosMiner linguistic processors, which are discussed in detail in sections 4.3 and 4.4. The output of these processors is a semantic graph (in RDF/XML, OWL, Turtle or N3 format) which represents named entities and relations recognized in the input text.
This graph is then stored in the knowledge base, where incoming knowledge is integrated with existing data. This process of integration is based on algorithms of object identification which make use of the Identification Knowledge Base (IKB). Properties of the Knowledge Base and the IKB employed in our system are discussed in more detail in section 4.5.
The data in the knowledge base is accessed by various web-oriented semantic applications, which were designed to provide end users with interesting and powerful services based on semantic metadata (see section 5 of the present chapter for a detailed discussion of some of these applications).

4.3 Information Extraction with Systems of the OntosMiner Family

4.3.1 Processors of the OntosMiner Family: Architecture and Basic Modules

Generally speaking, each IE-system of the OntosMiner family takes as input a plain text written in a natural language and returns a set of annotations, which are themselves sets of feature-value correspondences. Each annotation must have at least four features which define the type of annotation, its unique numerical identifier, and its start and end offsets (e.g. its placement in the input text). These output annotations represent the objects and relations which the processor was able to extract from the text.

Each OntosMiner linguistic processor (shortly, OntosMiner) consists of a set of specialized modules called 'resources' which are organized into 'resource chains' (Fig. 2). In this chain the resources are launched one after another and each subsequent resource has access to the output of previously launched resources. E.g. each resource modifies a common annotation set which is then fed as input to the next resource in the resource chain. Configurations of resource chains are created, edited and stored within the OntosMiner Domains Description database which is described below.

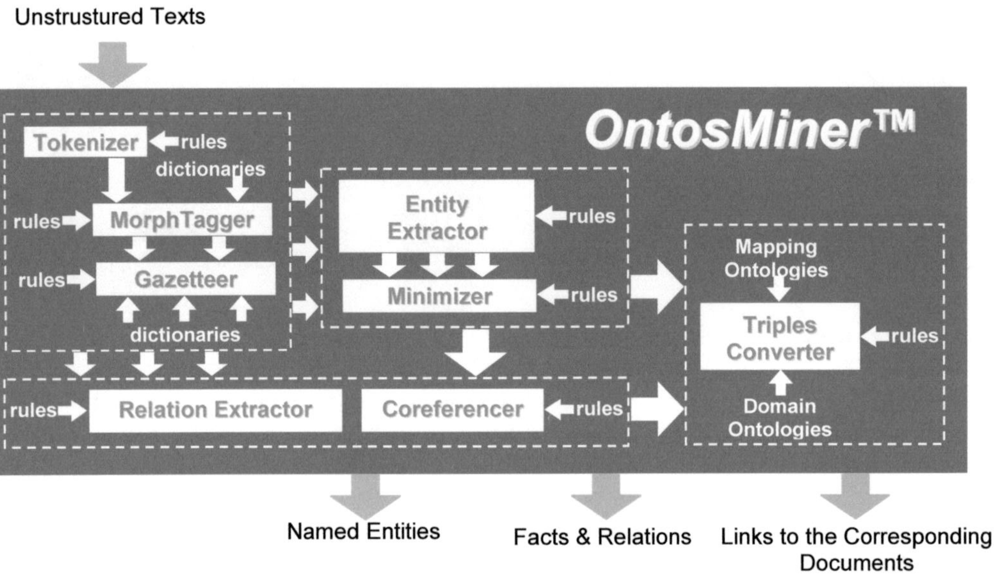

Fig. 2. Basic OntosMiner functionality and resource chain

We shall now give a short overview of the main types of resources employed in OntosMiner processors.

The first step is to determine word boundaries based on formal signs (spaces, paragraphs etc.) This is done by a resource called Tokenizer which generates a set of annotations of the type 'Token', corresponding to individual words in the input text. These annotations also contain some formal information about the corresponding words, e.g. length, distribution of uppercase and lowercase letters etc.

Next the set of Token annotations is fed to the Morphological Analyzer. This resource generates a set of annotations of the type 'Morph' which correspond to possible variants of morphological analysis for each word. Morphs include information about the word's base form and its morphological attributes (e.g. case, number, tense etc.), as well as formal features inherited from the corresponding Token annotations. One word (e.g. Token) can have several variants of morphological analysis; this is why the Morphological Analyzer often generates several Morphs with identical offsets. In certain processors we make use of statistical POS-tagging modules to reduce ambiguity in the morphological analysis.

The work of the Morphological Analyzer is based on dictionaries which store morphological information about individual words of a given language. These dictionaries can be accessed and updated via a specially developed user interface.

The set of Tokens and Morphs serves as input for the next resource - the Gazetteer. This resource annotates key words and key phrases which are later used for the recognition of named entities and relations (see below for more details). The key words and phrases are stored in special dictionaries in their base form. The developer has a possibility to semi-automatically determine the syntactic structure of a key phrase in the dictionary to reduce the risk of false recognition. This is useful when working with languages with rich inflectional morphology, such as Russian or German. For instance, if a key phrase consists of an adjective modifier X and a head noun Y the developer can indicate that the adjective must agree with the noun in certain morphological features (for instance gender and number). This means that only those sequences of adjective X and noun Y which fall under the restriction on agreement shall be annotated as a key phrase.

The annotations of key words and key phrases contain features which determine the role that these keys play in the recognition of named entities and relations, as well as the formal and morphological features inherited from the corresponding Morph annotations. They can also contain some additional information, such as the 'strength' of a specific key (see below).

These three modules - Tokenizer, Morphological Analyzer and Gazetteer - prepare the input for the two main modules of the system - Entity Extractor and Relation Extractor.

4.3.2 Named Entity Recognition

Named entity recognition is performed by the resource Entity Extractor. In this domain we have adopted the rule-based approach to NLP which means that named entities are identified according to rules defined by developers (Engels & Bremdal, 2000). Thus, the Entity Extractor consists of a set of rules divided into subsets called 'phases' which are applied sequentially to the annotation set. Rules from each subsequent phase have access to the output of rules in previous phases. Each rule consists of a pattern on the annotation set and a sequence of commands which define the action that has to be performed when the pattern is encountered. The pattern is written in the Jape+ language, which is an extended version of the Jape language developed by the Natural Language Processing Group at the University of Sheffield (Cunningham et al., 2002). The action parts of rules are mostly written in Java.

The main idea underlying the approach that we adopt is that named entities in natural language texts can be recognized based on two types of keys: internal and external keys (McDonald, 1996). Internal keys are key words and phrases which themselves form part of the named entity to be recognized. For instance, the key word *University* is an internal key for names of educational organizations such as *University of Michigan* or *Cornell University*. External keys, on the other hand, are not included into the named entity, but constitute the context for its recognition. For instance, job titles can be used as external keys for the recognition of persons' names, as in *Microsoft* ***CEO*** *Steve Ballmer*.

The list of possible keys for named entity recognition includes the key words and phrases annotated by the Gazetteer module, as well as annotations generated by previous phases of the Entity Extractor, and even specific features of annotations. For instance, the fact that a word begins with an upper case letter (this feature is supplied by the Tokenizer) can play a significant role in the recognition of proper names in languages like English and French.

Typically, the system of rules for the recognition of a certain type of named entity comprises several dozens of interlinked rules which 'build' the target annotations through a number of intermediate steps.

The table below contains two simple examples of patterns used for the identification of names of universities written in Jape+, and text fragments which correspond to these patterns.

Pattern	Text fragment
{Location} *// an annotation of the type 'Location'* {Lookup.majorType == "org_base", Lookup.minorType == "org_edu" Lookup.orth == "upperInitial"} *// a key word or phrase for educational organizations which starts with an uppercase letter* {Token.string == "of"} *// the word 'of'* {Token.orth == "upperInitial"} *// a word which starts with an uppercase letter*	Massachusetts Institute of Technology
{Lookup.majorType == "org_base", Lookup.minorType == "org_edu" Lookup.orth == "upperInitial"} *// a key word or phrase for educational organizations which starts with an uppercase letter* {Token.string == "of"} *// the word 'of'* {Location} *// an annotation of the type 'Location'* ({Token.string == "at"} {Location})? *// an optional sequence of the word 'at' and an annotation of the type 'Location'*	University of New York at Stony Brook

Table 1. Examples of patterns for named entity extraction

One of the main difficulties with the rule based approach that we adopt is the emergence of conflicts between different rules. For instance, one set of rules within the Entity Extractor can identify a certain text fragment as part of a person's name, while a different set of rules identifies it as part of a company name. We discovered that when the number of rules involved grows beyond one hundred, it becomes increasingly difficult and inconvenient to try to control for such conflicts within the rule system itself. This is why in OntosMiner processors we allow the rules for named entity extraction to apply freely, but complement the Entity Extractor with a special module called Minimizer which defines the policies for conflict resolution. The idea is that different rules have a varying measure of reliability (i.e. varying potential for overgeneration), and that the developer can evaluate this measure for each rule and state it as a feature of the annotation created by this rule using a common scale for all annotation types.

Thus, annotations generated by the Entity Extractor come with a feature called 'Weight' which has an integer value ranging from 0 to 100. This feature reflects the probability (as estimated by the developer) that this annotation is correct. One of the things that determine the weight of a rule is the measure of potential ambiguity of the keys employed in this rule (e.g. keys can be 'strong' or 'weak'). For key words and phrases generated by the Gazetteer this information can be tied to the key already in the dictionary.

The Minimizer resource contains a set of rules which describe different types of conflict and define which annotations should survive and which should be deleted, based on the types of annotations involved in the conflict and their weights. The resulting 'minimized' annotation set is passed on to the Relation Extractor.

4.3.3 Recognition of Semantic Relations

Semantic relations are certain facts or situations mentioned in the input text which relate one named entity to another, such as information about a person's employment in a company, about a meeting between two persons, or about a contract deal between two companies. The module which is responsible for the recognition of semantic relations in OntosMiner processors is the Relation Extractor. Just like the Entity Extractor, the Relation Extractor contains a set of rules written in Jape+ and Java, grouped into a sequence of phases.

Recognition of semantic relations differs from the recognition of named entities in that named entities are expressed by compact word groups, while the keys for semantic relations can be situated quite far apart from each other within one sentence or within the whole text. This is why in developing rules for relation recognition we exploit a different strategy: we reduce the set of annotations which is fed as input to the rules, so that it includes only key words and phrases needed to identify a particular relation, and conversely, 'stop-words' and 'stop-phrases' which should never interfere between the keys. All other annotations are not included into the input and are not 'visible' to the rules. For instance, there is a pattern for the recognition of the relation 'PersonalMetting' (a relation which connects two persons which are claimed to have met on some occasion) which includes an annotation of the type 'Person', an annotation for the key verb 'meet' and another 'Person' annotation, in that order. This pattern covers simple cases like *Barack Obama met Ehud Olmert in Jerusalem.* But it is obvious that different kinds of syntactic material can interfere between the elements of this pattern (for instance, *Barack Obama met* ***the Israeli Prime Minister*** *Ehud Olmert in Jerusalem,* or *Barack Obama* ***after landing in Jerusalem*** *met* ***the Israeli Prime Minister*** *Ehud Olmert*), and it is impossible to enumerate all such potential 'interveners'. This problem is solved if only the relevant annotation types are fed as input to the discussed rule, i.e. the type 'Person' and the type of annotation for the key verb 'meet'. In this case all irrelevant syntactic material becomes 'invisible' for the rule, and the pattern works in a desired fashion. If we leave it at that, our pattern would probably lead to overgeneration, that's why certain stop annotation types are also included into the input. If in some text an annotation of this type occurs between elements of the pattern, the relation will not be generated because the interfering annotation would be 'visible' to the rule.

A semantic relation extracted by the Relation Extractor can be codified in two different ways. It can either correspond to a separate annotation with two obligatory features ('to' and 'from') which contain unique identifiers of the named entities that are connected by this relation. Such relations can have features which carry certain additional information about the fact or situation in question. For instance, the relation 'BeEmployeeOf' which relates persons to organizations where they work has an additional feature 'JobTitle' which carries information about the person's position in the organization. The offsets of such annotations are not as important as the offsets of named entities and are usually taken to be equal either to the offsets of some key word or phrase, or to the offsets of one of the related entities, or alternatively, to the offsets of the sentence where the relation was recognized.

Another way to codify a semantic relation is by means of a feature in the annotation of a named entity. Such a feature would have as its name the type of relation and as its value a unique identifier of the related named entity. Thus, instead of creating a separate annotation for the relation 'BeEmployeeOf' we could create a feature with the name 'BeEmployeeOf' in the annotation of a person, and put the unique identifier of the corresponding organization as its value. The drawback is that in this case we cannot add any additional features to the relation, but the advantage is that such a way of codifying relations is more compact and requires less storage space.

4.3.4 Co-reference

A distinguished type of relation is the relation 'TheSame' (also called the 'identification relation') which is established between two co-referring occurrences of a named entity within a text. The resource which establishes relations of this type is called OntosCoreferencer. This resource builds a matrix of all the relevant annotations and compares them two by two to establish whether the annotations in each pair can count as two co-referring occurrences or not. Its work is based on a set of identification rules which determine what kinds of correspondences between features of two annotations are sufficient to establish an identification relation. For instance, consider the following text fragment:

Daimler AG *(DAI) Tuesday posted a worse-than-expected net loss in the first quarter as global demand for trucks and luxury cars collapsed, confirming that full-year revenue and vehicle sales will come in significantly lower than in 2008.*
*"**Daimler** anticipates a gradual improvement in operating profitability as the year progresses. Earnings in the second quarter are expected to be significantly negative once again, however," the German automaker said in a statement, adding that it targets EUR 4 billion in cost savings this year.*

This text mentions the same company 'Daimler AG' twice, but in slightly different form. The first occurrence contains the key word 'AG' which is often found at the end of company names, while the second occurrence does not contain this ending. To ensure that an identification relation is established in such cases two conditions must be met. First, the Entity Extractor which identifies the string 'Daimler AG' as a company name should add an additional feature to this annotation which is equal to the company name without the ending. We call this feature 'MatchName'. Thus, the annotation of the type 'Company' corresponding to 'Daimler AG' should contain both the full name 'Daimler AG' and the shorter MatchName 'Daimler'.
Second, the set of rules for the OntosCoreferencer should include a rule which establishes an identification relation between two annotations of the type 'Company' if the full name of one of these annotations matches the MatchName feature of the second annotation. In our example the full name of the second occurrence is equal the MatchName feature of the first occurrence, and so the necessary relation shall be established.
Similar rules are used on the Knowledge Base level for discovering multiple occurrences of the same named entity in different texts (see below). We employ a separate set of rules within OntosMiner processors primarily for two reasons. First, identification rules within a single text can be less restrictive than similar rules operating between different texts. For instance, if we discover two occurrences 'John Smith' and 'Mr. Smith' within a single text it is very likely that they refer to the same person. Thus, in the OntosCoreferencer resource we can state a rule that matches two annotations of the type 'Person' if they have identical family name features and non-conflicting first name features. On the other hand, if we formulate such an identification rule between different texts we face a significant risk of uniting objects which refer to completely different people.
The second reason is that on the Knowledge Base level we are much more restricted by productivity issues, because rules on that level generally apply to a much larger body of data. This means that within the OntosCoreferencer resource we can formulate complex conditional rules which on the Knowledge Base level would lead to an unacceptable slump of the system's productivity.

4.3.5 The Output

The final resource in the resource chain of every OntosMiner processor is the Triples Converter. This module takes as input the set of annotations created by previous modules and generates an output in the form of an RDF/XML, OWL, Turtle or N3 document. During its work the Triples Converter accesses the OntosMiner Domains Description database (see below) and replaces all the names of annotations generated by the OntosMiner processor with the names of corresponding concepts and relations of the Domain Ontology, using the mapping rules defined in the Mapping Ontology. All the OntosMiner annotations for which mapping rules have not been defined, are excluded from the output.

As was already mentioned above, the work of OntosMiner processors is defined by and based upon the information stored in the OntosMiner Domains Description database. We give an overview of its functions in section 4.4.

4.3.6 Language (In)Dependence of OntosMiner Processors

Within the OSSW we have developed several OntosMiner linguistic processors which work with English, German, Russian and French languages. All of these processors can make use of common domain ontologies which allows us to unify the results of processing multilingual text collections. On the other hand, the processors have to use language specific morphological modules and Gazetteers. The linguistic rules for entity and relation extraction have much in common, but there are also important differences which are due to differences in the syntactic structure of these languages, and even to orthographic peculiarities. For instance, as it was mentioned above, the fact that a certain word starts with an uppercase letter is an important key for the recognition of proper names in English, French and Russian, but this heuristic does not work for German because common noun are also written with an uppercase letter in German texts.

4.4 Ontological Engineering in the Ontos Solution

During the development of OntosMiner processors it is often necessary to work with new domains, to change or to make more exact existing domains' specifications or to tune these specifications to suit the needs of a certain customer. In all these cases efficiency plays a decisive role. Similar procedures have to be applied not only to ontological domain descriptions, but also to the sets of linguistic rules and resources, and to dictionaries and thesauri. This led us to develop an instrument which would support all the mentioned activities in a convenient way. This instrument is called OntosMiner Manager.

It is well known that ontological engineering is one of the core processes in the life cycle of semantic-oriented applications. Today there exist several methodologies, technologies and tools supporting this activity (Gómez-Pérez et al., 2004; Nicola et al., 2009). An overview of the most popular tools for ontological engineering is presented, for example, in (Simperl & Tempich, 2006). An overwhelming majority of them is oriented at creating and maintaining domain ontologies and doesn't have anything in common with editing linguistic dictionaries or developing natural language processors.

However, on the conceptual level, configuring a linguistic processor or a system of linguistic dictionaries may also be viewed upon as a new domain, the complexity of which is comparable with, for instance, political or business domains. This new domain in its turn may be modeled by an ontology. For example, while describing the workflow of a linguistic processor one can use such concepts as 'TextProcessingResource' and 'TextProcessingResourceChain'. Resources which are configured in a certain way will become instances of these concepts (e.g. Tokeniser configured to analyze the German language, Entity Extractor configured to extract organizations from French texts etc.). The list of upper concepts from dictionary ontologies includes, for instance, 'Dictionary' and 'DictionaryEntry' concepts. These ontologies also contain more specific concepts. For instance, concepts which describe the morphological categories of a given language.

Thus, a significant part of the information which determines the way an OntosMiner processor works may be represented using ontologies. All this information as a whole is called OntosMiner Domains Description (OMDD). On the physical level OMDD is the data, which is uploaded to an RDF-based triplestore (OMDD database). Ontological data in the OMDD is stored in a format which is completely compatible with OWL.

Generally speaking, OMDD is a system of ontologies which can be divided into 6 classes:

- Domain ontologies

These ontologies contain concepts and relations which are relevant for a certain domain (e.g. Politics, Business, Medicine etc.). Domain ontologies are interconnected by relations of inheritance. In OWL terms, one ontology can import concepts and relations from another ontology.

- Internal ontologies

These ontologies represent the sets of annotation types, features and possible feature values used in specific OntosMiner processors. Each annotation type corresponds to a concept in the internal ontology.

- Dictionary ontologies

These ontologies are used to store morphological dictionaries and dictionaries of key words and phrases. Each dictionary entry is linked to a concept from a certain thesaurus, which is also stored in the OMDD. Ontological dictionaries are used by the Gazetteer to recognize entities from thesauri in texts. Besides, dictionaries of a similar structure are used within a special component called OntoDix which allows end-users to add their personal instances and concepts to the set of objects recognized by OntosMiner.

- Resource ontologies

These ontologies represent sequences of text processing resources which are used by OntosMiner processors. Each resource type corresponds to a concept in a resource ontology. For instance the resource type 'JPlusTransducer' includes all the resources which are able to execute Jape+ rules.

- Mapping ontologies

These ontologies are accessed by OntosMiner processors in the course of generating the output document. Mappings ensure that concepts from the internal ontology are correctly replaced with concepts from the domain ontology.

- Other (auxiliary) ontologies

Each OntosMiner linguistic processor is defined by a group of ontologies which necessarily includes a domain ontology, an internal ontology, a resource ontology and a mapping ontology. Apart from that, it can include a dictionary ontology and one or more auxiliary ontologies (for instance, the ontology representing German morphological categories is included into the group of ontologies which defines the OntosMiner processor for the German language).

The current OMDD contains about 120 ontologies (around 2,5 million triples). Obviously, such level of complexity calls for an effective and convenient ontology management subsystem.

The core of OntosMiner Manager is an ontology editor which has the following characteristic features:

- effective work with complex multi-ontology systems
- capacity for automated ontology refactoring
- effective management of large sets of instances
- a flexible Graphical User Interface (GUI), which allows for easy automation of routine procedures
- convenient visual data representation specifically designed to work with complex graphs

OntosMiner Manager also includes the following extensions:

- a component for viewing and editing morphological dictionaries and dictionaries of key words and phrases
- a component for bulk dictionary extension

4.5 Ontos Semantic Knowledge Base

The Ontos Semantic Knowledge Base is one of the core components within the Ontos solution. Its main function is to provide effective storage of the RDF-graph which accumulates all the information extracted from large collections of texts by OntoMiner processors. Data in the Knowledge Base can be accessed via queries in the SPARQL query language. This task is facilitated by a special module called SPARQL Console which provides a GUI to query the knowledge base. It allows developers and knowledge managers to create and delete graphs, construct views based on SPARQL queries, export and import RDF data sets to/from files in standard RDF representation formats.

At the moment, we have two implementation of the Knowledge Base - one based on RDMS Oracle 11g and another one based on Open Source libraries and platforms for the implementation of RDF-stores.

A crucial problem in this regard is the presence of duplicate objects (i.e. objects that represent the same real world entities) within the accumulated RDF graph. For instance, if the linguistic processor identifies an object *Barack Obama* with the feature 'Status=president' in one text, and an object *Obama* with the feature 'Status=president' in another text, we need to have a mechanism that would enable us to merge these two objects, so that all the knowledge about one real world person Barack Obama would be related to a single object in our Knowledge Base. In our system this task is performed by algorithms of object identification which make use of Identification Knowledge Bases.

4.5.1 Object Identification and Identification Knowledge Bases

The task of object identification is performed in several steps. First, each object which is extracted from an input text receives a set of identifiers, which are calculated based on the values of the object's own features and on the values of features of other objects that are connected with this object by semantic relations. For instance, objects of the type 'Person' may receive identifiers based on the combination of values of the following features: FirstName + FamilyName, FamilyName + Status, FamilyName + name of the organization which is connected to the person via the 'BeEmployeeOf' relation etc. If an object has all the relevant features and relations it will receive several identifiers. Returning to an earlier example, the object *Barack Obama* with the feature 'Status=president' will receive two identifiers: one based on the combination 'Barack' + 'Obama', the other based on the combination 'Obama' + 'president'. On the other hand, the object *Obama* with the feature 'Status=president' will receive only one identifier, based on the combination 'Obama' + 'president'. Importantly, identical combinations of values give rise to identical identifiers. Thus these two objects shall have one identifier in common - the one generated from the values of 'FamilyName' and 'Status' features (i.e. 'Obama' + 'president').

Next, the identifiers of each object are compared with the identifiers of objects in the so called Identification Knowledge Bases (IKBs), and if a matching object (i.e. an object with an intersecting set of identifiers) is found, the objects are merged.

IKBs are databases which ideally contain validated objects with no duplicates. IKBs perform a dual role of filtering and merging the content generated by OntosMiner linguistic processors. There are several modes of initially building up IKBs. One possibility is to compose them manually, possibly taking as starting point all the objects extracted from a large collection of documents and then filtering them by hand, merging duplicates and removing errors. This approach guarantees high precision of the results, but it is labor-intensive and does not guarantee satisfactory recall, especially when we are dealing with a constant inflow of new content, for instance in case of processing news content. The problem is that if the set of objects in IKBs is fixed from the start based on some initial collection of texts, the system will never be able to identify objects which were not mentioned in that collection but became prominent in later texts. This is why we adopt a semi-automatic approach to composing IKBs. This means, that the initial set of objects is validated manually, but new objects which are not merged with objects from this initial set are not discarded, but placed in a secondary IKB database. Once the number of recognized occurrences of an object from the secondary IKB in different texts passes a certain threshold, it is transferred to the primary IKB. Functionally, the difference between primary and secondary IKBs is that only objects present in the primary IKB are accessible to end users via semantic applications (see below).

5. Intelligent Applications for the Next Generation Web

5.1 Own vs. Third-party Applications

The presented Ontos solution presumes two modes of access for external users: the accumulated semantic content can either be accessed via our own implemented semantic applications, or semantic content can be provided for use by third-party applications via an API.

There are three modes of access to Ontos semantic content for external systems:

- access to the output of OntosMiner which contains the results of processing separate documents;
- access to personalized content which is enriched with user-defined concepts by means of OntosDix (see above);
- access to identified content which appears as a result of filtering the content through the IKBs.

Conformity with W3C standards, flexibility and a wide range of output formats makes Ontos semantic content easy to use in external applications.
Our own solutions based on semantic content include, but are not limited to, packages for media-analysis, law enforcement, publishers, science & technology.

5.2 Semantic Portals for Innovative Fields

The main goals of "semantizing" NL-content are related to integrating pieces of information, identifying implicit connections, and providing the possibility to receive an object's profile, to find out trends, etc. All these issues are particularly important for innovative fields.
The OSSW underlies a number of portals for corporate customers and communities working in the fields of science and technology, including innovative fields, such as Nanotechnology, Nuclear energy, Power industry, Pharmacology, etc. The structure and functionality of these portals are similar in many respects, since users from different fields generally have common basic requirements.

5.2.1 Information Sources and Domain Models

In order to carry out a full-scale analysis of different aspects of any innovative field, one should integrate information from a variety of sources of different structure and content. This arduous work is among the daily tasks of researchers and analysts working on scientific papers, project appraisal, investment and patent analysis, etc. Thus, relevant information sources can include (but are not limited to) the following ones:

- Patent collections;
- Databases with descriptions of international projects and programmes;
- Conference materials and scientific papers;
- Blogs and forums in a specific domain;
- Regulatory documents;
- Opinion letters of analytic companies;
- Internet portals, news in technology, RSS feeds.

It is also worth mentioning that the most interesting data can be extracted from multilingual document collections, allowing users, above all, to get a picture of a certain field on an international scale.
This makes it evident that the technology underlying the knowledge extraction process should be as flexible as possible in order to be valuable for the users.
The OSSW possesses the needed level of flexibility due to the key features of its architecture, such as fine-tunable crawlers, powerful ontology-driven NLP engines and easy-to-combine components, as well as ontology editing tools supporting sophisticated techniques of inheritance and mapping.
The ontological system used for knowledge extraction is based on a combination of ontologies corresponding to specific domains and information sources. This means that each particular ontology is determined by concepts and relations relevant for the domain and typical for the considered source (e.g. "Inventors" and "Assignees" for Patent analysis).
An example of a system of domain models which underlie portals for innovative fields is presented below in Table 2. Points 2-7 correspond to ontologies, which inherit the so-called 'common' ontology, which in its turn inherits a domain-independent upper-ontology.

Partially, sub-ontologies can intersect, which is supported in OntosMiner Manager by a number of corresponding methods and tools.

№	Ontology	Description, Concepts, Relations
1	"Common"	"Basic" concepts and relations relevant for most of the ontologies in the considered domain. It can be viewed as an upper ontology specific for the domain of interest
2	Patents	Inventors, Inventions, Assignees, Agents, Key terms, Fields, etc.
3	Conferences	Events, Participants, Papers, Authors, Co-authors, etc.
4	News (specific for the field)	Mostly coinciding with the "Common" ontology; Sentiment
5	Projects	Projects, Investment, Programmes, Programme Types, etc.
6	Finance	Revenue, Shareholders, Producers, Customers, Stock information, Officers, etc.
7	Analytical research	Technology maturity, Producers, Customers, Competence, etc.

Table 2. Example of a system of domain ontologies for innovative fields

All the domain ontologies are language independent. This means that the NLP modules for any language relevant for the project are driven by the same ontologies. Language specificity is taken into consideration at the level of linguistic rules and linguistic (dictionary) ontologies.

5.2.2 Semantic Portals' Functionality

In this section we discuss a particular example of Web portal created on the basis of OSSW. This portal is oriented at users working in the field of innovative technologies. It includes the following sections: News/Monitoring, Experts, Companies and Institutions, Shadow groups, Analytics, "My Objects" analysis, Geographic Information System (GIS), Graph Navigation.

News/Monitoring. This page is meant for on-line monitoring of media-sources which are considered relevant by the customer/community. Objects and relations relevant for the field are extracted which makes it possible to form ratings, illustrate trends, and determine the semantic focus of processed documents. A multilingual thesaurus is integrated into the page. Filtering by categories, sources, object types, etc. is provided.

Experts. Companies and Institutions. Shadow groups. For the most part, the content for these sections is related to patents, scientific papers, PhD theses, and conference materials. OntosMiner extracts information about inventors, authors and co-authors, assignees, affiliations, etc. This allows users to find experts and leaders in the domain of their interest, and to look for shadow groups of people and institutions working in the domain, based on thesauri and objects of interest. Let us consider a typical task of finding a reviewer for a paper or for a project, which is relevant, say, for investment analysts, or finding scholars of authority, which is important for young researchers. In order to solve this task, one can select terms, objects of interest, nodes of the thesaurus, etc. and a collection of processed documents, e.g. conference materials. Based on a given input, the system helps the user to find personalities with proper reputation in the domain of interest. These are selected based on the number and status of publications or inventions, on the citation index, on a ranking of semantic relevance etc.

Analytics. "My Objects" analysis. These sections provide Business Intelligence (BI) tools for presenting a variety of views on the data stored in the Knowledge Base. Pie-charts, column diagrams, matrices help users to discover trends, areas of concentration of financial, intellectual and other resources, discover lacunae, etc. Ontos tools, as well as third-party instruments, can be used for presenting information in this section. Several standard formats such as RDF/XML, Turtle, etc. are supported for the output of the OSSW which facilitates integration with a variety of tools, and gives an opportunity to build knowledge-based analytics into the portals. "My Objects" functionality allows users to form personalized collections of objects, which are stored in user profiles, so that one can monitor their occurrence in the media and their public image (sentiment analysis is performed by OntosMiner), compare their ratings, discover the most interesting statements about them, etc.

GIS. Graph Navigation. The GIS section is designed for representing objects and facts from the Knowledge Base on geographic maps. Graph Navigation gives access to all objects and relations in the Knowledge Base, allowing users to discover connections between objects starting from an object of interest, with the possibility to filter relations by type, relevance, etc. (Fig. 3).

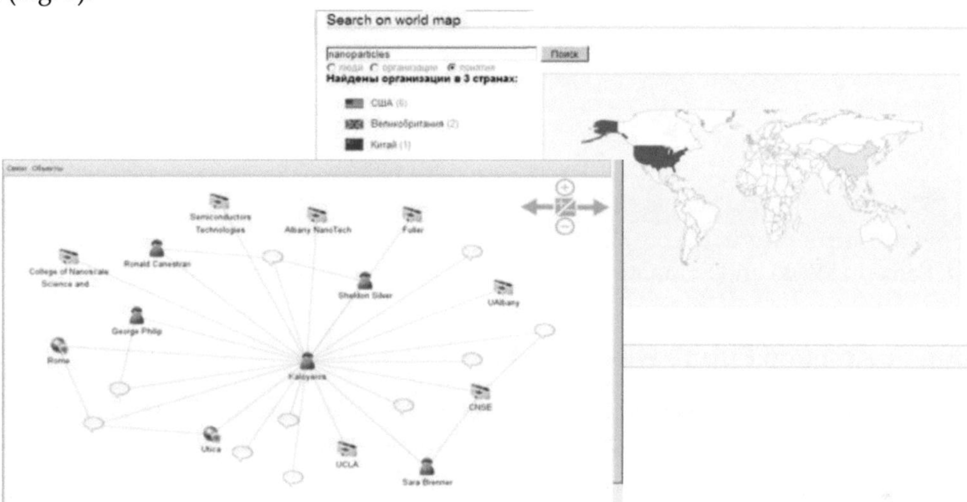

Fig. 3. Widgets within the Ontos Semantic Applications

5.2.3 Semantic Wiki, Bookmarking and Navigation

Ontos Portals for innovative fields are based on a wiki-engine, since one of their purposes is to create an environment for a community of experts. This functionality is in harmony with the Semantic Wiki approach. Initially the content of wiki-pages is generated in automated mode based on the accumulated semantic metadata. Later, these data can be supplemented manually by users in the standard wiki fashion. Semantic bookmarking tools are also integrated into these wiki-pages (Dudchuk & Minor, 2009). So, an object's wiki-page includes a semantic summary based on the facts present in the Knowledge Base, tags, relevant documents, graphics, etc., all generated automatically (Fig. 4). Experts with proper access rights can add their own texts and comments (which can then be processed by OntosMiner), as well as edit the semantic metadata.

Another option for the user is to install a specialized Semantic Navigation plug-in into the browser. This plug-in is able to superimpose semantic metadata upon the original content of processed web pages. This allows the user to get access to data stored in the Ontos Knowledge Base without leaving the original web page. Superficially, this looks similar to standard hypertext, but the functionality is different. Once the user clicks on a highlighted object a navigation card appears, which delivers accumulated information on the object's features and relations, and provides the possibility to navigate through the semantic graph starting from this object. We believe that this can be viewed as an implementation of the Semantic Web, since in this case navigation takes place via a web of data, not just a web of

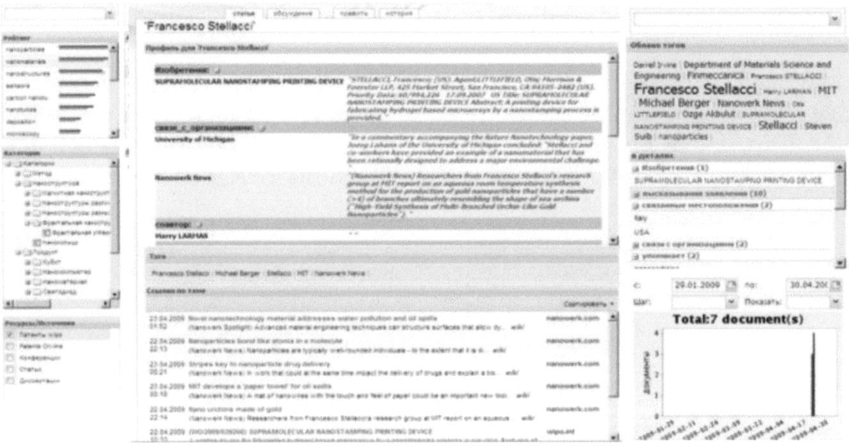

documents (http://www.w3.org/2001/sw/).
Fig. 4. Semantic Wiki and Semantic Bookmarking within the Ontos solution

6. Conclusion and Future R&D Trends

In this chapter we have presented the Ontos solution for the Semantic Web. This solution is based on automatic processing of large multilingual natural language text collections, gathered from Internet resources and corporate databases. This process is controlled by ontological representations of the domains of interest. The output of this analysis is represented in a standard format and stored in an RDF Knowledge Base, where data is merged and accumulated. Finally, we described a number of working Semantic Web Applications which are based on this accumulated semantic content.
Future steps in our view involve development and implementation of OntosMiner processors for new domains, and of new semantic services for the Internet community and corporative customers.

7. Acknowledgments

We would like to say many thanks to Alexander Alexeev, Igor Belopuhov, Maria Brykina, Philip Dudchuk, Oleg Ena, Daria Fadeeva, Polina Kananykina, Victor Klintsov, Daria Kondrashova, Alexander Pototsky, Alexander Ren, Vyacheslav Seledkin, Vitaly Volk, Vyacheslav Vorobyev, Natalia Zevakhina, Petr Zhalybin, and other specialists at Avicomp Services and Ontos AG. It is impossible to overestimate their contribution to the development and implementation of the presented Ontos solution.

8. References

Akkiraju, R.; Farrell, J.; Miller, J.A.; Nagarajan, M.; Schmidt, M-T.; Sheth, A. & Verma, K. (2005). Web Service Semantics - WSDL-S, Technical Note, Version 1.0, April 2005, *http://lsdis.cs.uga.edu/Projects/METEOR-S/WSDL-S*

Alesso, H.P. (2004). Developing the Next Generation Web Services - Semantic Web Services. *http://www.webservicessummit.com/Excerpts/BuildingSemanticWS.htm. A. K. Peters, Ltd.*

Beckett, D. (2001). Semantic Web Advanced Development for Europe (SWAD-Europe). *http://www.w3.org/2001/sw/Europe/reports/rdf_scalable_storage_report*

Benjamins R.; Decker S.; Fensel D. & Gomez-Perez A. (1999). (KA)2: Building Ontologies for the Internet: A Mid Term Report. *International Journal of Human Computer Studies (IJHCS)*. 51(3). September 1999.

Benjamins, V. R.; Contreras, J.; Corcho, O. & Gomez-Perez, A. (2002). Six Challenges for the Semantic Web, http://www.cs.man.ac.uk/~ocorcho/documents/KRR2002WS_BenjaminsEtAl.pdf

Berners-Lee, T. (2000). XML and the Web, *XML World 2000*, Boston, *http://www.w3.org/2000/Talks/0906-xmlweb-tbl/*

Berners-Lee, T., Hendler, J. and Lassila, O. (2001). The Semantic Web. Scientific American Magazine - May

Boguslavsky, I.; Frid, N.; Iomdin, L.; Kreidlin, L.; Sagalova, I. & Sizov, V. (2000). Creating a Universal Networking Language Module within an Advanced NLP System. *In Proceedings of the 18th International Conference on Computational Linguistics (COLING 2000)*, pp. 83-89

Boldasov, M.; Sokolova, E.; Malkovsky, M. (2002). User Query Understanding by the InBase System as a Source for a Multilingual NL Generation Module. *In Text, Speech and Dialogue*, Springer, Berlin, pp. 1-7

Bolshakova, E. (2001). Recognition of Author's Scientific and Technical Terms. *In Computational Linguistics and Intelligent Text Processing*, Springer, Berlin, pp. 281-290

Bolshakov, I.; Bolshakova, E. (2006). Dictionary-Free Morphological Classifier of Russian Nouns. *In Advances in Natural Language Processing*, Springer, Berlin, pp. 237-244

Bray, T. (1998). RDF and Metadata, June 09, 1998, *http://www.w3.org/RDF*

Broekstra, J. ; Kampman, A. ; van Harmelen, F. (2002). Sesame: A Generic Architecture for Storing and Querying RDF and RDF Schema. *In Proceedings of the First Internation Semantic Web Conference (ISWC'02)*. Sardinia, Italy

Cearley, D. W.; Andrews, W. & Gall, N. (2007). Finding and Exploiting Value in Semantic Technologies on the Web. 9 May 2007, ID №: G00148725. Gartner, Inc.

Çelik, T. (2008). microformats. 2008. *http://microformats.org/wiki/microformats*

Ciravegna, F. (2003). Designing adaptive information extraction for the Semantic Web in Amilcare. *In S. Handschuh and S. Staab, editors, Annotation for the Semantic Web, Frontiers in Artificial Intelligence and Applications*. IOS Press

CLEARFOREST. (2009). *http://www.clearforest.com/index.asp*

Cunningham, H.; Maynard, D.; Bontcheva, K. & Tablan, V. (2002). GATE: an Architecture for Development of Robust HLT Applications. *In Proceedings of the 40th Annual Meeting of the Association for Computational Linguistics (ACL)*, Philadelphia, July 2002

Cunningham, H.; Maynard, D.; Bontcheva, K. & Tablan, V. (2002). GATE: an Architecture for Development of Robust HLT Applications. *In Proceedings of the 40th Annual Meeting of the Association for Computational Linguistics (ACL)*, Philadelphia, July 2002

De Nicola, A.; Missikoff, M. & Navigli, R. (2009). A Software Engineering Approach to Ontology Building. *Information Systems, 34(2)*, Elsevier, 2009, pp. 258-275.

Decker, S.; Erdmann, M.; Fensel, D.; Studer, R. (1999). Ontobroker: Ontology Based Access to Distributed and Semi-Structured Information. *In R. Meersman et al. (eds.): Semantic Issues in Multimedia Systems. Proceedings of DS-8*. Kluwer Academic Publisher, Boston

Dudchuk, P. & Minor, S. (2009). In Search of Tags Lost: Combining Social Bookmarking and SemWeb Technologies, http://www.semanticuniverse.com/articles-search-tags-lost-combining-social-bookmarking-and-semweb-technologies.html

Efimenko I. ; Hladky D. ; Khoroshevsky V. & Klintsov V. (2008). Semantic Technologies and Information Integration: Semantic Wine in Media Wine-skin, *In Proceedings of the 2nd European Semantic Technology Conference (ESTC2008)*, Vienna

Efimenko, I.; Drobyazko, G.; Kananykina, P.; Khoroshevsky, V.; et. al.: Ontos Solutions for Semantic Web: Text Mining, Navigation and Analytics. *In Proceedings of the Second International Workshop "Autonomous Intelligent Systems: Agents and Data Mining" (AIS-ADM-07)*. St. Petersburg, Russia, June 3-5, 2007

Efimenko, I.V. (2007). Semantics of Time: Identification Models, Methods & Algorithms in Natural Language Processing Systems. *Vestnik of Moscow State Regional University. Vol. «Linguistics». – № 2, 2007*. Moscow State Regional University Publ., Moscow, 2007, p.p. 179-185 (in Russian)

Efimenko, I.V.; Khoroshevsky, V.F.; Klintsov, V.P. (2004). OntosMiner Family: Multilingual IE Systems. *In the Proceedings of International Conference SPECOM-2004*, St.-Petersburg, Russia

Engels R.; Bremdal B. (2000). Information Extraction: State-of-the-Art Report, *CognIT a.s., Asker*, Norway

Ermakov, A.E. (2007). Automatical Extraction of Facts from Texts of Personal Files: Experience In Anaphora Resolution. *In Proceedings of International Conference Computational Linguistics and Intellectual Technologies (Dialogue 2007)*. Bekasovo, 30 May - 3 June, 2007. p.p. 172-178 (in Russian)

Garrett, J.J. (2005). Ajax: A New Approach to Web Applications. February 18, 2005. *http://www.adaptivepath.com/publications/essays/archives/000385.php*

Gómez-Pérez, A.; Mariano Fernández-López, and Oscar Corcho Ontological engineering: with examples from the areas of knowledge management, e-commerce and the Semantic Web, Springer-Verlag New York, LLC, 2004, 403 p. ISBN-13: 9781852335519

Heflin, J. (ed.) (2004). OWL Web Ontology Language Use Cases and Requirements, W3C Recommendation, 10 February 2004, *http://www.w3.org/TR/2004/REC-webont-req-20040210/*

Hinchcliffe, D. (2005). Is Web 2.0 The Global SOA?, *SOA Web Services Journal, 28 October 2005*

Hladky, D. & Khoroshevsky V. (2007). Semantic Technologies for Real Commercial Applications: Experiences and Lessons based on Digesting and Summarization of Multilingual-Text Collections, *In Proceedings of International Conference "Semantic Technologies 2007" (SemTech-2007)*, San Jose, USA

Hladky, D. (2009) Sustainable Advantage for the Investor Relations Team through Semantic Content, *Chapter in this Book*

Hladky, D.; Ehrlich, C.; Khoroshevsky, V. (2007). Social and Semantic Web Technologies: Semantic Navigation, Digesting and Summarization. *In Proceedings of ESTC-2007*, Vienna, Austria

Iskold, A. (2008a). The Structured Web - A Primer. *http://www.readwriteweb.com/archives/structured_web_primer.php*

Iskold, A. (2008b). How YOU Can Make the Web More Structured. *http://alexiskold.wordpress.com/2008/01/31/how-you-can-make-the-web-more-structured/*

Karasev,V.; Mishchenko, O. & Shafirin, A. (2003). Interactive Debugger of Linguistic Programs in the GATE Environment, *In Proceedings of International Workshop "Information Extraction for Slavonic and Other Central and Eastern European Languages", IESL-2003*, Borovets, Bulgaria

Khoroshevsky, V.F. (2003). Shallow Ontology-Driven Information Extraction from Russian Texts with GATE. *In Proceedings of International Workshop "Information Extraction for Slavonic and Other Central and Eastern European Languages", IESL-2003*, Borovets, Bulgaria

Khoroshevsky, V.F. (2005). Semantic Indexing: Cognitive Maps Based Approach, *In the Proceedings of International Conference RANLP-2005*, Borovets, Bulgary

Khoroshevsky, V.F. (1998). Knowledge vs Data Spaces: How an Applied Semiotics to Work on Web, *In: Proceedings "3rd Workshop on Applied Semiotics", Proceeding of National Conference with International Participation (CAI'98)*, Pushchino, Russia

Khoroshevsky, V.F. (2002). Natural Language Texts Processing : From Models of Natural Language Understanding to Knowledge Extraction Technologies, *AI News, № 6* (in Russian)

Khoroshevsky, V.F. (2008). Knowledge Spaces in Internet and Semantic Web (Part 1), *Artificial Intelligence & Decision Support, N 1 2008*, p.p. 80-97 (In Russian)

Kleschev, A.S. & Shalfeeva, E.A. (2005). Ontologies Features Classification. Ontologies and Their Classifications. *NTI, seria 2, №9, 2005*, p.p. 16-22 (in Russian)

Kormalev, D.A.; Kurshev, E.P.; Syleymanova, E.A. & Trofimov, I.V. (2002). Data Extraction from Texts. Newsmaking Situations Analysis. *In Proceeding of 8-th Natiaonal Conference on Artificial Intelligence (CAI-2002)*. FizmatLit, Moscow, 2002, p.p. 199-206 (in Russian)

LREC. (2004). *Proc. 4th International Conference On Language Resources And Evaluation (LREC 2004)*, Lisbon, Portugal, 26-28 May 2004

LREC. (2004). *Proceedings of 4th International Conference On Language Resources And Evaluation (LREC 2004)*, Lisbon, Portugal, 26-28 May 2004

LT-CC. (2009). *http://www.lt-cc.org/index-e.html*

Maedche, A. & Staab, S. (2001). Learning Ontologies for the Semantic Web, *In: Proceedings Semantic Web WorkShop 2001*, Hongkong , China

Malkovskij M.; Starostin A. (2009). Treeton system: the analysis under penalty function control. *Sofware and Systems* 1(85). MNIIPU, Tver, p.p. 33-35 (in Russian)

Manning, C. ; Schütze, H. (1999). Foundations of Statistical Natural Language Processing, MIT Press. Cambridge, MA: May 1999

Maslov, M.; Golovko, A.; Segalovich, I.; Braslavski, P. (2009). Extracting News-Related Queries from Web Query Log. *In Proceedings of the 15th International World Wide Web Conference (WWW-2006)*

McDonald, D. (1996). Internal and External Evidence in the Identification and Semantic Categorisation of Proper Nouns. *In Corpus-Processing for Lexical Acquistion*, Pustejovsky J. and Boguraev B. (eds.), pp. 21-39, MIT Press

NLP-RG. (2009). *http://nlp.shef.ac.uk/*

ONTOPRISE. (2009). *http://www.ontoprise.com*

ORACLE. (2007a). Semantic Data Integration for the Enterprise. An Oracle White Paper. *http://www.oracle.com/technology/tech/semantic_technologies/pdf/semantic11g_dataint_twp.pdf*

ORACLE. (2007b). Innovate Faster with Oracle Database 11g. An Oracle White Paper. *http://www.oracle.com/technology/products/database/oracle11g/index.html*

Osipov, G.S. (2006). Linguistic Knowledge for Search Relevance Improvement. *Proceedings of Joint conference on knowledge-based software Engineering JCKBSE'06*, IOS Press

PARC. (2009). *http://www2.parc.com/isl/groups/nltt/*

Pautasso, C.; Zimmermann, O. & Leymann, F. (2008). RESTful Web Services vs. Big Web Services: Making the Right Architectural Decision, *In Proceedings of the 17th International World Wide Web Conference (WWW2008)*, Beijing, China

Poibeau, T.; Acoulon, A.; Avaux, C.; et. al. (2003). The Multilingual Named Entity Recognition Framework, *In the EACL 2003 Proceedings (European Conference on Computational Linguistics)*, Budapest, 15-17 April 2003

Poibeau, T.; Acoulon, A.; Avaux, C.; Beroff-Bénéat, L.; Cadeau, A.; Calberg, M.; Delale, A.; De Temmerman, L.; Guenet, A.-L.; Huis, D.; Jamalpour, M.; Krul, A.; Marcus, A.; Picoli, F. & Plancq, C. (2003). The Multilingual Named Entity Recognition Framework, *In the EACL 2003 Proceedings (European Conference on Computational Linguistics)*, Budapest, 15-17 April 2003

Popov, B.; Kiryakov, A.; Ognyanoff, D.; Manov, D. & Kirilov, A. (2004). KIM - a semantic platform for information extaction and retrieval, *Journal of Natural Language Engineering, Vol. 10, Issue 3-4, Sep 2004*, pp. 375-392, Cambridge University Press

Simperl, E.P.B. & Tempich, C. (2006). Ontology Engineering: A Reality Check. *OTM Conferences (1) 2006*, p.p. 836-854

SNLP. (2009). *http://nlp.stanford.edu/*

Suleymanov, D.Sh. (1997). The semantic analyzer as a part of the embedding Teacher's model in Intelligent Tutoring Systems. *In Proceedins of the Workshop: Embedding User Models in Intelligent Applications. Sixth International Conference on User Modeling (UM97) (Chia Laguna, Sardinia, Italy, 1-5 June, 1997)*. Chia Laguna, 1997. p.p. 48-53

TALENT. (2009). *http://www.research.ibm.com/talent/index.html*

TERAGRAM. (2009). *http://www.teragram.com/*

TREC. (2000). *Proceedings of the Eighth Text REtrieval Conference (TREC-8)*, E.M. Voorhees and D.K. Harman (eds), NIST Special Publication 500-246. *http://trec.nist.gov/pubs.html*

TREC. (2003). *Proceedings of the Twelfth Text Retrieval Conference (TREC 2003)*, http://trec.nist.gov/pubs/trec12/

Wood, D.; Gearon, P. & Adams, T. (2005). Kowari: A Platform for Semantic Web Storage and Analysis. *In Proceedings of XTech 2005*. 24-27 May 2005, Amsterdam, Netherlands

WWW. (2003). *Proceedings of The Twelfth International World Wide Web Conference*. Budapest Congress Centre, 20-24 May 2003, Budapest, HUNGARY

Xu, F.; Kurz, D.; Piskorski, J. & Schmeier, S. (2002). Term Extraction and Mining of Term Relations from Unrestricted Texts in the Financial Domain, *In Proceedings of BIS 2002*, Witold Abramowicz (ed.), Poznan, Poland

4

Sustainable Advantage for the Investor Relations Team through Semantic Content

Daniel Hladky and MBA
Ontos AG
Switzerland

1. Introduction

Semantic web technologies promise to bring companies closer to their customers and deliver to consumers more relevant content than ever before. Two technologies in particular will help build sustainable advantage for the investor relations team. The first is natural language processing and second content enhancement. Intuitively, semantic content should help establish a higher quality of communication between information providers and consumers. This chapter describes the state-of-the-art in digital text information extraction, specifically the application of semantic technology to confront the challenges of the investor relations department. We discuss the roots of human language technology and ontology-driven information extraction and how such extracted semantic metadata can be used for better decision making, market monitoring and competitor intelligence. We will consider ontology as a sound semantic platform for defining the meaning of content and consequently supporting the prudent access to data for business intelligence (Hladky, 2008). Examples are given on dynamic hypertext views (Staab et al. 2000), a solution that links different web pages together based on their semantic meaning. The foundation of the proposed solution relies on an ontology-driven information extraction approach, a framework that merges same entities and stores the semantic metadata in a knowledge base. This framework supports the complete transformation process, including web page crawling, the extraction of knowledge, the creation of unique identifiers and presentations offering access to the portal. In this context, we describe how these technologies are being used in real customer scenarios and compare the classical search approach to a more intelligent approach based on ontology and information extraction. In particular, we describe semantic indexing (Khoroshevsky, 2005), building a knowledge base from various sources and give an introduction on how to create domain ontology based on customer queries. Then we tackle issues of merging information from text with semi-structured information from the Web, highlighting the relation to Linked Data (Berners-Lee at al. 2006) using standards like RDF/XML. Finally, we present possible user interfaces which display the aggregated semantic metadata inside a portal and other third party software tools. The chapter concludes by looking beyond the current solution to how semantic technology will add more information in the near future, including a short survey of recent thinking that offers potential extensions to today's model.

2. Profile of Investor Relations

A company, public or private, has a duty to inform its shareholders about ongoing activities, and strategies as well as secure current investments or even raise new money. A large number of companies have introduced a new organizational unit called the investor relations (IR) department led by an Investor Relations Officer (IRO). While execution is key to a company's success, the way in which a public or private company communicates its value to potential investors or purchasers is central to the price individuals are willing to pay. If vital elements are omitted from a company's story, or if this story is not told convincingly, true value will most likely go unrecognized. The art of positioning and communicating a company's story and investment proposition to investors is at the heart of attaining fair value. The list below offers a cursory view of the IR team's major activities:

1. Determine the company's investment proposition.
2. Identify and target the appropriate investor audience.
3. Screen the competition and identify your company's position in relation to it.
4. Develop communications platforms for presentation to the targeted investor audience.
5. Build relationships with the targeted investor audience and maintain consistent communications

The IR team is at the centre of communications, building a company story and brand (Kotler, 2006). Imagine a scene where company executives explain the organization's actual position, value and strategy at the general meeting (GM) to the shareholders. It's natural that shareholders will ask critical questions or question elements of the presentation. It seems obvious that the IR team does their homework by analyzing all major forces (Porter, 1998) that can influence the company and be prepared to answer these questions. However, in order to prepare effectively, the team needs to understand the competitive environment. We will focus on the task of screening the environment and will not investigate other elements of the communication chain described in Fig. 1. In order to properly evaluate the competitive environment, the IR team needs to classify various areas and determine which parts require deeper analysis.

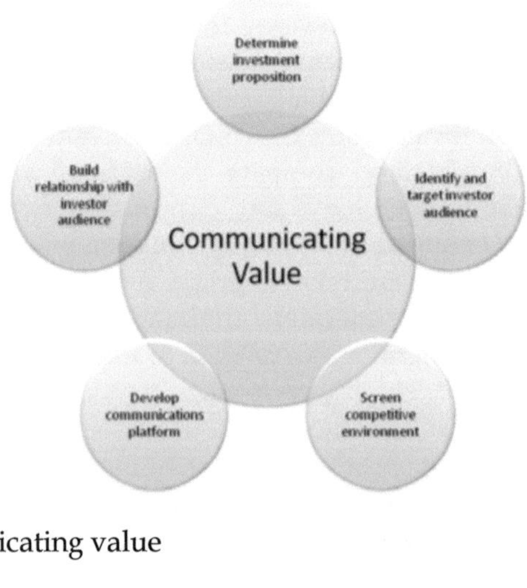

Fig. 1. The art of communicating value

Central to any company's success is the ability to sell products or services in a highly competitive marketplace. Achieving this objective leads to more revenue, better margins and a higher company value for shareholders. Consequently, the primary purpose of the IR team is to screen day-to-day information from external and internal sources and create an aggregate picture. The results of the screening are not only useful for IR but serve as input for the management team's daily tactical decisions.
Table 1 shows a list of variables that should be considered when screening the environment.

About the company	• Sell-side analyst opinions • Factors driving investor interest • Stock information • Media coverage • Blogs and chat rooms • Shareholders o Who are they o Where are they from o Investments in other companies
About competitors	• Shareholder information • Analyst coverage and comments • Stock information • Market share • Financial metrics • Changes in competitors o Key management o Business alliances o New product launches o Intellectual property • Conference participation • Lawsuits and litigation
About the industry	• General news • Trends • Identify new potential customers

Table 1. Competitive environment information

Having identified the main environmental factors requiring screening, the next task is identifying where such information can be retrieved. Obvious resources are search engines on the public internet. Additional special reports from analysts and company annual reports can be used for deeper analysis. However, most of the data that the IR team would like to investigate is unstructured. Gartner reported in 2002 that for at least the next decade more than 95% of human-to-computer information input will involve textual language. This large amount of information is growing, leading to the problem of keeping up with its pace. IR would need a huge number of people doing internet-based research to sort relevant from irrelevant information and compile findings into a complete knowledge database. All of this work is manual labour and time consuming. Knowledge Management (KM) and several other IT technologies have evolved that promise to facilitate this work, the latest being based on the semantic web (Berners-Lee, 2001) - a web of data that can be processed directly or indirectly by machines (computers). Semantic web technology promises to reduce people-hours and costs while accelerating decision-making.

3. Knowledge Management and Semantic Web Technology

Knowledge Management (Fensel, 2005) is concerned with acquiring, maintaining, and accessing the knowledge of an organization (Fig. 2). Knowledge is now seen as a basic resource (Drucker, 1993) for an organization and consequently we need to understand its main building blocks and how they can be put to use. The aim is to galvanize an organization's intellectual assets for greater productivity, increased competitiveness, and better decision-making support. Given the large number of documents put online by organizations and the public, classical Knowledge Management systems have severe weaknesses:

- Searching information is based typically on keyword-based approaches that return irrelevant information rather than desired content.
- Extracting information through meaning-based searches requires human browsing and reading in order to garner relevant information.
- Automatic aggregation from various sources requires fast crawlers and human language technology to understand texts, allowing knowledge acquisition based on semantic annotation.

The IR team is mainly interested in a set of information as shown in Table 1. In order to have this up-to-date information, the system should be able to extract a large volume of information.

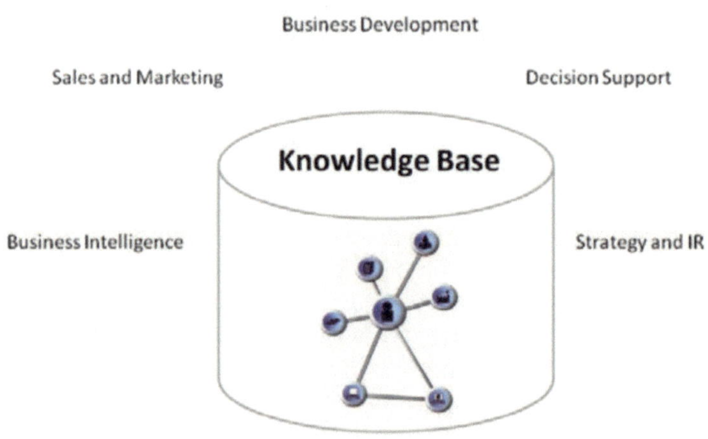

Fig. 2. Using the Knowledge Base within the organization

Thus, our Knowledge Management system needs to integrate heterogeneous, distributed and mostly unstructured or semi-structured information sources (Fensel, 2004). The core concern of our platform is steering clear of nonsense and maximizing computer support of the IR team in the aggregation and acquisition process. Before introducing the architecture's components, let's compare the keyword based search approach to the ontology driven information extraction approach.

3.1 Keyword based search approach

Imagine our IR team works for an automotive company and wants to analyze car news. A researcher might query the car brand "Jaguar" with a search engine (e.g. Google, Yahoo! or Live). The very rapid but imprecise result will be a huge set of pages containing the keyword "Jaguar" (Fig. 3). In many cases the user has to open the page in order to identify if the content is relevant. Recall is another weakness - it's unclear whether all relevant information has been found. To increase relevancy the user can extend his search expression by "jaguar+car" and reduce the result list dramatically. Let's take the example a step further and assume the researcher would like news about all car manufacturers that have reduced their working hours. What kind of search expression would the user need to find the relevant information? In this hunt, they would have to enter all relevant keywords that represent the meaning of reduced working hours.

¶

Fig. 3. Precision and recall in keyword based search

The user would then read the documents and extract the requisite information themselves. Then they might enter the data into the knowledge base system for additional analysis. In contrast to this information retrieval process (Davis, 2006) an ontology driven information extraction system would automatically populate the KM with the extracted data. Advantages of the information retrieval approach include speed and language independency. However, in situations where the user needs more precision and more complete recall without spending time reading text, another technology from the semantic web space offers relief. Information extraction systems based on natural language processing will not only improve the search results but also contribute to knowledge capturing and sharing (Davenport, 2008). Additional value is generated when the new acquired knowledge is merged. The system will be able to identify hidden links and relationships, contributing to company knowledge.

3.2 Knowledge generation from text

We have not yet described the complete search engine transformation made possible by the Semantic Web or the Web of data (Berners-Lee, 2007). Most web pages are not using the suggested standards by the W3C (World Wide Web Consortium) in order for people or machines to find and correlate the information they need. Web pages are still mainly based on HTML coding which allows Web browsers (e.g. Internet Explorer, Opera, Firefox) to display a given string. Web pages or documents primarily use natural language text that represents content's meaning in a manner understood only by humans. A person reading a web page understands that the content has semantic data which describes, for example, a person, a company or the relationship between them. The IR team pursues the creation of knowledge in order to answer the queries listed in Table 1. Therefore we need to extend the information retrieval approach to a strategy that can extract the semantic metadata from text. The solution proposed is ontology-driven information extraction using Natural Language Processing (NLP). NLP is a computerized approach to text analysis based on both a set of theories and a set of technologies. This application analyzes text and presents only the specific information in which the user is interested. The system identifies concepts and relationships based on a given domain ontology (Gruber, 1993). In order to demonstrate what an ontology-driven NLP system can extract let's consider the following text:

"Google's founders Larry Page and Sergey Brin developed a new approach for online search."

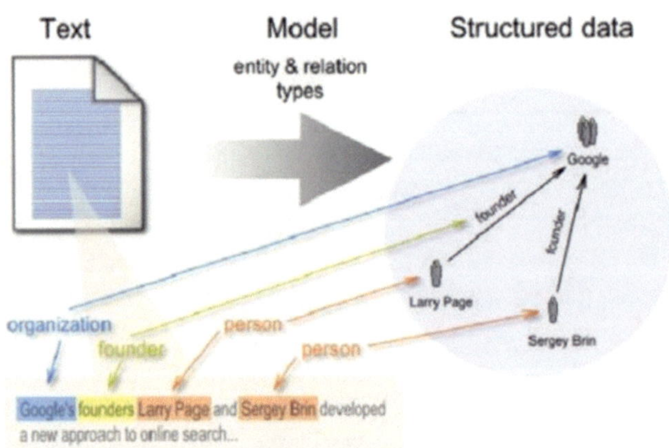

Fig. 4. Ontology-driven NLP

If a user wants to formulate a query like "Who founded Google?" than we need to understand the meaning of the text. Extracting the entities and the relationships (Fig. 4) from the text will help answer the query.
Based on a given domain ontology and set of rules the system will analyze the text and extract the information. The ontology-driven NLP will also create attributes like "FirstName", "FamilyName" and gender. Good NLP systems will also do reference resolution (e.g. discover that "he" in the following sentence is a reference to Larry Page: "Larry Page is working for Google. He also studied at Stanford University."). A substantial benefit of ontology-driven information extraction is that the system will automatically populate the ontology with new specific "instances" as they come up. Within the ontology, the system will describe concepts (e.g. person, location, company) and the relationships between the concepts. The semantic information extraction will then recognize these instances as persons (e.g. Larry Page, Sergey Brin) and populate the concept "person" with these names. Such an approach will allow queries to be formulated on an ontological level, for example "show all employees of company Google". The system will understand the query by recognizing that for the concept "company" and instance value "Google" we are looking for the concept "person" that is related via the semantic relationship "employees." Based on the extracted instances Larry Page and Sergey Brin, the query result will show those two values. Another crucial piece NLP can provide is a semantic graph (Khoroshevsky, 2005) or cognitive map for a single document at the end of the process. Such a process will merge "the same" instances together in order to grow the knowledge of connected information based on the semantic relations between the different ontology concepts. The same merging process can be executed for all documents in order to create a complete picture (Fig. 5).

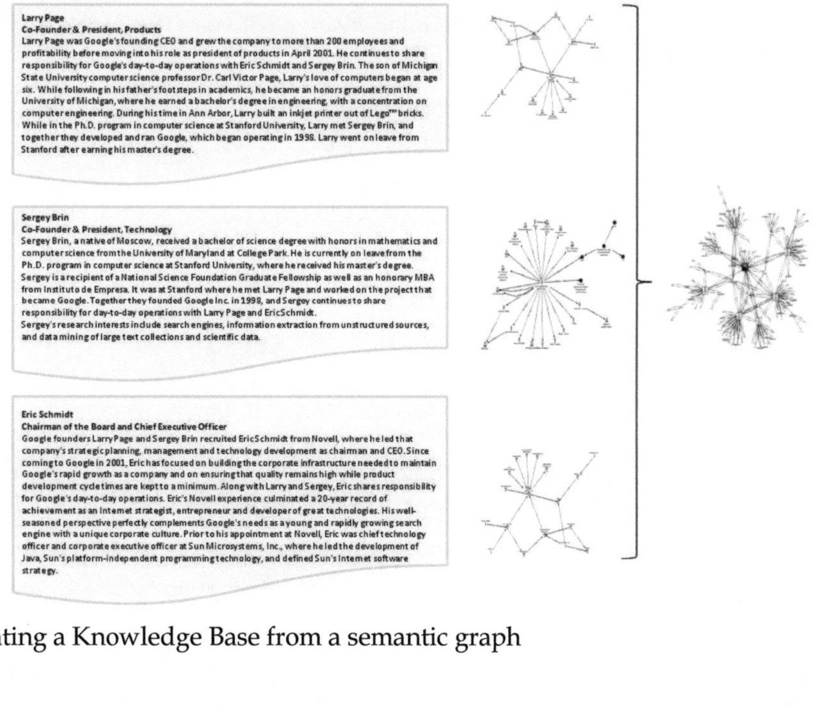

Fig. 5. Creating a Knowledge Base from a semantic graph

The final result of the merging process can be also described as the semantic index to all acquired information. NLP can be seen as the core process but in order to deliver a full solution we need another set of components in our framework.

4. Building the framework for IR

Because most web pages are still built with HTML, we need to define a framework that will allow the IR team to crawl, aggregate, merge and store semantic metadata. Besides analyzing text, we need a platform that can incorporate other data and convert it into new knowledge. The framework should work autonomously as much as possible and deliver the required background information to the IR user in a simple form through convenient user interfaces. As a first part of the framework, we need to define the knowledge model or domain ontology needed.

4.1 Building the domain ontology

Table 1's "competitive environment" assembled our main objects of interest. During the ontology engineering process (Fig. 6) we need to specify the domain ontology that we need in order to cover all possible user queries. Within the kick-off phase the main purpose is to define the general ontology application. This includes a list of possible dictionaries or a taxonomy related to the domain. After analyzing the input sources, the ontology engineer can decide which of them will be included. The lexical entries will be linked to the concepts/relations later on within the ontology. In this early stage one should also look for existing ontologies that can potentially be reused. The goal of the next phase is to develop the target ontology. This refinement takes the results of the kick-off phase as input, including the list of user queries, reusable ontologies and lexical data/dictionaries. The goal is to define the concepts and the semantic relationships between the concepts. Fig. 7 shows an extract of the domain ontology for competitive intelligence.

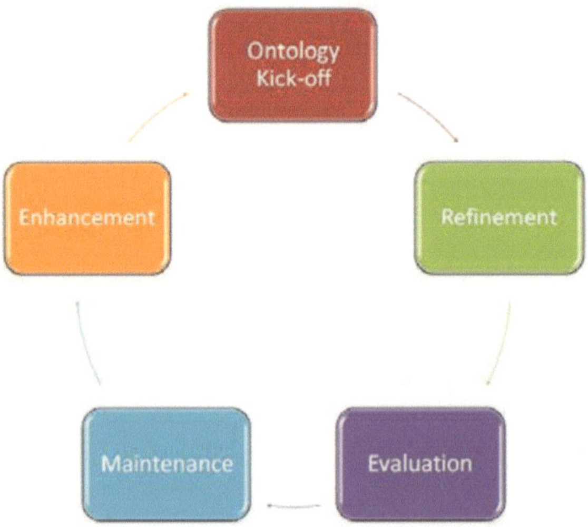

Fig. 6. Ontology engineering

The next step is the evaluation phase where we test the usefulness of the developed ontology. It is important to test the linguistic rules extracting objects/relationships from natural text, particularly when using NLP. During this phase it is also valuable to increase the quality of the NLP process. The main drivers for measurement are precision and recall (Porter & Cunningham, 2005). The goal is to tune the NLP system so both measures are high.

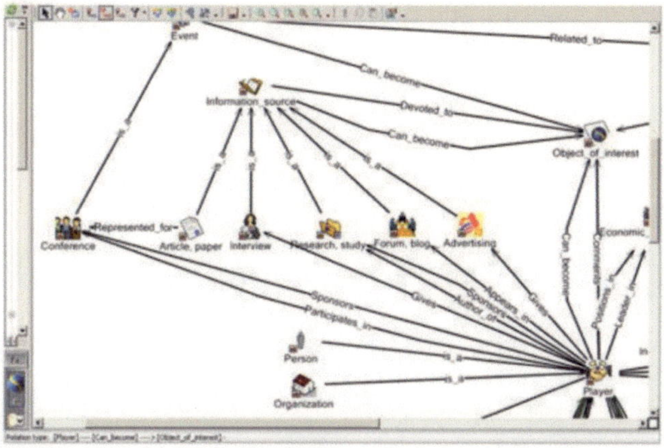

Fig. 7. CI domain ontology (extract)

In the case of this project, the testing of the NLP process was done using the environment of OntosMiner, the NLP engine from Ontos AG (see Fig. 8) and a simple web interface. The system shows the semantic annotation with mark-ups for the document. The left side panel shows the named entities that have been extracted and by clicking on marked text, the system shows the relevant facts on the right. Those facts are the extracted semantic relations of the text.

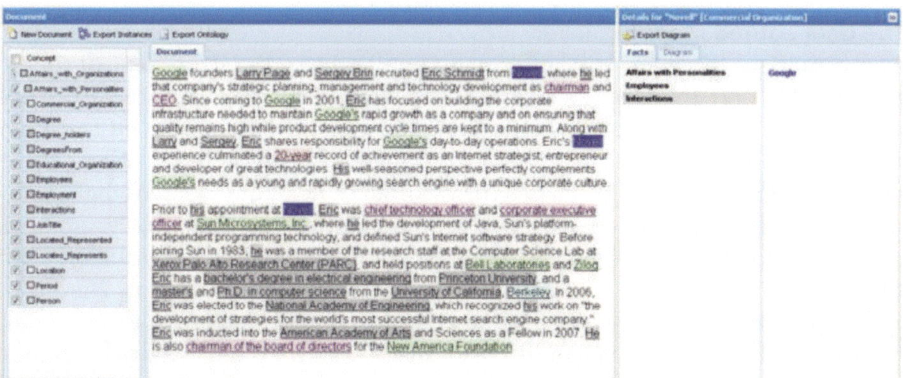

Fig. 8. NLP evaluation phase

After achieving a good level of quality with NLP, the next step of the evaluation phase is to link all components together by combining the framework's modules. The framework will then process the data and create valuable knowledge for the IR team.

4.2 Architecture

The Ontos Framework (Ontos Framework is provided by Ontos AG) that supports the solution for monitoring the competitive environment is based on a multi-layer architecture (see Fig. 9). Starting from the right, there is the presentation layer, the application layer (Web Services), the knowledge base, the semantic layer (OntosMiner) and the data source mapping section. This architecture provides the user functionality at run-time. A certain set of functions are used at configuration time, for example defining the external link to sources, creating the ontology engineering and the mapping of ontology to external databases.

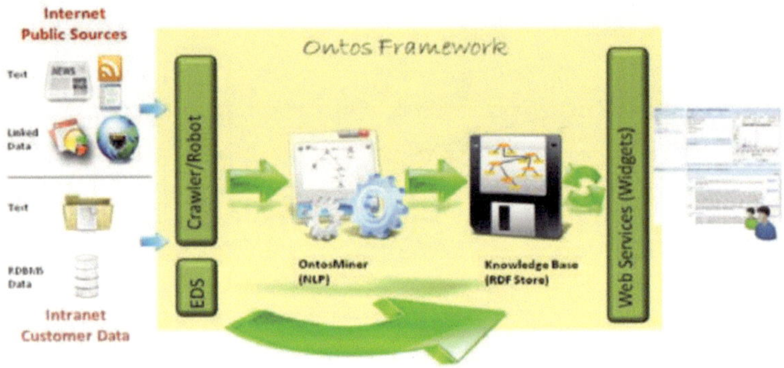

Fig. 9. Framework-Architecture

Access to the framework is based on web widgets. This allows embedding the user interface for web pages, portals, smart phones, and desktop tools like Outlook.

4.2.1 The data source mapping layer

This layer comprises three levels of information gathering - the list of text documents, the internal databases and the external sources that have semi-structured or structured data. The first category of text files can be further divided into a list of subscribed RSS items from trusted sources as well as a list of internal directories/folders with text files. The crawler that handles the RSS and text files passes the associated metadata to a tool that creates plain text, focusing on RSS and linked web pages. The plain text is then sent to an agent who allocates a task to the next available OntosMiner for semantic information extraction. Internal databases are mapped using the External Data Source (EDS) tool. The EDS system uses an ontology that describes concepts and relations, mapping them to external databases. This mechanism allows the system to read instances from the external database. The extracted information is then passed to the knowledge base directly without using the OntosMiner. In order to enhance the information, the framework can use an API (Application Programming Interface) to access other Web sources. Examples of such sources include "dbpedia", "freebase", "geonames" and other trusted sources. Most of them follow the guidelines of the W3C and provide information in RDF/XML and similar formats.

4.2.2 The semantic layer

The semantic layer core function is the OntosMiner engine. The majority of information on the Web is in unstructured format. The OntosMiner engine processes plain text and extracts the entities and facts based on the defined ontology (see section 3.2). Before the extracted metadata can be imported into the knowledge base, the semantic layer process needs to merge same entities and clean-up the semantic graph. By using this developing set of guiding parameters, the merger also resolves the problem of unique identifiers. For example, if the OntosMiner has extracted from the concept "company" the instance value "IBM" then the next step is to determine if such a value already exists. It is possible that in the knowledge base we have "International Business Machines" and the engine needs to merge "IBM" with the existing instance. This is how the semantic graph grows and with it our knowledge about a specific object.

4.2.3 The knowledge base layer

The knowledge base is a database which stores the extracted semantic information. Following the rules and standardization of the W3C, the metadata are stored as triples. These triples (subject predicate object) will be stored according to the Resource Description Framework (RDF). RDF storage benefits the user through scalability and performance.

4.2.4 The application layer

The application layer is mainly connected to the knowledge base through SPARQL access. The type of application depends on the user scenario but in most cases standard functions like search or query are included. The architecture also allows for applications to interface directly with semantic layer components when necessary.

4.2.5 The presentation layer

Client devices interact with the presentation layer of the architecture. The device's independent components show results in a suitable format according to the capabilities of the device. In the Ontos Framework, the presentation layer is based on web widget and JavaScript technology which has the flexibility integrating with different devices. In the IR solution, the user interface consists of a set of web widgets that are integrated with existing web pages. Microsoft Outlook is used as an additional desktop device.

4.3 User scenarios

The current IR solution consists of two distinct scenarios. The first solution is an intelligent way of collecting media information with the ability to search and filter according to desired topic. The underlying semantic technology allows the IR user to receive only relevant articles. This solution replaces the classical clipping service where external agencies read printed news and collect articles according to a set of key words.

4.3.1 News clipping for IR

The primary objective of this service is to collect all news relevant to IR. In order to facilitate this automated clipping, the IR team decides which trusted sources should be crawled. The sources could be RSS, URL or Blogs. A list of words is generated to define a given concept so irrelevant articles are filtered out. The system provides further possibilities for search and navigation within the user interface.

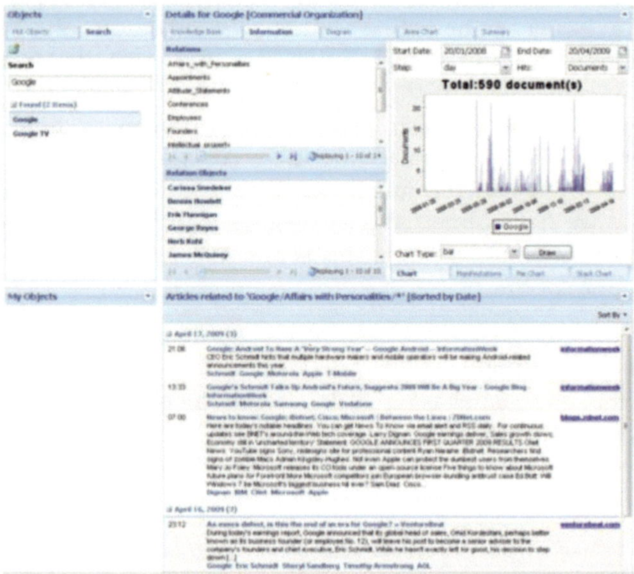

Fig. 10. News Clipping and Browsing

The described solution is a first step towards providing the IR team with more relevant information. The next level is to provide additional analytical functions to assist the team in the decision building process as well as supporting them in fact analysis.

4.3.2 Analytics for IR

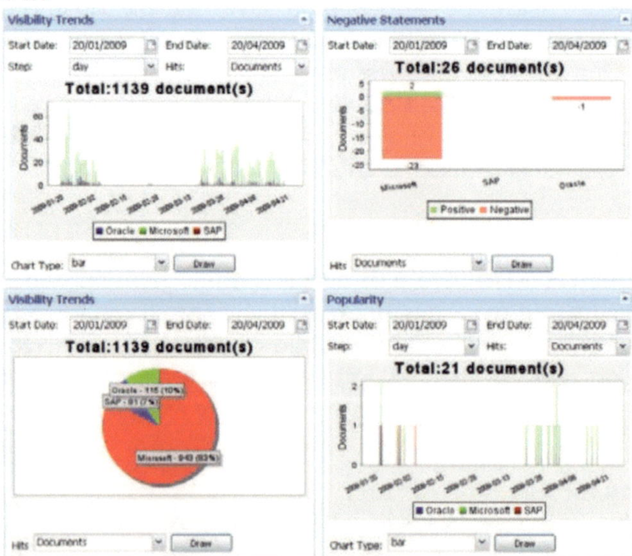

Fig. 11. Analytics

While using the clipping service, the user still makes their own conclusions about the content while browsing articles. However, analytical functions provide an additional option for examining the collected information. This analysis could involve the monitoring of media coverage, brand measurement, the analysis of individual sentiments or identifying management change at a specific company. The objective is for the system to create different graphs about situations of interest from the metadata. The competitive intelligence analysis is presented in a dashboard where each user can configure their own needs (see Fig. 11).
The web provides large amounts of data and it is impossible for a human to aggregate and analyze this kind of volume. The analytical functions described above provide a great support in creating a real-time situation snapshot and comparison between companies and their competitive environment. They also represent an improved way of working with multilingual texts - the ontology simplifies analysis by connecting the same concepts from various languages into one graph.

4.4 Lessons learned and future directions

Lessons have been learned by deploying the first IR solution. There is a strong need to analyze financial data, ideally extracted from annual reports. Once a competitor is identified, it is probably possible to receive their annual report and process the content. This scenario would involve the reading of a PDF document, transforming it into XBRL (eXtensible Business Reporting Language) and extracting the financial data of interest.
These days there is a lot of audio and video information on the Internet. A next point of interest is the creation of tools allowing the transformation of speech to text in order to use the NLP system to analyze the content and create semantic metadata for the knowledge base. In order to provide more flexibility, the NLP engine will be expanded to allow users to add their own personal concepts and instances. This process will contribute to the flexibility of extended domain ontology creation and facilitate keeping pace with a changing environment.

5. Conclusion

Semantic web technologies can be effectively employed in the area of investor relations and knowledge management. It is not enough to have tools for business intelligence that focus only on structured data. Increasing economic pressure, the growing weight of unstructured content and the difficulty of accessing relevant information underscore the need for a broader conception of business intelligence. The success of companies is correlated to the speed and and depth of their analysis of the changing environment. This involves the scanning of all trusted sources for a better understanding of the competitive landscape, serving not only to attract and retain investors but also for the growth and competitive advantage of the company. The same technology can benefit other departments like the sales and marketing division, management and the research team. Semantic web technology is concerned with the acquisition of information and its transformation into metadata that can be processed by computers in order to create sustainable advantage. Ontology-driven information extraction improves precision and recall while generating knowledge for the IR department. The World Wide Web provides a huge amount of data that needs to be processed effectively if companies want to benefit. Only companies that manage this process will create sustainable advantage over their competitors.

6. References

Berners-Lee, Tim (2001). *Weaving the Web,* Texere Publishing, ISBN 978-0752820903

Berners-Lee, T.; Chen, Y.; Chilton, L.; Connoly, D.; Dhanaraj, R.; Hollenbach, J.; Lerer, A. and Sheets, D. (2006). *Tabulator: Exploring and Analyzing linked data on the Semantic Web,* http://swui.semanticweb.org/swui06/papers/Berners-Lee/Berners-Lee.pdf, MIT, Cambridge, MA, USA

Berners-Lee, Tim (2007). *Q&A with Tim Berners-Lee,* BusinessWeek Online, April 9, 2007

Daconta, Michael C.; Obrst, Leo J.; Smith, Kevin T. (2003). *The Semantic Web,* Wiley Publishing Inc, ISBN 0-471-43257-1, Indianapolis, Indiana

Davenports, Tom (2008). *Enterprise 2.0: The New, New Knowledge Management,* Harvard Business Online, Feb. 19, 2008

Davis, John; Studer, Rudi; Warren, Paul (2006). *Semantic Web Technologies,* John Wiley & Sons Ltd, ISBN 978-0-470-02596-3, England

Drucker, Peter F. (1993). *Post-Capitalist Society,* HarperCollins Publishers Inc., ISBN 0-88730-620-9, New York, USA

Efimenko, Irina; Hladky, Daniel; Khoroshevsky V.F.; Klintsov, V. (2008). Semantic Technologies and Information Integration. *Proceedings of 2nd European Semantic Technology Conference (ESTC2008)*, Vienna, 2008

Fensel, Dieter, (2004). *Ontologies: A Silver Bullet for Knowledge Management and Electronic Commerce,* Springer, ISBN 3-540-00302-9, Germany

Fensel, Dieter; Hendler, James; Liebermann, Henry and Wahlster, Wolfgang (2005). *Spinning The Semantic Web,* First MIT Press, ISBN 0-262-06232-1, Cambridge, Massachusetts

Gruber, T. (1993). A translation approach to portable ontologies. Knowledge Acquisition 5(2):199-220. http://ksl-web.stanford.edu/KSL_Abstracts/KSL-92-71.html

Heyer, Gerhard; Quasthoff, Uwe; Wittig, Thomas (2008). *Text Mining,* W3L-Verlag, ISBN 978-3-937137-30-8, Germany

Hladky, Daniel; Khoroshevsky V.F. (2007). Semantic Technologies for Real Commercial Applications. *Proceedings of Semantic Technology Conference 2007,* San Jose, California, 2007

Hladky, Daniel (2008). Integration of Semantic Resources for Business Intelligence. *Proceedings of Semantic Technology Conference 2008,* San Jose, California, 2008

Khoroshevsky V.F. (2003). Shallow Ontology-Driven Information Extraction from Russian Texts with GATE. *Proceedings of IESL-2003,* Borovec, Bulgaria, 2003

Khoroshevsky V.F. (2005). Semantic Indexing: Cognitive Maps Based Approach. *Proceedings of RANLP-2005,* Borovec, Bulgaria, 2005

Khoroshevsky V.F. (2008). Knowledge Spaces in Internet and Semantic Web (Part 1). *Artifical Intelligence and Decision Making,* N 1, 2008

Kotler, Philip; Pfoertsch Waldemar, (2006). *B2B Brand Management,* Springer, ISBN 978-3-540-25360-0, New York

Porter, Alan; Cunningham, Scott (2005). *Tech mining: Exploiting new technologies for competitive advantage,* Wiley and Sons, ISBN 0-471-47567-X

Porter, Michael E. (1998). *Competitive Strategy,* The Free Press, ISBN 0-684-84148-7, New York

Staab, S.; Angele, J.; (2000). *Semantic Community Web Portals,* Computer Networks 33 (1-6), pp 473-491

5

Semantic Infrastructures

Jiří Dokulil, Jakub Yaghob and Filip Zavoral
Charles University in Prague
Czech Republic

1. Introduction

There is a well defined infrastructure (set of protocols and their implementations) for the current Internet. For example HTTP implemented by the Apache or IIS servers and in all internet browsers (clients). Or HTML, CSS and JavaScript for content presentation. While there is still room for improvement in standards conformance, the system works quite well.
The Semantic Web is not such case. Although there are many protocols and standards for data description, querying, semantic services etc., most of them have very few implementations, typically only prototypes. Many systems are developed without regard for interoperability, often as monolithic software.
But over the time, some prominent RDF handling systems have become increasingly popular, thus defining relatively stable and well accepted interfaces – both APIs and higher level interfaces. There are more such systems and there is no or limited interoperability among the systems, but thanks to their relatively wide adoption (compared to the state several years ago), they greatly improve the chance that two independently developed pieces of semantic web software can be made to work together.
Furthermore there are attempts by W3C to standardize some of the many interfaces such system requires to work. The most important is SPARQL query language together with SPARQL query protocol (Prud'hommeaux & Seaborne 2008). These standardize the whole process of making data queries. The standardized language is rather simple and the protocol may not be the most efficient one, but it still is a significant step towards a working, unified infrastructure.

2. Covered Systems

There is an abundance of existing systems supporting semantic web and semantization - a comprehensive list is maintained by W3C Consortium (Alexander 2009). Most of them are academic or scientific prototypes, many of which are unfortunately no longer supported. In this survey, we have included four most significant (in our opinion) systems that are still maintained and supported. In section 7, we also shortly mention some other systems.

2.1 Sesame
Sesame (Broekstra et al. 2002) is an open source RDF framework with support for RDF Schema inferencing and querying. Originally, it was developed as a research prototype for the EU research project On-To-Knowledge. Now, it is further developed and maintained by Aduna in cooperation with a number of volunteer developers. Sesame is one of the oldest systems, a lot of semantic projects used this infrastructure for storing their data. Currently, version 2.2.x is available, Sesame 3.0 with significant improvements in both API and implementation is pre-released.

2.2 Jena
Jena (Carrol et al., 2004) is a Java framework for building Semantic Web applications. It provides a programmatic environment for RDF, RDFS and OWL, SPARQL and includes a rule-based inference engine. Jena is open source and grown out of work with the HP Labs Semantic Web Programme.

2.3 Mulgara
The Mulgara Semantic Store is an Open Source, scalable, transaction-safe, purpose-built database for the storage and retrieval of metadata. It is an active fork of the Kowari (Wood 2005) project.

2.4 Redland
Redland (Beckett 2002) is a set of C libraries that provide support for RDF.

3. Architecture and Interfaces

In this section we explore the architecture and most important interfaces, both application and human-oriented.

3.1 Sesame
Sesame can be deployed on top of a variety of storage systems (relational databases, in-memory, filesystems, keyword indexers, etc.), and offers tools to developers to leverage the power of RDF and RDF Schema, such as a flexible access API, which supports both local and remote (through HTTP or RMI) access, and several query languages.
Figure 1 depicts the overall Sesame architecture. A central concept in the Sesame framework is the repository - a storage container for RDF. This can mean a set of Java objects in memory, or it can mean a relational database.
Sesame supports RDF Schema inferencing. Given a set of RDF and/or RDF Schema, Sesame can find the implicit information in the data. Sesame supports this by adding all implicit information to the repository as well when data is being added. Inferencing is supported only by a subset of repositories.
The Storage And Inference Layer, or SAIL API, is an internal API that abstracts from the storage format used, and provides reasoning support. SAIL implementations can also be stacked on top of each other, to provide functionality such as caching or concurrent access handling. Each Sesame repository has its own SAIL object to represent it. On top of the

SAIL, we find Sesame's functional modules, such as query engines, the admin module, and RDF export. Access to these functional modules is available through Sesame's Access APIs. Access APIs provide an access to Sesame functional modules. The Repository API provides high-level access to Sesame repositories, such as querying, storing of RDF files, extracting RDF, etc. The Graph API provides more fine-grained support for RDF manipulation, such as adding and removing individual statements, and creation of small RDF models directly from code.

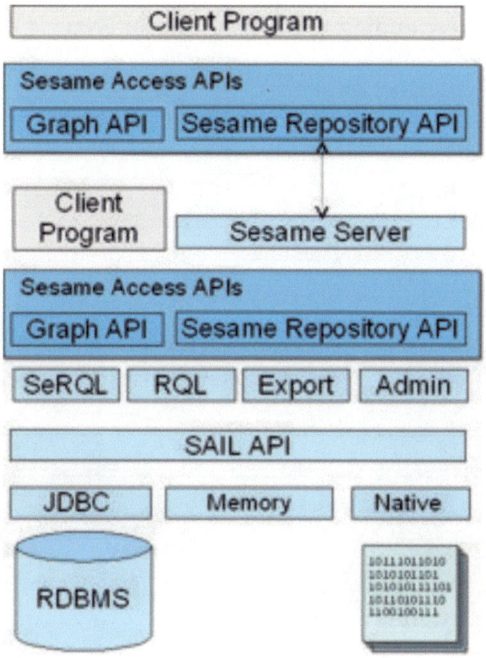

Fig. 1. Sesame Architecture

The Access APIs provide direct access to Sesame's functional modules, either to a client program, or to the next component of Sesame's architecture, the Sesame server. This is a component that provides HTTP-based access to Sesame's APIs. Then, on the remote HTTP client side, we again find the access APIs, which can again be used for communicating with Sesame as a server running on a remote location.

3.2 Jena

Jena is Semantic Web programmers' toolkit built upon RGF graph APIs. The Jena Framework includes: a RDF API, an OWL API, in-memory and persistent storage and SPARQL query engine.

The heart of the Jena2 architecture is the Graph layer containing the RDF graph. This layer is minimal by design, possible functionality is done in other layers. This permits a range of implementations of this layer such as in-memory or persistence triple stores.

The EnhGraph layer is the extension point on which to build APIs: within Jena2 the functionality offered by the EnhGraph layer is used to implement the Jena Model API and the new Ontology functionality for OWL and RDFS, upgrading the Jena DAML API.

I/O is done in the Model layer, essentially for historical reasons.
The Jena2 architecture supports fast path query that goes all the way through the layers from RDQL at the top right through to an SQL database at the bottom, allowing user queries to be optimized by the SQL query optimizer.
The Graph layer provides:

- triple stores, both in memory and backed by persistent storage;
- read-only views of non-triple data as triples, such as data read from a local file system, or scraped from a web page;
- virtual triples corresponding to the results of inference processes over some further set of triples.

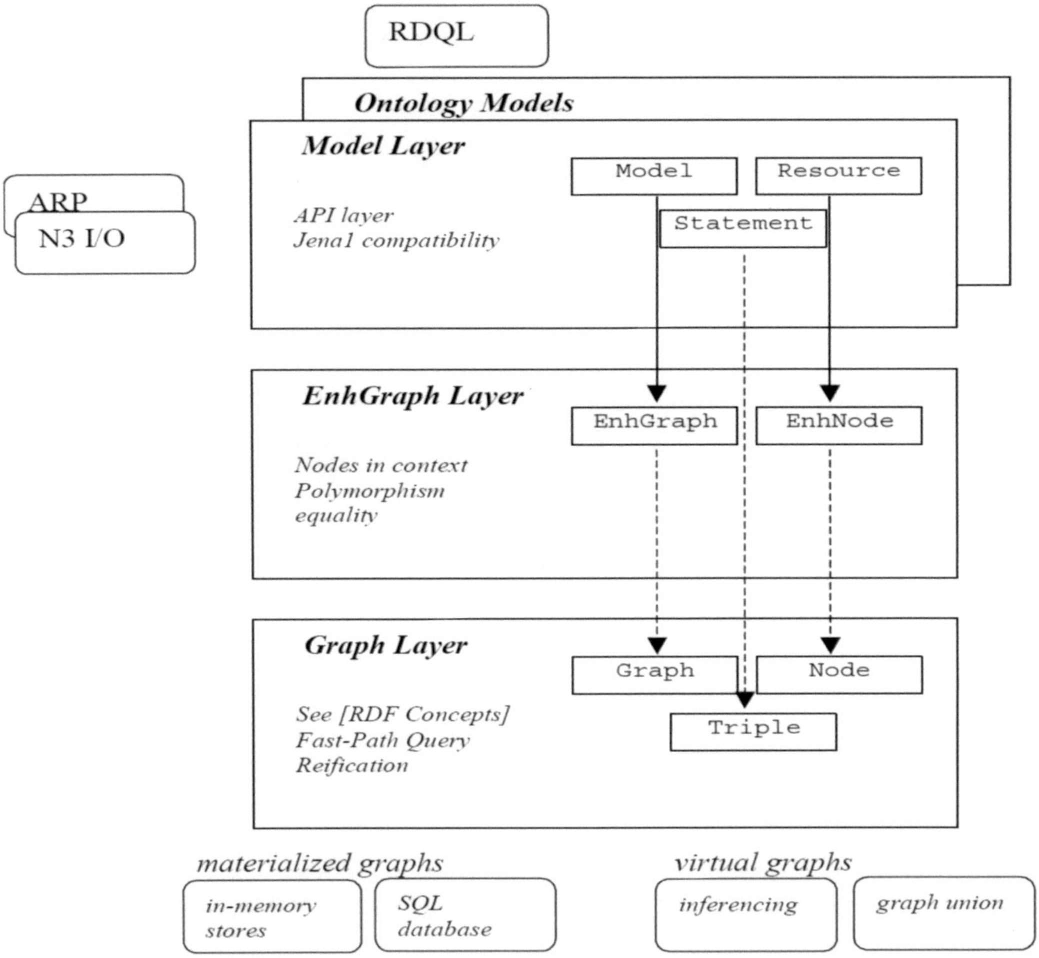

Fig. 2. Jena Architecture

Implementations of the Graph layer give a variety of concrete (materialized) triple stores, and built-in inference for RDFS and a subset of OWL.

The EnhGraph layer is designed to permit multiple views of graphs and nodes which can be used simultaneously. This allows the multiple inheritance and typing of RDFS to be reflected even in Java's single inheritance model.

The Model Layer maintains the Model API as the primary abstraction of the RDF graph used by the application programmer. This gives a much richer set of methods for operating on both the graph itself (the Model interface) and the nodes within the graph (the Resource interface and its subclasses). Further, the Ontology API can be realized as a DAML API or an OWL API.

The design goals for the Graph layer include:

- allowing collections of triples to be queried and updated efficiently. In particular, querying triples held in databases should be able to exploit the underlying database engine.
- being easy to reimplement, so that new triple collections can be represented by Graphs with minimal programming effort.
- supporting some specialist operations from the Model API when these cannot be easily constructed from the base functionality, reification in particular.

The elements within a Graph are Triples; each Triple comprises three Nodes, the subject, predicate, and object fields. A Node represents the RDF notion of a URI label, a blank node, or a literal; there are also two variable nodes, for named variables and a match-anything wildcard, for use in the Query interface.

The RDF restrictions that a literal can only appear as an object, and that a property can only be labelled with a URI, are not enforced by the Graph layer but by the Model layer. The core Graph interface supports modification (add and delete triples) and access (test if a triple is present or list all triples present matching some pattern). Graph implementations are free to restrict the particular triples they regard as legal and to restrict

3.3 Mulgara

Mulgara is a monolithic special-purpose database engine. The data access is provided using iTQL (Interactive Tucana Query Language).

Mulgara has an open API that supports various industry-standard programming languages and protocols. Different types of users interact with Mulgara in different ways depending on their needs:

- End users interact with Mulgara indirectly via applications that use Mulgara as the underlying data repository.
- System administrators use iTQL to load metadata into Mulgara, check its status, back up information held, or otherwise administer Mulgara databases.
- Programmers perform the integration between their own applications and Mulgara.

Queries to Mulgara databases can be issued alternatively using following mechanisms: iTQL shell, Simple Object Access Protocol (SOAP), iTQL JavaBean, or Mulgara Driver. Each of the above mechanisms connect to a Mulgara driver, which in turn connects to a Mulgara server over a separate communication channel. The communication channel is configurable and determines how a server exposes itself to the world, generally via RMI or SOAP.

Using SOAP allows Mulgara to run on a different server from an organizations' web application server, and still maintain accessibility through the regular corporate firewall. If this is not required (for example, the Java RMI port is opened on the firewall, or the Mulgara server and the web application server are running on the same machine) the JSP tag libraries can communicate with the driver directly using the iTQL bean, effectively removing a level of indirection. The JSP tag libraries and COM object provide convenient methods by which iTQL commands can be sent and answers parsed into suitable formats.

iTQL commands received by the SOAP endpoint are sent to the iTQL interpreter. The interpreter uses a driver to issue commands to Mulgara servers containing the models specified by the command. The driver is responsible for coordinating the distribution of commands to the appropriate servers, and collating the results into a single answer to be returned to the interpreter. The remote server receives method calls from the driver via RMI, and makes the appropriate method calls to the underlying Mulgara database.

Pluggable resolvers, provided with Mulgara or written by third parties, allow Mulgara to query different data source, including:

- local or distributed Mulgara native XA datastore
- Lucene models
- XSD datatype models
- Views
- External data sources such as relational databases or Mbox files

3.4 Redland

Unlike almost all other relevant projects that are written in Java, Redland RDF libraries are implemented in the C language. Its APIs enable manipulation with the RDF graph, triples, URIs and Literals. The RDF graphs can be stored either in memory or persistently using Sleepycat/Berkeley DB, MySQL, PostgreSQL, AKT Triplestore, SQLite, files or URIs. It supports multiple syntaxes for reading and writing RDF as RDF/XML, N-Triples and Turtle Terse RDF Triple Language, RSS and Atom syntaxes, and for querying with SPARQL and RDQL using the Rasqal RDF Query Library.

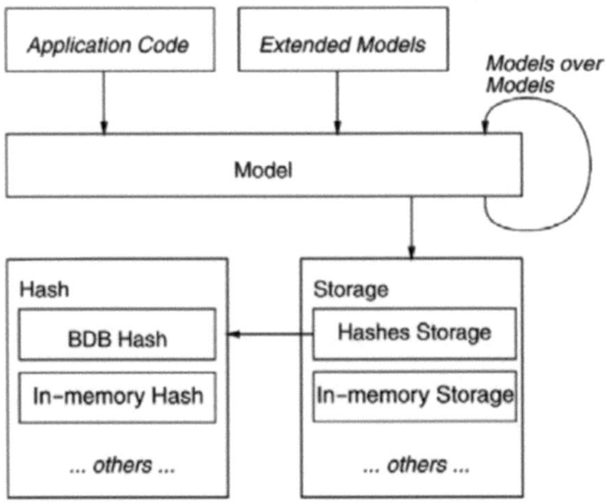

Fig. 3. Redland model layers

The library provides numerous bindings to other programming languages including Java, C#, Perl, PHP, Python and Ruby. The library is supplemented by a set of command line utilities for processing, parsing and querying RDF.

4. Query Languages and Reasoning

The ability to query the data stored in the repository is one of the key functions provided by all of the systems. However, the concrete implementation of this general task differs greatly from system to system. The systems usually provide some graph API to handle RDF graphs directly, but something more advanced is required for efficient application development. This role is performed by query languages, which define textual representation and more importantly the semantics of queries that the user can use to access data stored in the repository. A good parallel is the role of SQL in relational databases.

But since the very beginning, the Semantic web was supposed to do more than just return the data that was loaded into the database earlier. Semantic repositories are supposed to provide reasoning, i.e. the ability to infer new statements (knowledge) based on the statements that were loaded into the database. To do so, several technologies were developed or adopted for the use in the Semantic web. The most prominent are RDFS and OWL, the former being able to construct type hierarchies for resources and statements while the latter is a much more complex system based on the idea of description logics. The intricacy of OWL together with high time complexity results in varying degrees of adoption in different systems.

4.1 Sesame

Sesame supports two distinct query languages: SeRQL and SPARQL. SeRQL is a language developed by the Sesame team before the SPARQL standard was created. Its syntax is SQL-like, even more so than in the case of SPARQL. Even some advanced constructs of SQL have their parallels in SeRQL, for instance set operators (UNION, MINUS, INTERSECT, IN or EXISTS). The following query is an example of SeRQL:

```
SELECT DISTINCT
   label(ArtefactTitle), MuseumName
FROM
   {Artefact} arts:created_by {} arts:first_name {"Rembrandt"},
   {Artefact} arts:exhibited {} dc:title {MuseumName},
   {Artefact} dc:title {ArtefactTitle}
WHERE
   isLiteral(ArtefactTitle) AND
   lang(ArtefactTitle) = "en" AND
   label(ArtefactTitle) LIKE "*night*"
USING NAMESPACE
   dc   = <http://purl.org/dc/elements/1.0/>,
   arts = <http://example.org/arts/>
```

Fig. 4. SeRQL example

Overall, it is a pragmatic query language with clear syntax and relatively simple definition. Its complete specification is a part of the Sesame documentation. SeRQL is a viable option in cases where SPARQL compatibility is not necessary.
But Sesame also provides very advanced SPARQL implementation. According to W3C report (Harris 2008), it covers the whole specification.
Sesame only (optionally) supports RDFS reasoning. It is important to note that it is not handled by the "core" Sesame. Inferencing (reasoning) is supposed to be handled by the underlying storage system. This means that the RDFS reasoning is actually feature of the in-memory and native RDF repositories provided by Sesame and that different modules can provide more complex reasoning. One such example is OWLIM (http://www.ontotext.com/owlim), which implements the SAIL API and provides OWL reasoning.

4.2 Jena

Jena - the ARQ module, to be exact - provides full support for SPARQL (complete coverage according to W3C). It also offers several significant extensions that go beyond the SPARQL specification. These include:

- property paths - regular expressions over paths in the RDF graph,
- querying remote SPARQL endpoints - a query can specify URI of an endpoint that should be queried,
- group by, having and aggregation - very similar to SQL,
- selection list with expressions - queries can return computed values, e.g. sum of two variables,
- nested SELECTs - allows the use of sub-queries, especially powerful in combination with two extensions mention just above, and
- variable assignment - values of variables can be computed by an expression from other variable values.

Jena also implements the SPARQL/Update proposal, which allows insertion and deletion of values stored in the RDF store.
Jena supports RDFS and OWL reasoning "out of the box". Like in Sesame, other reasoners can be added thanks to an API provided by Jena. But unlike Sesame, Jena inference API does not combine storage with reasoning. It can even support stacked reasoners.
Built in reasoners are:

- transitive rasoner, which handles only subClassOf and subPropertyOf,
- RDFS reasoner, and
- Rubrik reasoner, which supports rule-based inferencing.

Jena contains RDFS and OWL Lite rule sets for the Rubrik reasoner, but application specific sets can be used as well.
Examples of external reasoners include the popular Racer reasoner or FaCT.

4.3 Mulgara

Mulgara supports two different query languages: SPARQL and TQL. The TQL language is specific to the Mulgara system and its syntax is also SQL-like. It offers some advanced features like graph traversing, transitive closure, set operations, ordering or sub-queries. It

also provides commands that allow the user to update the data and even to configure and manage the database. Unfortunately, the provided documentation is rather brief.
The SPARQL implementation is not complete (although thorough implementation report is unavailable) but the development team is improving it continually.
Mulgara uses the Krule rule engine developed as part of the original Kowari system. It is a general entailment system built around RLog logic language. The rule sets are then applied to graphs (data) in the system. An RDFS rule set is available in the Mulgara sources.

4.4 Redland

Redland provides the Rasqal RDF query library with support for SPARQL and RDQL. It is only partial implementation of the SPARQL standard but full support of RDQL. While the development of Rasqal seems to have slowed down over the last years, the project is still active and new releases are still being published.
Since Redland is designed purely as an RDF store, no reasoning is supported.

5. Data Engine

While the provided query capabilities are an important factor and define the system's ability to extract data, the storage of the data is also an important factor. It greatly affects the performance of queries and in some cases even influences the query capabilities by providing inferencing mechanism as part of the storage. It also defines system's ability to handle transactions and failure recovery.

5.1 Sesame

Sesame comes packed with two kinds of specialized native storage for RDF, two kinds of RDF storage built on top of a relational database and a general connection to a remote RDF repository.
Both native RDF storages offer different levels of inference. The first native RDF repository is an in-memory store. It offers very fast access to data, but has two serious disadvantages: it is not persistent and it takes a lot of memory. The second disadvantage becomes clearly visible when working with data of an average size (90MB RDF N3 file), where the memory has been exhausted and the whole Sesame system crashed including Apache Tomcat server.
The second native RDF storage is simply called "Native Java Store". It is persistent, offers very good performance, and consumes reasonable amount of memory. It is able to load and query larger data.
The second possibility is to use a relational RDF storage. Out of the box, Sesame supports two connectors to relational database engines common on Linux platforms: MySQL and PostgreSQL. Both of them offer reasonable performance, they are able to store large data, and they have decent memory requirements.
The last possibility is a connection to any RDF repository satisfying a HTTP-based protocol for Sesame, which is partially described in Sesame system documentation.
Other repositories can be added using the SAIL API. At least one notable example should be mentioned: OWLIM Semantic repository, which offers high-performance semantic repository services. A commercial version called BigOWLIM is available as well, which claims to operate upon billions of triples.

5.2 Jena

Jena itself is only a framework and the user needs to install additional storage subsystem. As usually, there are two kinds of storages: native RDF storage and SQL-based storages. Both subsystems are directly referenced from the Jena web site.

The native Java storage for Jena is called TDB and it performs very well. It is able to load and query large datasets and authors claim that it is able to operate upon billions of triples. Interestingly, the TDB behaves differently on 32-bit and 64-bit JVMs, where 32-bit version handles caching by itself, while 64-bit version utilizes memory-mapped files and caching is left to the operating system.

The second possibility is SDB storage, which is a storage subsystem built on top of a SQL database server. SDB supports variety of underlying SQL servers including commercial ones like Microsoft SQL Server or Oracle. Connection to the SQL server from SDB is described in one simple configuration file. Underlying SQL server brings robustness and well known practices for managing, maintenance, and backup of SQL databases, but at the price of lower performance in data loading, where known limitations of SQL servers arise.

5.3 Mulgara

Mulgara is primarily a native RDF database in Java, so the development is focused on storage and querying. As a successor of Kowari, it is high-performance RDF storage. Unfortunately, there is no documentation to the Mulgara internals. As the FAQ for Mulgara states, there are three possibilities, all of them quite inadvisable: read the source code, ask developers, or read Paul's blog.

5.4 Redland

Redland offers two kinds of storage engines: in-memory temporal storage with very fast query and access times and persistent storage with quite decent list of SQL database backends. The advantages and disadvantages of SQL backends are the same as in Jena.

5.5 Virtuoso

So far, we only dealt with the four systems and their different components. But since most of them are built as modular systems, some parts can be switched for modules, even from different authors. This is mostly used for data engines and OpenLink Virtuoso is a nice example of such module.

Virtuoso is a cross platform server to implement web, file, and database server functionality alongside native XML storage, and universal data access middleware. It supports many contemporary internet technologies and protocols as well as operating systems. Virtuoso provides transparent access to existing data sources, which are typically databases from different database vendors. Figure 5 depicts how applications that are built in conformance with industry standards. Virtuoso exposes its functionality to Web Services, it provides specialized providers for Sesame, Jena and Mulgara frameworks.

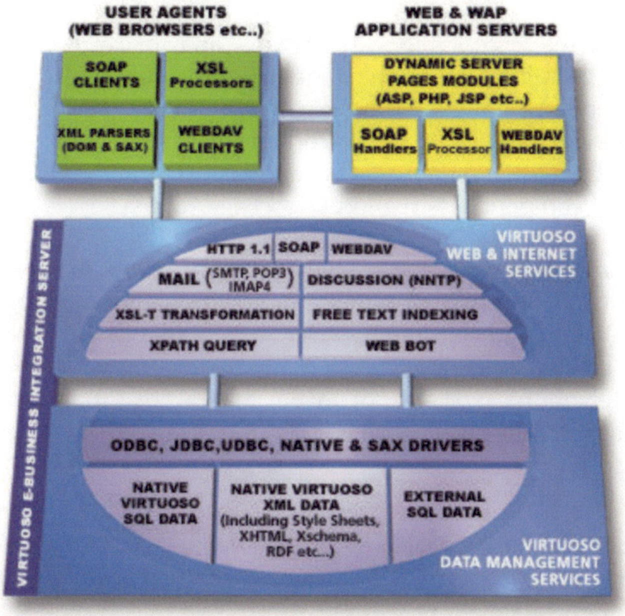

Fig. 5. Virtuoso architecture

6. Installation and Documentation

Most resources (papers and web pages) deal with performance, query languages, APIs and interfaces, but there are two other important aspects of any software. In order to operate such systems, one first has to install it. Since most Semantic web projects are built on top of many different libraries, the ease of installation may become a significant concern. The other aspects that often tends to be neglected by such projects is maintaining detailed and up-to-date documentation.

6.1 Sesame

The Sesame is delivered as a Java archive in two flavours. One of them is called "onejar" and it is a distribution best suitable for already compiled applications written for Sesame. The second flavour of the distribution is SDK, which contains all sources needed for developing Sesame applications as well as two .war files, which can be unpacked into Apache Tomcat application directory, where they create two applications: Sesame server with HTTP interface and Workbench, which is a web interface for playing with Sesame. We have to discover some nontrivial installation steps, like copying latest Apache Xalan-J distributable files into library directory of Tomcat, because the installation documentation is clearly outdated and short, and there is no notion about Xalan-J installation.

The documentation is in the form of HTML pages, either distributed in SDK distribution or reachable on the web pages of the Sesame project.

6.2 Jena

As mentioned above, the Jena is only a framework and for correct implementation more packages must be installed, although some of them are already contained in Jena downloadable package. All downloads are easily accessible from the Jena download page. At least two components are required for correct installation, the Jena framework and a storage subsystem. Currently there are two options: TDB and SDB. As an optional but highly recommended component is the Joseki package, which serves as an RDF publishing server.

The installation is smooth and easy as it only requires the user to set some environmental variables including CLASSPATH and sometimes edit a small number of configuration files. Moreover, the installation and configuration for each component is described in the project documentation very well.

The Jena documentation consists of web pages of the project, where each subproject/component has its own documentation.

6.3 Mulgara

Installation should be quite easy and straightforward, as it is shipped with variety of packages for different usage scenarios. The user can choose from complete package, package without third party dependencies, Web Archives, etc.

We have encountered interesting problem, as the current (at the time of writing of this text) version 2.0.9 had broken Web Archive distribution, but following versions 2.1.0 and 2.1.1 repaired this problem.

The documentation is rather brief, but it describes everything required to install and run the system.

6.4 Redland

Redland library requires two other libraries, Raptor and Rasqal, for compilation and runtime as well, and we will call these three libraries Redland libraries from now. All libraries are available for download at the Redland project page. The Redland libraries are (unlike all previously mentioned projects) written in C and are distributed in source code form with automake build system. Although creating make configuration using automake should be simple from user's point of view, in this case we have encountered some nontrivial problems.

The first problem has been caused by requirements on newer versions of some tools like flex, libtool, etc. We have used the latest RedHat Enterprise Linux 5.3 (RHEL) distribution and the required versions of the tools are not available. Manual installation of newer version has caused some dependency problems with existing software packages on RHEL.

The second problem has been linked to pkg-config tool, which couldn't find the already compiled Raptor and Rasqal libraries and failed to create configuration for Redland. Manual steps were required to correct this situation.

This somewhat limits the audience the library can target. It clearly isn't prepared for enterprise deployment, where stable versions of Linux (like RHEL) or Unix are usually used.

The documentation is surprisingly comprehensive and is provided separately for each library.

7. Other Projects

There are many other RDF repositories. We have only listed some of the most important ones. The others are either not as popular or their development was discontinued. One such example is the Kowari system (Wood 2005). While it was one of the earliest and very efficient RDF store with good scalability, its development stopped in 2005. Fortunately, the code base was later used to create the Mulgara project, which is still being very active.
Many of the projects have been created only as a scientific prototype, which means their development may easily stop at any time and their support can be very problematic. Examples include TAP from Stanford (Guha and McCool, 2003), Corese from INRIA (Corby et al., 2004), Trisolda (Dokulil et al., 2009), or Boca (Feigenbaum et al., 2007).
Comprehensive list of Semantic Web tools, including RDF repositories, is maintained by W3C (Alexander 2009). Unfortunately, it does not give current state of development of the individual systems and whether they are still being developed and supported.

8. Conclusion

Over time, a lot of projects aimed to be the framework for the Semantic Web. Only a few became stable and ready to use for diverse semantization projects. In this survey we described four such systems, their architecture, capabilities, strengths and limitations. Based on our practical experience, although these projects are not meant to became enterprise-level frameworks (e.g. none of them support access rights), they can be used as a platform for research of semantization.

9. References

Alexander, K. (2009) Semantic Web Development Tools, *http://esw.w3.org/topic/SemanticWebTools*, W3C Technical Report, 2009

Beckett, D. (2002). The design and implementation of the Redland RDF application framework, *Computer Networks*, Vol. 39, Issue 5, August 2002, pp. 577-588

Broekstra, J.; Kampman, A.; van Harmelen, F. (2002) Sesame: A Generic Architecture for Storing and Querying RDF and RDF Schema, *The Semantic Web – ISWC 2002*, Lecture Notes in Computer Science, vol. 2342, 2002, ISBN 978-3-540-43760-4

Carrol, J. J.; Reynolds, D.; Dickinson, I.; Seaborne, A.; Dollin, C.; Wilkinson, K. (2004). Jena: Implementing the Semantic Web Recommendations, *Proceedings of the 13th international World Wide Web conference*, 2004, New York, ISBN:1-58113-912-8

Corby, O.; Dieng-Kuntz, R. and Faron-Zucker, C. (2004) Querying the Semantic Web with Corese Search Engine, *Proc. 16th European Conf. Artificial Intelligence* (ECAI 04), 2004, IOS Press, pp. 705–709.

Dokulil, J.; Yaghob, J. and Zavoral, F. (2009) Trisolda: The Environment for Semantic Data Processing, *International Journal On Advances in Software*, 2008, vol. 1, IARIA, 2009

Feigenbaum, L.; Martin, S.; Roy, M. N.; Szekely, B. and Yung, W. C. (2007) Boca: an open-source RDF store for building Semantic Web applications, Briefings in Bioinformatics, Vol. 8, Issue 3, pp. 195-200, ISSN 1467-5463

Guha, R.; McCool, R. (2003) TAP: a Semantic Web platform, *Computer Networks*, Vol. 42, Issue 5, 2003, pp. 557-577

Harris, S. (2008) SPARQL Implementation Coverage Report, W3C Technical Report, *http://www.w3.org/2001/sw/DataAccess/tests/implementations*, 2008

Muys, A. (2006) Building an Enterprise-Scale Database for RDF Data, *Netymon technical paper*, 2006

Prud'hommeaux, E.; Seaborne, A. (2008) SPARQL Query Language for RDF, W3C Recommendation, W3C 2008

Wood D. (2005) Scaling the Kowari Metastore, *Lecture Notes in Computer Science,* Vol. 3807, pp. 193-198, Springer Verlag, 2005

6

Prime Number Labeling Scheme for Transitive Closure Computation

Gang Wu [1] and Juanzi Li [2]
[1] *Institute of Web Science, Southeast University, Nanjing 210096, P.R.China*
[2] *Knowledge Engineering Group, Tsinghua University, Beijing 100084, P.R.China*

1. Introduction

In the context of Semantic Web, subsumption, i.e., inference of implicit subclass relationship, owl:TransitiveProperty, and owl:inverseOf, is a kind of simple yet basic description logic reasoning [7]. It is usually solved as a transitive closure computation problem [4]. Directed Graph is an effective data structure for representing such subsumption hierarchies While, the growing number and volume of directed graphs involved greatly inspire the demands for appropriate index structures.

Labeling scheme[9] is a family of technologies widely used in indexing tree or graph structured data. It assigns each vertex a well-designed label with which relationship between any two vertices can be detected or filtered efficiently. This chapter concerns only about labeling scheme among diverse index technologies considering its avoiding expensive join operation for transitive closure computation. Determinacy, compaction, dynamicity, and flexibility are factors for labeling scheme design besides speedup [11]. However, the state of art labeling schemes for directed graph could not satisfy most above requirements at the same time. Even approaches for the directed acyclic graph (DAG) is few.

One major category of labeling schemes for DAG is spanning tree based. Most of them are developed from their tree versions. The first step of labeling is to find a spanning tree and assigning labels for vertices according to tree's edges. Next, additional labels are propagated to record relationships represented through non-tree edges. Christophides et al. surveyed and compared two such schemes [4], i.e. interval-based [8] and prefix-based [3]. Whereas, the weak point of above schemes is obvious. Evaluations to the relationships implied by non-tree edges cannot take advantage of the deterministic tree label characters. Non-tree labels need not only additional storage but also special efforts in query processing. Also interval-based scheme studied in [4] has a poor re-labeling ability for updates.

There are also labeling schemes having no concern with spanning tree. Such as bit vector [10] and 2-hops [5]. Though bit vector can process operations on DAG more efficiently, it is static and requires global rebuilding of labels when updates happen. Moreover, studies show that recent 2-hops approach introduces false positives in basic reachability testing.

A novel labeling scheme for XML tree depending on the properties of prime number is proposed in [11]. Prime number labeling scheme associates each vertex with a unique prime number, and labels each vertex with the product of multiplying parents' labels and the prime number owned by the vertex. The effect of updating on vertices is almost the same to that in prefix-based scheme. Moreover, the response time for queries and the size requirements are even smaller than those of prefix-based scheme. However no further work has been performed on extending the idea of prime number labeling scheme to the case of DAG.

In this research we expect to find out a labeling scheme for DAG to augment performance in all of the above requirements as much as possible. By taking a strong connected component in the graph as one vertex, arbitrary directed graphs (with cycles) can be treated with the proposed labeling scheme. We are stimulated by the virtues of prime number labeling scheme exhibited in indexing XML tree. We extend it by labeling each vertex in a DAG with an integer which equals to the arithmetic product of the prime number associating with the vertex and all the prime numbers associating with its ancestors. The scheme does not depend on spanning tree. Thus subsumption hierarchies represented in a DAG can be efficiently explored by checking the divisibility among the labels. It also inherits dynamic update ability and compact size feature from its predecessor. The major contributions are as follows.

- Extend original prime number scheme[11] for labeling DAG and to support the processing of typical operations on DAG.
- Optimize the scheme in terms of the characteristics of DAG and prime numbers. Topological sort and Least common multiple are used to prevent the quick expansion of label size; Leaves marking and descendants-label improve the performance of querying leaves and descendants respectively.
- A generator is implemented to generate arbitrary complex synthetic DAG for the extensive experiments. Space requirement, construction time, scalability, and impact of selectivity and update are all studied in the experiments.

Results indicate that prime number labeling scheme is an efficient and scalable scheme for indexing DAG with appropriate extensions and optimizations.

2. DAG and Typical Operations

Given a finite set V and a binary relation E on V, a *directed graph* can be represented as $G = (V, E)$. V and E consist of all the *vertices* and *edges* in G respectively. For any pair of vertices u and u' in G, vertices sequence $< v_0, v_1, v_2, \ldots, v_k >$ is called a *path*, if $u = v_0$, $u' = v_k$, and $(v_{i-1}, v_i) \in E$ for $i = 1, 2, \ldots, k + 1$. A directed graph is a *directed acyclic graph* (DAG) if there is no path returning to the same vertex. Figure 1(borrowed from [4]) is a DAG.

Reachability is a basic concept in DAG. Given two vertices v and w, if there exists a path p from v to w, we say that w is reachable from v via p, or $v \overset{p}{\rightsquigarrow} w$ (or as $v \rightsquigarrow w$ out of consideration of p). Known relations, such as *parent, child, ancestor, descendant, leaf, sibling, and nearest common ancestor(s) (nca)* are derived from this concept. Queries on these relations are typical operations on DAG. While, unlike trees, order-sensitive queries such as preceding/following are meaningless for DAG. In the following discussion, given vertices v and w in DAG G, we will use *parents(v), children(v), ancestors(v), descendants(v), leaves(v), siblings(v)* and *nca(v, w)* indicating the above queries respectively (See [4] for formal expressions). Update, including vertices insertions and deletions, is another kind of operation worthy of note because it usually brings reorganizations to the DAG storage and re-labelings to the index structure.

3. Prime Number Labeling Scheme for DAG

The first part of this section shows that the *divisibility* of integers still could be the evidence theory of the prime number labeling scheme for DAG. In the second part, we prove that all of the typical operations on DAG are solvable.

3.1 Prime Number Labeling Scheme for DAG - Lite

Few modifications are required to support DAG reachability testing.

Definition 1. *Let G = (V,E) be a directed acyclic graph. A* ***Prime Number Labeling Scheme for DAG - Lite****(PLSD-Lite for short) associates each vertex v ∈ V with an exclusive prime number p[v], and assigns to v a label* $L_{\text{lite}}(v) = (c[v])$, *where*

$$c[v] = p[v] \cdot \begin{cases} \prod_{v' \in parents(v)} c[v'], & in-degree(v)>0 \\ 1, & in-degree(v)=0 \end{cases} \quad (1)$$

In Figure 1, PLSD-Lite assigns each vertex an exclusive prime number increasingly from "2" with a depth-first traversal of the DAG. The first multiplier factor in the brackets of each vertex is the prime number assigned.

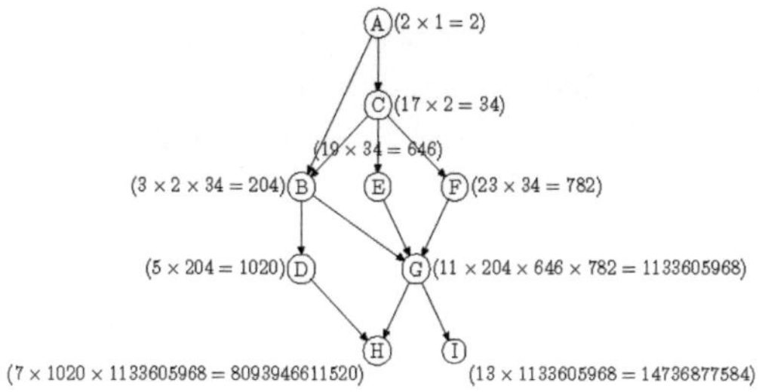

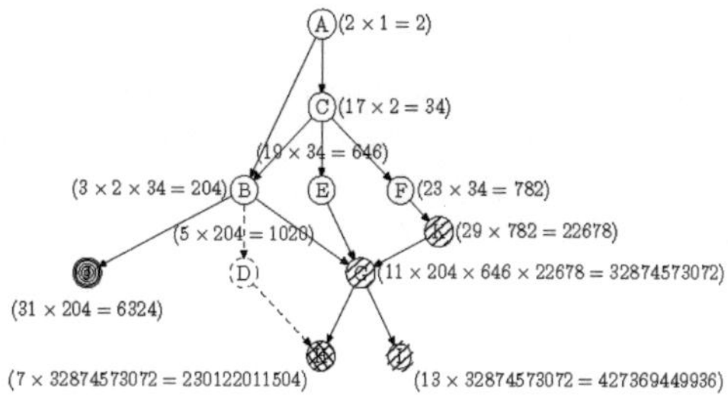

Fig. 1. Prime Number Labeling Scheme for DAG - Lite

Fig. 2. Updates in Prime Number Labeling Scheme for DAG - Lite

Lemma 1. *Let G =* (V, E) *be a directed acyclic graph. Composite number c[v] in the* $L_{\text{lite}}(v) = (c[v])$ *of a vertex v∈V can be written in exactly one way as a product ofthe form*

$$c[v] = p[v] \cdot \prod_{v' \in ancestors(v)} p[v']^{m_{v'}} \quad (2)$$

where $m_{v'} \in \mathbb{N}$.

Proof. Such a product expression can be constructed by performing transitive closure in terms of Definition 1. On the other hand, an integer has a unique factorization into primes, and hence the above product expression is unique. □

Lemma 1 implies that for any vertex in the DAG with PLSD-Lite, there is a bijection between an ancestor of the vertex and a prime factor of the label value.

Theorem 1. *Let G* = (V, E) *be a directed acyclic graph. For any two vertices v,w* ∈ *V where* $L_{lite}(v)$ = (c[*v*]) *and* $L_{lite}(w)$ = (c[*w*]), $v \rightsquigarrow w \Leftrightarrow c[v] \mid c[w]$.

Proof. Let $r = < v_0, ..., v_k >$ be one of the path length *k* from vertex *v* to vertex *w*, where $v_0 = v$, $v_k = w$ and $k >= 1$. By the definition of reachability, vertex *v* must be an ancestor of vertex *w* on r. Suppose $in - degree(w) > 0$, by Definition 1, composite number c[*w*] of label $L_{lite}(w)$ = (c[*w*]), could be represented as

$c[w] = \left(\prod_{i=1}^{k} p[v_i]\right) \cdot c[v_0] \cdot \prod_{v' \in parents(w) \wedge v' \neq v_{k-1}} c[v']$. Since $v_0 = v$, we conclude that $c[v] \mid c[w]$. On the other hand, $c[v] \mid c[w]$ implies $c[w] = k' \cdot c[v]$ for some integer k'. By Lemma 1, then we have that $c[w] = k' \cdot p[v] \cdot \prod_{v' \in parents(v)} p[v']^{m_{v'}}$. This factorization of *c[w]* implies that *p[v]* is a factor of *c[w]*. Therefore, vertex *v* is one of the ancestors of vertex *w*. The reachability from *v* to *w* is obvious. □

A consequence of Theorem 1 is that whether two vertices have the relation of ancestor/descendant can be simply determined with PLSD-Lite. For example, in Figure 1, we have $A \rightsquigarrow D$ because $2 \mid 1020$. Whereas there is no ancestor/descendant relation between *F* and *D* because $782 \nmid 1020$. In this way, finding out all the ancestors or descendants of a given vertex is realizable by testing the divisibility of the vertex's label with the other vertices' labels in the DAG or conversely. Averagely *(N* - 1)/2 divisibility testings have to be carried out to retrieve all the ancestors or descendants for any given vertex in a *N* vertices DAG. We can determine that *D* has three ancestors *B, C* and *A* by examining divisibility of each vertex that has label value less than "1020". Vertex *E* and *F* are not the ancestors of *D* because their label values cannot divide 1020. Moreover, a vertex is a leaf if any other vertex's label value could not be divided by its label value. There is also a naive solution to nca evaluating according to the definition of nca and Theorem 1. First put all the common ancestors of both vertices into a set. Then filter out vertices whose descendants are also within the set. Remainings in the set are the nca of the vertices.

PLSD-Lite is also a fully dynamic labeling scheme in the presences of updates as stated in [11]. Re-labeling happens with the insertion or deletion of a vertex, and only affects the descendants of the newly inserted vertex or the deleted vertex. After deleting vertex *D*, inserting leaf vertex *J* and non-leaf vertex *K*, we have Figure 2. As a new leaf, vertex *J* does not affect other vertex in the DAG. Insertion of vertex *K* only affects descendants G, *H, I* and *K* itself. Vertex *H* is affected by the deletion of ancestor *D* at the same time.

However PLSD-Lite lacks enough information to identify parents/child relation, not to mention finding all the siblings of a given vertex.

3.2 Prime Number Labeling Scheme for DAG - Full

In order to support all of the operations for DAG, PLSD-Lite should be extended by separately recording the prime number that identifies the vertex and the additional information about parents.

Definition 2. *Let* G = (V, E) *be a directed acyclic graph. A* ***Prime Number Labeling Scheme for DAG - Full****(PLSD-Full for short) associates each vertex* $v \in V$ *with an exclusive prime number* $p[v]$*, and assigns to* v *a label* $L_{full}(v) = (p[v], c_a[v], c_p[v])$*, where*

$$c_a[v] = p[v] \cdot \begin{cases} \prod_{v' \in parents(v)} c_a[v'], & in-degree(v)>0 \\ 1, & in-degree(v)=0 \end{cases} \tag{3}$$

$$c_p[v] = \begin{cases} \prod_{v' \in parents(v)} p[v'], & in-degree(v)>0 \\ 1, & in-degree(v)=0 \end{cases} \tag{4}$$

We term $p[v]$ as "self-label", $c_a[v]$ as "ancestors-label"(also $c[v]$ in Definition 1), and $c_p[v]$ as "parents-label". In Figure 3, three parts in one bracket is self-label, ancestors-label, and parents-label. Theorem 1 is still applicable. Moreover, all the operations on DAG are supported by the following theorem and corollary.

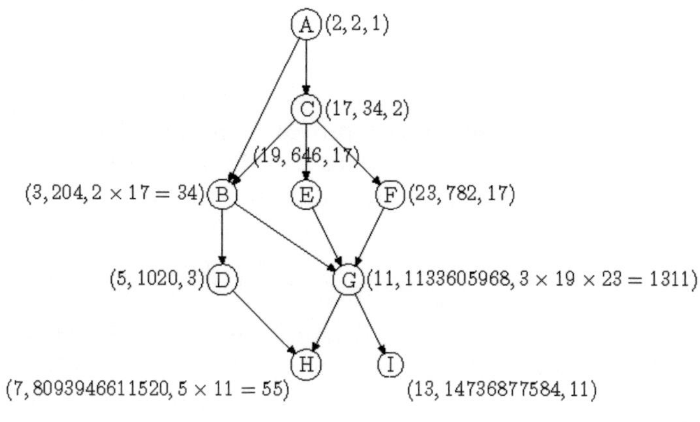

Fig. 3. Prime Number Labeling Scheme for DAG - Full

Theorem 2. *Let* G = (V, E) *be a directed acyclic graph, and vertex* $v \in V$ *has* $L_{full}(v) = (p[v], c_a[v], c_p[v])$. *If the unique factorization of composite integer* $c_a[v]$ *results* r *different prime numbers,* $p_1 < \ldots < p_r$*, then there is exactly one vertex* $w \in V$ *that takes* p_i *as the self-label for* $1 \le i \le r$*, and* w *is one of the ancestors of* v*. If the unique factorization of composite integer* $c_p[v]$ *results* s *different prime numbers,* $p'_1 < \ldots < p'_s$*, then there is exactly one vertex* $u \in V$ *that takes* p'_i *as the self-label for* $1 \le i \le s$*, and* u *is one of the parents of* v*.*

The proof of Theorem 2 is obvious according to Lemma 1, the definition of parents-label and the unique factorization property of integer. It implies that we can find out all the parents of any vertex by factorizing the parents-label. For instance, since vertex G in Figure 3 has a parents-label 1311 = 3 x 19x23, vertices B, E and F are considered to be all the parents of G. We still have the rights to determine the parent/child relation of two vertices by checking divisibility between one's parents-label and the other's self-label in terms of Definition 2. Corollary 1 further expresses PLSD-Full's sibling evaluation ability.

Corollary 1. *Let $G = (V, E)$ be a directed acyclic graph. For any two vertices $v,w \in V$ where $L_{full}(v) = (p[v], c_a[v], c_p[v])$ and $L_{full}(w) = (p[w], c_a[w], c_p[w])$, w and v are siblings ifand only ifthe greatest common divisor oftheir parents-label,* $\gcd(c_p[v], c_p[w]) \neq 1$.

Proof. Suppose vertex $u \in V$ is one of the parents of both v and w where $L_{full}(u) = (p[u], c_a[u], c_p[u])$. Then $c_p[v] = k_i\, c_p[u]$ and $c_p[w] = k_i\, c_p[u]$ hold where $k_i > 1, k_2 > 1 \in \mathbb{N}$. Therefore, $c_p[u]$ is the common divisor of $c_p[v]$ and $c_p[w]$ and hence the greatest common divisor $\gcd(c_p[v], c_p[w]) \neq 1$ since $c_p[u] \neq 1$. On the other hand, let $\gcd(c_p[v], c_p[w]) \neq 1$ be the greatest common divisor of $c_p[v]$ and $c_p[w]$, which implies that there exist $r \geq 1$ prime numbers $p_1^{\varepsilon_1} p_2^{\varepsilon_2} \dots p_r^{\varepsilon_r} = \gcd(c_p[v], c_p[w])$. According to Theorem 2, the vertices v and w have a set of parents whose self-labels are prime numbers $p_1, p_2, \dots, p_r$ respec-tively. Consequently, we conclude that vertices v and w are siblings. □

Corollary 1 enables us to discover the siblings of a vertex by testing whether the greatest common divisor of the parents-labels equals 1. In Figure 3, vertex *B* have two siblings *E* and *F* because $\gcd(34, 17) = 17 \neq 1$.

Theorem 2 provides us another measure to obtain ancestors besides doing divisibility testing one vertex after another. By applying unique factorization to the ancestors-label of vertex *D* in Figure 3, three ancestors *A*, *B* and *C* are thus identified by prime factors "3", "2" and "17" respectively. Though trial division itself could be used to do integer factorization, we can choose faster integer factorization algorithm alternately especially for small integers.

4. Optimization Techniques

As shown above, PLSD could perform all typical operations on DAG with elementary arithmetic operations such as divisibility testing, greatest common divisor evaluating, and integer factorization. Because these elementary arithmetic operations become time-consuming while their inputs are large numbers, running time is usually estimated by measuring the count of bit operations required in a number-theoretic algorithm. In other words, the more number of bits are required to represent the labels of PLSD, the more time will be spent on the operations. In this section we will introduce several optimization techniques to eliminate the count and the size of the prime factors involved in the multiplication for label generation of our scheme. Also another one is proposed at the end of this section as a complementarity of PLSD for querying descendants.

4.1 Least Common Multiple

In previous definitions, the value of a vertex's ancestors-label is constructed from multiplying its self-label by the parents' ancestors-labels. However, there is apparent redundancy in this construction of ancestors-label that power m_v' in Equation 2 magnifies the size of ancestors-label exponentially, but it is helpless for evaluating the operations of DAG. It is straightforward to remove the redundancy by simply setting m_v' to 1 in Equation 2. We have Equation 5 below.

$$c[v] = p[v] \cdot \prod_{v' \in ancestors(v)} p[v'] \quad (5)$$

The simplification is reasonable because in this case Theorems 1 and 2 still hold. Define $lcm(a_1,a_2,\ldots,a_n)$ to be the *least common multiple* of n integers $a_1, a_2,\ldots, a_n$. In particular, for an integer a we define $lcm(a) = a$ here. Thereafter we have the following equation for ancestors-label construction.

$$c[v] = p[v] \cdot \begin{cases} lcm(c[v'_1],\ldots,c[v'_n]), & in-degree(v)>0 \ and \ v'_1,\ldots,v'_n \in parents(v) \\ 1, & in-degree(v)=0 \end{cases} \quad (6)$$

The equivalence between Equation 5 and 6 can be proved with the property of least common multiple apparently. Equation 6 implies that an ancestors-label can be simply constructed by multiplying self-label by the least common multiple of all the parents' ancestors-labels. Thereafter, the value of an ancestors-label is the arithmetic product of its ancestors' as described in Equation 5. With this optimization technique, the max-length of ancestors-label in DAG is only on terms with the total count of vertices and the count of ancestors. Comparing with Figure 3, Figure 4 has a smaller max-length of ancestors-label.

4.2 Topological Sort

Previous selection of prime number for the self-label of a vertex is arbitrary only on condition that no two vertices have the same self-label. A naive approach is assigning each vertex met in depth-first search of DAG a prime number ascend-ingly. Unfortunately, Equation 5 and 2 imply that the size of a vertex's self-label has influence on all the ancestors-labels of its descendants. So vertices on the top of the hierarchy should be assigned small prime numbers as early as possible. Topological sort of a DAG can solve the problem.

"A *topological sort* of a dag *G* = (V, *E*) is a linear ordering of all its vertices such that if *G* contains an edge (*u*, *v*), then *u* appears before *v* in the ordering."[6]. Thus assigning prime numbers ascendingly to vertices with this ordering results in small self-labels precedences in the hierarchy. One of the topological sort of the DAG in Figure 1 is *"A, C, E, F, B, D, G, H,* I". Let the self-labels to be the first 9 prime numbers "2, 3, 5, 7,11,13,17,19, 23" respectively, then we get Figure 5.

4.3 Leaves Marking

As an optimization for reducing label size, even numbers such as $2^1, 2^2,\ldots, 2^n$ are used as self-labels for leaf vertices in [11], which gives us another method to identify leaves. However, the prime number theorem indicates that the growth of prime number is slower than that of power of 2, so self-labels of even number leaves increase dramatically. An alternative is to follow the rule of PLSD-FULL and simply setting leaf's ancestors-label to be negative. Then whether a vertex is a leaf could be determined by the sign of its ancestors-label. It is a meaningful technique in the case of existing large number of leaves in a DAG.

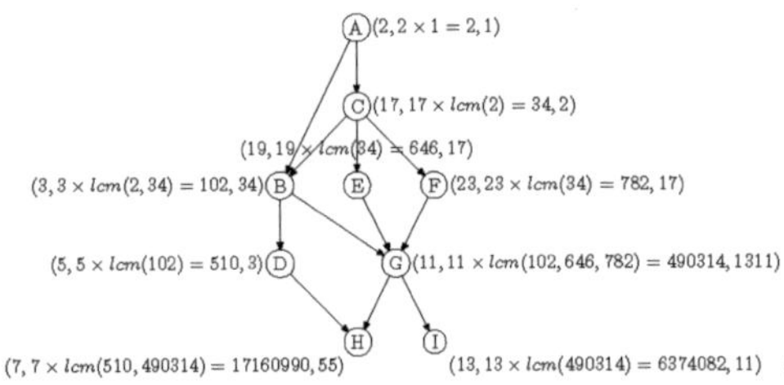

Fig. 4. PLSD-Full with Least Common Multiple Optimization

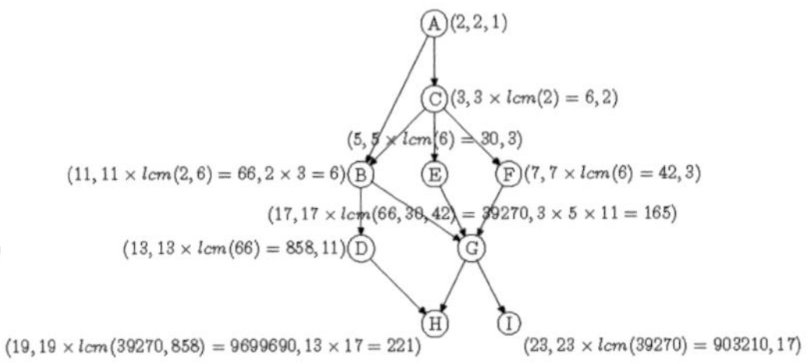

Fig. 5. PLSD-Full with Topological Sort Optimization

4.4 descendants-label

Divisibility testing and unique factorization both can be used for querying ancestors as discussed in section 3.It is feasible to spend more storage space on adding another label for helping to evaluate *descendants(v)* in consideration of existing timesaving integer factoring algorithms. In the same idea of ancestors-label, we extend PLSD-Full by adding the following so-called "descendants-label".

$$c_a[v] = p[v] \cdot \begin{cases} \prod_{v' \in children(v)} c_a[v'], & out{-}degree(v)>0 \\ 1, & out{-}degree(v)=0 \end{cases} \tag{7}$$

Clearly, Equation 7 is just like Equation 3 except in the reverse hierarchy. Now descendants query, *descendants(v),* can be evaluated by factoring descendants-label in the same way provided by Theorem 2. In section 5 we will give empirical results on querying descendants and leaves using this technique.

5. Performance Study

This section presents some results of our extensive experiments conducted to study the effectiveness of prime number labeling scheme for DAG (PLSD).

5.1 Experiment Settings

Taking the queries on RDF class hierarchies as an application background for DAG, we setup test bed on top of RDF Schema Specific DataBase(RSSDB v2.0) [2], which is a persistent RDF store that generates an Object-Relational (SQL3) representation of RDF metadata. In this case, each vertex in a DAG stands for a class in the RDF metadata, and each edge in a DAG stands for the hierarchy relationship between a pair of classes in the RDF metadata. In our configuration, RDF metadata is parsed and stored in PostgreSQL (win32 platform v8.0.2 with Unicode configuration) through the loader of RSSDB.

Though least common multiple, topological sort, and leaves marking are optional optimization techniques, they are integrated in our default PLSD-Full implementation. PLSD-Full without these optimizations and PLSD-Lite are ignored for their apparent defects. Furthermore, based on this default implementation of PLSDF-Full, descendants-label is employed to examine its effects on descendants query. We also provide the Unicode Dewey prefix-based scheme and the extended postorder interval-based scheme by Agrawal et al. The former is an implementation to the descriptions in [4], and the latter is a complementary to the scheme released with the source code of RSSDB v2.0. Hence, there are totally four competitors in our comparisons, namely, default PLSD-Full (PLSDF), PLSD-Full with descendants-label (PLSDF-D), extended postorder interval-based scheme (PInterval) and Unicode Dewey prefix-based scheme (UP-refix). All the implementations are developed in Eclipse 3.1 with JDK1.5.0. Database connection is constructed with PostgreSQL 7.3.3 JDBC2 driver build 110.

The relational representations of UPrefix and PInterval, including tables, indexes, and buffer settings, are the same to those in [4]. As for PLSDF, we create a table with four attributes: *PLSDF (self - label : text, label : text, parent - label : text, uri : text).* It is not surprising that we use PostgreSQL data type *text* instead of the longest integer data type *bigint* to represent the first three attributes considering that a vertex with 15 ancestors has an ancestors-label value 32589158477190044730 ($2 \times 3 \times 5 \times 7 \times 11 \times 13 \times 17 \times 19 \times 23 \times 29 \times 31 \times 37 \times 41 \times 43 \times 47 \times 53$) which easily exceeds the upper bound of *bigint* (8 bytes, between ±9223372036854775808). Fortunately, the conversion from text to number is available on host language Java. Thus the number-theoretic algorithms used for PLSDF could be performed outside PostgreSQL, and become main memory operations. Similarly, we use *PLSDF - D(self - label : text, label : text, parent - label : text, descendants - label : text, uri : text)* to represent PLSDF-D where attribute descendants-label is added. For PLSDF and PLSDF-D, we only build B-tree indexes on self-labels because of the limitation of B-tree on large size text column, though indexes are necessary on ancestors-label and parents-label. Buffer settings are the same to those of UPrefix and PInterval.

All the experiments are conducted on a PC with single Intel(R) Pentium(R) 4 CPU 2.66GHz, 1GB DDR-SDRAM, 80GB IDE hard disk, and Microsoft Windows 2003 Server as operating system.

5.2 Data Sets and Performance Metrics

To simulate diverse cases of DAG, we implement a RDF metadata generator that can generate RDF file with arbitrary complexity and scale of RDF class hierarchies. Generator's input includes 4 parameters that describe a DAG. They are the count of vertices, the max depth of DAG's spanning tree, the max fan-out of vertices, and the portion of fan-in *(ancestors/precedings).* The count of the edges changes with the adjustment to the above values. Though PLSDF and PLSDF-D depend only on the characters of DAG, parameters related to spanning tree are still employed here because Interval and UPrefix are all based on spanning tree. The output is a valid RDF file (conforming with W3C RDF/XML Syntax Specification) that satisfies the parameters. We concatenate the values of above four parameters and the count of edges with hyphens to identify a DAG.

RDF Metadata DAG	Size (MB)	Classes/ Vertices	SubClassOf/ Edges	Depth Max	Fan-out Max	Fan-in Portion	Fan-in Max
1300-8-4-0.2-50504	2.55	1300	50504	8	4	0.2	219
1300-8-4-0.4-100132	4.62	1300	100132	8	4	0.4	458
1300-8-4-0.6-149451	6.34	1300	149451	8	4	0.6	373
1300-8-4-0.8-199774	8.05	1300	199774	8	4	0.8	897
1300-8-4-1.0-250222	9.32	1300	250222	8	4	1.0	562
450-2-32-0.7-45525	2.78	450	45525	2	32	0.7	313
90000-16-2-0.000053-44946	16.3	90000	44946	16	2	0.000053	3

Table 1. Data Sets

Listed in Table 1, two groups of DAGs are generated for evaluating the performance of PLSDF, PLSDF-D, UPrefix, and PInterval. They are used for investigating the impacts of DAG size and shape respectively on the labeling schemes. Data in the first group indicates that the file size and the count of the edges are positively related, if we fix the other parameters. While the second group shows two DAGs with different shape of spanning trees.

5.3 Space Requirement and Construction Time

The first group of DAGs in Table 1 is used here. For space requirement, we has Figure 6(a) where PLSDF and PLSDF-D have much smaller average space requirement (size of both tables and indexes), and mild trend of increase. The underlying cause is twofold. First, PLSDF or PLSDF-D is so simple that it is composed of only one table, of whom the count of the tuples is just equal to the count of vertices in the DAG, and it has only one B-tree index built. In contrast, Interval and UPrefix both consist of three tables to record additional information besides spanning tree. Meanwhile, they need more indexes built on each table. Another cause is that all of the data type in the table of PLSDF or PLSDF-D is *text* which will be "compressed by the system automatically, so the physical requirement on disk may be less"[1]. On the other hand, Figure 6(b) illustrates that PLSDF and PLSFD-D have the same gentle tendency but less construction time to UPrefix, whereas the construction time of Interval is the worst. This can be explained with the different procedures of label constructions. PLSDF and PLSDF-D create labels on the fly while processing the RDF file. However, UPrefix or Interval has to wait to create additional labels for non-spanning tree edges until the whole spanning tree is constructed. It is obvious that the count of non-spanning tree edges impacts the space requirement and label construction time for UPrefix and Interval. Another observation is that PLSDF needs few space and construction time relative to PLSDF-D. This is reasonable considering that PLSDF-D equals to PLSDF plus descendants-label.

5.4 Response Time of Typical Operations

We present our experimental results of the typical operations on DAG in this section from several aspects.

Overall Performance DAG "9000-8-4-0.004-45182" is chosen to have an experience on overall performance. The operations are listed in Figure 7.

The total elapsed time are shown in Figure 8. Interval, UPrefix, PLSDF labeling schemes are tested for all of the five operations. Moreover, PLSDF-D is applied to Q2 and Q4 to examine the effectiveness of descendants-label, while Q1, Q3, and Q5 are not necessary for PLSDF-D because it is just the same to PLSDF in these operations. For the given selectivity, PLSDF processes all the operations faster than the others. PLSDF-D exhibits accepted performance in Q2 and Q4 as well. The reason is the concise table structure of PLSDF/PLSDF-D and computative elementary arithmetic operations which avoid massive database access. For instance, the evaluation of a vertex's ancestors includes only two steps. Firstly retrieve the self-label and ancestors-label of the vertex from the table. Next do factorization using the labels according to Theorem 2. Results are self-labels identifying the ancestors of the vertex. The only database access happens in the first step. In contrast, Interval and UPrefix need more database operations, such as join operations and nested queries (See [4]). Though it seems that PLSDF-D does not have advantage over PLSDF in this case, experiments in the next part will bring us elaborative effects of PLSDF-D in different selectivity.
Another observation is that UPrefix outperforms Interval in all of the typical operations, which conflicts with the results from [4]. The cause is that Interval generates more additional information to record non-spanning tree edges than UPrefix, which is counterevidence of the excellent speed of PLSDF/PLSDF-D.

Impact of varying DAG Shape and Selectivity Here we investigate the performance under different DAG shapes, i.e., DAG with short-and-fat spanning tree, and DAG

	Operation Type	Selectivity
Q1	Ancestors	2.53%
Q2	Descendants	20.08%
Q3	Siblings	2.98%
Q4	Leaves	38.67%
Q5	nea	0.011%

Fig. 7. Test Typical Operations for Overall Performance

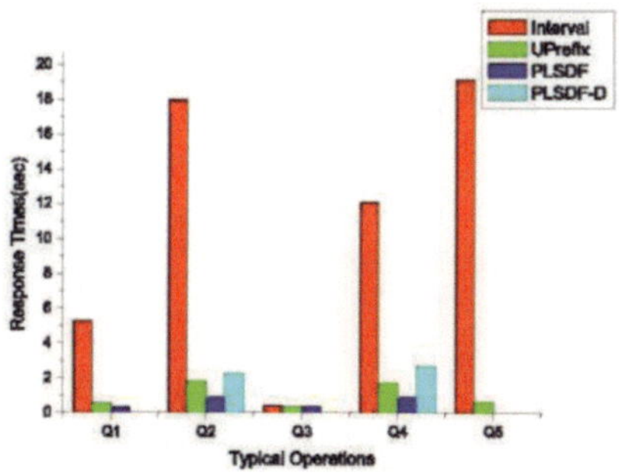

Fig. 8. Overall Performance

with tall-and-thin spanning tree. They are shown in Figure 9 to 10. Diagrams in each figure correspond to operations from Q1 to Q5 respectively. The metric of X-axis is the results selectivity of the operation except that the fifth diagram for nca uses X-axis to indicate the vertices' average length from the root of spanning-tree. The metric of Y-axis is the response time.

PLSDF displays almost constant time performance for all kinds of DAG shapes and operations. Because it does the chief computations with main memory algorithms instead of time-consuming database operations. The change of response time is indistinguishable in some extensions. The side effect is that PLSDF stays at a disadvantage at a very low selectivity especially for Q2 and Q4, e.g. in Figure 9(b) below selectivity 40%. Fortunately, PLSDF-D counterbalances this difficulty by trading off time to space with descendants-label. PLSDF-D almost has the same effect to UPrefix. Thus, it is a better plan to choose PLSDF-D at a low selectivity and switch to PLSDF when the selectivity exceeds some threshold. However, no good solution is found for PLSDF in Q3 where it costs more response time at a low selectivity. Interval and UPrefix could make use of the indexes on the parent label. Whereas PLSDF has to traverse among the vertices and compute greatest common divisor one at a time.

Scale-up Performance We carried out scalability tests of the four labeling schemes with the first group of DAGs in Table 1. Operations are made to have the equal selectivity (equal length on path for nca) for each scale of DAG size. Five diagrams in Figure 11 corresponds to operations from Q1 to Q5 respectively.

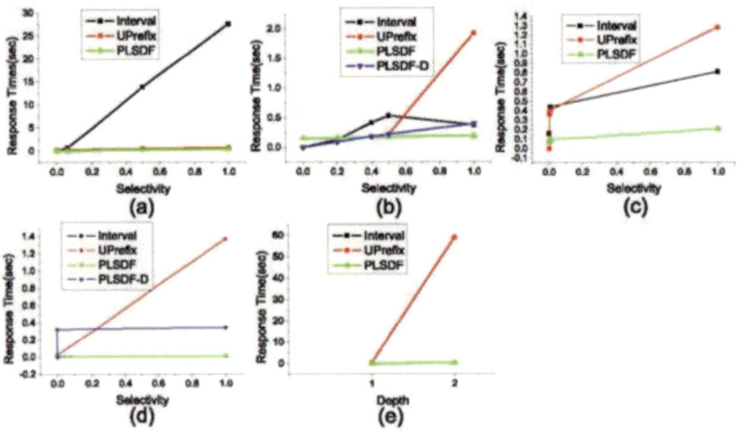

Fig. 9. DAG Shape and Selectivity of 450-2-32-0.7-45525

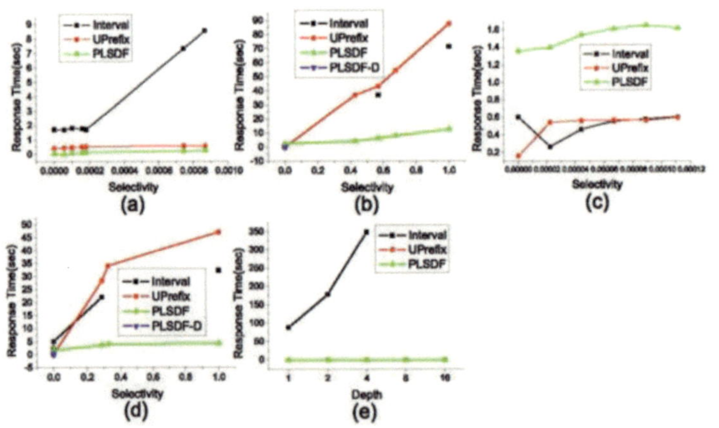

Fig. 10. DAG Shape and Selectivity of 90000-16-2-0.000053-44946

Interval and UPrefix are affected by both the size and the internal structure of the DAG (Note that the DAG is generated randomly). Unlike the other two labeling schemes, PLSDF and PLSDF-D perform good scalability in all cases.

5.5 Effect of Updates

To examine the dynamic labeling ability inherited from original prime number labeling scheme, we repeated the "Un-ordered Updates" experiments exhibited in [11], while "Order-Sensitive Updates" experiments are meaningless to our research subject. It is evident that updates on leaf vertices of DAG will have the same experimental results to that of XML tree with our analysis at the end of Section 3.1. Here we only give the results of updates on non-leaf vertices.

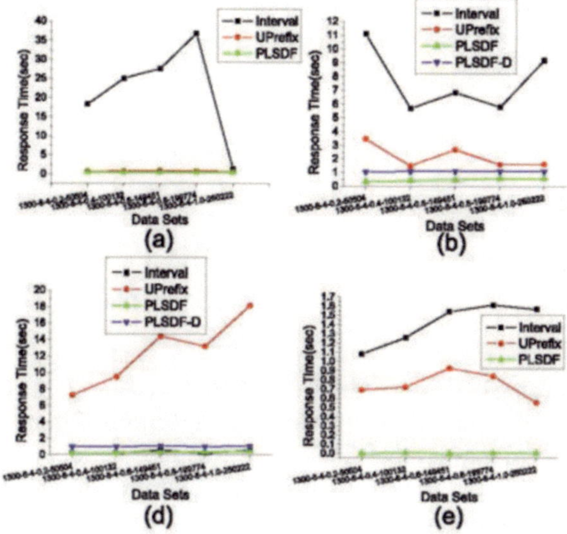

Fig. 11. Scale-up Performance

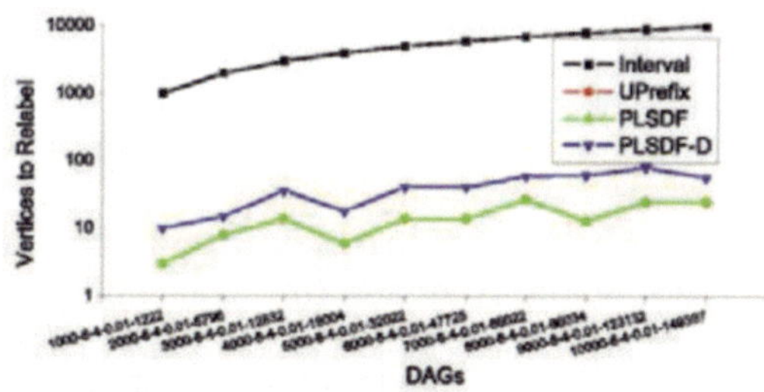

Fig. 12. Effect of Updates

Ten DAGs whose vertices increase from 1000 to 10000 are generated. We insert a new vertex into each DAG between bottom left leaf and the leaf's parent in the spanning tree. Figure 12 shows our experimental results for Interval, UPrefix, PLSDF, and PLSDF-D, which coincide with that of XML tree. PLSDF has exactly the same effect of update as Uprefix. While additional label of PLSDF-D questionless causes more vertices, the ancestors vertices, to be re-labeled.

6. Prime Number Labeling Scheme for Arbitrary Directed Graph

DAG is a special kind of directed graph. For arbitrary directed graph, containing cycles is very common. The labeling scheme discussed above need some modifications to deal with arbitrary directed graphs. There are two steps to construct a more general labeling scheme. First, preprocess all the strong connected components in the graph. Then, construct prime number labeling scheme on the preprocessed graph.

Definition 3. *Let G = (V, E) be an arbitrary directed graph. A* ***Prime Number Labeling Scheme for Arbitrary Directed Graph****(PLSD-General for short) associates each vertex $v_i \in V$ with an exclusive prime number p_i, and assigns to v_i a label $L_{general}(v) = (p_i, ca_i, cp_i)$, where*

$$ca_i = lcm\left(\prod_{v_j \in comp(v_i)} p_j, \; lcm_{v_j \in parents(v_i)} ca_j\right) \tag{8}$$

$$cp_i = \begin{cases} \prod_{v_j \in parents(v_i)} p_j, & inDegree(v_i) > 0 \\ 1, & in-degree(v_i) = 0 \end{cases} \tag{9}$$

According to Theorem 2 and Corollary 1, with the help of PLSD-General, all operations mentioned in Section 2 can be implemented. The following algorithm describes a three stages generation process for PLSD-General label. First (line 1 to line 4), topologically sort the vertices in the directed graph where the orders of vertices within a strong connected component are ignored. We also assign the self-labels at this stage. Second (line 5 to line 12), compute the value of *comp(vi)*. Finally (line 13 to line 17), compute the values of ancestors-label and parents-label.

7. Conclusion and Future Work

Prime number labeling scheme for DAG takes full advantage of the mapping between integers divisibility and vertices reachability. Operations on DAG, such as querying ancestors, descendants, siblings, leaves and nca could be easily converted to elementary arithmetic operations. The space requirement and time consuming are further reduced with the optimization techniques. Analysis also indicates that re-labeling only happens when a non-leaf vertex is inserted or removed, and affects its descendants (and ancestors if descendants-label used). By taking a strong connected component in the graph as one vertex, arbitrary directed graphs (with cycles) can be treated with the proposed labeling scheme.

Our implementation of prime number labeling scheme for DAG has least space requirement, construction time, and typical operations response time compared to interval-based and prefix-based labeling scheme in almost all of the experiments in our test bed.

```
input  : A directed graph G = (V, E)
output: The graph G with PLSD labels on each vertex
TopoOrder [] ← TOPOLOGICAL-SORT (G);
for i ← 0 to (|V| − 1) do
    Vertices [TopoOrder [i]].self-label ← NEXT-PRIME();
end
Components [] ← STRONGLY-CONNECTED-COMPONENTS(G);
for i ← 0 to SIZE-OF(Components ) − 1 do
    ComponentsLabel [i] ← 1 ;
    for j ← 0 to SIZE-OF(Components [i]) − 1 do
        Components [i][j].component-id ← i ;
        ComponentsLabel [i] ← Components [i][j].self-label ×
        ComponentsLabel [i] ;
    end
end
for i ← 0 to (|V| − 1) do
    v ← Vertices [TopoOrder [i]];
    v.ancestors-label ← LCM(ComponentsLabel [v.component-id ],
    LCM_{vj∈Parents(v)} vj.ancestors-label);
    v.parents-label ← ∏_{vj∈Parents(v)} vj.self-label ;
end
```

Algorithm 1: BuildPLSD

The main reason is that no additional information is required to be stored for non-spanning tree edges and that the utilizations of elementary arithmetic operations avoid time-consuming database operations. The extensive experiments also show good scalability and effect of update of prime number labeling scheme for DAG. The shape of DAG and the selectivity of operation results has little effect on the response time of our labeling scheme. Doubtless, a polynomial time quantum algorithm for factoring integers is expectative. Factoring in parallel may be another more practical technology nowadays for prime number labeling scheme for DAG.

8. References

[1] Postgresql 8.0.3 documentation, 2005. Available at http://www.postgresql.0rg/docs/8.O/ interactive/ index.html.

[2] D. Beckett. Scalability and storage: Survey of free software/ open source rdf storagesystems. Technical Report 1016, ILRT, June 2003. http://www.w3.org/2001/sw/Europe/ reports/ rdLscalable_storage_report/.

[3] O.C.L. Center. Dewey decimal classification, 2009. Available at http://www.oclc.org/ dewey

[4] V. Christophides, G. Karvounarakis, D. Plexousakis, M. Scholl, and S. Tourtounis.Optimizing taxonomic semantic web queries using labeling schemes. *Journal of Web Semantics,* 11(001):207-228, November 2003.

[5] E. Cohen, E. Halperin, H. Kaplan, and U. Zwick. Reachability and distance queries via 2-hop labels. *SIAM J. Comput.,* 32(5):1338-1355, 2003. T. H. Cormen, C. E. Leiserson, R.L. Rivest, and C. Stein. *Introduction to Algorithms, Second Edition.* The MIT Press,September 2001.

[6] Y. Guo, Z. Pan, and J. Heflin. LUBM: A benchmark for OWL knowledge base systems. *Journal of Web Semantics,* 3(2-3):158-182, 2005.

[7] Q. Li and B. Moon. Indexing and querying xml data for regular path expressions. In P. M. G.Apers, P. Atzeni, S. Ceri, S. Paraboschi, K. Ramamohanarao, and R. T. Snodgrass, editors, *Proceedings of the 27th International Conference on Very Large Data Bases,* pages 361-370, Roma, Italy, 2001.

[8] N. Santoro and R. Khatib. Labelling and implicit routing in networks. *Comput. J.,* 28(1):5-8, 1985.

[9] N. Wirth. Type extensions. *ACM Trans. Program. Lang. Syst.,* 10(2):204-214, 1988.

[10] X. Wu, M.-L. Lee, and W. Hsu. A prime number labeling scheme for dynamic ordered xml trees. In *ICDE,* pages 66-78. IEEE Computer Society, 2004.

7

Towards an Automatic Semantic Data Integration: Multi-agent Framework Approach

Miklos Nagy and Maria Vargas-Vera
The Open University
United Kingdom

1. Introduction

The continuously increasing semantic meta data on the Web will soon make it possible to develop mature Semantic Web applications that have the potential to attract commercial players to contribute to the Semantic Web vision. This is especially important because it will assure that more and more people will start using Semantic Web based applications, which is a pre condition for commercial viability. However the community expectations are also high when one thinks about the potential use of these applications. The vision of the Semantic Web promises a kind of "machine intelligence", which can support a variety of user tasks like improved search and question answering. To develop such applications researchers have developed a wide variety of building blocks that needs to be utilised together in order to achieve wider public acceptance. This is especially true for ontology mapping (Euzenat & Shvaiko, 2007), which makes it possible to interpret and align heterogeneous and distributed ontologies on the Semantic Web. However in order to simulate "machine intelligence" for ontology mapping different challenges have to be tackled.

Consider for example the difficulty of evaluating ontologies with large number of concepts. Due to the size of the vocabulary a number of domain experts are necessary to evaluate similar concepts in different ontologies. Once each expert has assessed sampled mappings their assessments are discussed and they produce a final assessment, which reflects their collective judgment. This form of collective intelligence can emerge from the collaboration and competition of many individuals and is considered to be better at solving problems than experts who independently make assessments. This is because these experts combine the knowledge and experience to create a solution rather than relying on a single person's perspective. We focus our attention how this collective intelligence can be achieved by using software agents and what problems need to be addressed before one can achieve such machine intelligence for ontology mapping. Our work DSSim (Nagy et al., 2007) tries to tackle the different ontology representation, quality and size problems with providing a multi-agent ontology mapping framework, which tries to mimic the collective human actions for creating ontology mappings.

This chapter is organised as follows. In section 2 we describe the challenges and roadblock that we intend to address in our system. In section 3 the related work is presented. Section 4 describes our core multi agent ontology mapping framework. In section 5 we introduce how uncertainty is represented and in our system. Section 6 details how contradictions in belief similarity are modelled with fuzzy trust. Section 7 explains our experimental results and section 8 outlines the strengths and weaknesses of our system. In section 9 we draw our conclusions and discuss possible future research directions.

2. Challenges and roadblocks

Despite the fact that a number of ontology matching solutions have been proposed (Euzenat & Shvaiko, 2007) in the recent years none of them have proved to be an integrated solution, which can be used by different user communities. Several challenges have been identified by Shvaiko and Euzenat (Euzenat & Shvaiko, 2007), which are considered as major roadblocks for successful future implementations. To overcome a combination of these challenges was the main motivation of our work. It is easy to foresee that the combination of these challenges might differ depending on the different requirements of a particular ontology mapping solution. In the context of Question Answering, we have identified some critical and interrelated challenges, which can be considered as roadblocks for future successful implementations (Nagy et al., 2008). The main motivation of our work, which is presented in this chapter, was to overcome the combination of these challenges.

2.1 Representation problems and uncertainty

The vision of the Semantic Web is to achieve machine-processable interoperability through the annotation of the content. This implies that computer programs can achieve a certain degree of understanding of such data and use it to reason about a user specific task like question answering or data integration.

Data on the semantic web is represented by ontologies, which typically consist of a number of classes, relations, instances and axioms. These elements are expressed using a logical language. The W3C has proposed RDF(S) (Beckett, 2004) and OWL (McGuinness & Harmelen, 2004) as Web ontology language however OWL has three increasingly-expressive sublanguages(OWL Lite, OWL DL, OWL Full) with different expressiveness and language constructs. In addition to the existing Web ontology languages W3C has proposed other languages like SKOS (Miles & Bechofer, 2008), which is a standard to support the use of knowledge organization systems (KOS) such as thesauri, classification schemes, subject heading systems and taxonomies within the framework of the Semantic Web. SKOS are based on the Resource Description Framework (RDF) and it allows information to be passed between computer applications in an interoperable way. Ontology designers can choose between these language variants depending on the intended purpose of the ontologies. The problem of interpreting semantic web data however stems not only from the different language representations (Lenzerini et al., 2004) but the fact that ontologies especially OWL Full has been designed as a general framework to represent domain knowledge, which in turn can differ from designer to designer. Consider the following excerpts **Fig. 1** from different FAO (Food and Agricultural Organization of the United Nations) ontologies. Assume we need to assess similarity between classes and individuals between the two ontologies. In fragment one a class *c_8375* is modelled as named OWL individuals. In the class description only the ID is indicated therefore to determine the properties of the class one needs to extract the necessary information from the actual named individual. In **Fig. 1** (right) the classes are represented as RDF individuals where the individual properties are defines as OWL data properties. One can note the difference how the class labels are represented on **Fig. 1** (left) through *rdfs:label* and **Fig. 1** (right) through through *hasNameScientific* and *hasNameLongEN* tags.

```
...
<owl:Class rdf:ID="c_8375">
  <rdfs:subClassOf>
    <owl:Class rdf:ID="c_7033"/>
  </rdfs:subClassOf>
</owl:Class>
...
< c_8375 rdf:ID="i_8375">
  <aos:hasScopeNote xml:lang="EN">Isscaap group
b-52</aos:hasScopeNote>
  <aos:hasScopeNote xml:lang="FR">Groupe b-52 de
la csitapa</aos:hasScopeNote>
...
  <rdfs:label xml:lang="en">Demospongiae</rdfs:label>
</c_8375>
...
```

```
...
<owl:Class rdf:about="#species">
  <rdfs:subClassOf rdf:resource="#biological_entity"/>
  <owl:disjointWith rdf:resource="#family"/>
  <owl:disjointWith rdf:resource="#order"/>
  <owl:disjointWith rdf:resource="#group"/>
</owl:Class>
...
<rdf:Description rdf:about="http://www.fao.org/aims
/aos/fi/species_v1.0.owl#31005_17431">
  <j.0:hasNameLongEN>Barrel
sponge</j.0:hasNameLongEN>    <j.0:hasMeta>31005
  </j.0:hasMeta>    <j.0:hasNameScientific>
  DEMOSPONGIAE</j.0:hasNameScientific>
</rdf:Description> ...
```

Fig. 1. Ontology fragments from the AGROVOC and ASFA ontology

From the logical representation point of view both ontologies are valid separately and no logical reasoner would find inconsistency in them individually. However the problem occurs once we need to compare them in order to determine the similarities between classes and individuals. It is easy to see that once we need to compare the two ontologies a considerable amount of uncertainty arises over the classes and its properties and in a way they can be compared. This uncertainty can be contributed to the fact that due to the different representation certain elements will be missing for the comparison e.g. we have label in fragment **Fig. 1** (left) but is missing from fragment **Fig. 1** (right) but there is *hasNameLongEN* tag in fragment **Fig. 1** (right) but missing in fragment **Fig. 1** (left). As a result of these representation differences ontology mapping systems will always need to consider the uncertain aspects of how the semantic web data can be interpreted.

2.2 Quality of Semantic Web Data

Data quality problems (Wang et al., 1993) (Wand & Wang, 1996) in the context of database integration (Batini et al., 1986) have emerged long before the Semantic Web concept has been proposed. The major reason for this is the increase in interconnectivity among data producers and data consumers, mainly spurred through the development of the Internet and various Web-based technologies. For every organisation or individual the context of the data, which is published can be slightly different depending on how they want to use their data. Therefore from the exchange point of view incompleteness of a particular data is quite common. The problem is that fragmented data environments like the Semantic Web inevitably lead to data and information quality problems causing the applications that process this data deal with ill-defined inaccurate or inconsistent information on the domain. The incomplete data can mean different things to data consumer and data producer in a given application scenario. In traditional integration scenarios resolving these data quality issues represents a vast amount of time and resources for human experts before any integration can take place. Data quality has two aspects

- Data syntax covers the way data is formatted and gets represented
- Data semantics addresses the meaning of data

Data syntax is not the main reason of concern as it can be resolved independently from the context because it can be defined what changes must occur to make the data consistent and standardized for the application e.g. defining a separation rule of compound terms like "MScThesis", "MSc_Thesis". The main problem what Semantic Web applications need to solve is how to resolve semantic data quality problems i.e. what is useful and meaningful because it would require more direct input from the users or creators of the ontologies. Clearly considering any kind of designer support in the Semantic Web environment is unrealistic therefore applications itself need to have built in mechanisms to decide and reason about whether the data is accurate, usable and useful in essence, whether it will deliver good information and function well for the required purpose. Consider the following example **Fig. 2** from the directory ontologies.

```
...
<owl:Class        rdf:about="http://matching.com/source
  /3887.owl#Windows_Vista">
  <rdfs:label xml:lang="en"> Windows Vista Home
Edition </rdfs:label>
  <j:hasSerialNumber>
    <rdfs:label >00043-683-036-658</rdfs:label>
  </j:hasSeriamNumber>
  <rdfs:subClassOf>
    <owl:Class         rdf:about="http://matching.com
    /source/3887.owl#Operating_Systems">
    </owl:Class>
  </rdfs:subClassOf>
</owl:Class>
...
```

Fig. 2. Ontology fragments from the Web directories ontology

As figure **Fig. 2** shows we can interpret Windows Vista as the subclass of the Operating systems however the designed has indicated that it has a specific serial number therefore it can be considered as an individual. At any case the semantic data quality is considered as low as the information is dubious therefore the Semantic Web application has to create its own hypothesises over the meaning of this data.

2.3 Efficient ontology mapping with large scale ontologies

Ontologies can get quite complex and very large, causing difficulties in using them for any application (Carlo et al., 2005) (Flahive et al., 2006). This is especially true for ontology mapping where overcoming scalability issues becomes one of the decisive factors for determining the usefulness of a system. Nowadays with the rapid development of ontology applications, domain ontologies can become very large in scale. This can partly be contributed to the fact that a number of general knowledge bases or lexical databases have been and will be transformed into ontologies in order to support more applications on the

Semantic Web. Consider for example WordNet. Since the project started in 1985 WordNet[1] has been used for a number of different purposes in information systems. It is popular general background knowledge for ontology mapping systems because it contains around 150.000 synsets and their semantic relations. Other efforts to represent common sense knowledge as ontology is the Cyc project[2] , which consists of more than 300.000 concepts and nearly 3.000.000 assertions or the Suggested Upper Merged Ontology (SUMO)[3] with its 20.000 terms and 70.000 axioms when all domain ontologies are combined. However the far largest ontology so far (according to our knowledge) in terms of concept number is the DBPedia[4] , which contains over 2.18 million resources or "things", each tied to an article in the English language Wikipedia. Discovering correspondences between these large-scale ontologies is an ongoing effort however only partial mappings have been established i.e. SUMO-Wordnet due to the vast amount of human and computational effort involved in these tasks. The Ontology Alignment Initiative 2008 (Caracciolo et al., 2008) has also included a mapping track for very large cross lingual ontologies, which includes establishing mappings between Wordnet, DBPedia and GTAA (Dutch acronym for Common Thesaurus for Audiovisual Archives) (Brugman et al., 2006), which is a domain specific thesaurus with approximately 160.000 terms. A good number of researchers might argue that the Semantic Web is not just about large ontologies created by the large organisations but more about individuals or domain experts who can create their own relatively small ontologies and publish it on the Web. Indeed might be true however from the scalability point of view it does not change anything if thousands of small ontologies or a number of huge ontologies need to be processed. Consider that in 2007 Swoogle (Ding et al., 2004) has already indexed more than 10.000 ontologies, which were available on the Web. The large number of concepts and properties that is implied by the scale or number of these ontologies poses several scalability problems from the reasoning point of view. Any Semantic Web application not only from ontology mapping domain has to be designed to cope with these difficulties otherwise it is deemed to be a failure from the usability point of view.

3. Related Work

Several ontology-mapping systems have been proposed to address the semantic data integration problem of different domains independently. In this paper we consider only those systems, which have participated in the OAEI (Ontology Alignment Evaluation Initiative) competitions and has been participated more than two tracks. There are other proposed systems as well however as the experimental comparison cannot be achieved we do not include them in the scope of our analysis. Lily (Wang & Xu, 2008) is an ontology mapping system with different purpose ranging from generic ontology matching to mapping debugging. It uses different syntactic and semantic similarity measures and combines them with the experiential weights. Further it applies similarity propagation

[1] http://wordnet.princeton.edu/
[2] http://www.cyc.com/
[3] http://www.ontologyportal.org/
[4] http://dbpedia.org/About

matcher with strong propagation condition and the matching algorithm utilises the results of literal matching to produce more alignments. In order to assess when to use similarity propagation Lily uses different strategies, which prevents the algorithm from producing more incorrect alignments.

ASMOV (Jean-Mary & Kabuka, 2007) has been proposed as a general mapping tool in order to facilitate the integration of heterogeneous systems, using their data source ontologies. It uses different matchers and generates similarity matrices between concepts, properties, and individuals, including mappings from object properties to datatype properties. It does not combine the similarities but uses the best values to create a pre alignment, which are then being semantically validated. Mappings, which pass the semantic validation will be added to the final alignment. ASMOV can use different background knowledge e.g. Wordnet or UMLS Metathesaurus (medical background knowledge) for the assessment of the similarity measures.

RiMOM (Tang et al., 2006) is an automatic ontology mapping system, which models the ontology mapping problem as making decisions over entities with minimal risk. It uses the Bayesian theory to model decision-making under uncertainty where observations are all entities in the two ontologies.

Further it implements different matching strategies where each defined strategy is based on one kind of ontological information. RiMOM includes different methods for choosing appropriate strategies (or strategy combination) according to the available information in the ontologies. The strategy combination is conducted by a linear-interpolation method. In addition to the different strategies RiMOM uses similarity propagation process to refine the existing alignments and to find new alignments that cannot be found using other strategies. RiMOM is the only system other than DSSim in the OAEI contest that considers the uncertain nature of the mapping process however it models uncertainty differently from DSSim. RiMOM appeared for first time in the OAEI-2007 whilst DSSim appeared in the OAEI-2006.

MapPSO (Bock & Hettenhausen, 2008) is a research prototype, which has been designed to address the need for highly scalable, massively parallel tool for both large scale and numerous ontology alignments. MapPSO method models the ontology alignment problem as an optimisation problem. It employs a population based optimisation paradigm based on social interaction between swarming animals, which provides the best answer being available at that time. Therefore it is especially suitable for providing answers under time constraint like the ontology mapping. MapPSO employs different syntactic and semantic similarity measures and combines the available base distances by applying the Ordered Weighted Average(OWA) (Ji et al., 2008) aggregation of the base distances. It aggregates the components by ordering the base distances and applying a fixed weight vector. The motivation of the MapPSO system is identical with one of the motivations of the DSSim namely to address the need of scalable mapping solutions for large-scale ontologies. Surprisingly MapPSO did not participate in the Very Large Cross Lingual Resources track (especially designed for large scale thesauri) therefore experimental comparison cannot be achieved from this point of view.

TaxoMap (Hamdi at al., 2008) is an alignment tool, which aims is to discover rich correspondences between concepts with performing oriented alignment from a source to a target ontology taking into account labels and sub-class descriptions. It uses a part-of-speech

(Schmid 1994) and lemma information, which enables to take into account the language, lemma and use word categories in an efficient way. TaxoMap performs a linguistic similarity measure between labels and description of concepts and it has been designed to process large scale ontologies by using partitioning techniques. TaxoMap however does not process instances, which can be a drawback in several situations.
SAMBO and SAMBOdtf (Lambrix & Tan, 2006) is a general framework for ontology matching. The methods and techniques used in the framework are general and applicable to different areas nevertheless SAMBO has been designed to align biomedical ontologies. Their algorithm includes one or several matchers, which calculate similarity values between the terms from the different source ontologies. These similarities are then filtered and combined as a weighted sum of the similarity values computed by different matchers.

4. Multi agent ontology mapping framework

For ontology mapping in the context of Question Answering over heterogeneous sources we propose a multi agent architecture (Nagy et al., 2005) because as a particular domain becomes larger and more complex, open and distributed, a set of cooperating agents are necessary in order to address the ontology mapping task effectively. In real scenarios, ontology mapping can be carried out on domains with large number of classes and properties. Without the multi agent architecture the response time of the system can increase exponentially when the number of concepts to map increases. The main objective of DSSim architecture is to be able to use it in different domains for creating ontology mappings. These domains include Question Answering, Web services or any application that need to map database metadata e.g. Extract, Transform and Load (ETL) tools for data warehouses. Therefore DSSim is not designed to have its own user interface but to integrate with other systems through well defined interfaces. In our implementation we have used the AQUA (Vargas-Vera & Motta, 2004) Question Answering system, which is the user interface that creates First Order Logic(FOL) statements based on natural language queries posed by the user. As a consequence the inputs and outputs for the DSSim component are valid FOL formulas.

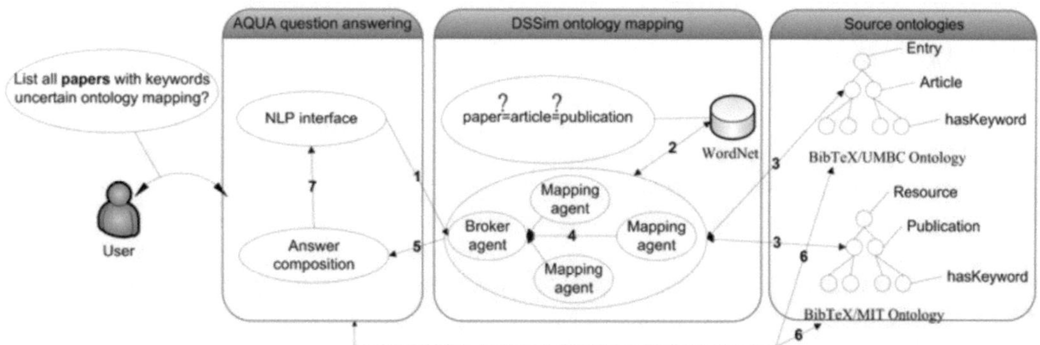

Fig. 3. Overview of the mapping system

An overview of our system is depicted on **Fig. 3** The two real word ontologies[5][6] describe BibTeX publications from the University of Maryland, Baltimore County (UMBC) and from the Massachusetts Institute of Technology (MIT).
The AQUA (Vargas-Vera & Motta, 2004) system and the answer composition component are described just to provide the context of our work (our overall framework) but these are not our major target in this paper. The user poses a natural language query to the AQUA system, which converts it into FOL (First Order Logic) terms.
The main components and its functions of the system are as follows:

1. Broker agent receives FOL term, decomposes it(in case more than one concepts are in the query) and distributes the sub queries to the mapping agents.
2. Mapping agents retrieve sub query class and property hypernyms from WordNet.
3. Mapping agents retrieve ontology fragments from the external ontologies, which are candidate mappings to the received sub-queries. Mapping agents use WordNet as background knowledge in order to enhance their beliefs on the possible meaning of the concepts or properties in the particular context.
4. Mapping agents build up coherent beliefs by combining all possible beliefs over the similarities of the sub queries and ontology fragments. Mapping agents utilize both syntactic and semantic similarity algorithms build their beliefs over the correctness of the mapping.
5. Broker agent passes the possible mappings into the answer composition component for particular sub-query ontology fragment mapping in which the belief function has the highest value.
6. Answer composition component retrieves the concrete instances from the external ontologies or data sources, which is included into the answer.
7. Answer composition component creates an answer to the user's question.

The main novelty in our solution is that we propose solving the ontology mapping problem based on the principles of collective intelligence, where each mapping agent has its own individual belief over the solution. However before the final mapping is proposed the broker agent creates the result based on a consensus between the different mapping agents. This process reflects well how humans reach consensus over a difficult issue.

4.1 Example scenario

Based on the architecture depicted on **Fig. 3** we present the following simplified example, which will be used in the following sections of the paper in order to demonstrate our algorithm. We consider the following user query and its FOL representation as an input to our mapping component framework:
List all papers with keywords uncertain ontology mapping?

$$(\exists x)paper(x) \text{ and } hasKeywords(x,[uncertain, ontology\ mapping]) \quad (1)$$

[5] http://ebiquity.umbc.edu/ontology/publication.owl
[6] http://visus.mit.edu/bibtex/0.01/bibtex.owl

- Step 1: Broker agent distributes (no decomposition is necessary in this case) the FOL query to the mapping agents.
- Step 2: Mapping agents 1 and 2 consult WordNet in order to extend the concepts and properties with their inherited hypernym in the query. These hypernyms serve as variables in the hypothesis. For the concepts "paper" e.g. we have found that "article" and "communication" or "publication" are possible concepts that can appear in any of the external ontologies.
- Step 3: Mapping agents iterate through all concepts and properties from the ontologies and create several hypothesises that must be verified with finding evidences e.g.

$$Agent\,1: H_n(mapping) = Query\{paper, article, communication, publication\} \Leftrightarrow Ontology_{MIT}\{Article\} \quad (2)$$

and

$$Agent\,2: H_n(mapping) = Query\{paper, article, communication, publication\} \Leftrightarrow Ontology_{UMBC}\{Publication\} \quad (3)$$

where H is the hypothesis for the mapping.

Further, we find supporting evidences for hypothesis. In this phase different syntactic and semantic similarity measures are used (see subsection 5.1, 5.2). These similarity measures are considered as different experts determining belief functions for the hypothesis. The last phase of this step is to combine the belief mass functions using Dempster's combination rule in order to form a coherent belief of the different experts on the hypothesises.

- Step 4: Mapping agents select the hypothesis in which they believe in most and sent it back to the broker agent. In our example the following mappings have been established:

$$Mapping_{Query,MIT\ ontology}(paper \leftrightarrow article) \quad (4)$$
$$Mapping_{Query,UMBC\ ontology}(paper \leftrightarrow publication)$$

- Step 5-6: The answer is composed for the user's query, which includes the relevant instances from the ontologies.

5. Uncertain reasoning and agent belief

Our proposed method works with two ontologies, which contain arbitrary number of concepts and their properties.

$$O_1 = \{C_1,..,C_n; P_1,..,P_n; I_1,..,I_n\} \quad (5)$$
$$O_2 = \{C_1,..,C_m; P_1,..,P_m; I_1,..,I_m\}$$

where *O* represents a particular ontology, *C, P* and *I* the set of concepts, properties and instances in the ontology.

In order to assess similarity we need to compare all concepts and properties from O_1 to all concepts and properties in O_2. Our similarity assessments, both syntactic and semantic produce a sparse similarity matrix where the similarity between C_n from O_1 and C_m in O_2 is represented by a particular similarity measure between the i and j elements of the matrix as follows:

$$SIM := \left(s_{i,j}\right)_{n\times m} \tag{6}$$
$$1 \le i \le n \quad and \quad 1 \le j \le m$$

where *SIM* represents a particular similarity assessment matrix, *s* is a degree of similarity that has been determined by a particular similarity e.g. Jaccard or semantic similarity measure. We consider each measure as an "expert", which assess mapping precision based on its knowledge. Therefore we assume that each similarity matrix is a subjective assessment of the mapping what needs to be combined into a coherent view. If combined appropriately this combined view provides a more reliable and precise mapping that each separate mapping alone. However one similarity measure or some technique can perform particularly well for one pair of concepts or properties and particularly badly for another pair of concepts or properties, which has to be considered in any mapping algorithm. In our ontology mapping framework each agent carries only partial knowledge of the domain and can observe it from its own perspective where available prior knowledge is generally uncertain. Our main argument is that knowledge cannot be viewed as a simple conceptualization of the world, but it has to represent some degree of interpretation. Such interpretation depends on the context of the entities involved in the process. This idea is rooted in the fact the different entities' interpretations are always subjective, since they occur according to an individual schema, which is than communicated to other individuals by a particular language. In order to represent these subjective probabilities in our system we use the Dempster-Shafer theory of evidence (Shafer, 1976), which provides a mechanism for modelling and reasoning uncertain information in a numerical way, particularly when it is not possible to assign belief to a single element of a set of variables. Consequently the theory allows the user to represent uncertainty for knowledge representation, because the interval between support and plausibility can be easily assessed for a set of hypothesizes. Missing data (ignorance) can also be modelled by Dempster-Shafer approach and additionally evidences from two or more sources can be combined using Dempster's rule of combination. The combined support, disbelief and uncertainty can each be separately evaluated. The main advantage of the Dempster-Shafer theory is that it provides a method for combining the effect of different learned evidences to establish a new belief by using Dempster's combination rule. The following elements have been used in our system in order to model uncertainty:

Frame of Discernment(Θ): finite set representing the space of hypothesizes. It contains all possible mutually exclusive context events of the same kind.

$$\Theta = \{H_1,..,H_n,..,H_N\} \tag{7}$$

In our method Θ contains all possible mappings that have been assessed by the particular expert.

Evidence: available certain fact and is usually a result of observation. Used during the reasoning process to choose the best hypothesis in Θ.

We observe evidence for the mapping if the expert detects that there is a similarity between C_n from O_1 and C_m in O_2.

Belief mass function (m): is a finite amount of support assigned to the subset of Θ. It represents the strength of some evidence and

$$\sum_{A\subseteq\Theta} m_i(A) = 1 \tag{8}$$

where $m_i(A)$ is our exact belief in a proposition represented by A that belongs to expert *i*. The similarity algorithms itself produce these assignment based on different similarity measures. As an example consider that O_1 contains the concept "paper", which needs to be mapped to a concept "*hasArticle*" in O_2. Based on the WordNet we identify that the concept "article" is one of the inherited hypernyms of "paper", which according to both JaroWinkler(0.91) and Jaccard(0.85) measure (Cohen et al., 2003) is highly similarity to "has Article" in O_2. Therefore after similarity assessment our variables will have the following belief mass value:

$$m_{\exp ert1}(O_1\{paper, article, communication, publication\}, O_2\{hasArticle\}) = 0.85 \quad (9)$$

$$m_{\exp ert2}(O_1\{paper, article, communication, publication\}, O_2\{hasArticle\}) = 0.91$$

In practice we assess up to 8 inherited hypernyms similarities with different algorithms (considered as experts), which can be combined based on the combination rule in order to create a more reliable mapping. Once the combined belief mass functions have been assigned the following additional measures can be derived from the available information.
Belief: amount of justified support to A that is the lower probability function of Dempster, which accounts for all evidence E_k that supports the given proposition A.

$$belief_i(A) = \sum_{E_k \subseteq A} m_i(E_k) \quad (10)$$

An important aspect of the mapping is how one can make a decision over how different similarity measures can be combined and which nodes should be retained as best possible candidates for the match. To combine the qualitative similarity measures that have been converted into belief mass functions we use the Dempster's rule of combination and we retain the node where the belief function has the highest value.
Dempster's rule of combination: Suppose we have two mass functions m_i (E_k) and m_j ($E_{k'}$) and we want to combine them into a global m_{ij}.(A). Following Dempster's combination rule

$$m_{ij}(A) = m_i \oplus m_j = \sum_{E_k E_{k'}} m_i(E_k) * m_j(E_{k'}) \quad (11)$$

where *i* and *j* represent two different agents.
The belief combination process is computationally very expensive and from an engineering point of view, this means that it not always convenient or possible to build systems in which the belief revision process is performed globally by a single unit. Therefore, applying multi agent architecture is an alternative and distributed approach to the single one, where the belief revision process is no longer assigned to a single agent but to a group of agents, in which each single agent is able to perform belief revision and communicate with the others. Our algorithm takes all the concepts and its properties from the different external ontologies and assesses similarity with all the concepts and properties in the query graph.

5.1 Syntactic Similarity

To assess syntactic similarity between ontology entities we use different string-based techniques to match names and name descriptions. These distance functions map a pair of strings to a real number, which indicates a qualitative similarity between the strings. To achieve more reliable assessment and to maximize our system's accuracy we combine different string matching techniques such as edit distance like functions e.g. Monger-Elkan (Monge & Elkan, 1996) to the token based distance functions e.g. Jaccard (Cohen et al., 2003) similarity. To combine different similarity measures we use Dempster's rule of combination. Several reasonable similarity measures exist however, each being appropriate to certain situations. At this stage of the similarity mapping our algorithm takes one entity from Ontology 1 and tries to find similar entity in the extended query. The similarity mapping process is carried out on the following entities:

- Concept name similarity
- Property name and set similarity

The use of string distances described here is the first step towards identifying matching entities between query and the external ontology or between ontologies with little prior knowledge. However, string similarity alone is not sufficient to capture the subtle differences between classes with similar names but different meanings. Therefore we work with WordNet in order to exploit hypernymy at the lexical level. Once our query sting is extended with lexically hypernym entities we calculate the string similarity measures between the query and the ontologies. In order to increase the correctness of our similarity measures the obtained similarity coefficients need to be combined. Establishing this combination method was our primary objective that had been included into the system. Further once the combined similarities have been calculated we have developed a simple methodology to derive the belief mass function that is the fundamental property of Demster-Shafer framework.

5.2 Semantic Similarity

For semantic similarity between concept, relations and the properties we use graph-based techniques. We take the extended query and the ontology input as labelled graphs. The semantic matching is viewed as graph like structures containing terms and their inter-relationships. The similarity comparison between a pair of nodes from two ontologies is based on the analysis of their positions within the graphs. Our assumption is that if two nodes from two ontologies are similar, their neighbours might also be somehow similar. We consider semantic similarity between nodes of the graphs based on similarity of leaf nodes, which represent properties. That is, two non leaf schema elements are semantically similar if their leaf sets are highly similar, even if their immediate children are not. The main reason why semantic heterogeneity occurs in the different ontology structures is because different institutions develop their data sets individually, which as a result contain many overlapping concepts. Assessing the above mentioned similarities in our system we adapted and extended the SimilarityBase and SimilarityTop algorithms (Vargas-Vera & Motta, 2004) used in the current AQUA system for multiple ontologies. Our aim is that the similarity algorithms (experts in terms of evidence theory) would mimic the way a human designer would describe a domain based on a well-established dictionary. What also needs to be considered when the two graph structures are obtained from both the user query fragment and the representation of the subset of the source ontology is that there can be a generalization or specialization of a specific concepts present in the graph, which was obtained from the external source and this needs to be handled correctly. In our system we adapted and extended the before mentioned SimilarityBase and SimilarityTop algorithms, which has been proved effective in the current AQUA system for multiple ontologies.

6. Conflict resolution with fuzzy voting model

The idea of individual voting in order to resolve conflict and choose the best option available is not rooted in computer but political science. Democratic systems are based on voting as Condorcet jury theorem (Austen-Smith & Banks, 1996) (Young, 1988) postulates that a group of voters using majority rule is more likely to choose the right action than an arbitrary single voter is. In these situations voters have a common goal, but do not know how to obtain this goal. Voters are informed differently about the performance of alternative ways of reaching it. If each member of a jury has only partial information, the majority decision is more likely to be correct than a decision arrived at by an individual juror. Moreover, the probability of a correct decision increases with the size of the jury. But things become more complicated when information is shared before a vote is taken. People then have to evaluate the information before making a collective decision. The same ideas apply for software agents especially if they need to reach a consensus on a particular issue. In case of ontology mapping where each agent can built up beliefs over the correctness of the mappings based on partial information we believe that it is voting can find the socially optimal choice. Software agents can use voting to determine the best decision for agent society but in case voters make mistakes in their judgments, then the majority alternative (if it exists) is statistically most likely to be the best choice. The application of voting for software agents is a possible way to make systems more intelligent i.e. mimic the decision making how humans reach consensus decision on a problematic issue.

6.1 Fuzzy voting model

In ontology mapping the conflicting results of the different beliefs in similarity can be resolved if the mapping algorithm can produce an agreed solution, even though the individual opinions about the available alternatives may vary. We propose a solution for reaching this agreement by evaluating trust between established beliefs through voting, which is a general method of reconciling differences. Voting is a mechanism where the opinions from a set of votes are evaluated in order to select the alternatives that best represent the collective preferences. Unfortunately deriving binary trust like trustful or not trustful from the difference of belief functions is not so straightforward since the different voters express their opinion as subjective probability over the similarities. For a particular mapping this always involves a certain degree of vagueness hence the threshold between the trust and distrust cannot be set definitely for all cases that can occur during the process. Additionally there is no clear transition between characterising a particular belief highly or less trustful. Therefore our argument is that the trust membership or belief difference values, which are expressed by different voters can be modelled properly by using fuzzy representation as depicted on **Fig. 4**. Before each agent evaluates the trust in other agent's belief over the correctness of the mapping it calculates the difference between its own and the other agent's belief. Depending on the difference it can choose the available trust levels e.g. if the difference in beliefs is 0.2 then the available trust level can be high and medium. We model these trust levels as fuzzy membership functions. In fuzzy logic the membership function $\mu(x)$ is defined on the universe of discourse U and represents a particular input value as a member of the fuzzy set i.e. $\mu(x)$ is a curve that defines how each point in the U is mapped to a membership value (or degree of membership) between 0 and 1. Our ontology mapping system models the conflict resolution as a fuzzy system where the system components are described in the following subsections.

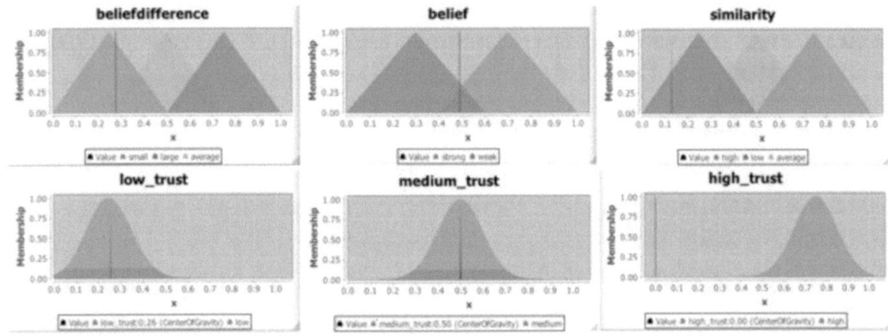

Fig. 4. Example fuzzy membership functions

6.1.1 Fuzzification of input and output variables

Fuzzification is the process of decomposing a system input and/or output into one or more fuzzy sets. We have experimented different types of curves namely the triangular, trapezoidal and gauss shaped membership functions. **Fig. 4** shows a system of fuzzy sets for an input with triangular and gauss membership functions. Each fuzzy set spans a region of input (or output) value graphed with the membership. Our selected membership functions overlap to allow smooth mapping of the system. The process of fuzzification allows the system inputs and outputs to be expressed in linguistic terms so that rules can be applied in a simple manner to express a complex system.

Belief difference is an input variable, which represents the agents own belief over the correctness of a mapping in order to establish mappings between concepts and properties in the ontology. During conflict resolution we need to be able to determine the level of difference. We propose three values for the fuzzy membership value $\mu(x)$=*{small, average, large}*

Belief is an input variable, which described the amount of justified support to A that is the lower probability function of Dempster, which accounts for all evidence E_k that supports the given proposition A.

$$belief_i(A) = \sum_{E_k \subseteq A} m_i(E_k) \tag{12}$$

where m Demster's belief mass function represents the strength of some evidence i.e. $m(A)$ is our exact belief in a proposition represented by A. The similarity algorithms itself produce these assignment based on different similarity measures. We propose three values for the fuzzy membership value $\nu(x)$=*{weak, strong}*

Similarity is an input variable and is the result of some syntactic or semantic similarity measure. We propose three values for the fuzzy membership value $\zeta(x)$=*{low, average, high}*

Low, medium and high trusts are output variables and represent the level of trust we can assign to the combination of our input variables. We propose three values for the fuzzy membership value $\tau(x)$=*{low, medium, high}*

6.1.2 Rule set

Fuzzy sets are used to quantify the information in the rule-base, and the inference mechanism operates on fuzzy sets to produce fuzzy sets. Fuzzy systems map the inputs to the outputs by a set of *condition ⇒ action* rules i.e. rules that can be expressed in *If-Then* form. For our conflict resolution problem we have defined four simple rules Fig. 5. that ensure that each combination of the input variables produce output on more than one output i.e. there is always more than one initial trust level is assigned to any input variables.

```
RULE 1 : IF ( beliefdifference IS large OR beliefdifference IS average ) AND belief IS weak AND
(similarity IS low OR similarity IS average ) THEN low_trust IS low;
RULE 2 : IF ( beliefdifference IS large OR beliefdifference IS average ) AND belief IS weak AND
(similarity IS low OR similarity IS average ) THEN medium_trust IS medium;
RULE 3 : IF ( beliefdifference IS small OR beliefdifference IS average ) AND belief IS strong AND
(similarity IS high OR similarity IS average ) THEN high_trust IS high;
RULE 4 : IF ( beliefdifference IS small OR beliefdifference IS average ) AND belief IS strong AND
(similarity IS high OR similarity IS average ) THEN medium_trust IS medium;
```

Fig. 5. Fuzzy rules for trust assessment

6.1.3 Defuzzification method

After fuzzy reasoning we have the linguistic output variables, which need to be translated into a crisp (i.e. real numbers, not fuzzy sets) value. The objective is to derive a single crisp numeric value that best represents the inferred fuzzy values of the linguistic output variable. Defuzzification is such inverse transformation, which maps the output from the fuzzy domain back into the crisp domain.

In our ontology mapping system we have selected the Center-of-Area (C-o-A) defuzzification method. The C-o-A method is often referred to as the Center-of-Gravity method because it computes the centroid of the composite area representing the output fuzzy term. In our system the trust levels are proportional with the area of the membership functions therefore other defuzzification methods like Center-of-Maximum (C-o-M) or Mean-of-Maximum (M-o-M) does not correspond well to our requirements. For representing trust in beliefs over similarities we have defined three membership functions, $\tau(x)=\{low, average, high\}$ in the beliefs over concept and property similarities in our ontology mapping system. Our main objective is to be able to resolve conflict between two beliefs in Dempster-Shafer theory, which can be interpreted qualitatively as one source strongly supports one hypothesis and the other strongly supports another hypothesis, where the two hypotheses are not compatible. Consider for example a situation where three agents have used WordNet as background knowledge and build their beliefs considering different concepts context, which was derived from the background knowledge e.g. agent 1 used the direct hypernyms, agent 2 the sister terms and agent 3 the inherited hypernyms. Based on string similarity measures a numerical belief value is calculated, which represent a strength of the confidence that the two terms are related to each other. The scenario is depicted in Table 1.

CONFLICT DETECTION	BELIEF 1	BELIEF 2	BELIEF 3
Obvious	0.85	0.80	0.1
Difficult	0.85	0.65	0.45

Table 1. Belief conflict detection

The values given in **Table 1** are demonstrative numbers just for the purpose of providing an example. In our ontology mapping framework DSSim, the similarities are considered as subjective beliefs, which is represented by belief mass functions that can be combined using the Dempster's combination rule. This subjective belief is the outcome of a similarity algorithm, which is applied by a software agent for creating mapping between two concepts in different ontologies. In our ontology mapping framework different agents assess similarities and their beliefs on the similarities need to be combined into a more coherent result. However these individual beliefs in practice are often conflicting. In this scenario applying Dempster's combination rule to conflicting beliefs can lead to an almost impossible choice because the combination rule strongly emphasizes the agreement between multiple sources and ignores all the conflicting evidence through a normalization factor. The counter-intuitive results that can occur with Dempster's rule of combination are well known and have generated a great deal of debate within the uncertainty reasoning community. Different variants of the combination rule (Sentz & Ferson, 2002) have been proposed to achieve more realistic combined belief. Instead of proposing an additional combination rule we turned our attention to the root cause of the conflict itself namely how the uncertain information was produced in our model.
The fuzzy voting model was developed by Baldwin (Baldwin, 1999) and has been used in Fuzzy logic applications. However, to our knowledge it has not been introduced in the context of trust management on the Semantic Web. In this section, we will briefly introduce the fuzzy voting model theory using a simple example of 10 voters voting against or in favour of the trustfulness of an another agent's belief over the correctness of mapping. In our ontology mapping framework each mapping agent can request a number of voting agents to help assessing how trustful the other mapping agent's belief is. According to Baldwin (Baldwin, 1999) a linguistic variable is a quintuple $(L,T(L),U,G,\mu)$ in which L is the name of the variable, $T(L)$ is the term set of labels or words (i.e. the linguistic values), U is a universe of discourse, G is a syntactic rule and μ is a semantic rule or membership function. We also assume for this work that G corresponds to a null syntactic rule so that $T(L)$ consists of a finite set of words. A formalization of the fuzzy voting model can be found in (Lawry, 1998). Consider the set of words *{Low_trust (L_t), Medium_trust (M_t) and High_trust (H_t) }* as labels of a linguistic variable trust with values in $U=[0,1]$. Given a set "m" of voters where each voter is asked to provide the subset of words from the finite set $T(L)$, which are appropriate as labels for the value u. The membership value $\chi_{\mu(w)(u)}$ is taking the proportion of voters who include u in their set of labels, which is represented by w. The main objective when resolving conflict is to have sufficient number of independent opinions that can be consolidated. To achieve our objective we need to introduce more opinions into the system i.e. we need to add the opinion of the other agents in order to vote for the best possible outcome. Therefore we assume for the purpose of our example that we have 10 voters (agents). Formally, let us define

$$V = A_1, A_2, A_3, A_4, A_5, A_6, A_7, A_8, A_9, A_{10} \qquad (13)$$
$$T(L) = \{L_t, M_t, H_t\}$$

The number of voters can differ however assuming 10 voters can ensure that

1. The overlap between the membership functions can proportionally be distributed on the possible scale of the belief difference [0..1]
2. The work load of the voters does not slow the mapping process down

Let us start illustrating the previous ideas with a small example. By definition consider three linguistic output variables *L* representing trust levels and *T(L)* the set of linguistic values as *T(L)={Low_trust, Medium_trust, High_trust}*. The universe of discourse is *U*, which is defined as *U=[0,1]*. Then, we define the fuzzy sets per output variables μ (Low_trust), μ(Medium_trust) and μ(High_trust) for the voters where each voter has different overlapping trapezoidal, triangular or gauss membership functions as depicted on **Fig. 4.** The difference in the membership functions represented by the different vertices of the membership functions in **Fig. 14** ensures that voters can introduce different opinions as they pick the possible trust levels for the same difference in belief. The possible set of trust levels *L=TRUST* is defined by the **Table 2.** Note that in the table we use a short notation *L_t* means *Low_trust*, *M_t* means *Medium_trust* and *H_t* means *High_trust*. Once the input fuzzy sets (membership functions) have been defined the system is ready to assess the output trust memberships for the input values. Both input and output variables are real numbers on the range between [0..1]. Based on the difference of beliefs, own belief and similarity of the different voters the system evaluates the scenario. The evaluation includes the fuzzification which converts the crisp inputs to fuzzy sets, the inference mechanism which uses the fuzzy rules in the rule-base to produce fuzzy conclusions (e.g., the implied fuzzy sets), and the defuzzification block which converts these fuzzy conclusions into the crisp outputs. Therefore each input (belief difference, belief and similarity) produces a possible defuzzified output (low, medium or high trust) for the possible output variables. Each defuzzified value can be interpreted as a possible trust level where the linguistic variable with the highest defuzzified value is retained in case more than one output variable is selected. As an example consider a case where the defuzzified output has resulted in the situation described in **Table 2.** Note that each voter has its own membership function where the level of overlap is different for each voter. Based on a concrete input voting agent nr 1 could map the defuzzified variables into high, medium and low trust whereas voting agent 10 to only low trust.

A1	A2	A3	A4	A5	A6	A7	A8	A9	A10
L_t	L_t	L_t	L_t	L_t	L_t	L_t	L_t	L_t	L_t
M_t	M_t	M_t	M_t	M_t	M_t				
H_t	H_t	H_t							

Table 2. Possible values for voting

Note that behind each trust lever there is a real number, which represents the defuzzified value. These values are used to reduce the number of possible linguistic variables in order to obtain the vote for each voting agent. Each agent retains the linguistic variable that represents the highest value and is depicted in **Table 3.**

A1	A2	A3	A4	A5	A6	A7	A8	A9	A10
H_t	M_t	L_t	L_t	M_t	M_t	L_t	L_t	L_t	L_t

Table 3. Voting

Taken as a function of x these probabilities form probability functions. They should therefore satisfy:

$$\sum_{w \in T(L)} P_r(L = w \mid x) = 1 \tag{14}$$

which gives a probability distribution on words:

$$\sum P_r(L = Low\_trust \mid x) = 0.6 \tag{15}$$
$$\sum P_r(L = Medium\_trust \mid x) = 0.3$$
$$\sum P_r(L = High\_trust \mid x) = 0.1$$

As a result of voting we can conclude that given the difference in belief *x=0.67* the combination should not consider this belief in the similarity function since based on its difference compared to another beliefs it turns out to be a distrustful assessment. The before mentioned process is then repeated as many times as many different beliefs we have for the similarity i.e. as many as different similarity measures exist in the ontology mapping system.

7. Experimental analysis

Experimental comparison of ontology mapping systems is not a straightforward task as each system is usually designed to address a particular need from a specific domain. Authors have the freedom to hand pick some specific set of ontologies and demonstrate the strengths and weaknesses of their system carrying out some experiments with these ontologies. The problem is however that it is difficult to run the same experiments with another system and compare the two results. This problem has been acknowledged by the Ontology Mapping community and as a response to this need the Ontology Alignment Evaluation Initiative[7] has been set up in 2004. The evaluation was measured with recall, precision and F-Measure, which are useful measures that have a fixed range and meaningful from the mapping point of view.

Precision: A measure of the usefulness of a hit list, where hit list is an ordered list of hits in decreasing order of relevance to the query and is calculated as follows:

$$\mathrm{Pr}ecision = \frac{\left|\{relevant\ items\} \cap \{retrieved\ items\}\right|}{\left|\{retrieved\ items\}\right|} \tag{16}$$

Recall: A measure of the completeness of the hit list and shows how well the engine performs in finding relevant entities and is calculated as follows:

$$\mathrm{Re}call = \frac{\left|\{relevant\ items\} \cap \{retrieved\ items\}\right|}{\left|\{relevant\ items\}\right|} \tag{17}$$

[7] http://oaei.ontologymatching.org/

F-Measure: The weighted harmonic mean of precision and recall and is calculated as follows:

$$F - measure = \frac{2 * (Precision * Recall)}{(Precision + Recall)} \tag{18}$$

Recall is 100% when every relevant entity is retrieved. However it is possible to achieve 100% by simply returning every entity in the collection for every query. Therefore, recall by itself is not a good measure of the quality of a search engine. Precision is a measure of how well the engine performs in not returning non-relevant documents. Precision is 100% when every entity returned to the user is relevant to the query. There is no easy way to achieve 100% precision other than in the trivial case where no document is ever returned for any query. Both precision and recall has a fixed range: 0.0 to 1.0 (or 0% to 100%). A good mapping algorithm must have a high recall to be acceptable for most applications. The most important factor in building better mapping algorithms is to increase precision without worsening the recall. In order to compare our system with other solutions we have participated in the OAEI competitions since 2006. Each year we have been involved in more tracks than the previous year. This gave us the possibility to test our mapping system on different domains including medical, agriculture, scientific publications, web directories, food and agricultural products and multimedia descriptions. The experiments were carried out to assess the efficiency of the mapping algorithms themselves. The experiments of the question answering (AQUA) using our mappings algorithms are out of the scope of this paper. Our main objective was to compare our system and algorithms to existing approaches on the same basis and to allow drawing constructive conclusions.

7.1 Benchmarks

The OAEI benchmark contains tests, which were systematically generated starting from some reference ontology and discarding a number of information in order to evaluate how the algorithm behave when this information is lacking. The bibliographic reference ontology (different classifications of publications) contained 33 named classes, 24 object properties, 40 data properties. Further each generated ontology was aligned with the reference ontology. The benchmark tests were created and grouped by the following criteria:

- Group 1xx: simple tests such as comparing the reference ontology with itself, with another irrelevant ontology or the same ontology in its restriction to OWL-Lite
- Group 2xx: systematic tests that were obtained by discarding some features from some reference ontology e.g. name of entities replaced by random strings, synonyms, name with different conventions, strings in another language than English, comments that can be suppressed or translated in another language, hierarchy that can be suppressed, expanded or flattened. Further properties that can be suppressed or having the restrictions on classes discarded, and classes that can be expanded, i.e. replaced by several classes or flattened
- Group 3xx: four real-life ontologies of bibliographic references that were found on the web e.g. BibTeX/MIT, BibTeX/UMBC

Fig 6 shows the 6 best performing systems out of 13 participants. We have ordered the systems based on the their the F-Value of the H-means because the H-mean unifies all results for the test and F-Value represents both precision and recall.

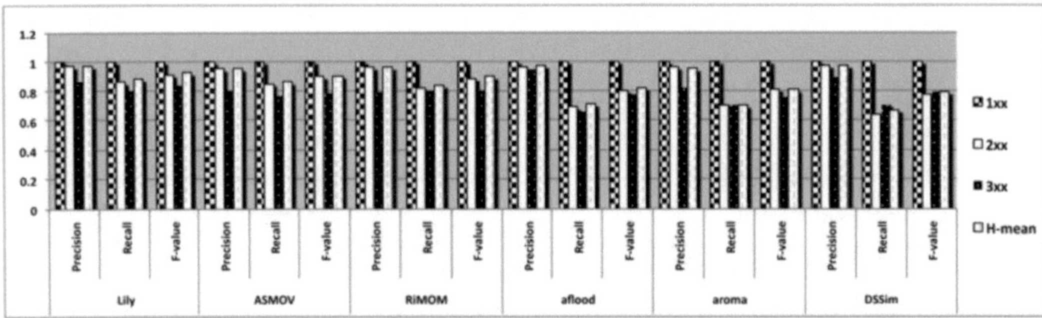

Fig 6. Best performing systems in the benchmarks based on H-mean and F-value

In the benchmark test we have performed in the upper mid range compared to other systems. Depending on the group of tests our system compares differently to other solutions:

- Group 1xx: Our results are nearly identical to the other systems.
- Group 2xx: For the tests where syntactic similarity can determine the mapping outcome our system is comparable to other systems. However where semantic similarity is the only way to provide mappings our systems provides less mappings compared to the other systems in the best six.
- Group 3xx: Considering the F-value for this group only 3 systems SAMBO, RIMOM and Lily are ahead.

The weakness of our system to provide good mappings when only semantic similarity can be exploited is the direct consequence of our mapping architecture. At the moment we are using four mapping agents where 3 carries our syntactic similarity comparisons and only 1 is specialised in semantics. However it is worth to note that our approach seems to be stable compared to our last year's performance, as our precision recall values were similar in spite of the fact that more and more difficult tests have been introduced in this year. As our architecture is easily expandable with adding more mapping agents it is possible to enhance our semantic mapping performance in the future.

7.2 Anatomy

The anatomy track (**Fig 7**) contains two reasonable sized real world ontologies. Both the Adult Mouse Anatomy (2.744 classes) and the NCI Thesaurus for Human Anatomy (3.304 classes) describes anatomical concepts. The classes are represented with standard *owl:Class* tags with proper rdfs:label tags. Besides their large size and a conceptualization that is only to a limited degree based on the use of natural language, they also differ from other ontologies with respect to the use of specific annotations and roles, e.g. the extensive use of the *partOf* relations, *owl:Restriction* and *oboInOwl: hasRelatedSynonym* tags. Our mapping algorithm has used the labels to establish syntactic similarity and has used the *rdfs:subClassOf* tags to establish semantic similarities between class hierarchies. For this track we did not use any medical background knowledge but the standard WordNet dictionary. Three systems SAMBO, SAMBOdtf and ASMOV have used domain specific background knowledge for this track.

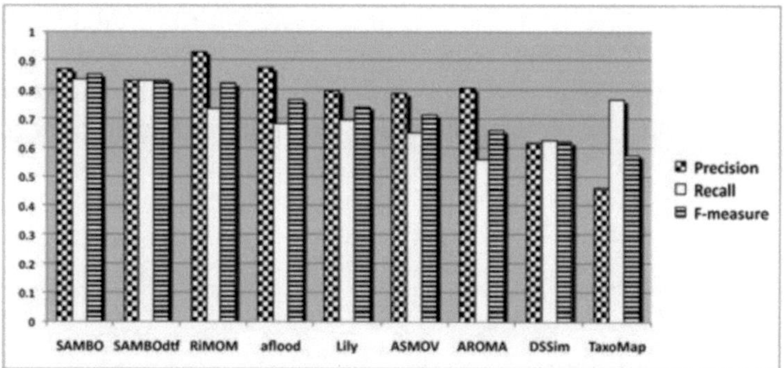

Fig 7. All participating systems in the anatomy track ordered by F-value

The anatomy track represented a number of challenges for our system. Firstly the real word medical ontologies contain classes like "outer renal medulla peritubular capillary", which cannot be easily interpreted without domain specific background knowledge. Secondly one ontology describes humans and the second describes mice. To find semantically correct mappings between them requires deep understanding of the domain. According to the results our system DSSim did not perform as we expected in this test compared to the other systems, as we do not use any domain specific background knowledge or heuristics. The best performing system was SAMBO, which has been designed specifically for the biomedical domain. In order to improve our performance we consider to experiment with medical background knowledge in the future.

7.3 Fao

The Food and Agricultural Organization of the United Nations (FAO) track contains one reasonable sized and two large real world ontologies.

1. The AGROVOC describes the terminology of all subject fields in agriculture, forestry, fisheries, food and related domains (e.g. environment). It contains around 2.500 classes. The classes itself are described with a numerical identifier through *rdf:ID* attributes. Each class has an instance, which holds labels in multiple languages describing the class. For establishing syntactic similarity we substitute the class label with its instance labels. Each instance contains a number of additional information like *aos:hasLexicalization* of *aos:hasTranslation* but we do not make use of it as it describes domain specific information.
2. ASFA contains 10.000 classes and it covers the world's literature on the science, technology, management, and conservation of marine, brackish water, and freshwater resources and environments, including their socio-economic and legal aspects. It contains only classes and its labels described by the standard *owl:Class* formalism.
3. The fisheries ontology covers the fishery domain and it contains a small number of classes and properties with around 12.000 instances. Its conceptual structure is different from the other two ontologies. These differences represented the major challenge for creating the alignments.

For the OAEI contest three sub tracks were defined as follows:

- agrafsa: create class to class mapping between the AGROVOC and ASFA ontologies
- agrorgbio: create class to class mappings between the AGROVOC organism module and fisheries biological entities where the fisheries instances are matched against classes.
- fishbio: create class to class mappings between fisheries commodities and biological entities where the instances are matched against classes

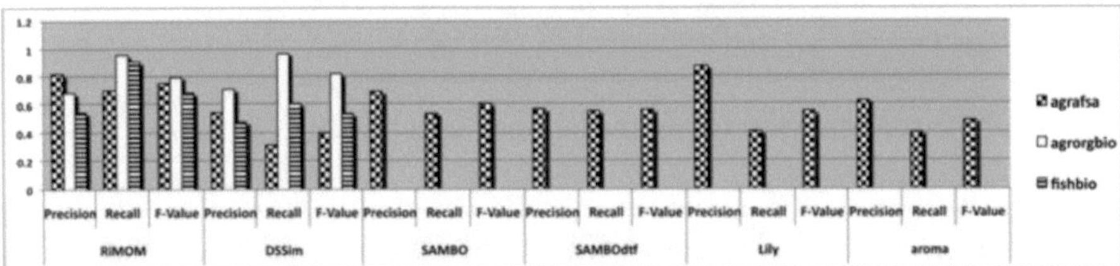

Fig. 8. All participating systems in the FAO track ordered by F-value

The FAO track (**Fig. 8**) was one of the most challenging ones as it contains three different sub tasks and large scale ontologies. As a result DSSim was one of the two systems, which could create complete mappings. The other systems have participated in only one sub task. In terms of overall F-Value RiMOM has performed better than DSSim. This can be contributed to the fact that the FAO ontologies contain all relevant information e.g. *rdfs:label, hasSynonym, hasLexicalisation* on the individual level and using them would imply implementing domain specific knowledge into our system. Our system has underperformed RiMOM because our individual mapping component is only part of our whole mapping strategy whereas RiMOM could choose the favour instance mapping over other strategies. However in the agrorgbio sub task DSSim outperformed RiMOM, which shows that our overall approach is comparable.

7.4 Directory

The purpose of this track was to evaluate performance of existing alignment tools in real world taxonomy integration scenario. Our aim is to show whether ontology alignment tools can effectively be applied to integration of "shallow ontologies". The evaluation dataset was extracted from Google, Yahoo and Looksmart web directories. The specific characteristics of the dataset are:

- More than 4500 of node matching tasks, where each node matching task is composed from the paths to root of the nodes in the web directories. Expert mappings for all the matching tasks.
- Simple relationships. Basically web directories contain only one type of relationship so called "classification relation".
- Vague terminology and modelling principles: The matching tasks incorporate the typical "real world" modelling and terminological errors.

These node matching tasks were represented by pairs of OWL ontologies, where classification relation is modelled as OWL *subClassOf* construct. Therefore all OWL ontologies are taxonomies (i.e. they contain only classes (without Object and Data properties) connected with subclass relation.

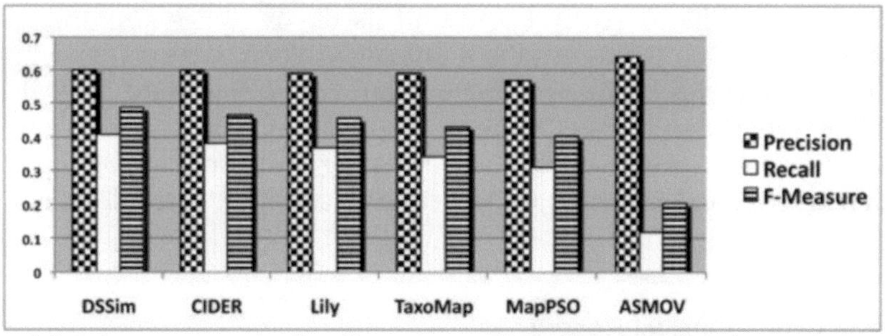

Fig 9. All participating systems in the directory track ordered by F-value

In the library track only 6 systems (**Fig 9**) have participated this year. In terms of F-value DSSim has performed the best however the difference is marginal compared to the CIDER (Gracia & Mena, 2008) or Lily systems. The concepts in the directory ontologies mostly can mostly be characterised as compound nouns e.g. "News_and_Media" and we need to process(split) them properly before consulting background knowledge in order to provide better mappings in the future.

7.5 Library

The objective of this track was to align two Dutch thesauri used to index books from two collections held by the National Library of the Netherlands.

Each collection is described according to its own indexing system and conceptual vocabulary. On the one hand, the Scientific Collection is described using the GTT, a huge vocabulary containing 35.000 general concepts ranging from "Wolkenkrabbers (Sky-scrapers)" to "Verzorging (Care)". On the other hand, the books contained in the Deposit Collection are mainly indexed against the Brinkman thesaurus, containing a large set of headings (more than 5.000) that are expected to serve as global subjects of books. Both thesauri have similar coverage (there are more than 2.000 concepts having exactly the same label) but differ in granularity. For each concept, the thesauri provide the usual lexical and semantic information: preferred labels, synonyms and notes, broader and related concepts, etc. The language of both thesauri is Dutch, but a quite substantial part of Brinkman concepts (around 60%) come with English labels. For the purpose of the alignment, the two thesauri have been represented according to the SKOS model, which provides with all these features.

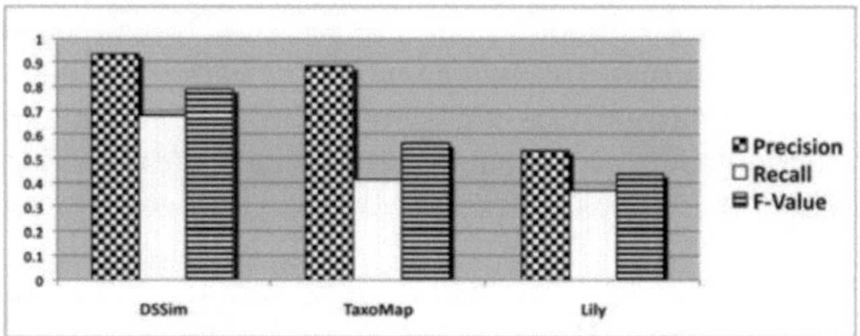

Fig. 10. All participating systems in the library track ordered by F-value

In the library track DSSim has performed the best (**Fig. 10**) out of the 3 participating systems. The track is difficult partly because of its relative large size and because of its multilingual representation. However these ontologies contain related and broader terms therefore the mapping can be carried out without consulting multi lingual background knowledge. This year the organisers have provided instances as separate ontology as well however we did not make use of it for creating our final mappings. For further improvements in recall and precision we will need to consider these additional instances in the future.

7.6 Very Large Cross-Lingual Resources

This vlcr track was the most complex this year. It contains 3 large ontologies. The GTAA thesaurus is a Dutch public audiovisual broadcast's archive, for indexing their documents, contains around 3.800 subject keywords, 97.000 persons, 27.000 names and 14.000 locations. The DBPedia is an extremely rich dataset. It contains 2.18 million resources or "things", each tied to an article in the English language Wikipedia. The "things" are described by titles and abstracts in English and often also in Dutch. We have converted the original format into standard SKOS in order to use it in our system. However we have converted only the labels in English and in Dutch whenever it was available. The third resource was the WordNet 2.0 in SKOS format where the synsets are instances rather than classes. In our system the WordNet 3.0 is included into as background knowledge therefore we have converted the original noun-synsets into a standard SKOS format and used our WordNet 3.0 as background knowledge. Unfortunately DSSim was the only system, which participated in this track therefore we cannot make qualitative comparisons. Nevertheless in this track our precision has ranged from 10% to 94% depending on the test and facet. The lowest precision 0.1 occurred on the GTAA-Wordnet mapping for the persons facet. This can be explained because the GTAA contains nearly hundred thousand persons, which does not have at all correspondence in WordNet. In fact WordNet contains very few persons. As the number of entities in these ontologies are very large only an estimation was can be calculated for the recall/coverage and for not all the facets. The estimated recall values for the evaluated samples were relatively low around 20%. For more advanced evaluation more test will be carried out in order to identify the strengths and weaknesses of our system.

8. Strengths and weaknesses of our solution

Based on the OAEI experiments, we can conclude that our solution compares and scales well to other well established ontology mapping systems. Nevertheless it is clear (OAEI seems to share our opinion) that it is not possible to clearly define a "winner" on these yearly competitions. Each system has its strengths and weaknesses and they tend to perform differently on different domains. However we can define some criteria to determine where we perform well and on which areas do we need to make further progress.

1. Domain independence: This is a definite strength of our system. Our solution does not rely on pre-defined thresholds or parameters that needs to be changed from domain to domain. Several mapping systems utilise machine learning in order to determine these parameters however these solutions are likely to be dependent on

the training set. DSSim uses WordNet as the background knowledge. This ensures that we can provide equivalent mappings on different domains. Nevertheless domain specific background knowledge can influence the results positively. The anatomy track has proved that systems that use domain specific background knowledge are far superior compared to the systems with general background knowledge. Nevertheless the drawback of these systems is that they cannot produce equally good results once the domain is changing. For example the AOAS system (Zhang & Bodenreide, 2007) performed the best on the anatomy track on the OAEI 2007 but they did not produce result in any other track as their system was fine tuned for the medical domain.

2. Conflict management: This area needs to be improved in our system. DSSim do manage conflicting beliefs over a particular mapping, which can occur when different agents have built up conflicting beliefs for the correctness of a mapping candidate. The problem occurs when we have already selected a mapping candidate and later on in the mapping process we add an another mapping that contradicts the previous one. Systems e.g. ASMOV, which try to detect conflicting mappings in the result-set can provide better overall results compared to our solution.
3. Mapping quality: DSSim does not produce always the best precision and recall for each track however our mapping quality is stable throughout different domains. We consider this as a strength of our system because we foresee different application domains where our solution can be used. In this context it is more important that we can produce equally good enough mappings.
4. Mapping performance: Due to our multi-agent architecture our solution scales well with medium and large domains alike. For example in the OAEI 2008 the largest ontologies were in the Very Large Cross-Lingual Resources track. DSSim was the only system that has participated in this track. Our solution can scale well for large domains because as the domain increases we can distribute the problem space between an increasing number of agents. Additionally our solution fits well to current hardware development trends, which predicts an increasing number of processor core in order to increase the computing power.
5. Traceability of the reasoning: Unfortunately this is a weakness of our system as we cannot guarantee that running the algorithm twice on the same domain we will always get exactly the same results. The reason is that our belief conflict resolution approach (Nagy et al., 2008) uses fuzzy voting for resolving belief conflicts which can vary from case to case. Additionally beliefs are based on similarities between a set of source and target variables. The set of variables are deducted from the background knowledge, which can differ depending on the actual context of our query. Therefore it is not feasible to trace exactly why a particular mapping has been selected as good mapping compared to another candidate mappings.

9. Conclusions

In this paper we have investigated a combination of 3 challenges that we think is crucial to address in order to provide an integrated ontology mapping solution. We have provided

our solution DSSim, which is the core ontology mapping component for our proposed architecture that integrates with question answering at the moment. However our system is easily expandable, layered with clear interfaces, which allows us to integrate our solution into different context like Semantic Web Services (Vargas-Vera et al., 2009). Further in this paper we have shown how the fuzzy voting model can be used to resolve contradictory beliefs before combining them into a more coherent state by evaluating fuzzy trust.
We have proposed new levels of trust for resolving these conflicts in the context of ontology mapping, which is a prerequisite for any systems that makes use of information available on the Semantic Web. Our system is conceived to be flexible because the membership functions for the voters can be changed dynamically in order to influence the outputs according to the different similarity measures that can be used in the mapping system. We have described initial experimental results with the benchmarks of the Ontology Alignment Initiative, which demonstrates the effectiveness of our approach through the improved recall and precision rates. There are many areas of ongoing work, with our primary focus considering the effect of the changing number of voters and the impact on precision and recall or applying our algorithm in different application areas. We continuously evaluate the performance of our system through OAEI competitions (Nagy et al., 2006) (Nagy et al., 2007) (Nagy et al., 2008) that allows us to improve, evaluate and validate our solution compared to other state of the art systems. So far our qualitative results are encouraging therefore we aim to investigate further the belief combination optimisation, compound noun processing and agent communication strategies for uncertain reasoning in the future.

10. References

Austen-Smith, D.; Banks, J.S. (1996). Information Aggregation, Rationality, and the Condorcet Jury Theorem, pp-34-45, The American Political Science Review

Baldwin, J.F. (1999). Mass assignment Fundamentals for computing with words, pp 22-44, Springer-Verlag, vol 1566

Batini, C.; Lenzerini, M.; Navathe, S.B. (1986). A comparative analysis of methodologies for database schema integration, pp 323-364, ACM Computing Surveys

Beckett, D. (2004). RDF/XML Syntax Specification, http://www.w3.org/RDF/

Bock, J.; Hettenhausen, J. (2008). MapPSO Results for OAEI 2008, *Proceedings of the 3rd International Workshop on Ontology Matching,* Germany, Karlsruhe

Brugman, H.; Malaisé, V.; Gazendam, L. (2006). A Web Based General Thesaurus Browser to Support Indexing of Television and Radio Programs, *Proceedings of the 5th international conference on Language Resources and Evaluation (LREC 2006)* , Italy Genoa

Carlo, W.; Tharam, D.; Wenny, R.; Elizabeth, C. (2005). Large scale ontology visualisation using ontology extraction, pp 113-135, International Journal of Web and Grid Services, vol 1

Caracciolo, C.; Euzenat, J.; Hollink, L.; Ichise, R. (2008). First results of the Ontology Alignment Evaluation Initiative 2008, *Proceedings of the 3rd International Workshop on* Ontology Matching, Germany, Karlsruhe

Cohen, W.; Ravikumar, P.; Fienberg, S.E. (2003). A comparison of string distance metrics for name-matching tasks, *Proceedings of Information Integration on the Web (IIWeb 2003)*, Indonesia, Jakarta

Ding, L.; Finin, T.; Joshi, A. (2004). Swoogle: A Search and Metadata Engine for the Semantic Web, *Proceedings of the Thirteenth ACM Conference on Information and Knowledge Management*, USA, Washington DC

Euzenat, J.; Shvaiko, P. (2007). Ontology matching, Springer-Verlag, 3-540-49611-4, Heidelberg, Germany

Flahive, A.; Apduhan, B.O.; Rahayu, J.W.; Taniar, D. (2006). Large scale ontology tailoring and simulation in the Semantic Grid Environment, pp 256-281, International Journal of Metadata, Semantics and Ontologies, vol 1

Gracia, J.; Mena, E. (2008). Ontology Matching with CIDER:Evaluation Report for the OAEI 2008, *Proceedings of the 3rd International Workshop on Ontology Matching*, Germany, Karlsruhe

Hamdi, F.; Zargayouna, H.; Safar, B.; Reynaud, C. (2008). TaxoMap in the OAEI 2008 alignment contest , *Proceedings of the 3rd International Workshop on Ontology Matching*, Karlsruhe, germany

Jean-Mary Y.R; Kabuka, M.R. (2007). ASMOV: Ontology Alignment with Semantic Validation, *Proceedings of Joint SWDB-ODBIS Workshop*, Austria, Vienna

Ji, Q. ; Haase, P. ;Qi, G. (2008). Combination of Similarity Measures in Ontology Matching by OWA Operator, *Proceedings of the 12th International Conference on Information Processing and Management of Uncertainty in Knowledge-Based Systems (IPMU'08)*, Spain, Malaga

Lambrix, P.; Tan, H. (2006). SAMBO - a system for aligning and merging biomedical ontologies, pp 196-206, Journal of Web Semantics, Special issue on Semantic Web for the Life Sciences, vol 4

Lawry, J. (1998). A voting mechanism for fuzzy logic, pp 315-333, International Journal of Approximate Reasoning, vol 19

Lenzerini, M.; Milano, D.; Poggi, A. (2004). Ontology representation and reasoning, NoE InterOp (IST-508011), WP8, subtask 8.2

McGuinness, D.L; Harmelen, F. (2004). OWL Web Ontology Language, http://www.w3.org/TR/owl-features/

Miles, A.; Bechhofer, S. (2008). SKOS Simple Knowledge Organization System, http://www.w3.org/TR/skos-reference/

Monge, A.E.; Elkan, C.P. (1996). The field matching problem: Algorithms and applications, *Proceedings of the Second International Conference on Knowledge Discovery and Data Mining*, USA, Portland

Nagy, M. ; Vargas-Vera, M. ; Motta, E. (2006). DSSim-ontology Mapping with Uncertainty, *Proceedings of the 1st International Workshop on Ontology Matching*, USA, Georgia

Nagy, M. ; Vargas-Vera, M. ; Motta, E. (2005). Multi Agent Ontology Mapping Framework in the AQUA Question Answering System, pp 70-79, *Proceedings of MICAI 2005 : Advances in Artificial Intelligence, 4th Mexican International Conference on Artificial Intelligence*, Mexico, Monterrey

Nagy, M. ; Vargas-Vera, M. ; Motta, E. (2007). DSSim - managing uncertainty on the semantic web, *Proceedings of the 2nd International Workshop on Ontology Matching,* South Korea, Busan

Nagy, M. ; Vargas-Vera, M. ; Stolarski, P. (2008). DSSim results for the OAEI 2008, *Proceedings of the 3rd International Workshop on Ontology Matching,* Germany, Karlsruhe

Nagy, M. ; Vargas-Vera, M. ; Motta, E. (2008). Introducing Fuzzy Trust for Managing Belief Conflict over Semantic Web Data, *Proceedings of 4th International Workshop on Uncertain Reasoning on the Semantic Web,* Germany, Karlsruhe

Sentz, K.; Ferson, S. (2002). Combination of Evidence in Dempster-Shafer Theory, Systems Science and Industrial Engineering Department, Binghamton University

Schmid, H. (1994). Probabilistic part-of-speech tagging using decision trees,pp 25-36, *Proceedings of the International Conference on New Methods in Language Processing,* UK, Manchester

Shafer, G. (1976). A Mathematical Theory of Evidence, 978-0691081755, Princeton University Press

Tang, J.;Li, J.; Liang, B.; Li, Y. (2006). Using Bayesian decision for ontology mapping, pp 243-262, Web Semantics: Science, Services and Agents on the World Wide Web, vol 4

Vargas-Vera, M. ; Motta, E. (2004). AQUA - Ontology-based Question Answering System, *Proceedings of the 3rd International Mexican Conference on Artificial Intelligence (MICAI-2004*), Mexico, Monterrey

Vargas-Vera, M. ; Motta, E. (2004). An Ontology-driven Similarity Algorithm, KMI-TR-151, Knowledge Media Institute, The Open University, UK, Milton Keynes

Vargas-Vera, M.;Nagy, M.; Zyskowski, D.; Haniewicz, K.;Abramowicz, W.; Kaczmarek, M. (2009). Challenges on Semantic Web Services, 978-1-60566-650-1, Handbook of Research on Social Dimensions of Semantic Technologies and Web Services, Information Science Reference

Wand, Y.; Wang, R.Y. (1996). Anchoring data quality dimensions in ontological foundations, pp 86-95, Communications of the ACM, vol 39

Wang, P.; Xu, B. (2008). Lily: Ontology Alignment Results for OAEI 2008, *Proceedings of the 3rd International Workshop on Ontology Matching,* Germany, Karlsruhe

Wang, R.Y.;Kon, H.B.; Madnick, S.E. (1993). Data Quality Requirements Analysis and Modeling, *Proceedings of the 9th International Conference on Data Engineering,* Austria, Vienna

Zhang, S.; Bodenreide, O. (2007). Hybrid Alignment Strategy for Anatomical Ontologies Results of the 2007 Ontology Alignment Contest, Proceedings of the 2nd International Workshop on Ontology Matching, South Korea, Busan

Young, H.P. (1988). Condorcet's Theory of Voting, pp 1231-1244, The American Political Science Review, vol 82

8

Using Semantic Technology to Enable Behavioural Coordination of Heterogeneous Systems

Artem Katasonov
VTT Technical Research Centre Finland
Vagan Terziyan
University of Jyväskylä Finland

1. Introduction

Coordination is one of the fundamental problems in systems composed of multiple interacting processes (Tamma et al., 2005). Coordination aims at avoiding negative interactions, e.g. when two processes conflict over the use of a non-shareable resource, as well as exploiting positive interactions, e.g. when an intermediate or final product of one process can be shared with another process to avoid unnecessary repetition of actions. A classic example of a negative interaction from the field of agent-based systems is two robots trying to pass thorough a door at the same time and blocking each other. A corresponding example of a positive interaction is a robot opening and closing the door when passing it while also letting the other robot to pass, in so saving it the need of opening/closing the door by itself. On the Web, the coordination has not yet been treated much as traditional Web applications and services are normally isolated from each other, run on separate computing systems and, therefore, do not do not have other types of interaction beyond *using* each other. However, as the Internet grows towards the Internet of Things, where the physical and digital worlds will be interconnected, where e.g. Web services will control various physical processes, the problem of coordination becomes more and more critical also in the Web domain.

The predominant approach to coordination has been to hard-wire the coordination mechanism into the system structure (Tamma et al., 2005). Synchronization tools such as semaphores have been traditionally used to handle negative interactions, requiring every process to be programmed to check the semaphore before accessing the resource (like checking if there is an "occupied" light over a lavatory door). If a resource is occupied by a process for a significant time, it would be clearly better for the other process to work on another its task rather than just wait. Under the traditional approach, realizing that, as well as attempting to exploit any positive interactions, is possible only through additional hard-wiring: the programs of the processes must have incorporated some knowledge about the behaviours of each other.

This traditional approach becomes insufficient when considering more open systems, where the processes and resources composing the system may be unknown at design time (Decker & Lesser, 1995). In such systems, we ideally want computational processes to be able to reason about the coordination issues in their system, and resolve these issues autonomously (Decker & Lesser, 1995). We would like to even allow ad-hoc interaction, where two stand-alone independently-designed systems are able to coordinate whenever a need arises. One way towards achieving this is to enable the relevant processes to *communicate their intentions* with respect to future activities and resource utilization (Moyaux et al., 2006). Jennings at al. (1998) present this as an issue of enabling individual agents to represent and reason about the actions, plans, and knowledge of other agents to coordinate with them. In other words, there is a need for the interacting processes, e.g. software agents, Web services, etc, to be able to communicate not only about the external world, i.e. the domain, but also about their own abilities, goals, as well as the current and intended actions.

In the case of highly heterogeneous systems, enabling such a dynamic coordination among them is an even harder problem than more traditional problems of data-level or protocol-level heterogeneity. Tamma and colleagues (Tamma et al., 2005; Moyaux et al., 2006) developed *an ontological framework* for dynamic coordination. They stated the need for an agreed common vocabulary, with a precise semantics, that is therefore suitable for representation as an ontology. Tamma et al. (2005) provided such an ontology that defined coordination in terms of *agents* carrying out *activities* involving some *resources*, which can be non-shareable, consumable, etc. Moyaux et al. (2006) described then the rules for checking for conflicts among activities: e.g. if two activities overlap in time and require the same resource that is known to be non-shareable, they are mutually-exclusive. They also described some possible coordination rules to be followed when a conflict of a certain type is detected.

The ontology of Tamma et al. is an *upper ontology*, i.e. an ontology which attempts to describe the concepts that are the same across all the domains of interest. Roughly speaking, the idea is to make the agents to communicate their intentions and actions using the upper-ontology concepts (i.e. "resource", "activity") rather than the domain-ontology concepts (e.g. "printer", "printing document") and in so to resolve the problem of evolving domains or domains not fully known at design time.

We build on this work of Tamma and colleagues. We, however, observe a few drawbacks of the current solution:

- The traditional approach to coordination in a sense involves hard-wiring the domain ontology concepts into both agents that want to coordinate with each other. In the approach of Tamma et al., the upper ontology concepts are hard-wired into both instead. The latter is better than the former, yet still requires a design-phase ontological alignment of agents and does not support for coordination with agents for which this was not done.
- Translating all coordination messages into the upper ontology may make them significantly longer. Also, when considering that in some cases the agents may actually share the domain ontology and in some other cases the receiver of the message may be familiar with a super-class of the unknown concept used in the message, bringing every conversation down to the upper ontology sounds somewhat unnatural.

On the other hand, we observe that the Semantic Web research explicitly addresses the possibility of multi-ontology systems. In open or evolving systems, different components would, in general, adopt different ontologies as either knowledge models of the environment or as knowledge models of own configuration, capabilities and behaviour. Therefore, practical Semantic Web applications have to operate with heterogeneous data, which may be defined in terms of many different ontologies and may need to be combined, e.g., to answer specific queries (Motta & Sabou, 2006). At present, the standard technologies of the Semantic Web, such as RDF Schema (RDF-S) and Web Ontology Language (OWL), on the level of hierarchies of entities' classes, enable communications in which (we will discuss an example in Section 2):

- The sender of a message can express it in its own domain ontology and does not need to know any integrating upper ontology.
- Only the receiver of the message has to know the upper ontology and to have access to a formal definition of the domain ontology of the sender that links the concepts from that ontology to the upper ontology.

We would like to disclaim that we do not imply here the use of any automated ontology mapping (also known as ontology matching and ontology alignment, see Tamma & Payne, 2008; Shvaiko & Euzenatsh, 2008), which is an imprecise, e.g. statistical, process of identifying relationships between concepts in two domain ontologies. We speak of a case where the concepts from both domain ontologies were manually, by human designers, linked to a single upper ontology. Then, the needed automatic process consists only of locating, accessing and use of relevant ontology specifications. This process we refer to in this chapter as *ontology linking*. The definition of a domain ontology in terms of an upper ontology acts as an annotation, i.e., is external to the agents and therefore may be added when an agent is already in the operation. Therefore, an intelligent agent can potentially communicate with a "stupid" agent (e.g. from a legacy system). It is even possible to connect two "stupid" agents by putting an intelligent middleware in between.

Our approach to ontological coordination aims at enabling exactly the same: so that an agent can express its action intention according to its own domain ontology. Then, assuming that this ontology has a formal definition in terms of an upper ontology such as one by Tamma et al., the agent receiving the message will be able to interpret it and understand if there is any conflict with its own actions or if there is a possibility to re-use any of the shareable results. In this chapter, we describe this approach. In particular, we show how we realize it with the *Semantic Agent Programming Language (S-APL)* (Katasonov & Terziyan, 2008).

2. Ontological coordination principles

Let us consider the following communication scenario, which is readily enabled by the standard technologies of the Semantic Web, namely RDF-S and OWL. Assume there are two agents; let us call one Enquirer and another Responder. Assume the Responder knows the following facts: *org:Mary rdf:type person:Woman ; person:hasSon org:Jack*, meaning that Mary is a woman and has a son Jack. (The syntax for RDF we use here is one of Turtle and of Notation3, see Berners-Lee, 2000a. We assume that the namespace *org:* refers to all entities related to an organization and *person:* denotes an ontology of people and relationships that is used in that organization).

Now assume that the Enquirer issues a SPARQL (W3C, 2008) query *SELECT ?x WHERE {?x rdf:type family:Mother}* (definition of prefixes is omitted), i.e. "give me all entities that belong to the class *family:Mother*". The result of executing this query is an empty set - the Responder does not have any facts that would directly match the pattern given. The Responder can, however, analyze the query and notice that the concept *family:Mother* is unknown to him. This can be done, e.g., by simply checking if he has any RDF triple involving this concept. So, the Responder decides to look for the ontology that defines it. In the simplest and common case, the definition of the prefix *family:* in the query will give the URL of the online OWL document defining the ontology in question. So, the Responder downloads it and obtains the information that *family:Mother* is a subclass of *human:Human* with the restriction that it must have a property *human:hasSex* with the value *human:FemaleSex* and must also have at least one property *human:hasChild*. (We assume that the namespace *human:* denotes some general upper ontology for describing human beings.) This additional information does not yet change the result of the query execution, because the Responder does not have a definition of his own *person:* ontology in terms of *human:* ontology. However, let us assume that he is able to locate (e.g. from a registry) and download such a definition. In so, the Responder obtains information that *person:Woman* is a subclass of *person:Person* which is in turn a subclass of *human:Human*, and that *person:Woman* has a restriction to have a property *human:hasSex* with the value *human:FemaleSex*. Also, he obtains the fact that *person:hasSon* is a sub-property of *human:hasChild*.
Then, the application of the standard RDF-S and OWL reasoning rules will infer that *org:Mary human:hasSex human:FemaleSex* (because she is known to be a woman) and also that *org:Mary human:hasChild org:Jack* (because having a son is a special case of having a child). Immediately, the OWL rules will conclude that *org:Mary rdf:type family:Mother* and this information will be sent back to the Enquirer. As can be seen, the concepts from the domain ontology used by the Enquirer were, through an upper ontology, dynamically linked to the concepts from the domain ontology used by the Responder. In so, the Enquirer was able to use his own concepts when formulating a question and, yet, the Responder was able to answer the question correctly.

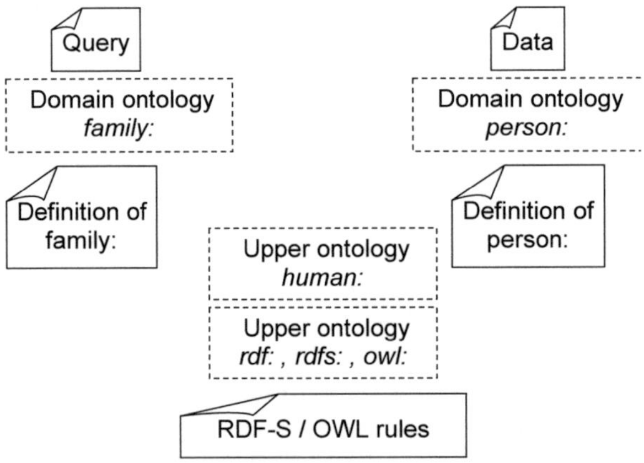

Fig. 1. The logical components of the example

Figure 1 depicts the logical components involved in this example. There are two upper ontologies involved. One is the ontology of RDF-S/OWL itself - one operating with concepts such as class, subclass, property, restriction on property, etc. The other one is a basic agreed common vocabulary about human beings. Then, there should be a specification for each domain ontology involved - a definition that links the concepts from that ontology to an upper ontology (*human:* in this case), normally using concepts from another upper ontology (RDF-S/OWL properties in this case). Finally, at least one of the upper ontologies (RDF-S/OWL in this case) must come with a set of rules defined. These rules, when applied to the existing facts and domain ontologies' definitions, are supposed to infer new facts and in so to enable the understanding between agents.
In the simple example above, the RDF graph we obtain after merging all sub-graphs in question (data plus two ontology specifications) is a sufficiently connected one, so that all the needed interpretations are directly possible. In many practical cases, this will not be a case, thus requiring *ontology alignment* (also known as ontology matching or ontology mapping). For example, we might not to know the fact that *person:hasSon* is a sub-property of *human:hasChild*. Ontology alignment is an important open challenge in the Semantic Web research (see e.g. Tamma & Payne, 2008; Shvaiko & Euzenatsh, 2008) and is outside the scope of this chapter. Note that we include "attempt ontology alignment" in Figure 3 below as the last resort for a case when ontology linking did not succeed; we do not discuss, however, how this can be done.

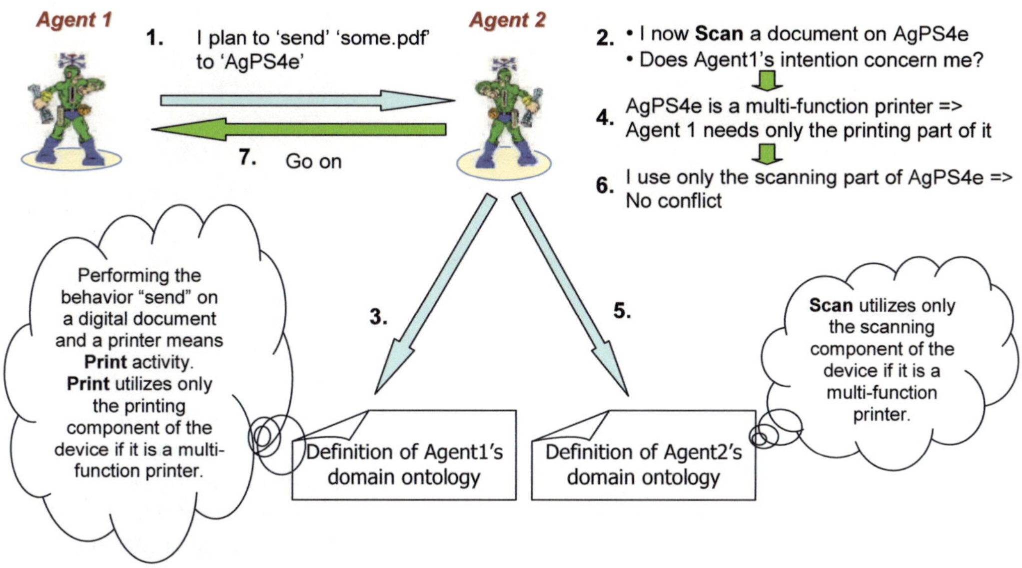

Fig. 2. Ontological coordination situation

As was stated in Section 1, our goal is to enable more flexible and dynamic ontological coordination among agents, at least at the level of how RDF-S and OWL enable dynamic linking of entities' class hierarchies. Figure 2 depicts an example situation. Agent1 informs Agent2 that he plans to "send" some resource called "some.pdf" to some resource called "AgPS4e". Let us assume that Agent2 can recognize the former resource as a digital

document and the latter resource as a multi-function printer. Agent2 is currently utilizing (or plans to) the scanning function of AgPS4e. So, an obvious question appears is there any conflict between this activity and Agent1's intention.
Following a similar workflow as in RDF-S/OWL example earlier, Agent2 could try to locate a specification of the domain ontology of activities used by Agent1. From such a specification, he would receive information that, in the vocabulary of Agent1, sending a document to a printer corresponds to executing *Print* activity, that *Print* holds the printer for the whole time of the activity, and that if a multi-function printer is in question (that can also scan, copy, etc.) *Print* requires only the printing component of it. Then, if this has not been done yet, Agent2 would have to locate the definition of his own domain ontology of activities to obtain similar information about his own ongoing activity *Scan*. Finally, combining all this information, Agent2 would infer that he and Agent1 need different components of the multi-function printer AgPS4e that can be engaged independently and, therefore, there is no conflict.

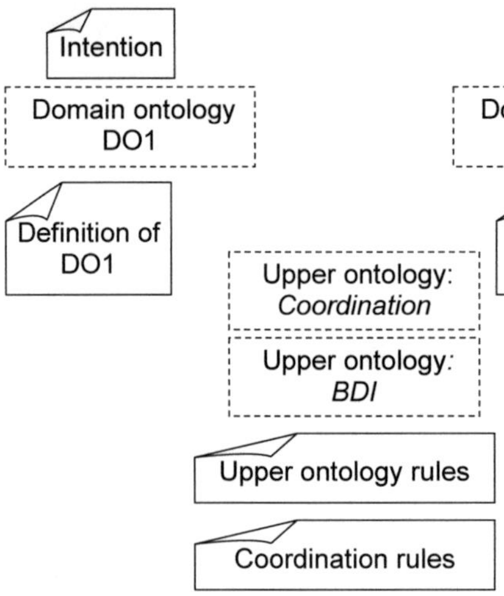

Fig. 3. Ontological coordination framework

By the analogy with Figure 1, Figure 3 depicts the logical components needed to realize this. Let us assume that an agent communicates to another agent his intentions with respect to future actions, and let us assume that he does this using a vocabulary unknown to the receiver. There are two upper ontologies involved. One is the *coordination ontology*, i.e. one that operates with the concepts such as activity and resource, like one provided by Tamma and colleagues (Tamma et al., 2005; Moyaux et al., 2006). The other upper ontology is the ontology of *mental attitudes* of agents. Since the Beliefs-Desires-Intentions (BDI) architecture (Rao & Georgeff, 1991) is quite a standard approach, Figure 3 assumes the BDI ontology in place of this ontology of mental attitudes. The definition of a domain ontology have to therefore link it to these two upper ontologies, in a way that will enable the *upper ontology rules* to do the following:

1. Interpret an expression of a mental attitude conveying an action intention to obtain the identifier of the intended activity.

2. Match the activity description in the domain ontology definition with the intention to understand what resources will be utilized and results produced by the intended action.

For example, in FIPA SL communication content language (FIPA, 2002), an action intention is expressed using a construct like *(I (agent-identifier :name agent1) (done (action (agent-identifier :name agent1) (print some.pdf AgPS4e))))*. In a simplest case, the upper ontology rules have to extract the name of the activity "print" and then, from the semantic definition of that activity, understand that "AgPS4e" is the identifier of the resource (printer) that is going to be utilized by the intended action. As can be seen, these rules, as well as corresponding activities' definitions, have to be tailored to a particular language used in communication. In addition, more complex cases are likely and have to be handled, where the activity name as modelled in the ontology is not present directly in the expressed intention but has to be inferred from the action parameters. As in the example depicted in Figure 2, the intention could have been given as "send some.pdf AgPS4e". Then, the fact that the printing activity is meant has to be inferred from combining a more general and ambiguous "send" with known classes of the resources some.pdf (a document) and AgPS4e (a printer).

In our work, we utilize the Semantic Agent Programming Language (S-APL) (Katasonov & Terziyan, 2008) instead of SL or similar. An S-APL expression is an RDF graph itself, which greatly simplifies describing activities in an ontology to enable the rules to match them with expressed intentions and to do all needed interpretations (see Section 4).

Figure 3 also includes the *coordination rules* as the part of the framework. Those rules operate on the output of the upper ontology rules in order to e.g. identify conflicts between activities and propose resolution measures, like those described in Moyaux et al. (2006).

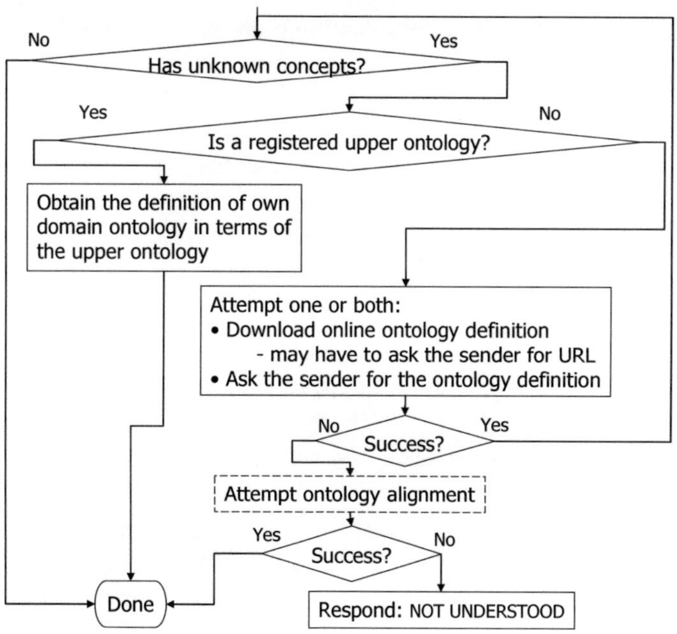

Fig. 4. Dynamic ontology linking process

Assuming that an agent received a message and identified it as conveying an action intention of another agent, the flowchart of the ontology linking process is depicted in Figure 4. The terminator 'Done' implies only the end of this particular process. The upper ontology rules and the coordination rules can then trigger some follow-up actions.

3. Semantic Agent Programming Language (S-APL)

The main motivation for the development of the Semantic Agent Programming Language (S-APL) (Katasonov & Terziyan, 2008) was to facilitate the dynamic coordination of heterogeneous systems according to the principles presented in Section 2. S-APL provides a common medium for realizing all the stages of the ontological coordination framework described.

S-APL is an RDF-based language that integrates the semantic description of domain resources with the semantic prescription of the agents' behaviours. S-APL is a hybrid of semantic rule-based reasoning frameworks such as N3Logic (Berners-Lee et al., 2008) and agent programming languages (APLs) such as e.g. AgentSpeak(L) (Rao, 1996). From the semantic reasoning point of view, S-APL is an extension of CWM (Berners-Lee, 200b) with common APL features such as the BDI architecture, which implies an ability to describe goals and commitments - data items presence of which leads to some executable behaviour, and an ability to link to sensors and actuators implemented in a procedural language, namely Java. From the APL point of view, S-APL is a language that has all the features (and more) of a common APL, while being RDF-based and thus providing advantages of semantic data model and reasoning. S-APL can be used as a programming language as well as the content language in the inter-agent communications: in querying for data, in requesting for action, as well as in communicating plans and intentions.

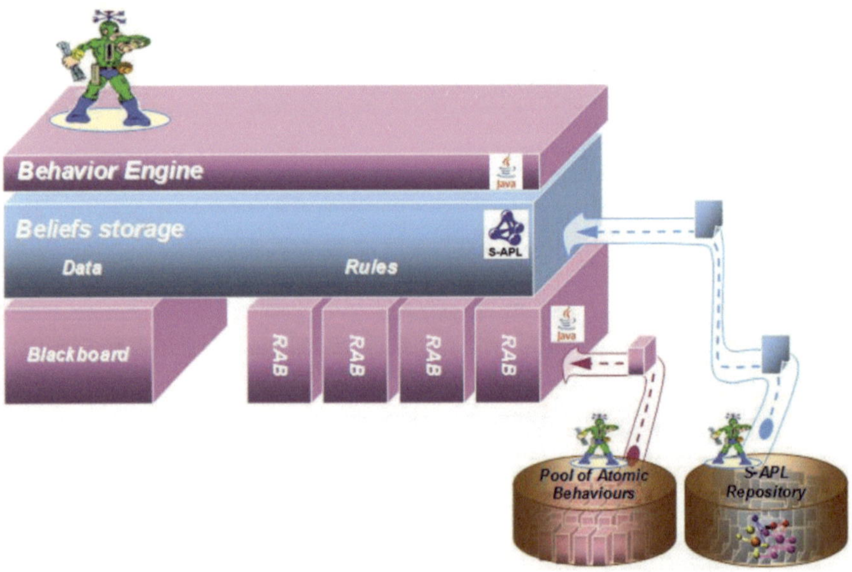

Fig. 5. Architecture of an S-APL agent

The architecture of an S-APL agent is depicted in Figure 5. The basic 3-layer structure is common for the APL approach. There is the behaviour engine implemented in Java, a declarative middle-layer, and a set of sensors and actuators which are again Java components. The latter we refer to as *Reusable Atomic Behaviours (RABs)*. We do not restrict RABs to be *only* sensors or actuators, i.e. components concerned with the agent's environment. A RAB can also be a reasoner (data-processor) if some of the logic needed is impossible or is not efficient to realize with S-APL, or if one wants to enable an agent to do some other kind of reasoning beyond the rule-based one. We also equip each agent with a blackboard, through which RABs can exchange arbitrary Java objects, for cases where the use of semantic data is not possible.

The middle layer is the agent' beliefs storage. What differentiates S-APL from traditional APLs is that S-APL is RDF-based. In addition to the advantages of the semantic data model and reasoning, an extra advantage is that in S-APL the difference between the data and the program code is only logical but not any principal. Data and code use the same storage, not two separate ones. This means that a rule upon its execution can add or remove another rule, the existence or absence of a rule can be used as a premise of another rule, and so on. None of these is normally possible in traditional APLs treating rules as special data structures principally different from normal beliefs which are n-ary predicates. S-APL is very symmetric with respect to this - anything that can be done to a simple RDF statement can also be done to any belief structure of any complexity.

As Figure 5 stresses, an S-APL agent can obtain the needed data and rules not only from local or online documents, but also through querying S-APL repositories. Such a repository, for example, can be maintained by some organization and include prescriptions (lists of duties) corresponding to the organizational roles that the agents are supposed to play. In our implementation, such querying is performed as inter-agent action with FIPA ACL messaging but does not involve any query or content languages beyond S-APL itself. As can be seen from Figure 5, agents also can load RABs remotely. This is done as an exception mechanism triggered when a rule prescribes engaging a RAB while the agent does not have it available. Thus, organizations are able to provide not only the rules to follow but also the tools needed for that.

Our implementation of the S-APL platform is built on the top of the Java Agent Development Framework (JADE) (Bellifemine et al., 2007). JADE provides communication infrastructure, agent lifecycle management, agent directory-based discovery and other standard services.

The syntax for RDF used in S-APL is one of Notation3 (N3) (Berners-Lee, 2000a) and S-APL utilizes the syntax for rules very similar to that of N3Logic (Berners-Lee et al., 2008). N3 was proposed as a more compact, better readable and more expressive alternative to the dominant notation for RDF, which is RDF/XML. One special feature of N3 is the concept of formula that allows RDF graphs to be quoted within RDF graphs, e.g. *{org:room1 org:hasTemperature 25} org:measuredBy org:sensor1*. An important convention is that a statement inside a formula is not considered as asserted, i.e., as a general truth. In a sense, it is a truth only inside a context defined by the statement about the formula and the outer formulas. In S-APL, we refer to formulae as *context containers*. The top level of the S-APL beliefs storage, i.e. what is the general truth for the agent, we refer to as *general context* or just *G*.

The technical details of S-APL can be found in Katasonov (2008). Below, we describe the main constructs of S-APL. We use three namespaces: *sapl:* for S-APL constructs, *java:* for

RABs, and *p:* for the parameters of standard (being a part of the S-APL platform) atomic behaviours. The namespace *org:* is used for resources that are assumed to be defined elsewhere.
The two constructs below are equivalent and define a simple belief. The latter is introduced for syntactic reasons.

```
org:room1 org:hasTemperature 25.
{org:room1 org:hasTemperature 25} sapl:is sapl:true.
```

The next two constructs add context information:

```
{org:room1 org:hasTemperature 25} org:measuredBy org:sensor1.
{org:room1 org:hasTemperature 25} sapl:is sapl:true;
                                    org:measuredBy org:sensor1.
```

The former states that "sensor1 measured the temperature to be 25" without stating that "the agent believes that the temperature is 25". In contrast, the latter states both. This demonstrates a specific convention of S-APL: rather than doing several statements about one container, "{...} P1 O1; P2 O2" leads to linking the statements inside the formula to two separate containers. Then, using *sapl*:true it is also possible to link some statements to a container and to one of its nested containers.
The goals of the agent and the things that the agent believes to be false (not just unknown) are defined, correspondingly, as:

```
sapl:I sapl:want {org:room1 org:hasTemperature 25}.
{org:room1 org:hasTemperature 25} sapl:is sapl:false.
```

sapl:I is an indicative resource that is defined inside the beliefs of an agent to be *owl*:sameAs the URI of that agent. A specific convention of S-APL is that e.g. "sapl:I sapl:want {A B C}. sapl:I sapl:want {D E F}" is the same as "sapl:I sapl:want {A B C. D E F}". In other words, the context containers are joined if they are defined through statements with the same two non-container resources.
The commitment to an action is specified as follows:

```
{sapl:I sapl:do java:ubiware.shared.MessageSenderBehavior}
     sapl:configuredAs {
          p:receiver sapl:is org:John.
          p:content sapl:is {org:room1 org:hasTemperature 25}.
          sapl:Success sapl:add
               {org:John sapl:is org:notified}
     }
```

The *java:* namespace indicates that the action is a RAB. Otherwise, the action would correspond to an S-APL plan (kind of subprogram) specified elsewhere. When the behaviour engine finds such a belief in G, it executes the RAB and removes the commitment. In the configuration part, one may use special statements to add or remove beliefs. The subject can be *sapl*:Start, *sapl*:End, *sapl*:Success, *sapl*:Fail. The predicate is either *sapl*:add or *sapl*:remove. Using such statements, one can also easily specify sequential plans: *{sapl:I sapl:do ...} sapl:configuredAs {... sapl:Success sapl:add {{sapl:I sapl:do ...} sapl:configuresAs {...}}}.*
Beliefs can also be added or removed through explicit mental actions:

```
sapl:I sapl:remove {?x sapl:is org:notified}
```

```
sapl:I sapl:add {org:John sapl:is org:notified}
```

sapl:remove uses its object as a pattern that is matched with G and removes all beliefs that match. Use of variables (as ?x above), filtering conditions, etc. is possible. *sapl*:add adds its object to G. It does not need to be normally used, since just stating something is the same as adding it to G. This construct is only needed when one wants to postpone the creating of the belief until the stage of the agent run-time cycle iteration when commitments are treated, or when one uses as the object a variable holding the ID of a statement or a container (see below).
The conditional commitment is specified as:

```
{
    {?room org:hasTemperature ?temp} org:measuredBy ?sensor.
    ?temp > 30
} => {...}
```

=> and > are shorthands for *sapl*:implies and *sapl*:gt, correspondingly. The object of *sapl*:gt and other filtering predicates (>=, <, <=, =, !=) is an expression that can utilize arithmetic operations, functions like *abs, floor, random,* etc. and string-processing functions like *length, startsWith, substring,* etc. When the behaviour engine finds in G a belief as above and finds out that all the conditions in the subject context container are met, it copies to G all the beliefs from the object container substituting variables with their values. Those can be simple beliefs and/or commitments, unconditional or conditional. S-APL allows a variable value to substitute a part of a resource, e.g. "logs/?today/received". Such a liberty is in contrast with, e.g., N3Logic approach where a variable value can only be a substitute for the whole resource; however, it was shown to greatly simplify the programming.
As with any commitments, the conditional commitment is removed after successful execution. In order to create a persistent rule, the => statement has to be wrapped as:

```
{ {...} => {...} } sapl:is sapl:Rule
```

A specific convention of S-APL is that if there are several possible solutions to the query in the left side of =>, the right side is copied by default for the first-found solution only. One can use *sapl*:All wrappings to define that the right part has to be copied several times: for every unique value of some variable of every unique combination of the values of some variables. These wrapping can be used in either the left or the right side:

```
{ {{ ... } sapl:All ?x} sapl:All ?y } => {...}
{...} => { {{...} sapl:All ?x} sapl:All ?y }
```

sapl:All on the right side is allowed to enable defining different wrappings for different (top-level) resulting statements, e.g. *{...} => {X Y Z . {{?x L ?y} sapl:All ?y. A B ?x} sapl:All ?x}*. On the left side of =>, *sapl*:All must always wrap the whole contents of the container.
Other solutions set modifiers are also available, namely *sapl*:OrderBy, *sapl*:OrderByDescending, *sapl*:Limit, and *sapl*:Offset. The meaning of those are the same as of their equivalents in SPARQL. One can also wrap a condition in the left side of => with *sapl*:Optional to have the same effect as SPARQL's OPTIONAL, and connect two conditions with *sapl*:or to have the same effect as SPARQL's UNION. It is also possible to specify exclusive conditions, i.e. ones that must not be know to be true, by using the wrapping *sapl*:I *sapl*:doNotBelieve {...}.
There are also several of alternatives to =>, including:

```
{...} -> {...} ; sapl:else {...}
{...} ==> {...}
```

-> and ==> are the shorthands for *sapl*:impliesNow and *sapl*:infers. -> specifies a conditional action rather than a commitment: it is checked only once and removed even if it was false. One can also combine it with *sapl*:else to specify the beliefs that have to be added if the condition was false. ==> works almost the same as => with the following difference. If one uses => inside a persistent rule for semantic inference (generating new facts from existing ones), one needs to: (1) add to the head of the rule the negation of the tail the rule - to avoid continuous non-stop execution of the rule; (2) use a set of *sapl*:All wrappings - for all relevant variables - to enforce that the rule infers all possible facts in one iteration. When using ==>, these two things are done automatically - negation of the tail is checked and the rule is executed for every solution found.
One can also define new calculated variables:

```
{?person org:hasHeight ?h. ?feet sapl:expression ''?h/0.3048''.
     ?m sapl:min ?feet } => {...}
```

sapl:expression gives to the new variable the value coming from evaluating an expression. *sapl*:min is a special predicate operating on the set of matching solutions rather than on a particular solution - it determines the minimum value of the variable. The other predicates from the same group are *sapl*:max, *sapl*:sum, *sapl*:count (number of groups when grouped by values of one or several variables) and *sapl*:countGroupedBy (number of members in each group).
Variable can also refer to IDs of statements and context containers, and one can use the predicates *sapl*:hasMember, *sapl*:memberOf, *rdf*:subject, *rdf*:predicate and *rdf*:object. After obtaining the ID of the container with *?x org:accordingTo org:Bill*, one can do the following things:

```
{... {?x sapl:is sapl:true} org:accordingTo org:John} => {...}
?x sapl:is sapl:true
sapl:I sapl:add ?x
sapl:I sapl:remove ?x
sapl:I sapl:erase ?x
?x sapl:hasMember {org:room1 org:hasTemperature 25}
```

The first construct defines a query that is evaluated as true iff any belief that is found in the context container ?x has a match in the context container {} org:accordingTo org:John. The second one links the statements from ?x to G, while the third copies them to G. The fourth uses the contents of ?x as the pattern for removing beliefs from G, while the fifth erases the container ?x itself. Finally, the sixth adds to the container ?x a new statement.
There are several ways to create a variable holding IDs of some statements:

```
{{?room org:hasTemperature 25} sapl:ID ?x}
                                 org:accordingTo org:Bill
{?x rdf:predicate org:hasTemperature} org:accordingTo org:Bill
{?x sapl:is sapl:true} org:accordingTo org:Bill
?c org:accordingTo org:Bill. ?c sapl:hasMember ?x
```

The first will find all the statements inside the container {} org:accordingTo org:Bill that match the pattern given, while the second all the statements with the predicate org:hasTemperature. The third and the fourth will find all the statements in that container. One can then use a query like *{{?x sapl:is sapl:true} org:accordingTo org:Bill. {?x sapl:is sapl:true} org:accordingTo org:John} => {...}*, which is evaluated as true if there is at least one belief from the first container that has a match in the second container. One can also use *sapl*:true, *sapl*:add, *sapl*:remove, *sapl*:erase, *sapl*:hasMember and *sapl*:memberOf to do the same things as listed above for containers, but for a single statement.

4. Defining classes of activities

In this and the following sections, we show how the general ontological coordination framework described in Section 2 is realized with the Semantic Agent Programming Language (S-APL) (see Section 3) plus a set of additional concepts we refer to as S-APL Schema (SAPL-S).

In this context, we are mostly interested in one S-APL construct - *intention (commitment) to perform an action*. As described in Section 3, such an intention is encoded in S-APL as:

```
{ sapl:I sapl:do <action name> } sapl:configuredAs
     { <parameter> sapl:is <value>. ... }
```

Such a construct, when found in the agent's beliefs, leads to execution of the specified action. *sapl*:I is an indicative resource that is to be defined in the beliefs of an agent to be *owl*:sameAs the URI of that agent. Obviously, substituting *sapl*:I with an URI of another agent in the construct above would result in a description of somebody's else intention. A simple example of an intention to send a message to another agent was provided in Section 3. Note that one can easily put a construct specifying another action intention as the contents of the message (in place of the single triple in that example) - in order to communicate that intention to the other agent.

An intention to perform an action, as any other S-APL construct, is just a logically connected set of RDF triples (Notation3 allows to have a compact representation but does not change the data model). If one wants to check if a larger S-APL dataset, e.g. the contents of a message, includes an intention to perform a particular action, one can simply run a query against the dataset. That query is given as a pattern, i.e. another set of RDF triples with some of the resources being variables. For instance, the pattern matching any own action intention is *{sapl:I sapl:do ?x} sapl:configuredAs ?y*. This is the same principle as followed in SPARQL for querying general RDF datasets.

Moreover, we can make the following observations. First, a pattern that is universally quantified by using variables can be seen as the definition of a *class* of S-APL constructs, i.e. a class of agents' mental attitudes. Second, when considering inheritance (class-subclass) hierarchies of mental attitudes, the definition of a subclass, in most cases, only introduces some additional restrictions on the variables used in the definition of the super-class. If, e.g. *{sapl:I sapl:do ?x} sapl:configuredAs ?y* is the definition of a general action, adding a statement *?x rdf:type org:PrintAction* may be used to create the definition of a class of printing actions.

In S-APL, it is easy to record such patterns as data, merge patterns when needed, and use patterns as queries against any given dataset - thus giving us all the needed means for modelling classes of agents' activities and utilizing them in rules.

S-APL Schema (namespace *sapls:* below) defines a set of concepts needed for such modelling. First, SAPL-S introduces a set of general classes of BDI mental attitudes, such as a goal or an action intention. SAPL-S ontology defines these classes using the statements of the type <*class*> *sapl:is* <*pattern*>. Second, SAPL-S provides a property *sapls*:restriction that enables one to describe some additional restrictions on the pattern of a class to define some subclasses of it.
An action intention is defined in SAPL-S as:

```
sapls:Action sapl:is {
     {{?subject sapl:do ?behavior}
          sapl:configuredAs ?parameters} sapl:ID ?id
}
```

The wrapping with the property *sapl*:ID is included in order to, when an action class definition is used as a query pattern, receive the identifier of the matching action statement – to enable removing or modifying it if wished.
One can then define a subclass of *sapls*:Action, for example:

```
org:Scan rdfs:subClassOf sapls:Action;
     sapls:restriction {
          ?behavior rdf:type org:ScanAction.
          ?parameters sapl:hasMember
                    {org:device sapl:is ?device}.
          {?device rdf:type org:ScanDevice.
               ?scanner sapl:expression ?device}
          sapl:or {?device org:hasPart ?scanner.
               ?scanner rdf:type org:ScanDevice}
     }
```

This definition specifies that *org*:Scan is an action intention to perform an atomic behaviour or a plan that is known to belong to the class *org*:ScanAction, and that has a parameter *org*:device referring to a device that either belongs to the class *org*:ScanDevice (a stand-alone scanner) or has a part that belongs to that class (a multi-function printer). This definition is made taking into account that we need to be able to specify which resource gets occupied by the activity in question. In this case, it is one whose URI will be bound to the variable ?scanner (note that *sapl*:expression as used above works as simple assignment). In Section 6, we will present the syntax for describing activities, including the resources they require.
Let us assume that we also define *org*:Print in exactly the same way as *org*:Scan, only with *org*:PrintAction, *org*:PrintDevice and ?printer in places of *org*:ScanAction, *org*:ScanDevice and ?scanner correspondingly. Then, we can also define *org*:Copy as intersection of both without additional restrictions:

```
org:Copy rdfs:subClassOf sapls:Scan, sapl:Print
```

Logically, the pattern defining a mental attitude class is obtained by merging its own *sapls*:restriction with all *sapls*:restriction of its super-classes and with *sapl*:is of the top of the hierarchy. Therefore, an activity is classified as *org*:Copy if it is implemented with a plan that is assigned to both *org*:ScanAction and *org*:PrintAction classes and that is performed on a device that has both an *org*:ScanDevice part and an *org*:PrintDevice part. Of course, the pattern will also match with a case where the whole device is tagged as both *org*:ScanDevice and *org*:PrintDevice. However, the latter would not be a good domain model since the scanning component and the printing component of a multi-function printer are normally independent resources, i.e., e.g., scanning a document does not block simultaneous printing of another document by another process.

The reason for separating the base part of a pattern given as *sapl*:is from the restrictions given as *sapls*:restriction is that the base part can be evaluated against any given dataset, e.g. the contents of a received message, while the restrictions are always evaluated against the general beliefs base of the agent.

5. Using activity classes in policies

Before continuing discussion of the main topic of this chapter, namely dynamic coordination over shared resources and shareable results, let us briefly discuss the utilization of the basic definitions of activity classes in definitions of access control policies.

Semantic Web based approaches to access control policies have been developed in recent years (Finin et al., 2008; Naumenko, 2007). In both Finin et al. (2008) and Naumenko (2007), the access control policies are defined in terms of *prohibitions* or *permissions* for certain actors to perform certain operations. Such policies may have a number of reasons behind them, with one of the reasons being coordination over shared resources. Such coordination is not dynamic, i.e. the conflicts are not resolved on per-instance basis. Rather, an agent with authority imposes some restriction on other agents' behaviours to avoid the conflicts as such. An example of such a policy could be "no employee other than the management is allowed to use company printers for copying". According to the syntax given in Finin et al. (2008), such a policy could easily be defined by two statements (*rbac:* stands for role-based access control):

```
org:Employee rbac:prohibited org:Copy.
org:Management rbac:permitted org:Copy
```

This definition assumes that *org*:Management is a subclass of *org*:Employee and that permissions have priority over prohibitions (this is not discussed in Finin et al., 2008), i.e. that the permission given to the management staff overrules the restriction put on a more general class of employees.

Combining policy definitions with definitions of the activity classes (Section 3) enables enforcement of the policies. An agent itself of an external supervisor can match the plans or intentions of the agent with the activity classes and then check if those are in the scopes of some defined policies. As a simplest reaction, an action that contradicts a policy can be blocked.

Dynamic ontology linking is also enabled. This means that a policy can be formulated using concepts originally unknown to the agent in question. For example, one may be informed about a prohibition to *org*:Copy while one may not know what *org*:Copy means. Yet, following the process sketched in Figure 3, one will be able to link this concept to *org*:Print and *org*:Scan and, if those are also unknown, link them to the upper S-APL BDI concepts.

In contrast to Finin et al. (2008), Naumenko (2007) uses the concepts of prohibition and permission as the statement classes rather than predicates. The activity class is used as the predicate, and the policy statement is extended by specifying the class of the activity object.

We utilize this approach in our work and represent an access control policy as in the example above in the form (*sbac:* stands for semantics-based access control):

```
{org:Employee org:Copy org:Printer}
                   sapl:is sbac:Prohibition.
{org:Management org:Copy org:Printer}
                   sapl:is sbac:Permission
```

By substituting *org*:Printer with e.g. *org*:PrinterAg4, the policy can be modified into "no employee other than the management is allowed to use for copying printers located on the 4th floor of the Agora building". Such policy is probably more realistic than the former because it may have a rationale that the managers use those printers for their higher-priority tasks and want to avoid possible delays.

In order to enable such policy statements with objects, the definitions of *org*:Scan and of *org*:Print in Section 3 have to be extended with the statement *?object sapl:expression ?device*, so that, after the matching an intention with the pattern, the variable ?object would be bound to the activity object. Note that the variable ?subject, which is needed for both ways of defining policies, was already included in the definition of *sapls*:Action.

6. Annotating activities for coordination

In terms of Figure 2, the approach to defining activity classes described in Section 4 enables linking domain ontologies of activities to the upper BDI ontology and, therefore, the interpretation of expressed mental attitudes. The interpretation may give information about what activity is intended, by who (i.e. who is the subject), and on what object. As we discussed in Section 4, the ability of making such basic interpretations can already be utilized in policy mechanisms, such as those of access control. In order to enable more complex and dynamic coordination schemes, however, the definition of activities have to be also linked to *the upper coordination ontology*.

In this section, we describe such an ontology and show how coordination-related properties are linked to basic definitions of the activity classes as presented in Section 4. We use the namespace *coord:* to denote concepts belonging to this ontology. As was mentioned in Section 1, with respect to a coordination ontology, we build on the work of Tamma and colleagues (Tamma et al., 2005; Moyaux et al., 2006). Below, we first describe concepts that correspond directly to those of Tamma et al. After that, we comment on limitations of the ontology of Tamma et al. and present few extensions to it.

The central concepts of the coordination ontology are:

- *coord:Agent* – a thing that able of performing some actions that may require coordination.
- *coord:Process* – something that that changes the state of the environment in some way.
- *coord:NonCoordinableActivity* – a subclass of coord:Process for which coordination is not possible. Non-coordinable activities can be natural events or other processes that are outside of control of the agents comprising the system in question.
- *coord:CoordinableActivity* – a process performed by an agent that is a part of the system in question, which therefore can be coordinated.
- *coord:Resource* – something that may be required to expedite an activity.

When two activities require the same resource, the type and the effect of the interaction depends on what resource is in question. The set of important subclasses of the class *coord*:Resource are (note that Tamma et al. model these as boolean properties of *coord*:Resource rather than subclasses of it):

- *coord:ShareableResource*. The resource that can be simultaneously used by two activities, e.g. a computing unit. Simultaneous use normally results in activities impeding, but not blocking, each other.
- *coord:NonShareableResource*. The resource that can only be used by one activity at a time.
- *coord:ConsumableResource*. A special type of a non-shareable resource that is also consumed when used, i.e. not available for any other activity afterwards.
- *coord:CloneableResource*. The resource that can be duplicated for use in several activities, e.g. an electronic document.

The set of properties used to describe activities follows:

- *coord:actor* – the agent performing the activity
- *coord:requires* – a resource utilized by the activity.
- *coord:shareableResult* – a result produced by the activity that is in principle shareable with another activities.
- *coord:earliestStartDate* – the earliest time at which the activity may begin; null indicates that this information is not known. There are also similar predicates *coord:latestStartDate, coord:latestEndDate, coord:expectedDuration* as well as *coord:actualStartDate* and *coord:actualEndDate.*
- *coord:status* – the execution status of the activity, which can be one of the following: requested, proposed, scheduled, continuing, suspended, failed, succeeded.

These properties have a double use: in operational data to describe the instances of *coord*:CoordinableActivity and in activity ontologies to describe subclasses of *sapls*:Action. The former use is straightforward, e.g:

```
_:act397 rdf:type coord:CoordinableActivity;
           coord:requires org:AgPS4e
```

On the other hand, it would be uncommon for an ontological description of an activity class to have a defined resource URI (i.e. always the same resource), defined start time, etc. Therefore, in this use, the objects of all the properties above are allowed to be variables which are to be initialized when matching the class definition with an expressed action intention. For example, the *org*:Scan activity from Section 4 can be described with a statement:

```
org:Scan coord:requires ?scanner.
```

As commented earlier, during the matching the variable ?scanner will be given the URI of a stand-alone scanner or the scanning part of a multi-function printer. The statement above simply puts that this URI corresponds to a resource that is utilized by the activity.

We could also define a subclass of *org*:Scan, *org*:ScanToFile, which allows saving the result of scanning into a file whose name is given as the parameter *org*:saveTo, and then add a description that this file is shareable with other activities and agents:

```
org:ScanToFile rdfs:subClassOf org:Scan;
     sapls:restriction {
```

```
            ?parameters sapl:hasMember
                  {org:saveTo sapl:is ?file}.
      };
      coord:shareableResult ?file.
```

Similarly, if the parameters of the action intention include the timestamp when the action is planned to be executed, one could use a variable receiving this timestamp when annotating the activity class with time-related properties. Here, arithmetic expressions are allowed, e.g. *?time+1000* (in milliseconds).
Given such annotations of activity classes, the interpretation rules in S-APL are to have the basic form as follows:

```
{     ...
      ?x rdfs:subClassOf sapls:Action.
      sapls:Action sapl:is ?base.
      ?x sapls:restriction ?restriction.
      ?dataset sapl:hasMember {?base sapl:is sapl:true}.
      ?restriction sapl:is sapl:true.
      {     ?x coord:requires ?res.
            ?resource sapl:expression ''valueOf(?res)''
      } sapl:is sapl:Optional.
      ...
} => {
      _:?id rdf:type coord:CoordinableActivity; rdf:type ?x;
      coord:actor ?subject; coord:requires ?resource ...

}
```

Here, for the sake of brevity, we assume that there exist additional rules that do the pre-processing of the activity class hierarchies. These rules extend *sapls*:restriction of an activity class with *sapls*:restriction of its super-classes and also extend the activity class annotation with *coord*:requires, *coord*:sharedResult, etc. of the super-classes. (It is also possible, of course, to write a longer interpretation rule that does not require such pre-processing). The variable ?dataset is assumed to refer to the dataset which is being searched for an action intention, e.g. the contents of a message. *sapl*:Optional wraps a non-mandatory part of the query, similarly to a corresponding construct in SPARQL. If the variable ?resource will not get bound, the statement in the right hand of the rule that uses this variable will not be created. In this example, the activity URI is generated as the blank node prefix *_:* plus the identifier of the intention statement.
One limitation of the ontology of Tamma et al. is that it does not provide for explicit modelling of the effect of activities on the resources they utilize. The ontology includes a possibility to define a resource as being *consumable* (see above). However, there is no way of distinguishing between activities that consume the resource, e.g. printing on paper, and activities that reserve the resource (make unavailable to other activities) without the consumption, e.g. transporting a package of paper from one place to another. Similarly, in many cases, it is needed to distinguish between an activity that destroys a resource (e.g. erases a file) and an activity that uses it (e.g. reads the file). Additionally, one may want to be able to distinguish between consuming/destroying a resource and changing it. For example, printing on a sheet of paper does not destroy it. It consumes it in the sense that it makes the sheet unavailable for future printing activities; however the sheet remains usable

for other activities that do not depend on the sheet being clean. In short, the coordination ontology has to be extended with constructs that will enable describing the effect of an activity on a resource or an attribute of that resource.

There is also a challenge related to increasing the flexibility of the approach by allowing some of an activity's parameters to come from the background knowledge of the listener agent rather than from the expressed action intention directly. For example, an agent X can inform an agent Y about the intention to print a document without specifying the printer. Yet, Y could know what printer X normally uses and make the interpretation based on that. An even more interesting scenario is where X informs Y about an intention to ask some third agent, Z (e.g. a secretary), to print a document for him. In addition, some of the resources used by an activity might not be mentioned in the action intention. For example, a printing intention would not normally mention paper in the expressed parameters. Yet, we may want to be able to specify that the paper will be consumed in the activity. The ontology of Tamma et al. does not include concepts or properties to enable this.

Finally, we may want to be able to connect the parameters of an action intention with time-related estimates. For example, the expected duration of the printing activity is related to the number of pages to print. Realizing this is possible by including an extra statement like *?file org:hasPages ?pages* into the activity class definition, and then by annotating the activity class as *<activity> coord:expectedDuration "?pages*1000"*. We can also wrap this extra statement with {} *sapl*:is *sapl*:Optional, so that absence of information about the number of pages of the printed document would not lead to not counting the action as printing, but only to inability to provide the duration estimate. However, we believe that the definition of an activity class and its coordination-related annotation should not be mixed in such a way. Rather, a separate construct is needed.

For these reasons above, we extended the coordination ontology with the following properties that are to be used in activity ontologies to describe subclasses of *sapls*:Action:

- *coord:assumption* – a pattern for querying the beliefs storage of the agent to extend the information given explicitly in the action intention. In principle, this construct is very similar to the concept of *precondition* of an activity. However, the statements given are not treated as required since we can not assume the agent to be omniscient.
- *coord:effect* – the expected rational effect of the activity. Specifies changes to the resources that the activity uses or other environment entities.

The definition below of a subclass of *org*:Print, *org*:PrintFile, provides an example of using these two properties:

```
org:PrintFile rdfs:subClassOf org:Print;
     sapls:restriction {
          ?parameters sapl:hasMember
               {org:input sapl:is ?file}.
     };
     coord:assumption {
          ?file org:hasPages ?pages.
          ?printer org:hasSheetsOfPaper ?sheets.
          ?remain sapl:expression ''?sheets-?pages''
     };
     coord:expectedDuration "?pages*1000";
     coord:effect {?printer org:hasSheetsOfPaper ?remain}
```

The last element in the ontological coordination framework presented in Section 2 and depicted in Figure 3 is the coordination rules. Those rules attempt to identify conflicts between activities and propose resolution measures. An example of a coordination rule in S-APL follows:

```
{
        ?x rdf:type coord:Activity; coord:actor sapl:I;
             coord:requires ?r.
        ?y rdf:type coord:Activity; coord:actor ?agent;
             coord:requires ?r.
        ?r rdf:type coord:NonShareableResource.
        ?ca rdf:type org:ContractualAuthority;
             org:hasSourceAgent ?agent;
             org:hasTargetAgent sapl:I
} => {... postpone or suspend own activity ...}
```

This example uses the concept of the *operational relationship* from Moyaux et al. (2006). An operation relationship is a relationship between agents that implies the priority of one over the other. ContractualAuthority is a subclass of OperationalRelationship that implies that the "source" agent has the priority over the "target" agent. Moyaux et al. (2006) put these concepts as part of the coordination ontology. The operational relationship concept is important for coordination, however, we believe that it should be a part of a larger organizational ontology rather than embedded into the coordination ontology. This is why in the example above we did not put these concepts into the *coord:* namespace.

7. Conclusions

When considering systems where the agents and resources composing them may be unknown at design time, or systems evolving with time, there is a need to enable the agents to communicate their intentions with respect to future activities and resource utilization and to resolve coordination issues at run-time. In an ideal case, we would like also to allow ad-hoc interaction of systems, where two stand-alone independently-designed systems are able to communicate and coordinate whenever a need arises. Consider, for example, two robots with totally unrelated goals who need to coordinate their activities when they happen to work in the same physical space.

Enabling such a dynamic coordination among highly heterogeneous applications is an even harder problem than more traditional problems of data-level or protocol-level heterogeneity. While the Semantic Web technologies are designed to handle the latter problems, they also provide a basis for handling the coordination problem.

The Semantic Web based approach presented in this chapter aims at enabling agents to coordinate without assuming any design-time ontological alignment of them. An agent can express an action intention using own vocabulary, and through the process of dynamic ontology linking other agents will be able to arrive at a practical interpretation of that intention. The definition of the domain ontology in terms of an upper ontology must be provided. However, such a definition is external to the agents and may be added later, when an agent is already in the operation.

In result, an intelligent agent can potentially communicate with a "stupid" agent, e.g. from a legacy system. It is also possible to connect two "stupid" agents by putting an intelligent middleware in between. This work has been performed in a research project UBIWARE (Katasonov et al., 2008) where the latter case is a major motivation. The interests of the project industrial partners are in Enterprise Application Integration and data integration, with an accent on enabling new intelligent business processes in systems created by interconnecting independently-designed applications and data sources that often do not share a common data model or even ontology.

In this chapter, we first described our general framework for dynamic ontological coordination. Then, we showed how we realize this framework on top of the Semantic Agent Programming Language. In so, this chapter provided a functional vertical solution. One can develop agents with S-APL and instruct them to communicate their intentions using S-APL as the communication content language, i.e. basically send to other agents small pieces of their own code. Then, one can develop needed definitions of the ontologies of activities (Section 4), extend them with coordination-related properties (Section 6) and implement various coordination rules (Section 6), thus getting a fully working solution. Additionally, one can specify and enforce access control policies (Section 5). Of course, the value of the general framework goes beyond this particular S-APL implementation.

One limitation of our present approach, which poses an important challenge to be addressed in the future work, is the following. We assumed so far that the conflicts among activities are identifiable from the activities' descriptions alone. However, if an activity changes an attribute of a resource, the resource may undergo some follow-up changes due to environmental causes, thus leading to a conflict. For example, the activity of opening a food container would not be seen as conflicting with a later activity of consuming the food in the container, unless considering that the food in an open container will spoil faster than in a closed one. This implies that for many practical cases the identification of conflicts has to be performed as reasoning or planning process rather than based on straightforward rules.

8. References

Bellifemine, F. L., Caire, G. & Greenwood, D. (2007). *Developing Multi-Agent Systems with JADE*, Wiley

Berners-Lee, T. (2000a) *Notation 3: A readable language for data on the Web*, online: http://www.w3.org/DesignIssues/Notation3.html

Berners-Lee, T. (2000b) *CWM: A general-purpose data processor for the semantic web*, online: http://www.w3.org/2000/10/swap/doc/cwm

Berners-Lee, T., Connoly, D., Kagal, L., Scharf, Y. & Hendler J. (2008). N3Logic: A logical framework for the World Wide Web, *Theory and Practice of Logic Programming*, Vol.8, No.3, pp. 249–269

Decker, K. & Lesser, V. (1995) Designing a family of coordination algorithms. *Proceedings of 1st Intl. Conf. on Multi-Agent Systems*, pp. 73–80. AAAI Press

Finin, T., Joshi, A., Kagal, L., Niu, J., Sandhu, R., Winsborough, W. & Thuraisingham, B. (2008). ROWLBAC: Role based access control in OWL, *Proceedings of ACM Symposium on Access Control Models and Technologies*, pp. 73–82

Foundation for Intelligent Physical Agents (2002). *FIPA SL Content Language Specification*, online: http://www.fipa.org/specs/fipa00008/SC00008I.pdf

Jennings, N., Sycara, K. P. & Wooldridge, M. (1998). A roadmap of agent research and development, *Autonomous Agents and Multi-Agent Systems*, Vol. 1, No.1, pp.7–38

Katasonov, A. (2008). *UBIWARE Platform and Semantic Agent Programming Language (S-APL). Developer's guide*, online: http://users.jyu.fi/~akataso/SAPLguide.pdf

Katasonov, A., Kaykova, O., Khriyenko, O., Nikitin, S. & Terziyan, V. (2008). Smart semantic middleware for the internet of things, *Proceedings of 5th International Conference on Informatics in Control, Automation and Robotics, Vol. ICSO*, pp. 169–178

Katasonov A. & Terziyan, V. (2008) Semantic agent programming language (S-APL): A middleware platform for the Semantic Web, *Proceedings of 2nd IEEE International Conference on Semantic Computing*, pp. 504–511

Motta, E. & Sabou, M. (2006). Next generation semantic web applications, *Proceedings of ACM Asian Semantic Web Conference, LNCS vol.4185*, pp. 24–29

Moyaux, T., Lithgow-Smith, B., Paurobally, S., Tamma, V. & Wooldridge, M. (2006). Towards service-oriented ontology-based coordination, *Proceedings of IEEE International Conference on Web Services*, pp. 265–274

Naumenko, A. (2007). Semantics-based access control – Ontologies and feasibility study of policy enforcement function, *Proceedings of 3rd ACM International Conference on Web Information Systems and Technologies, Vol. Internet Technologies*, pp. 150–155

Rao, A. (1996). AgentSpeak(L): BDI agents speak out in a logical computable language, *Proceddings of 7th European Workshop on Modelling Autonomous Agents in a Multi-Agent World, LNCS vol.1038*, pp. 42–55

Rao, A. & Georgeff, M. (1991). Modeling rational agents within a BDI architecture, *Proceedings of 2nd International Conference on Principles of Knowledge Representation and Reasoning*, pp. 473–484

Shvaiko, P. & Euzenat, J. (2008). Ten challenges for ontology matching, *Proceedings of 7th Conference on Ontologies, Databases, and Applications of Semantics*

Tamma, V., Aart, C., Moyaux, T., Paurobally, S., Lithgow-Smith, B. & Wooldridge, M. (2005). An ontological framework for dynamic coordination, *Proceedings of 4th Semantic Web Conference, LNCS vol. 3729*, pp. 638–652

Tamma, V. & Payne, T. (2008). Is a Semantic web agent a knowledge-savvy agent? *IEEE Intelligent Systems*, Vol. 23, No.4, pp. 82–85

W3C (2008). *SPARQL Query Language for RDF*, W3C Recommendation 15 January 2008, online: http://www.w3.org/TR/rdf-sparql-query/

9

Leveraging Semantic Web Computing for Context-Aware Software Engineering Environments

Roy Oberhauser
Aalen University
Germany

1. Introduction

The increasing and ongoing need for and reliance on software in almost all industries, coupled with increasing code volume and complexity and changing technologies, results in increasing productivity pressure on software engineers to deliver greater software functionality within stringent cost, time, and quality constraints. Moreover, the software maintenance phase is affected by these pressures, and new approaches are also needed for improving the efficiency and effectiveness of corrective and progressive maintenance activities. The nature of many software engineering (SE) projects, especially in small and medium enterprises (SMEs), often undergo rapid technology, tool, and process changes. Although coupled with ever shorter delivery cycles, this area has, however, not yet lent itself to the type of optimization that business process management (BPM) has succeeded in achieving in other industries and disciplines. It is somewhat ironic that software and IT technology has played a significant role in achieving results for BPM, yet the application to SE processes has not succeeded. Among the various challenges, software engineering environments (SEEs) typically consist of heterogeneous tool environments not optimally tuned to leveraging the semantic value of data that become available in these SEEs during a SE project.

Computer-Aided Software Engineering (CASE) tools are software applications that support software engineering activities within a software development process. Due to the incessant lack of standardization in data formats, interfaces, protocols, and agreed upon (common) data models, tools have typically been created with their own internal interaction and data model paradigms. Yet the focus of industry on BPM systems (BPMS) via Enterprise Application Integration (EAI) with Service-Oriented Architecture (SOA) has fueled a wide adoption of web service (WS) toolkits, and has recently had a ripple effect in SE with an increasing provision of RESTful and SOAP-based WS access to tool functionality and data. However, the access to this functionality and data has not been exploited via Semantic Web (SemWeb) technologies, and herein lies potential. SemWeb adds machine-processable semantics to data (Berners-Lee et al., 2001). SemWeb computing (SWC) allows for greater and improved automation and integration of information due to its formal structuring of information, clearly defined meanings and properties of domain concepts, and standardized exchange formats. The application of SWC within a confined heterogeneous SEE setting where external interchange of data is not a primary concern can provide certain advantages, for example for context-aware computing (CAC).

This chapter explores CoSEEEK (Context-aware Software Engineering Environment Event-driven frameworK), a hybrid semantic web computing approach towards improved context-aware SEEs. The approach is based on an event-based computing paradigm, utilizing multi-agent computing for active SE processing components. Space-based computing is used as a common data repository, decoupling the interaction and data of tools and agents and supporting heterogeneous and flexible configurations. A process-aware information system (PAIS) is utilized to support adaptable SE processes, giving SE engineers process support while supporting the degree of adaptability appropriate for the organization. A conjunction of paradigms enables CAC to be applied in heterogeneous SEE settings and exhibit proactive and reactive behaviors that can improve the effectiveness and efficiency of SEEs. The hybrid SemWeb focus avoids the perhaps unjustifiable time and resource investments that a comprehensive integration would require for the tool, artifact, person, process, project, measure, practice, event, and data models in an SEE along with the inevitable continual changes, while leveraging the noticeable benefits for software engineers in responsiveness of the SEE. The experimental results validate the current feasibility and potential benefits that such a distributed, decentralized, event-based, hybrid semantic web approach can bring to SEEs. The chapter is organized as follows: section 2 reviews the current literature; section 3 discusses the requirements and constraints; section 4 describes the solution approach while section 5 details a current realization; section 6 then discusses the results which are followed by a conclusion in section 7.

2. Literature Review

With regard to SE tool interoperability in SEEs, one attempt at standardization was the Portable Common Tool Environment (H-PCTE) ISO/IEC 13719:1998, "a distributed object management system (OMS) standardized by ISO/IEC and ECMA which is intended to be used as a basis of distributed software development environments (SDE), or, more generally, distributed document editing systems." It specifies various services such as data management, schema management, access and concurrency controls, notifications, and bindings for C, Ada, and IDL (CORBA). At this point it is not relevant to the industry, as no commonly used SE tools today utilize or promote this or alternative standards.

(Arbaoui et al., 2002) and (Gruhn, 2002) provide an overview of Process-Centered Software Engineering Environments (PCSEEs). (Adams et al., 2006) describes worklets, a SOA-based extensible repertoire of self-contained sub-processes aligned to each task, from which a dynamic runtime selection is made depending on the context of the particular work instance. An example of a metamodel-based PCSEE framework is OPEN (Object-oriented Process, Environment and Notation), which addressed business, quality, model, and reuse issues (Henderson-Sellers, 2002) and is based on CORBA and not on WS. It has not been active since 2006. Another example is DiME, which is a proprietary, integrated, collaborative environment for managing product definition, development and delivery processes and information (Koenig, 2003).

As to integration of SemWeb technologies in the SE lifecycle, (Oberhauser & Schmidt, 2007) discuss a holistic approach. (Calero et al., 2006) includes ontology work on SWEBOK (Software Engineering Body of Knowledge), software maintenance, software measurement, and other related SE ontologies. (Happel & Seedorf, 2006) describe the application of ontologies in SE and a framework for classifying them. With regard to software artifacts, (Bontcheva & Sabou, 2006) present an ontology learning approach that exploits a range of information sources associated with software projects. Work utilizing the Semantic Web for automated software engineering purposes includes (Dinger et al., 2006).
While it appears that relatively little work on context-aware SEEs has been done, much work regarding context-awareness has been done in the area of ubiquitous and pervasive computing, e.g., (Ferscha et al., 2004). Examples of frameworks for building context-aware applications include the Java Context-Awareness Framework (JCAF) (Bardram, 2005) and the ContextToolkit (Dey & Abowd, 2000). Considering the combination of SWC with CAC, (Adi et al., 2000) describe a semantic data modeling approach for situation detection that defines and describes events and their relationships to other events, objects, and tasks. (Christopoulou et al., 2005) describe Context Meta-Model (CMM), an ontology-based three layer metamodel for context with a formal mapping to OWL DL.

3. Requirements and Constraints

For creating a solution approach for context-aware SEEs, specific requirements and constraints must be considered. As shown in the context diagram of Fig. 1, for typical SE projects, artifacts are retained in a configuration management (CM) tool-based repository, e.g., CVS, Subversion, etc., and thus changes to artifacts can be readily detected and SE events can be generated. People involved in SE activities interact with the SEE primarily via the use of SE tools (shown as SE Tool Services), and to support context-awareness these interactions should generate SE events transparently. SE actions may also be directed to appropriate SE tools or tool services. Other project-specific inputs into the SEE are tailored SE processes, workflows, and best practices, as well as general and domain-specific SE knowledge and quality assurance methods.

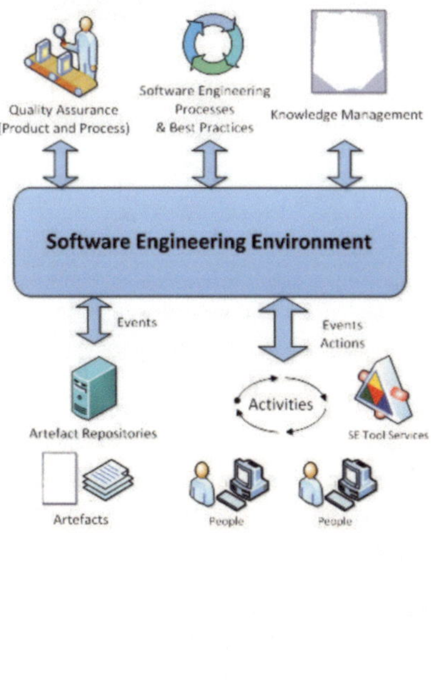

Fig. 1. SEE context diagram

While numerous and various requirements for a context-aware SEE may be considered due to the diversity in SEEs, the following general requirements were important to shaping the solution approach (the square brackets below indicate the abbreviated form):

- Automatic selection of proposed quality measures should be based on contextual problems or risks [Req:AutoQM]
- Quality measures should be adjusted based on new events and states across the project [Req:QMAdj]
- Automated project task assignment for a software engineer should be based on task difficulty (which maps to skill level), employee availability, and roles [Req:AutoTask]
- Tasks to be performed by a software engineer shall be adjusted based on context within the realm of constraints allowed in the process workflow [Req:TaskAdj]
- The black-box view of solution use cases should demonstrate context-awareness not otherwise currently easily provided [Req:BlackBox]
- Support for heterogeneous operating systems and SE tool implementations [Req:Heterog]
- Avoid internal access to SE tools [Req:Encap]
- Support for distributed SEEs [Req:Dist]

4. CoSEEEK Solution Approach

To achieve improved and more holistic solutions for SEEs, the CoSEEEK approach is a synthesis of various areas of computing shown in (Fig. 2), specifically semantic web computing (SWC), service-oriented computing (SOC), space-based computing (SBC), multi-agent computing (MAC), event-based computing (EBC), complex-event processing (CEP), context-aware computing (CAC), rule-based computing (RBC), and process-aware information systems (PAIS). These will be discussed below.

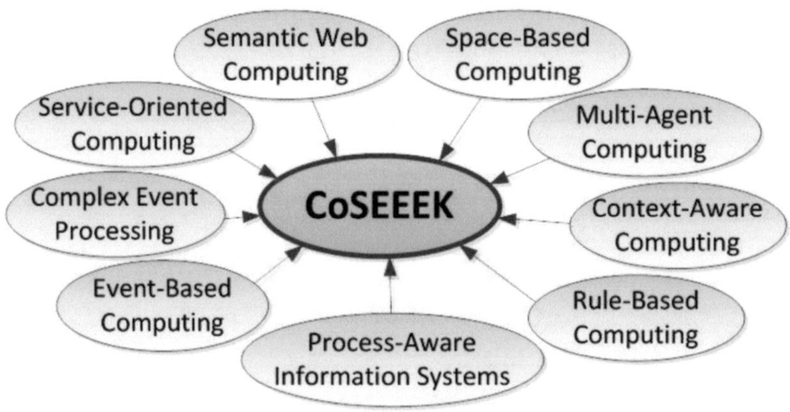

Fig. 2. The CoSEEEK synergistic solution approach to SEE

Semantic web computing, with its formal structuring of information and machine-processable semantics, has the potential to improve SE automation and information integration. One of the issues facing SWC is the creation and adoption of standardized ontologies in OWL (Web

Ontology Language) (Horrocks et al., 2004) for the various industry domains to precisely define the semantic meaning of the domain-specific concepts. The additional modeling effort incurred by ontologies must result in savings elsewhere (Oberle, 2006). Coupled with customized SEEs needs and the rapidly changing and specialized nature of many SE tools, a transitional hybrid stage is proposed. CoSEEEK utilizes the advantages of the distributed and heterogeneous support OWL provides, and relies on defining the semantic meaning of a common subset of the key concepts necessary to adjust quality measures, project task assignments, or workflows based on events within a shared agent-accessible context.

Service-oriented computing, with its reliance on Web Services (WS), provides platform-neutral integration for arbitrary applications (Alonso et al., 2003). The advantages of WS for SE are discussed in (Dinger et al., 2006). Some SE tools already support WS via SOAP or REST, and this access to data and functionality produced or consumed by the SEE tools can be leveraged, e.g., by agents, for enhanced collaboration and distributed data exchange across heterogeneous services in a loosely-coupled fashion. All CoSEEEK inter-process communication is via WS in support of [Req:Dist] and [Req:Heterog].

Space-based computing is a powerful paradigm for coordinating autonomous processes by accessing tuples (an ordered set of typed fields) in a distributed shared memory (called a tuple space) via messaging (Gelernter, 1985), thereby exhibiting linear scalability properties by minimizing shared resources. Work on semantic enhancement of tuple spaces includes sTuples (Khushraj et al., 2004), which extends the object-oriented JavaSpace implementation (Freeman et al., 1999) with an object field of type DAML-OIL Individual. (Tolksdorf et al., 2005) and (Tolksdorf et al., 2005a) describe work on Semantic Tuple Spaces. The Triple Space Computing (TSC) project[1] aims to develop a communication and coordination framework for the WSMX Semantic Web Service platform (Bussler et al., 2005) (Simperl, 2007). CoSEEEK leverages a non-SemWeb XML-based SBC to support a common shared context accessible by loosely-coupled agents. This also supports [Req:Dist] [Req:Heterog] as well as the hybrid SemWeb approach.

Multi-agent computing or Multi-Agent Systems (MAS) have been researched extensively[2] [3]. Agent-based event management approaches includes Sense, Think & Act (ST&A), which exhibits function-driven, goal-driven (local goals), and collaborative goal-driven (global goals) behaviors. Tool-specific agents are used to invoke tool functionality, retrieve data, or provide event sources. In CoSEEEK, the agents are employed in the style of the blackboard architecture pattern (Hayes-Roth, 1985); thus agents do not interact directly, resulting in loose-coupling and functional flexibility. SBC is utilized and events are placed in spaces where subscribing agents are notified of changes. This supports [Req:Encap] and [Req:Dist].

Event-based computing allows the flow of the software functionality to be determined by events, supporting context-awareness with temporal data and allowing reactive and proactive behaviors. Proactive in this sense is behavior that is preventative in regard to SE problems, and may still be a response to some event and not necessarily self-triggered.

Complex event processing (Luckham, 2002) or event stream processing (ESP) is a concept to deal with meaningful event detection and processing using pattern detection, event

---

[1] http://tsc.deri.at

[2] *The Journal of Autonomous Agents and Multiagent Systems*, Publisher: Springer Science+Business Media B.V.

[3] *Whitestein Series in Software Agent Technologies and Autonomic Computing*, published by Springer Science+Business Media Group

correlation, and other techniques to detect complex events from simpler events. With CoSEEEK, once complex events are detected, workflow adjustments can be made in a PAIS, and developers are informed about changes via Task Management.

Context-aware computing is concerned with the acquisition of context (e.g., using sensors to perceive a situation), the abstraction and understanding of context (e.g., matching a perceived sensory stimulus to a context), and application behavior based on the recognized context (e.g., triggering actions based on context) (Schmidt, 2003). Event Condition Actions (ECA) is enabled via a semantic reasoner. CoSEEEK utilizes CAC to support the requirements [Req:AutoQM][Req:QMAdj][Req:AutoTask][Req:BlackBox].

In *rule-based computing* a collection of rules is applied to a collection of facts via pattern matching using efficient algorithms such as Rete (Forgy, 1982). It may be advantageous with regard to the transitional hybrid SemWeb support that non-context-specific rules (e.g., artifact quality rules) be maintained separately. CoSEEEK sees advantages to utilizing RBC for such purposes, for example triggering quality events at certain thresholds. This also reduces the ontology complexity.

Process-aware information systems separate process logic from application code while avoiding data- or function- centricity. Workflow management systems (van der Aalst & van Hee, 2002) can be viewed as an enabling PAIS technology, whereas a key feature of PAIS is to support process change (Reichert & Dadam, 1997; Müller et al., 2004; Pesic et al., 2007). Since SE in a project setting is in view for this chapter, the uniqueness of each project and the complexity will likely cause unforeseen changes to become necessary in a subset of SE processes. The CoSEEEK approach utilizes PAIS to support the requirement for adaptable SE processes [Req:TaskAdj].

The combination of these various computing paradigms enhances the ability of the CoSEEEK approach to deal with various difficulties that arise in supporting context-aware SEEs while fulfilling the requirements. The following discussion describes considerations regarding the key aspects of event processing, the conceptual architecture, and the context model.

4.1 Event Processing

Due to the very heterogeneous nature of SE tooling, today's available tools are typically built with an information island mentality, and at best integration into a widely-used IDE (Integrated Development Environment) is considered, e.g., Eclipse[4]. Given the lack of standards and support for sourcing tool SE events, various techniques such as proxies, tool agents, plugins, or wrappers may be used to generate such SE events.

As illustrated in Fig. 3, events from SE tooling are acquired and then stored in the common space, where it may optionally be annotated with any relevant contextual information by any agent after this point. Event processing mainly includes CEP to detect higher level events. Agents with subscriptions to the space are notified if appropriate, and proactive and reactive behaviors are supported. This may result in workflow adjustment, and the software engineer is informed of a change in tasks or measures via task management. The responses and actions by software engineers to task management via SE tools cause further event acquisition, and so on.

[4] http://eclipse.org

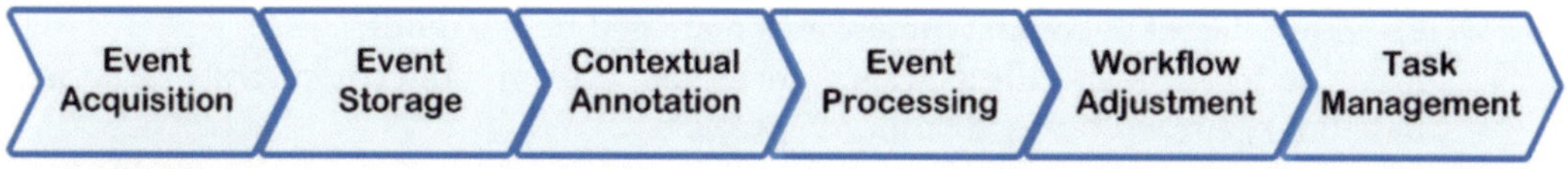

Fig. 3. Event flow

4.2 Solution Architecture

The conceptual view of the CoSEEEK solution architecture is shown in Fig. 4. *Artifacts* is a placeholder for the artifacts that are produced or used in a software project. These are accessed usually via tools directly or indirectly on a file system. *SE Tools* is a placeholder for independent development and testing tools that are tied into CoSEEEK. *Agents* provides behavior agents as well as management agents for each SE tool and CoSEEEK process for application control and integration in the architecture. The *Event Extraction* consists primarily of event sensors and data collection for SE tools. *Data Storage* provides event and data storage in a loosely-coupled fashion via an XML Space implementation. This allows CoSEEEK (e.g., the agents) to be reactive to event or data changes and still be loosely-coupled, thus enabling integration without dependencies. *Event Processing* applies CEP and any contextual annotation to events. *Process Management* is aware of and responsible for SE process conformance of activities and supports adaptive task management. *Context Management* contains a semantic reasoner that tracks and adapts the context as needed and generates appropriate events to initiate behavior. The *SemWeb Integration* module is OWL-aware and is responsible for loading, storing, and synchronizing OWL between the space and the Context Management module, e.g., using Jena or Protégé generated Data Access Objects (DAOs).

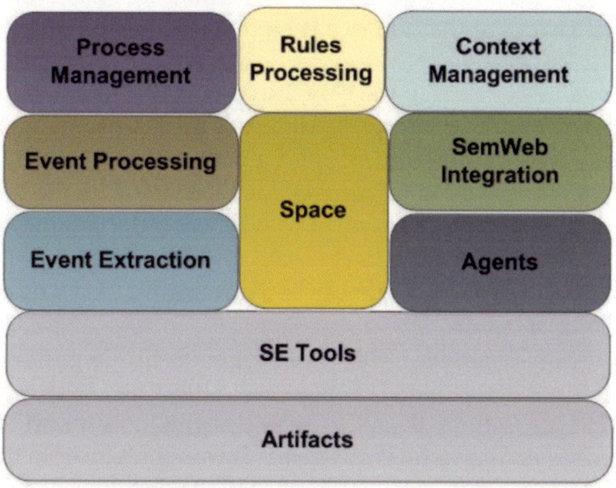

Fig. 4. Conceptual view of CoSEEEK architecture

4.3 Context Model

The context model developed for CoSEEEK will be described in conformance with the context model analysis framework presented in (Bolchini et al., 2007) and is summarized in Table 1.

Modeled aspects are the set of context dimensions managed by the model:

- *Space*: no location-specific aspects were as yet necessary, but could easily be added to handle geographically distributed projects.
- *Time*: temporal aspects are managed, e.g., the timeframes allowed or available for certain tasks or quality measures.
- *Absolute/relative space and time*: Both absolute and relative time aspects are needed. The absolute time is needed for logging and archival purposes as well as supporting traceability. Relative time is used for determining the time available for tasks or measures.
- *Context history*: The context history is used as experience to adjust and improve current and future relations between problems, risks, and preemptive and reactive measures
- *Subject*: the point of view of the context is both the user and the application.
- *User profile (Role or Features based):* The profile of the user, e.g., their experience, is considered explicitly in the context.

Representation features are the general characteristics of the model itself:

- *Type of formalism*: Ontology-based
- *Formality level*: OWL-Lite compatibility was achieved and results in the best performance and computability characteristics.
- *Flexibility*: the context is bound to the SE domain. However, an adaptation to new SE concepts is supported
- *Variable context granularity*: aspects deal with different abstraction levels, e.g., artifacts, activities, persons, and the project.
- *Valid context constraints*: the number of admissible contexts is constrained, e.g., a person executes an activity within a project

Context management and usage refers to the way the context is built, managed and exploited:

- *Context construction:* the context description is built centrally at design-time, rather than dynamic run-time agreement among partners.
- *Context reasoning*: reasoning on context data is enabled by the model to infer properties. Current usage is however rule-based, but inference of new facts is foreseen for future usage.
- *Context quality monitoring*: the quality of the retrieved context information is not considered or managed.
- *Ambiguity/Incompleteness management*: ambiguous, incoherent or incomplete context information is not interpolated or mediated. Only valid data is accepted.
- *Automatic learning features*: the model was designed to support this aspect, and although it does not yet exhibit automatic learning features in the currently supported use cases, this is desirable and will be developed in the future
- *Multi-context model*: All contexts are represented in a single central model instance, with the advantage that the reasoning has access to all the possible data.

In summary, the essence of the CoSEEEK approach is the conjointment of the computing paradigms of Fig. 2. The event processing flow, the space-centric solution architecture, and the SEE-specific context model elaborate on how these can be combined in order to fulfill the requirements for SEEs described in section 3.

Category	**Context**
Space	Future
Time	Supported
Space/Time coordinates (Relative or Absolute)	A,R
Context history	Supported
Subject (User or Application)	Projects, Activities, Artifacts Employees, Risks, Problems, Measures
User profile (Role or Features based)	Supported
Variable context granularity	Supported
Valid context constraints	Supported
Type of formalism	Ontology via OWL
Formality level	OWL-Lite or OWL-DL
Flexibility	Only within the domain
Context construction (Distributed or Centralized)	Centralized
Context reasoning	Future
Context quality monitoring	-
Ambiguity/Incompleteness mgmt.	-
Automatic learning features	Future
Multi-context model	-

Table 1. CoSEEEK context model support

5. Solution Realization

The primary focus of the initial solution realization was sufficient technical validation of the CoSEEEK approach.

5.1 Realization Requirements

For a realization of CoSEEEK, further requirements were elaborated and an extract thereof is listed in simplified form:

- Utilization of OpenUP[5] for SE processes in the PAIS. OpenUP is a lean Unified Process that applies iterative and incremental approaches within a structured SE lifecycle.
- Generate dynamic checklist items based, e.g., on code complexity and test coverage
- Assignment of quality measures:
    - Effort (Low/Med/Hi) can be different conceptual instances with any granularity (e.g., person hours, Low/Med/Hi, or based on a worker formula) and can be made equivalent for a query.
    - Assign an artifact review if quality rules triggered a quality event and the risk is high. If time allows within the iteration, assign an inspection.
    - Assign refactoring as needed
    - Quality measures for the future (list of open measures)
- Remember problems and unfinished measures.
- Report "Top 10" problems periodically.
- Considers person availability
- Suggests proactive measures (for risks) and reactive measures (for problems)
- Developer receives notifications via emforge and mylyn, including checklists
- Web Service-based XML Space implementation with different collections for events, context, and the ontology

Following are some key functional scenarios that incorporate a subset of the above context-aware requirements. The Automatic Assignment Scenario Fig. 5 assigns a qualified worker to a task based on their role, skill level, and current availability. SOC is supported for direct assignment retrieval by a tool.

In the automatic quality measure scenario of Fig. 6, a new problem event is generated and placed in the Space, e.g., by the Rules Processing Agent, whereby the Context Management is notified due to its Space subscription and retrieves and processes the event. SemWeb Integration is used to instantiate a new problem in the ontology. The semantic reasoner is then invoked which has a rule that is triggered when a Problem exists with the status new in the ontology. A countermeasure is chosen based on various criteria and the ontology in the Space is synchronized via SemWeb Integration. Other subscribed agents are notified of an ontology change and may then respond to the new measures, e.g., the rule agent.

[5] http://epf.eclipse.org/wikis/openup/

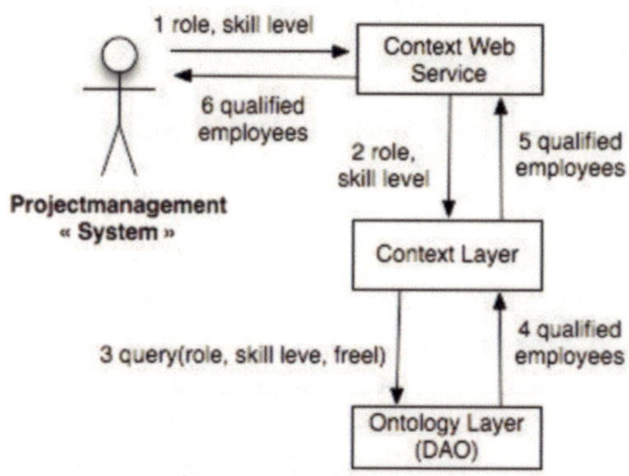

Fig. 5. Context-aware automatic assignment scenario [Req:AutoTask]

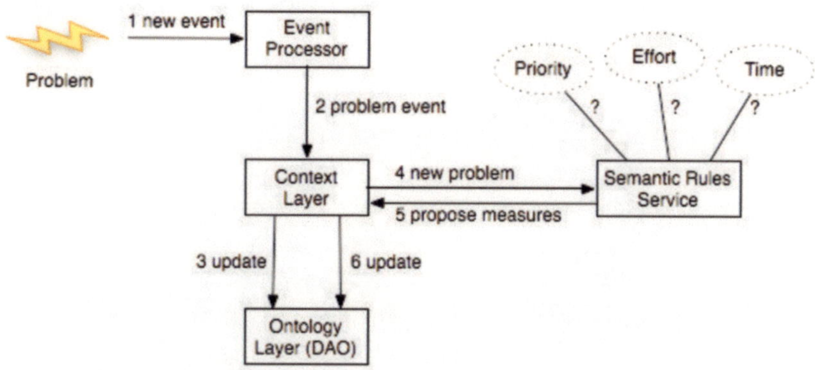

Fig. 6. Context-aware automatic quality measure scenario [Req:AutoQM]

In the scenario of Fig. 7, a list of the top 10 problems may be retrieved via SOC, for display by a tool.

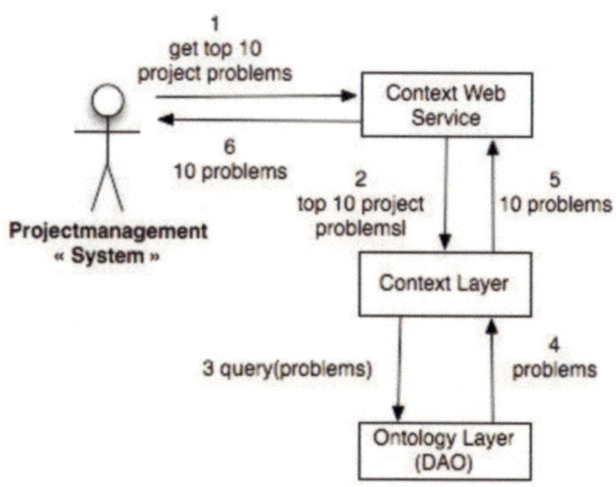

Fig. 7. Context-aware top 10 problems [Req:Top10]

5.2 Implementation Architecture

The CoSEEEK Implementation Architecture is shown in Fig. 8. The *Artifacts* consist of source code and test code. The *SE Tools* consisted of Eclipse as a representative for Integrated Development Environments (IDEs), JUnit[6] to represent SE test tools, Subversion[7] to represent version control systems for artifacts, PMD[8] and Metrics[9] for static analysis tools, and EmForge[10] and Mylyn[11] for task management tools. *Event Extraction* utilized Hackystat sensors (Johnson, 2007) for event extraction, an agent forwarding the events to the XML Space implementation which uses eXist[12] as a storage backend. *Event Processing* utilized Esper[13] for CEP. As an agent platform, WADE (Workflows and Agents Development Environment) was used (Caire et al., 2008). With regard to *Process Management*, ADEPT2 (Dadam et al., 2007) was utilized as PAIS technology. *Rules Processing* was performed by Drools[14]. For *Context Management* and semantic reasoning, the Rete-based inference engine Bossam (Jang & Sohn, 2004) was employed. It supports reasoning over OWL and SWRL ontologies and RuleML rules. *SemWeb Integration* for loading, storing, and synchronizing OWL between the space and the Context Management module was achieved using Java-based Data Access Objects (DAOs) generated using the Protégé ontology editor.

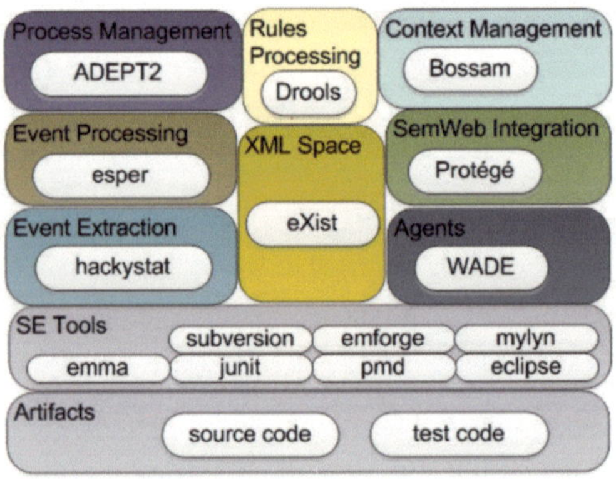

Fig. 8. CoSEEEK implementation architecture

No suitable XML Space implementation was found, thus an XML Space was realized in keeping with SOC using Apache CXF[15] for SOAP-based WS and eXist as a backend. Since in CoSEEEK SBC is used for storage, retrieval, and change notification of key shared data such as events, context, and ontologies, its performance was evaluated in section 6.

[6] http://junit.org
[7] http://subversion.tigris.org
[8] http://pmd.sourceforge.net
[9] http://metrics.sourceforge.net/
[10] http://www.emforge.org
[11] http://www.eclipse.org/mylyn/
[12] http://exist.sourceforge.net/
[13] http://esper.codehaus.org
[14] http://www.jboss.org/drools/
[15] http://cxf.apache.org/

5.3 Leveraging CAC and SWC

To achieve context-awareness, an analysis of common SE concepts was performed and then incorporated into the ontology shown in Fig. 9. The modeling focused on high-value and reusable SE concepts such as activities, problems, risks, and quality measures and practices. Relations to artifacts are used, but artifact details are maintained outside of the ontology. Tools are minimally modeled in their relation to events.

The concept of a Template was introduced for denoting prescribed relationships and properties, e.g., by predefined processes such as OpenUP. A Template contains generic metadata such as preconditions, postconditions, required artifacts, produced artifacts, responsible roles, etc.

For example, an instance of the ActivityTemplate would have this specific metadata for "Design the Solution" activity. Once this activity is actually started, an Activity class is instantiated that is based on this ActivityTemplate (and remains after completion for historical context). This allows a comparison of the actual activity state vs. the prescribed state and allows common problems and risks associated with the activity to be tied to the ActivityTemplate, while real problems are tied to the Activity instance.

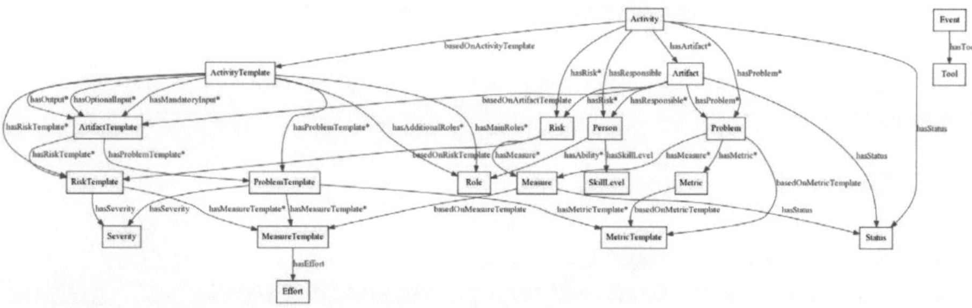

Fig. 9. CoSEEEK implemented ontology

The SemWeb Integration and Context Management design components are shown in Fig. 10, while Fig. 11 shows the dynamic interactions for an activity event with ontology synchronization and context processing.

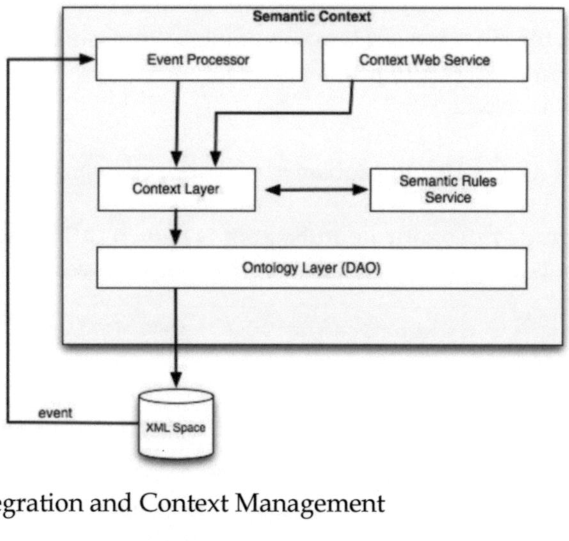

Fig. 10. SemWeb Integration and Context Management

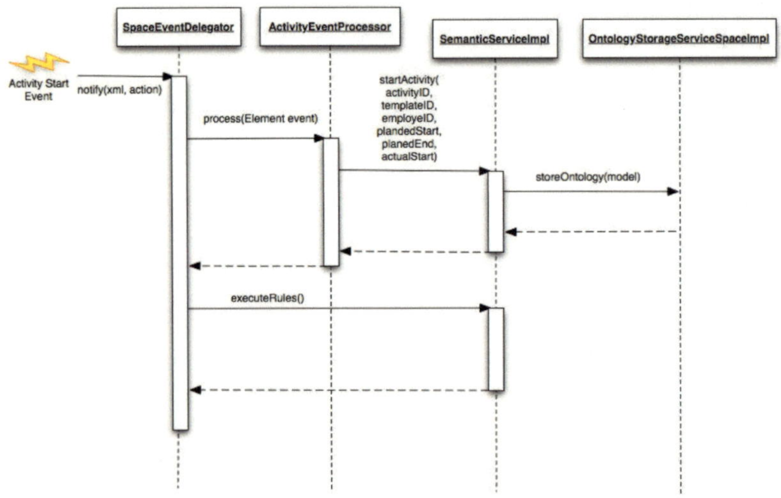

Fig. 11. Activity event ontology update and context processing

Events necessary to support the prescribed level of context-awareness had the following contextual relevance:

Activity Begin and End events:
- Logging
- Relevant for task assignment
- Provides the current context for a person and the project

Artifact Begin and End events:
- Logging
- Relevant for task assignment
- Provides the current context for a person and the project

New Problem event:
- Logging
- Triggers the automatic suggestion of quality measures
- Relevant for the Top 10 problems

Completed Measure event:
- Logging
- Relevant for the Top 10 problems

An example of a semantic reasoner rule in Bossam is shown in Listing 1. This rule ensures that a quality measure is assigned when a new problem is detected.

```
reasoner.tell("rule ruleMeasuresForNewProblems is"
+ " if Problem(?p) and sem:class(?o)"
+ " and hasProblemStatus(?p, ?status) and
[?status=problemStatus_New]"
+ " and hasProblem(?thing, ?p)"
+ " then sem:assignMeasureForNewProblem(?o, ?p, ?thing)");
```

Listing 1. Example context-based quality measure assignment rule

5.4 Leveraging rule-based computing

The rules engine Drools was used to address areas where semantic-agnostic rules excel, e.g., to assess the quality of artifacts or to generate dynamic checklists. The rules engine does not have direct access to Context Management, but rather to non-SWC context that is available to all agents in the XML Space. This separation of responsibilities allows context-centric processing not to be burdened with tool-specific and lower-level quality processing functionality, and thus permit the focus on ontology-centric higher-level intricate context and relation-centric support via SWC. This is the essence of the hybrid SWC approach in CoSEEEK, leveraging SWC technologies for common and high-value SE areas as seen in the ontology of Fig. 9. Benefits include lower maintenance and training costs compared to comprehensive SWC.

For the realization, events generated by Hackystat sensors due to invocation of the PMD and Metrics tools causes the rule agent to take the output of the tools in XML form and transform them via XSLT into an intermediate simplified XML form for parsing by the rule engine. Any negative results cause the artifact context in the space to be adjusted with the actual quality problems, see Fig. 13 for an example.

```
- <context category="Artifact" id="artifact_3" type="Code">
  - <recipients>
      <recipient email="foo.bar@xy.com" language="en"/>
      <recipient email="blubb.bar@xy.com" language="de"/>
    </recipients>
  - <q-evaluation>
      <risk level="medium"/>
    - <q-measures>
        <q-measure measure="measureTemplate_Review" status="proposed"/>
      </q-measures>
    - <q-checklist>
        <q-checklist-item name="EFGH"/>
        <q-checklist-item name="CCUI"/>
        <q-checklist-item name="CCMN"/>
      </q-checklist>
      <testingNeeded level="Low"/>
      <size>358</size>
    </q-evaluation>
  </context>
```

Fig. 13. Artifact context

The rules primarily determine quality problems, and during checklist generation a map of quality problems to checklist items is referenced with a set of locale-specific checklist items serving as a basis for the natural language checklist items. Quality measures assigned by Context Management are also incorporated when these are not already addressed by task assignment, e.g., assigning refactoring and testing tasks. A dynamic customized checklist is generated in XHTML and a link sent to the software engineer as a task via emforge in order to address the quality issues, see Fig. 14. When the engineer processes the checklist, the XML is archived in a collection in the XML Space.

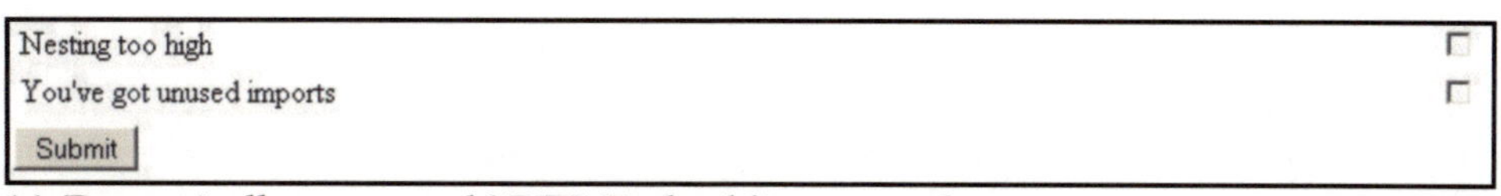

Fig. 14. Dynamically generated XHTML checklist screenshot

The choice of checklist items is dynamically generated, temporally context-dependent and containing items deemed applicable. The software engineer is thus not bothered by irrelevant checklist issues, and as such perceives the SEE as context-aware in regard to quality management behavior [Req:AutoQM][Req:BlackBox].

5.5 Leveraging Process-Awareness

For SEE process support, OpenUP processes were mapped to ADEPT2 process templates as illustrated in the figure below.

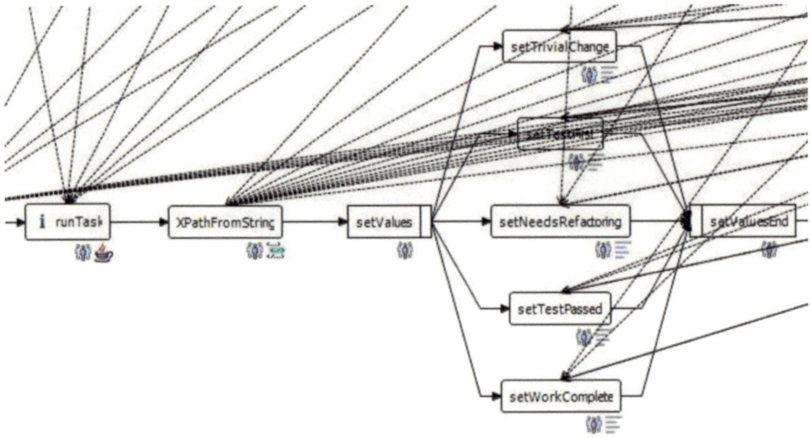

Fig. 15. Start Task Template

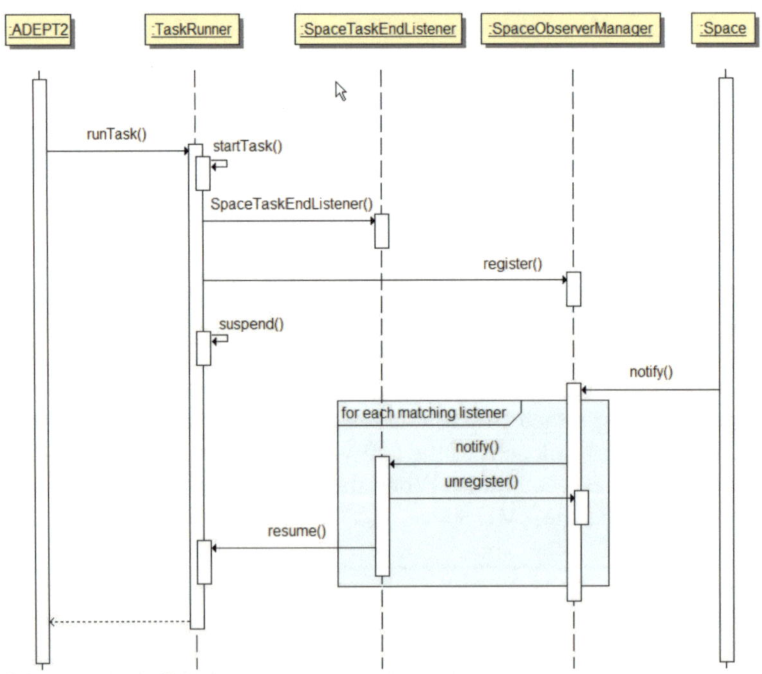

Fig. 16. Task Management Sequence

The ADEPT2 process templates required an integration mechanism to place new tasks events in the Space for retrieval and processing by the EmForge task management agent, and then wait for their notification of task completion. A component TaskRunner was developed that provides two methods: runTask which starts a new task and waits for the end event in the Space, and the method stopTask which removes an open task. A sequence diagram for runTask is shown in the figure below.
The software engineer perceives changes in the IDE, in this case Mylyn displays the emforge task list as shown below. Any changes to the tasks or usage of tools by the software engineer generate events that adjust the context and possibly process and may result in task adjustments. Since CoSEEEK is aware of all open tasks, and to allow for assignment flexibility and maintain focus, the software engineer typically sees only the current task and optionally next one (to allow for mental preparation and reduce surprises).

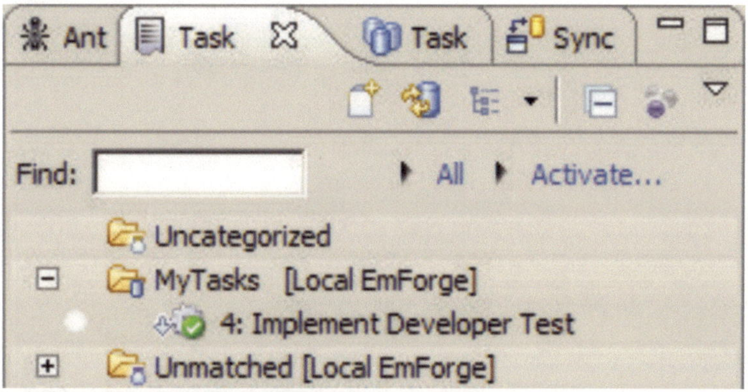

Fig. 17. Mylyn Task List showing OpenUP task via emforge

6. Results

The preliminary results for this research focused on the viability of the CoSEEEK approach, with the realization meeting its functional scenario goals, general requirements, and detailed realization requirements. As to any performance and scalability limitations, the performance evaluation principally has SWC and CAC limitations in view. Due to the centricity and dependency on the new SBC implementation, sufficient performance in this area was also verified.

6.1 SBC Performance

For measuring the SBC performance of the CoSEEEK XML Space implementation, the configuration consisted of 10 AMD Opteron 180 Dual Core 2,4 GHz 3GB PCs running Windows XP Pro SP2, Java JDK 1.6.0_06, and Apache CXF 02.01.03 on a 100MBit/s Ethernet network. 1 PC was configured as the Space server with eXist 1.2.5-rev8668 as a backend. For the read or write operations, up to 8 PCs (each with a client) were used as space clients all performing the same operation. For notifications, 1 PC wrote 1000 events in the space and up to 8 clients received notifications. The measurements were repeated 3 times and the averages presented in the following tables.

Clients	Write time (ms)	% increase	Notification time (ms)	% increase
1	14.0	-	14.7	-
2	14.1	0%	14.4	-2%
4	15.0	7%	15.0	4%
8	17.0	13%	17.0	13%

Table 2. Average notification performance for 1000 events

Clients	Write time (ms)	% increase
1	13.9	-
2	16.3	18%
4	23.0	41%
8	61.7	168%

Table 3. Average write performance for 1000 events

Clients	Read time (ms)	% increase
1	10.7	-
2	9.5	-11%
4	12.4	31%
8	41.8	237%

Table 4. Average read performance for 1000 events

Table 2 shows that notification performance was not significantly affected by an increase in peers, and the scalability is sufficient for SEE purposes. The results for writing into the space in Table 3 show the bottleneck effect of the chosen data consistency limitation of allowing only sequential writes. Since the space is used primarily as a blackboard coordination mechanism, such heavy parallel writing by multiple agents is not expected. Table 4 shows the read performance, but again due to the chosen data consistency mechanism, the reads are synchronized to wait until the write completes, and vice versa. If this becomes a serious bottleneck in industrial settings, various optimizations are possible.

6.2 SWC and CAC Performance

For measuring the semantic reasoner performance and scalability, the test configuration consisted of an Intel Core 2 Duo 2,0 GHz PC running Mac OS X 10.5.6, 2 GB RAM, Java JRE 1.5.0, Bossam 0.9b45, and Protégé 3.3.1. The averages from 3 measurements are shown in the following tables.

```
resultPossibleEmployee = reasoner.ask("query q is Person(?employee)"
+ " and available(?employee, 1)"
+ " and hasAbility(?employee, " + role + ")"
+ " and hasSkillLevel(?employee," + skillLevel + ");");
```

Listing 2. Example context-based task assignment rule

Person instances	Time (ms)	Factor increase in time
10	60	-
100	83	1.4
1000	274	3.3
10000	7397	27.0

Table 5. Query performance vs. person instances

```
resultArtifact=reasoner.ask("query q is Artifact(?artifact)"
+ " and basedOnArtifactTemplate(?artifact, ?template);");
```

Listing 3. Artifact rule

Artifact instances	Time (ms)	Factor increase in time	Factor increase in artifacts
10	55	-	
100	62	1.1	10
1000	137	2.2	10
10000	1578	11.5	10
20000	3936	2.5	2
40000	10793	2.7	2

Table 6. Query performance vs. artifact instances

In the person query, the effect of the multiple conditions shows a larger impact to the performance than for the artifact query for the cases of 100 and 1000 instances. Since overall time was measured, in both cases the jump from 1000 to 10000 instances caused the time to jump from the millisecond range to seconds, at which point operating system multitasking and scheduling may play a more significant factor and account for the anomaly in the factor

increases in time. The 20000 and 40000 artifact instance measurements show that this remains consistent thereafter for larger sets.
Since the current usage of the reasoner and context-awareness is supportive and requires no hard real-time user or system response latencies, these results show that current usage of such an approach for typical SE project sizes with typical SE IT hardware is feasible.

7. Conclusion

To deal with the current and coming challenges facing SE, new approaches for SEEs are needed that coalesce the heterogeneous and distributed tool data and events that occur, contextualize them, and then proact or react to provide software engineers with a cohesive and improved SEEs. While semantic web computing is an obvious candidate, due to the uniqueness of each project context, the advantages of must be weighed against some of the difficulties and the investments required, and a pragmatic hybrid approach may be reasonable in the interim.
The CoSEEEK approach, with its synthesis of various computing paradigms, provides advantages for addressing this situation. The semantic meanings of a common subset of the key concepts are used to adjust quality measures, project task assignments, or workflows based on events within a shared agent-accessible context. Combined with a semantic reasoner, context-aware proactive and reactive behaviors that can improve the effectiveness and efficiency of SEEs are exhibited. The reduced ontology focus avoids the perhaps unjustifiable time and resource investments in SWC that a comprehensive integration would require for the tool, artifact, and data models in an SEE along with their continuous changes, while leveraging the visible benefits in responsiveness of the SEE. Context-aware behavior is perceived by humans via task assignments and dynamically generated checklists.
The event processing flow coupled with the solution architecture provides flexibility and loose-coupling in the processing of events. The current CoSEEEK ontology and context model supported the SE scenarios, and additional ontologies can be incorporated for expanded reasoning if desired. As a side note, by utilizing EDA, RBC, and PAIS, no sequential process logic was needed to support the scenarios, which furthers flexibility and potential reuse and is a key for the adaptability of the infrastructure in ever-changing SEEs. The results validated the current technical feasibility and potential benefits that the CoSEEEK approach can bring to SEEs. Future work includes planned empirical studies of CoSEEEK in SE industrial settings.

8. Acknowledgements

The author thanks Tobias Gaisbauer, Michael Vögeli, and Daniel Sebel for their assistance with the experiments, implementation, and figures.

9. References

Adams, M.; ter Hofstede, A.H. M.; Edmond, D. & van der Aalst, W. M. P. (2006). Worklets: A Service-Oriented Implementation of Dynamic Flexibility in Workflows, In: *Lecture Notes in Computer Science*, Vol. 4275, Springer Berlin / Heidelberg, ISSN 0302-9743

Adi, A.; Borzer, D. & Etzion, O. (2000). Semantic Event Model and its Implication on Situation Detection. In *Proceedings of the Eighth European Conference on Information Systems* (Hansen HR, Bichler M, Mahrer H eds.), Vienna, pp. 320-325

Alonso, G.; Casati, F.; Kuno, H. & Machiraju, V. (2003). *Web Services – Concepts, Architectures and Applications*, Springer Verlag, Berlin

Arbaoui, S.; Derniame, J.; Oquendo, F. & Verjus, H (2002). A Comparative Review of Process-Centered Software Engineering Environments, In: *Annals of Software Engineering*, Vol. 14, Issue 1-4 (December 2002), J. C. Baltzer AG, Science Publishers Red Bank, NJ, USA, ISSN:1022-7091

Bardram, J. (2005). The Java Context Awareness Framework (JCAF) - A Service Infrastructure and Programming Framework for Context-Aware Applications, in *Lecture Notes in Computer Science*, Springer Berlin / Heidelberg, Vol. 3468/2005, ISBN 978-3-540-26008-0

Berners-Lee, T.; Hendler, J. & Lassila, O. (2001). The Semantic Web, *Scientific American*, May 2001, pp. 28-37

Bolchini, C.; Curino, C. A.; Quintarelli, E.; Schreiber, F. A. & Tanca, L. (2007). A data-oriented survey of context models. SIGMOD Rec. 36, 4 (Dec. 2007), pp. 19-26

Bontcheva, K. & Sabou, M. (2006). Learning Ontologies from Software Artifacts: Exploring and Combining Multiple Sources, In: *Proceedings of 2nd International Workshop on Semantic Web Enabled Software Engineering (SWESE 2006)*

Bussler, C.; Kilgarriff, E.; Krummenacher, R.; Martin-Recuerda, F.; Toma, I. & and Sapkota, B. (2005). WSMX Triple-Space Computing, http://wsmo.org/TR/d21/v0.1, June 2005, D21 v0.1

Caire, G.; Gotta, D. & Banzi, M. (2008). WADE: a software platform to develop mission critical applications exploiting agents and workflows. In *Proceedings of the 7th International Joint Conference on Autonomous Agents and Multiagent Systems: Industrial Track*, pp. 29-36.

Calero, C.; Ruiz, F. & Piattini, M. (Eds.) (2006). *Ontologies for Software Engineering and Software Technology*, ISBN: 978-3-540-34517-6

Christopoulou, E.; Goumopoulos, C. & Kameas, A. (2005). An ontology-based context management and reasoning process for UbiComp applications, In: *Proceedings of the 2005 Joint Conference on Smart Objects and Ambient intelligence: innovative Context-Aware Services: Usages and Technologies* (Grenoble, France, October 12 - 14, 2005). sOc-EUSAI '05, vol. 121. ACM, New York, NY, pp. 265-270

Dadam, P.; Reichert, M.; Rinderle, S.; Jurisch, M.; Acker, H.; Göser, K.; Kreher, U. & Lauer, M. (2007). ADEPT2 - Next Generation Process Management Technology. *Heidelberger Innovationsforum*, Heidelberg, April 2007

Dey, A. & Abowd, G. (2000). The Context Toolkit: Aiding the Development of Context-Aware Applications, in *Proceedings of the Workshop on Software Engineering for Wearable and Pervasive Computing*, Limerick, Ireland

Dinger, U.; Oberhauser, R. & Reichel, C. (2006). SWS-ASE: Leveraging Web Service-based Software Engineering, In: *Proceedings of the International Conference on Software Engineering Advances (ICSEA'06)*, IEEE Computer Society Press.

Ferscha, A.; Hechinger, M.; Mayrhofer, R.; dos Santos Rocha, M.; Franz, M.; and Oberhauser, R. (2004). Digital Aura, In: *Advances in Pervasive Computing*, Vol. 176, Austrian Computer Society (OCG), pp. 405-410

Forgy, C. (1982). "Rete: A Fast Algorithm for the Many Pattern/Many Object Pattern Match Problem", *Artificial Intelligence*, 19, pp 17–37, 1982.

Gelernter, D. (1985). Generative communication in Linda, *ACM Transactions on Programming Languages and Systems*, volume 7, number 1, January 1985, pp. 80-112

Gruhn, V. (2002). Process-Centered Software Engineering Environments, A Brief History and Future Challenges, In: *Annals of Software Engineering*, Springer Netherlands, Vol. 14, Numbers 1-4 / (December 2002), J. C. Baltzer AG, Science Publishers Red Bank, NJ, USA. ISSN:1022-7091, pp. 363-382

Happel, H. & Seedorf, S. (2006). Applications of Ontologies in Software Engineering, In: *Proceedings of the Workshop on Semantic Web Enabled Software Engineering (SWESE)* at the 5th International Semantic Web Conference (ISWC 2006)

Hayes-Roth, B. (1985). A blackboard architecture for control, *Artificial Intelligence*, Volume 26, Issue 3 (July 1985), pp. 251-321.

Henderson-Sellers, B. (2002). Process Metamodelling and Process Construction: Examples Using the OPEN Process Framework (OPF), In: *Annals of Software Engineering*, Vol. 14, Issue 1-4, (December 2002), ISSN:1022-7091, pp. 341–362

Horrocks, I.; Patel-Schneider, P.; McGuinness, D. & Welty, C. (2007). OWL: a Description Logic Based Ontology Language for the Semantic Web. In: *The Description Logic Handbook: Theory, Implementation, and Applications (2nd Edition)*, chapter 14. Cambridge University Press

Jang, M. & Sohn, J. (2004). Bossam: an extended rule engine for OWL Inferencing, *Proceedings of RuleML 2004* (LNCS Vol. 3323), Nov. 8, 2004

Johnson, P. (2007). Requirement and Design Trade-offs in Hackystat: An in-process software engineering measurement and analysis system, *Proceedings of the 2007 International Symposium on Empirical Software Engineering and Measurement*, Madrid, Spain, September, 2007.

Khushraj, D.; Lassila, O. & Finin, T. (2004). sTuples: Semantic Tuple Spaces, In: Proceedings of the First Annual International Conference on Mobile and Ubiquitous Systems: Networking and Services (MobiQuitous'04), pp. 268-277

Koenig, S. (2003). Integrated Process and Knowledge Management for Product Definition, Development and Delivery, In: *Proceedings of the IEEE International Conference on Software-Science, Technology & Engineering (SWSTE)*, pp.133

Koenig, Shai (2003). "Integrated Process and Knowledge Management for Product Definition, Development and Delivery," swste, pp. 133, *IEEE International Conference on Software-Science, Technology & Engineering*

Luckham, D. (2002). *The Power of Events - An Introduction to Complex Event Processing in Distributed Enterprise Systems*, Addison-Wesley, ISBN 0-201-72789-7

Müller, R.; Greiner, U. & Rahm, E. (2004). AgentWork: A workflow system supporting rule-based workflow adaptation. *Data and Knowledge Engineering*, 51 (2), pp. 223-256

Oberhauser, R. & Schmidt, R. (2007). Towards a Holistic Integration of Software Lifecycle Processes using the Semantic Web, In: *Proceedings of the 2nd International Conference on Software and Data Technologies (ICSOFT 2007)*, Vol. 3 - Information Systems and Data Management, 2007, pp. 137-144

Oberle, D. (2006). *Semantic Management of Middleware*, The Semantic Web and Beyond, Vol. 1, Springer, New York, ISBN 0387276300

Pesic, M.; Schonenberg, M.; Sidorova, N. & van der Aalst, W. (2007). Constraint-based workflow models: change made easy. In: *Proceedings of the 15th Int'l Conf. on Cooperative Information Systems (CoopIS'07)*, Vilamoura, Algarve, Portugal, LNCS 4803, pp. 77-94

Reichert, M. & Dadam, P. (1997). A framework for dynamic changes in workflow management systems. In: *Proc. 8th Int'l Workshop on Database and Expert Systems Applications*, Toulouse, pp. 42–48.

Schmidt, A. (2003). Ubiquitous Computing - Computing in Context, PhD dissertation, Lancaster University, U.K.

Simperl, E.; Krummenacher, R. & Nixon, L. (2007). A coordination model for triplespace computing, *Proceedings of the 9th International Conference on Coordination Models and Languages (Coordination)*, Springer Verlag, June 2007

Tolksdorf, R.; Bontas, E. P. & Nixon, L. J. (2005). Towards a Tuplespace-Based Middleware for the Semantic Web, *Proceedings of the 2005 IEEE/WIC/ACM international Conference on Web intelligence*, (September 19 - 22, 2005). Web Intelligence. IEEE Computer Society, Washington, DC, pp. 338-344

Tolksdorf, R.; Nixon, L.; Bontas, E. P.; Nguyen, D. M. & Liebsch, F. (2005a). Enabling real world Semantic Web applications through a coordination middleware, *Proceedings of the 2nd European Semantic Web Conf.* ESWC'05, 2005

Van der Aalst, W. & van Hee, K. (2002). Workflow management: models, methods, and systems, MIT Press.

10

Reasoning and Representing Viewpoints on the Semantic Web

Christiana Panayiotou
University of Leeds
UK.

1. Introduction

Pertaining to the process of critical thinking is the ability to analyse, assess and discern different points of view that are either explicitly or implicitly expressed in resources. Examples of explicitly represented viewpoints are viewpoints of historical value expressing standpoints or theses which had been recognised as significant for the development of a given area and are based on known theories and assumptions. Explicit representation and comparison of these viewpoints is particularly useful in the learning domain, where different theories and theses may have been advocated based on different and possibly conflicting contextual assumptions with advantages and disadvantages for each. Exposition of the learner to these theories helps to broaden understanding, enables the learner to construct new knowledge and motivates the critical thinking activity of the learner. Implicitly recorded viewpoints appear as manifestations of evaluative assessments or outcomes of higher cognitive processes, like comparison, decision making, choice etc. Resources on the web are underpinned by ontologies which may be considered as particular theories of the world. Although ontologies were originally intended to be shareable conceptualizations of the world, particular ontologies usually represent only partially a domain and do so in a way that addresses the needs of particular users and reflects the experience, perspective and personal judgment of particular experts. In this case, the viewpoints of the domain experts are implicit to the design of domain knowledge. Differences in points of view inherent in different ontologies may give rise to inconsistencies in the representation of domain knowledge and need to be made explicit. Otherwise, differences in domain representation may be explained as differences in the local meaning of concepts used by different resources rather than positions which may be defended by sound arguments rooted in coherent theories, judgements, assumptions, or other contextual factors narrowing the scope of reasoning.
So, what is a viewpoint (or point view)? Intuitively, we understand a viewpoint as the position held about an issue which may be disputed, supported by a coherent set of beliefs, theory, etc. Obviously, the notion of viewpoint may be used in natural language to express different things, e.g. a spatial viewpoint which refers to what an agent can see from a particular spatial point. There is something common with this interpretation of viewpoint and the viewpoint we discuss in this chapter. The commonality is based on the fact that the

validity of a particular viewpoint may be verified with reference to: The scope of perception of the agent, the actual point where she stands -this would mean cognitive state, mental state, attitude etc, the ability to place herself relative to the surrounding objects and reflect on her relative position, the ability to place herself outside this setting and compare with other viewpoints. A viewpoint in this chapter is represented as a structure consisting of a set of statements, a distinct formula representing the position or standpoint of the viewpoint, the resource of the assertions, axioms, rules, etc from which a viewpoint derives its position, a set of arguments defending the position, any set of relevant assumptions and the vocabulary used in the viewpoint. As argued in (Panayiotou & Dimitrova, 2007), awareness of a position or viewpoint does not necessarily imply agreement with it. An agent may accept more than one points of view without necessarily supporting a particular one. Also, for the purposes of this chapter we make the assumption, that the beliefs of an agent are consistent, and an agent may believe at most one position about a particular topic of dispute. Further we assume that each resource is consistent.

In (Panayiotou & Bennett, 2009 : © 2009 IEEE), the notion of reason was defined as a propositional modal logic formula. The intention of the definition of reason there, was to represent the situation where the truth of a proposition is sufficient to deduce the truth of another proposition. Also, in (Panayiotou & Bennett, 2008) we addressed the problem of necessary and sufficient conditions for the classification of an object: if an individual of the domain satisfies a set of properties that sufficiently define a class then the individual belongs to that class. Satisfaction of sufficient conditions (properties) may be interpreted as another way of expressing the fact that a formula a reason for deducing a classification. So, reason, can be used to represent this situation too. Propositional logic is not expressive enough to capture the types of discrepancies that can arise in concept definitions and individual classification problems. The alternative would be to use a modal logic approach. First order modal logic approaches need careful consideration with regard to domain assumptions over quantified formulas. For example, the intuitive interpretation of the Barcan formula (Blackburn et al., 2001) requires that it is valid in case where the (possible) worlds' domains are invariant.

An alternative to the modal approach has been a purely syntactic approach. The syntactic approach has attracted much interest and has been used to address the problem of relativized truth. McCarthy (McCarthy, 1994), and Konolige (Konolige, 1983), were among the first who experimented with the syntactic approach. Giunchiglia and Serafini (Giunchiglia & Serafini, 1994) argued that problems encountered by modal logic can be avoided by using Multilanguage logical systems (ML) (Serafini & Giunchiglia, 2000). Moreover, they proved that the theorems of the most common modal logics can be embedded into their corresponding ML systems. ML systems also follow a syntactic approach to relativized truth of formulas resulting from hierarchical models (Serafini & Giunchiglia, 2000; Giunchiglia & Serafini, 1994). The notion of viewpoint is relevant to the notion of context and relativized truth: In order to evaluate a viewpoint it is necessary to evaluate the truth of its formulas with respect to its local vocabulary definition, assumptions and theoretical underpinnings, in the context in which valuation takes place. Context-based reasoning has its roots in reasoning with micro-theories (Guha, 1991). Contexts are local models describing a local view about a domain. Microtheories and local contexts can be reused to provide information and draw inferences in other contexts (Guha, 1991). The same applies to viewpoints. Unlike theories and contexts which are assumed to be complete and use the closed world assumption (CWA) to draw inferences, ontologies underpinning resources on the web are assumed to be incomplete. This raises new challenges with regard to deciding the compatibility of different points view of resources where either assertions or axioms important for checking compatibility are missing from some of them. The rest of the chapter is outlined as follows. Section 2 discusses some basic notions concerning ontology entailment and reasons.

2. Background

In (Panayiotou & Bennett, 2009; © 2009 IEEE) we defined a language L_{ARG} of argumentation using propositional logic. L_{ARG} uses the notion of reason to account for sentences of the form 'p is a reason for q', represented as $(p \hookrightarrow q)$ where p and q are propositions. Intuitively, a reason is an instance of a rule $A \Rightarrow B$ where all variables in the formula schemata A and B are instantiated and which, in natural language takes the form of an IF ... THEN statement. Propositional logic, may be extended to allow for formulas of the form: $Q \Rightarrow P$ where Q and P represent propositional formula schemata. The double arrow notation aims to show that a rule in strict sense cannot be described as a material conditional. For example, $A \Rightarrow B$ would not make sense if B was always true independently of A. In order to be able to determine how reasons are related, we need to determine the syntax and semantics of the language in which reasons and rules are represented. In Description Logics (DL) inclusion terminological axioms may be considered as rules whose formulas may be expressed in first-order logic. For example, for any two atomic concepts A, and B such that $A \sqsubseteq B$, we may derive the rule $A(x) \Rightarrow B(x)$. It is also important to be able to determine conflicting formulas. For example if DL is used and the axiom $A \sqsubseteq B$ is used in the construction of a reason then its important to be able to deduce that $A \sqsubseteq \neg B$ is a conflicting axiom, and hence a reason based on the latter axiom conflicts with a reason based on the first. The logic developed in (Panayiotou & Bennett, 2009; © 2009 IEEE) to give a semantic account of the notion of reason, like many well known relevance and conditional logics, suffers from some drawbacks. For example it allows for formulas of the form $\alpha \hookrightarrow (\alpha \vee \beta)$. One reason for this result is that $\hookrightarrow$ is defined in terms of a modal formula involving necessary material implication within a set of worlds. Thus, within this set of worlds (which are assumed to be normal (Blackburn et al., 2001) and compatible with the actual world of the reasoning agent), every valid propositional logic formula holds, e.g. $\alpha \rightarrow (\alpha \vee \beta)$.

In this chapter we focus on a syntactic axiomatization of reasons using *ALC*. Concept languages, like *ALC* are uniquely identified by its set of concept-forming and role-forming constructors that permit the creation of concept expressions and role expressions (Patel-Schneider, 1990). The syntax and semantics of concept-forming constructors and role-forming constructors are shown in tables 1 and 2. The terminology adopted is identical to (Patel-Schneider, 1990). That is, concept names are denoted with the letters A, B, role names with P and individual names with a, b,... , possibly with subscripts. Concept expressions and role expressions (typically referred to as concepts and roles) are denoted with the letters C, D and Q, R, respectively. The notion of satisfiability is defined on the statements of ontology as usual. An interpretation I is a model of an ontology O = <T, A> if and only if it is both a model of T and a model of A. An ontology O logically implies a formula α (either an assertion or a T-axiom) if and only if α is true in every model of O. We denote this as: O |= a. A set of statements F satisfies a, denoted as F |= a if and only if whenever O |= F then O |= a. *ALC* is a decidable fragment of first order logic. The language of arguments described above can be extended to cover first order statements in schematic form with two variables. Therefore, we argue that we can determine the association between DL statements and schematic statements with the 'reason for' operator as will be shown below.

CONSTRACTOR NAME	SYNTAX	SEMANTICS
Concept name	A	$A^I \subseteq \Delta^I$
Top	$\top$	Δ^I
bottom	$\bot$	$\varnothing$
conjunction	$C \sqcap D$	$C^I \cap D^I$
disjunction	$C \sqcup D$	$C^I \cup D^I$
negation	$\neg C$	$\Delta^I \backslash C^I$
Universal quantification	$\forall R.C$	$\{d_1 \mid \forall d_2 : (d_1,d_2) \in R^I \rightarrow d_2 \in C^I\}$
Existential quantification	$\exists R.C$	$\{d_1 \mid \exists d_2 : (d_1,d_2) \in R^I \wedge d_2 \in C^I\}$
Number restrictions	$\geq nR$	$\{d_1 \mid \#\{d_2 : (d_1,d_2) \in R^I\} \geq n\}$
	$\leq nR$	$\{d_1 \mid \#\{d_2 : (d_1,d_2) \in R^I\} \leq n\}$
Collection of individuals	$\{a_1,\ldots,a_n\}$	$\{a^I_1,\ldots,a^I_n\}$

Table 1. Syntax and Semantics of concept-forming operators

CONSTRUCTOR NAME	SYNTAX	SEMANTICS
Role name	P	$P^I \subseteq \Delta^I \times \Delta^I$
Role conjunction	$Q \sqcap R$	$Q^I \cap R^I$

2.1 Reasons, in DL Ontologies

Consider an ontology O = <T, A> where T is the set of terminological axioms in O and A the set of assertions in O. Further assume that O comes with a vocabulary $\Sigma = C \cup R \cup I$ and domain D, where C denotes the set of concept names, R the set of role names and I the set of individual names used in the ontology O, respectively. An interpretation function $\cdot I$ assigns to each name in Σ an individual of the domain, to each concept a subset of the domain and to each role a subset of D×D. A reason is entailed from a (set of) assertions and axioms in the following way:

Definition 2.1

If O = <T, A>, then we say that a reason $\alpha \hookrightarrow \beta$ is valid in O and denote it as O:[$\alpha \hookrightarrow \beta$] if and only if there is a subset of formulas,

1. $T \models \Phi$

2. $A \models \alpha$
3. $\Phi \cup \alpha \models_{min} \beta$

where $\models_{min}$ is interpreted as 'minimally entails'.
We note that although the above definition for reason is different from the one given in (Panayiotou & Bennett, 2009; © 2009 IEEE), it is nonetheless equivalent since in (Panayiotou & Bennett, 2009) 'reason' is defined within an S5 modal logic system.

2.2 Computing the Closure of an Ontology

One way to deduce all relevant information in order to construct reasons is to obtain the closure of T∪A which is computed as follows.

Definition 2.1 (Closure of an Ontology)
If O = <T, A>, then we say that the closure of the union of a set of terminological axioms T and assertions A of is computed as follows:

1. CL := { T ∪ A }
2. If (A ⊓ B)(a) ∈ CL then CL := CL ∪ { A(a), B(a) }
3. If {(A ⊔ B)(a) , ¬A(a)} ⊆ CL then CL := CL ∪ { B(a) }; else if ¬B(a) ∈ A then CL := CL ∪ { A(a) }
4. If {A ⊑ B, A(a)} ⊆ CL then CL := CL ∪ { B(a) }
5. If {A ⊑ B , B ⊑ C} ∈ T then CL := CL ∪ { A ⊑ C }
6. If { R(a, b), ∀R.C } ⊆ CL then CL := CL ∪ { C(b) }
7. If {R1 ⊑ R2, (a, b)} ⊆ CL then CL := CL ∪ { R2(a, b) }
8. If Q ⊓ R).C(a) ∈ CL then CL := CL ∪ { R.C(a), Q.C(a)}
9. If { A ⊑ B, R.A(a) } ⊆ CL then CL := CL ∪ { R.B (a)}
10. If { R1⊑ R2 , R1.C(a)} ⊆ CL then CL := CL ∪ { R2.C(a) }
11. If {A⊑ B⊓C} ⊆ CL then CL := CL∪ {A⊑ B, A⊑ C}
12. If { A ⊔ B ⊑ C} ⊆ CL then CL := CL∪ {A⊑ B, A⊑ C}

2.3 Rewriting

Computing the closure of ontology statements is not very efficient, especially for large ontologies. The task becomes even harder when we need to compare the closures of different ontologies. To increase the efficiency of computation we need to extract only those assertions and terminological axioms from an ontology that are relevant to the formula under consideration. Consider the following ontological statements:

Example 2.1
Suppose we have a small ontology about male workers in UK as shown below and we wish to determine whether MALE(John) is relevant to MWUK(John).

1. MWUK = MLE ⊓ WORK.UK
2. MLE = MALE ⊓ EMPLOY EE
3. MWUK(John)

Then, obviously MWUK $\sqsubseteq$ MLE and MLE $\sqsubseteq$ MALE. Therefore, MWUK $\sqsubseteq$ MALE and since MWUK(John) then MALE(John) follows. It turns out that not only MALE(John) is relevant to MWUK(John) but one is the *reason for* the other (i.e. the truth of the first is a sufficient reason to conclude the truth of the second) as will be discussed later. In natural language terms we can say that: MALE(John) because MWUK(John), or, equivalently that MWUK(John) is a reason for MALE(John).

Example 2.2

Suppose we wish to determine what assertions are related to the assertion A(a) in the small ontology below. The letters A, B, C, D below denote generic concepts.

1. $A \sqsubseteq (B \sqcup C)$
2. $\neg B(a)$
3. $D(a)$

In the above example, it should be possible to identify the relevance between A(a) and ¬B(a) and C(a). The problem with subsumption relation is monotony: If we assume that $A \sqsubseteq B$ then we may deduce that $A \sqsubseteq B \sqcup C$ although concept C may not be related to concept A. Item 1 above, implies that either $A \sqcap B \neq \emptyset$, or, $A \sqsubseteq B$ or $A \sqsubseteq C$. Thus, if B and C are disjoint (i.e. $B^I \cap C^I = \emptyset$) then $A \sqsubseteq (B \sqcup C)$ is superfluous to one of $(A \sqsubseteq B)$ or $(A \sqsubseteq C)$, i.e. $A \sqsubseteq (B \sqcup C)$ is 'too general'. Similarly if we have two axioms: $(A \sqcap B \sqcap C) \sqsubseteq D$ and $(A \sqcap B) \sqsubseteq D$ then the former axiom is 'unnecessarily restricted'.

Definition 2.2 (Minimal Subsumption)

Assume we have an axiom of the form: $\Phi \sqsubseteq \Lambda$. Then, we say that Φ is subsumed minimally by Λ if and only if the following conditions hold:

1. If $\Lambda = \Lambda 1 \sqcup \cdots \sqcup \Lambda n$ and $n \geqq 2$ then Φ is subsumed minimally if and only if $\Phi \not\sqsubseteq [\Lambda \backslash \Lambda j]$ for any $j \in \{1 \ldots n\}$.
2. If $\Lambda = \Lambda 1 \sqcap \cdots \sqcap \Lambda n$ and $n \geqq 2$ then Φ is subsumed minimally if and only if $\Phi \not\sqsubseteq \Lambda \sqcap \Psi$ for any Ψ.

Definition 2.3 We say that an axiom is *too generous* if it is subsumed by a non-minimal disjunction.

Definition 2.4 We say that an axiom is *too restricted* if it is subsumed by a minimal conjunction.

When an axiom is neither too generous nor too restricted, then it can be used to create reasons which are valid within an ontology. For example, although $C \sqsubseteq D \sqcup E$ is not inconsistent with $C \sqsubseteq D \sqcup E \sqcup F$ and both can be true, only the first one would be used to determine E: $C \sqcap \neg B \sqsubseteq C$. Since different ontologies may be expressed at different levels of granularity, reasons giving rise to arguments may conflict; thus, reasoning with 'reasons' gives rise to defeasible reasoning. In order to facilitate the matching of statements within an ontology we devised a rewriting mapping that transforms axioms as described below. After this transformation function is applied, all the upper lever conjunctions of the formula will have been eliminated.

Definition 2.5 (Rewriting function - τ)
To ease the task of searching statements relevant to reasons the following rewriting rules are applied on the definitional and terminological axioms of the ontology being considered:

1. Each terminological axiom of the form $A \sqsubseteq B \sqcup C$ where A, B, C denote simple concepts, is translated into $A \sqcap \neg B \sqsubseteq C$.
2. Each terminological axiom of the form $\Phi \sqsubseteq C \sqcup D$ where Φ is not a simple concept is re-written so that Φ has a $\sqcup$ at the top level (the equivalent of disjunctive normal form) i.e. Φ has the form $\Phi = A1 \sqcup A2 \sqcup \cdots \sqcup An$
3. Each axiom of the form $\Phi 1 \sqcup \cdots \sqcup \Phi n \sqsubseteq \Lambda 1 \sqcap \cdots \sqcap \Lambda n$ is translated into a set of axioms: $\Phi i \sqsubseteq \Lambda j$ for all $j \in \{1 \dots k\}$ and $i \in \{1 \dots n\}$.
4. Each axiom of the form: $\Phi \sqsubseteq \Lambda$ where Λ is not a simple concept is re-written so that Λ has a $\sqcap$ at the top level, i.e. into a form equivalent to conjunctive normal form in first-order logic.
5. Definitional axioms of the form: $\Phi = \Lambda 1 \sqcap \cdots \sqcap \Lambda n$ are rewritten into the following two axioms:
    a. $\Phi \sqsubseteq \Lambda 1 \sqcap \cdots \sqcap \Lambda n$
    b. $\Lambda 1 \sqcap \cdots \sqcap \Lambda n \sqsubseteq \Phi$

The above definition is particularly useful since as I argued in the propositional case (Panayiotou & Bennett, 2009 : © 2009 IEEE): $(\alpha \vee \beta) \hookrightarrow \gamma$ if and only if $(\alpha \hookrightarrow \gamma)$ and $(\beta \hookrightarrow \gamma)$, where α, β, and γ denote formula schemata. Intuitively, this rule aims to establish that a disjunction of formulas can only give rise to another formula if both disjuncts are sufficient reasons on their own to cause γ (i.e. the consequent). Implicit to this rule is the assumption that there can be more than one propositions constituting a sufficient reason for a claim.

2.4 Relevance Relation

Statements related to each other have some properties that enable us to locate them more easily. For example, if an assertion is related to another assertion then it is also related to its negation. Thus, when two ontologies are compared, it is not only important to be able to recognize agreements but also disagreements between them. With hindsight on axioms of relevance theory, relevance between formulas is represented as a relation $\Re$, satisfying the following properties:

1. **(R1)** $\Re(A,A)$
2. **(R2)** $\Re(A, \neg A)$
3. **(R3)** $\Re(A, B)$ if and only if $\Re(B, A)$
4. **(R4)** $\Re(A, B)$, $\Re(B, C)$ implies $\Re(A, C)$.
5. **(R5)** $\Re(A, D \wedge E)$ if and only if $\Re(A, D)$ and $\Re(A, E)$

where A, B, D, E are formula schemata.

Proposition 2.1

Let O = < T, A> and f : T ↦ T' which translates O into O' according to the rewriting rules stated above. Then, $O \models \varphi$ if and only if $O' \models \varphi$.

The proof is easy since rewriting preserves satisfiability between the original and the rewritten axioms. Proposition 2.1 refers to ontologies that do not include too generous or too restricted axioms. If this were not the case then reasons entailed by the original ontology might not have been entailed from the translated ontology. Notably, definition 2.1 defines reason as part of an inclusion or subsumption entailment. This is not necessarily the case. Reasons may be defined in different logical languages differently. The main point made here is that inclusion or definitional axioms that can be translated to rules, can give rise to reasons. For example, if we assume that $Ax \Rightarrow Bx$ denotes a rule then when its variables are substituted by names of individuals of the domain, it gives rise to reasons. Next, we show how to deduce reasons from ontological axioms and assertions. After the definition of **T** (please refer to definition 2.5), it is possible to select from the knowledge base those axioms and assertions that give rise to reasons.

In order to draw inference using formulas that include 'reasons', we need to define a new inference relation that uses first order formulas and 'reasons' to derive new inferences. We define the *cumulative* inference relation $\vdash_{\mathbf{R}}$, which is a supraclassical non-monotonic inference relation which draws inferences using 'reason' formulas. Studying the meta-theoretic properties of inference (with the term metatheoretic meaning drawing inferences or studying the properties of the inference relation of a language) was originally done by (Szabo, 1969) for the sequent calculus inference relation. Later results for the non-monotonic inference relations were obtained by Gabbay (Gabbay, 1984), by Makinson (Makinson, 1989), by Kraus (Krause et al., 1990) and others. A *cumulative* inference relation is an inference relation satisfying the principles of: *Inclusion*, *Cut* and *Cautious Monotony*. Obviously, the first two properties are satisfied by the classical inference relation as well. The definition of a cumulative inference relation as defined in (Brewka et al., 1997) is given below:

Definition 2.6 (Cumulative Inference Relation) (Brewka et al., 1997)

An Inference relation, $|\sim$ is cumulative if and only if it satisfies the following properties:

1. Supraclassicality: $$\frac{X \vdash \alpha}{X \mid\sim \alpha}$$
2. Inclusion: $X, \alpha \mid\sim \alpha$
3. Cut: $$\frac{X \mid\sim \alpha \quad X, \alpha \mid\sim y}{X \mid\sim y}$$
4. Cautious Monotony: $$\frac{X \mid\sim \alpha \quad X \mid\sim y}{X, \alpha \mid\sim y}$$ instead of monotony: ($X \mid\sim \alpha$ implies $X, y \mid\sim \alpha$)

The fact that $\vdash_R$ is a cumulative relation follows from the properties of $\hookrightarrow$ and the definition of well formed formulas of the language used to represent reasons. We define this language to be $\mathcal{L}_R$, which is a metatheoretic logical language, including rules for deriving 'reason' expressions from other languages, like DL. $\mathcal{L}_R$ includes rules for deriving reason schemata from DL ontologies and may be extended to include reason schemata from other languages. In addition it includes a set of properties about the 'reason for' operator. Both rule schemata for deriving reasons and properties of $\hookrightarrow$ are discussed below.

Definition 2.7 (Rules for deriving reason schemata applicable to DL ontologies)
Assume an ontology O. Further assume that the inference relations $\vdash_S$ and $\vdash_R$ correspond to subsumption inference in DL and reason inference in $\mathcal{L}_R$ we have the following rules for deriving reasons from O.

1. $\underline{O \vdash_S A \sqsubseteq B}$
   $O \vdash_R A(x) \hookrightarrow B(x)$
2. $\underline{O \vdash_S A \sqsubseteq \forall R.C}$
   $O \vdash_R (A(x) \wedge R(x,y)) \hookrightarrow B(y)$
3. $\underline{O \vdash_S R1 \sqsubseteq R2}$
   $O \vdash_R R1(x,y) \hookrightarrow R2(x,y)$
4. $\underline{O \vdash_S A \sqcup B \sqsubseteq C}$
   $O \vdash_R (A(x) \vee B(x)) \hookrightarrow C(x)$

Properties of $\hookrightarrow$ are discussed below:
1. $(A(x) \hookrightarrow B(x)) \wedge (B(x) \hookrightarrow C(x)) \rightarrow (A(x) \hookrightarrow C(x))$ ($\hookrightarrow$ transitivity)
2. If $\vdash_C A(x) \rightarrow B(x)$ then $\vdash_R \neg (A(x) \hookrightarrow B(x))$

Also we have the following two rules about reasons, which we refer to as (R1) and (R2), respectively.
(R1) $[A(x) \hookrightarrow B(x)] [y \backslash x] \equiv A(y) \hookrightarrow B(y)$ if and only if $x^I = y^I \in A^I$
(R2) $O \vdash_R (A(x) \vee B(x)) \hookrightarrow C(x)$ if and only if $O \vdash_R A(x) \hookrightarrow C(x)$ and $O \vdash_R B(x) \hookrightarrow C(x)$.

Note that item 4 above is particularly important since after the translation function **T** is applied on the ontology, the resulting formulas are in disjunctive form.

Definition2.7 (Conflicts between reasons)
Two reasons $\Gamma 1 \hookrightarrow \alpha$ and $\Gamma 2 \hookrightarrow \beta$ conflict if and only if:
1. $\Gamma 1 \wedge \Gamma 2 \nvdash_R \bot$ and $\alpha \wedge \beta \vdash_R \bot$
2. $\Gamma 1 \wedge \Gamma 2 \vdash_R \bot$ and $\alpha \wedge \beta \nvdash_R \bot$

It is important to mention that $\vdash_R$ is a supraclassical inference relation, which means that it includes classical inferences.

Proposition 2.2
Let O = <T, A>. Then O is inconsistent only if there are conflicting reasons r1 and r2 such that O $\vdash_R$ r1 and O $\vdash_R$ r2.

The proof follows easily by referring to definition 2.7 above and considering each formula type by induction. Note the 'only if' site.

Example 2.3
Let O = <A, T > and { D(a) } = A and $\{A \sqsubseteq C, D \sqsubseteq \neg C\} \subseteq T$. Then O $\vdash_R$ A(x) $\hookrightarrow$ C(x) and O $\vdash_R$ D(x) $\hookrightarrow$ ¬C(x).

2.4 Arguments

In this section we discuss the notion of argument and its relevance to reason. Argumentation is a popular field of study in AI and has been researched extensively by many researchers. Among the most important contributions can be traced in the works of Parsons (Parsons et al., 1998), Jennings (Jennings et al., 2001), and Wooldridge (Wooldridge, 2002) and in the area of multi-agent reasoning, Walton (Walton, 2006) and Toulmin (Toulmin, 2005) in the area of philosophy, etc. These approaches provided us with a solid theoretical background in what is now legitimately referred to as the area of argumentation. Apart from very few approaches, the vast majority of work on argumentation focuses on the relationships between arguments and the argument's semantic status (in particular whether it is acceptable or not) and not so much on the internal structure of arguments themselves. Besnard and Hunter (Besnard & Hunter, 2008), are among the exceptions since their work elaborates on the structure of deductive arguments. Below we give our definition of an ontology argument.

Definition 2.8 (Ontology Argument) An ontological argument is a structure < Γ, ∏, C > where:

- C is a claim,
- Γ is a set of assertions or instantiated reason schemata { γ1,...,γn }
- ∏ = { R1,... Rk } is a set of rules (including axioms),
- ∃γk, γm ∈ Γ such that ∃Ri ∈ ∏ and Ri(γk, γn, γi) where i ∈ { 1,…,k }.

We now elaborate on the structure of arguments. In the previous section we presented reasons as grounded instances of rules where the antecedent was the reason for the consequent. In terms of ontologies, grounded instances of rules can take the form of instantiated terminological axioms. For example, $(A \sqsubseteq B)(a)$ implies that A(a) $\hookrightarrow$ B(a) holds in logic R. The claim of an argument may represent a derived assertion or a derived axiom. If Σ is a set of statements in an ontology O, then, obviously if $\Sigma \vdash_S \alpha$ where α is an assertion, $\vdash_S$ denotes the subsumption inference relation and Σ is minimal, then $\Sigma \hookrightarrow \alpha$. Further, $\Sigma \wedge (\Sigma \hookrightarrow \alpha) \vdash_R \alpha$. So, in logic R, we assume an inference rule similar to modus ponens in classical logic which we shall call RMP (from Reason Modus Ponens) and which takes the form:

$$\frac{A(x) \wedge (A(x) \hookrightarrow B(x))}{B(x)}$$

and may be expressed as the relation: RMP(A(a), A(a) $\hookrightarrow$ B(a), B(a)).
Following the above definition of argument we have that < { A(a) }, { MPR }, B(a) > is an argument. The rules included in argumentation logic do not have to be the inference rules of classical logic and reason logic R, alone. Argumentation permits itself a wide range of rule schemata that can be used to derive claims. For example, Walton defines a number of argumentation schemes for arguments (Walton, 2006). One such scheme is the argumentation scheme for appeal to expert opinion, which says that: (i) if source E is an expert in subject domain D containing proposition A and (ii) E asserts that proposition A (in domain D) is true (false), then A may plausibly be taken to be true (Walton, 2006). A rule can be anyone of these schemes.

2.4 Conflicts between Arguments

Assume two ontologies O1 and O2 and α = < Γ1, Π1, C1 > and β = < Γ 2, Π2, C2 > entailed from O1 and O2, respectively. Then α conflicts with β if:

1. The claims of the arguments, i.e. C1 and C2 are inconsistent,
2. The claim of one argument is inconsistent with the premises of the other argument. For example, $A(d) \hookrightarrow B(d) \in \Gamma 1$ and $\{A(d), \neg B(d)\} \subseteq \Gamma 2$.

Proposition 2.3
Suppose that both arguments α and β are entailed from ontology O. Argument α conflicts with argument if β and only if the ontology is inconsistent.

3. Viewpoints

In this section we discuss a structural definition of viewpoint. Let us first discuss the characteristics of viewpoints.

3.1 Characteristics of Viewpoints

A viewpoint consists of a set of reasons or arguments, a set of labeled beliefs describing the underlying ontological theory used in the construction of arguments, mapping rules that map concepts and relations between terminologies from different ontologies used in the viewpoint, a formula representing the position expressed by the viewpoint, the set of resources that are used in the construction of beliefs and arguments and any other contextual beliefs used in the construction of arguments/reasons. Thus, a viewpoint is defined as follows:

Definition 3.1 (Structural definition of a Viewpoint)

A viewpoint is defined as a structure V = < Φ, p, A, R, υ > where

1. Φ is a set of formulas which we assume to be consistent and relevant.
2. p is the formula representing the position of the viewpoint - assume for the time being that the position refers to an ontological assertion.

3. R is the union of a set of rules and reasons.
4. A is a set of arguments supporting position p.
5. υ is an interpretation, assigning to each constant used in the viewpoint an individual of a domain D, to each concept a subset of a domain and to each role a subset of the Cartesian product of the domain D x D.

Each viewpoint uses a vocabulary, denoted as L_V consisting of concept names, individual names and role names from possibly more than one ontology. Below we define the notion of inconsistency between different viewpoints.

Definition 3.2 (Viewpoint inconsistency)

A viewpoint Vi = < Φi, pi, Ai, Ri, υi > is inconsistent with a viewpoint Vj = < Φj, pj, Ai, Rj, υj > if and only if anyone of the following situations hold:

1. There exists rk ∈ Ri and rm ∈ Rj such that rk conflicts with rm.
2. There exists ψ ∈ Φi which is inconsistent with χ ∈ Φj.
3. There is an argument α in Ai and an argument β in Aj such that α and β conflict.

We also say that a viewpoint *attacks* another viewpoint if the former position supports a position which is conflicting to the latter.

Definition 3.3 (Viewpoint attack)

A viewpoint Vi = $< \Phi_i, p_i, A_i, R_i, \upsilon_i >$ attacks a viewpoint $V_j = < \Phi_j, p_j, A_j, R_j, \upsilon_j >$ if and only if $p_i \vdash \neg p_j$.

Intuitively a viewpoint is *plausible* if it can survive the attacks of other viewpoints. We have the following definition of a plausible viewpoint:

Definition 3.4 (Plausible Viewpoint)

A plausible viewpoint is a viewpoint V = < Φ, p, A, R, υ > where:

1. The reasons supporting a conflicting viewpoint do not *defeat* any reason r ∈ R.
2. The set R is *admissible.*
3. The set A is *admissible.*
4. Any other relevant belief in the viewpoint that underpins the context in which beliefs, arguments or reasons are evaluated *is* compatible with the actual context in which the viewpoint is evaluated. (e.g. domains overlap, vocabulary compatibility or mapping, constraints in the context in which the argument is valid, etc).

The notion of admissibility used in the definition of a plausible viewpoint above is defined below and is based on the notion of acceptability as defined by Dung in (Dung, 1995) with slight verbal adaptation to fit the current context:

Definition 3.5 (Acceptability of arguments) (Dung, 1995)

An argument A is acceptable with respect to a set S of arguments if and only if for each argument B that can be raised: if B attacks A the B is attacked by an argument in S (we say simply say that A is attacked by S).

Definition 3.6 (Acceptability of reasons, rules and arguments)
In this chapter, an argument, rule, or reason A is acceptable with respect to a set of arguments, reasons or rules S if for each argument, reason or rule that follows from the knowledge base of the software agent, if A conflicts with B then S conflicts with B, in the sense of definition 3.5 above.

Definition 3.6 (Admissibility of arguments) (Dung, 1995)
A conflict-free set of arguments S (i.e. one that does not contain arguments A and B such that A attacks B) is admissible if and only if each argument in S is acceptable with respect to S.

The above definition can be extended to cover reasons and rules as in definition 3.6 above.

3.2 Viewpoints created from multiple ontologies

In order to represent viewpoints from multiple ontologies, we first need to define a language for representing reasons, arguments and viewpoints from different ontologies. Let us call this language, $\mathcal{L}_{MV}$, The vocabulary of $\mathcal{L}_{MV}$, henceforth referred to as V($\mathcal{L}_{MV}$), consists of:

1. A set of labels, $\lambda = \{\lambda 1, \ldots \lambda n\}$, where each label refers to a resource,
2. Reason expressions,
3. Rule expressions,
4. The predicate *Trust*,
5. A partial order relation $\prec$ on resources,
6. The relations *contradicts*,
7. Argument expressions,
8. The inference relation $|\sim$

where each label is a type of unique resource identifier, reason expressions are formulas of the form $\alpha \hookrightarrow \beta$ where α and β are formula schemata, rule expressions are domain rules of the form $\alpha \Rightarrow \beta$ used to denote natural language statements of the form 'IF α THEN β', the predicate *Trust* shows whether the reasoning agent trusts a resource, $\prec$ is a partial order on resources (preference relation); the relations *contradicts* shows whether viewpoints contradict to each other or attack each other respectively, and the inference relation $|\sim$ enables reasoning over formulas of $\mathcal{L}_V$. Further, we assume that if $\alpha \vdash_R \beta$ then $\alpha \; |\sim \beta$. An expression of the form: $\lambda_i{:}\varphi$ means φ holds in the ontology which is uniquely identified by the label λ_i.
A viewpoint may be derived from the statements of a single resource or from the combined statements of multiple resources. Let us first represent entailment for a single resource. Semantic entailment may be defined as follows: Assume resource R1 is underpinned by an ontology O = < T, A > with an interpretation I = < D, I > where D represents the domain of the ontology. Then $T \cup A$ models φ, denoted as $T \cup A \vDash \varphi$, if and only if φ is true whenever $T \cup A$ is true. We say that any set of statements $S \subseteq (T \cup A)$ models ϕ if and only if whenever O models S it also models φ. We denote this as: $S \vDash \varphi$. Then, we may derive 'reasons' as in definition 2.6 from $\tau(O) = O'$.

Definition 3.5 (DOAF)

Let I be a finite non-empty set of indices {1,..., n}. Further assume that {...,Oi,...}, $i \in I$, is a set of ontologies with at least overlapping domains Δ_i where $i \in I$, respectively. Then a distributed ontology argumentation system DOAF is a tuple < {...,λi,...}, {...,Ti,...}, {...,Ai,...}, IR, DR > where

1. λi is the label of the ith ontology, Oi.
2. Ti is the set of terminological axioms of Oi
3. Ai is the set of assertions of Oi
4. IR is the set of inference rules and bridge axioms (Ghidini et al., 2007) employed by DOAF.
5. DR is the set of default rules for reasoning with concepts in different ontologies of the same or overlapping domain.

A set of default rules and inference rules is in DOAF are shown below. A substantial amount of work has been done by Giunchiglia (Giunchiglia & Serafini,), Serafini and Giunchiglia (Serafini & Giunchiglia, 2000), Ghidini (Ghidini et al., 2007) on the proof theory of multi-language systems, hierarchical contexts, distributed ontologies, and mappings between ontologies. Our work on the construction of inference rules and natural deduction from assumptions and axioms from different ontologies is very much influenced by this work. However, although a distributed ontology argumentation framework takes into account known mappings between concepts of different ontologies, in case where explicit mappings are not available we employ default rule (D1) shown below. In addition the rule (↪ Ei) is used to draw inferences

(D1) $\dfrac{i{:}A,\ j{:}(A \hookrightarrow B) \mid i{:}A \leftrightarrow j{:}A}{[i+j]{:}A}$ **(↪ Ei)** $\dfrac{i{:}A \quad i{:}(A \hookrightarrow B)}{i{:}B}$

where A, B and C are formula schemata. Note that i:(A ↪ B) is equivalent to (i:A ↪ i:B)

(M1) $\dfrac{i{:}C \sqsubseteq j{:}D}{i{:}C(x) \hookrightarrow j{:}D(x)}$

where C and D are concepts in ontologies uniquely identified by labels i and j respectively and i:C(x) and j:D(x) are the unary predicates corresponding to these concepts.

In addition, the local context of a reasoning agent is defined as follows:

Definition 3.6 (CSWA)

The (reasoning) context of a semantic web agent, CSWA consists of:

1. A topic, T, under consideration,
2. A set of reasoning rules: R,
3. A set of local judgments J,
4. Inferences from DOAF.

5. A Local vocabulary with mappings from its local vocabulary to the vocabulary of the ontologies.

Notably, local judgements, reasoning rules and inferences from DOAF need to be relevant to a particular topic at each instance.

We may consider the above logic as a hierarchical logic (Serafini & Giunchiglia, 2000), capable of using formulas from other logics or theories to infer arguments and viewpoints.

4. Application Issues and Potentialities

Up to now we've taken a rather abstract view of the notion of viewpoints without mentioning how this notion could be applied in practice to benefit applications. My work on viewpoint representation and reasoning aimed to be applied in the identification of discrepancies of viewpoints in the learning domain. For example, in trying to model the initial concepts involved in the introduction section of a programming language course on the web, it became obvious that viewpoints could play a role in constructing an orderly investigation of different ideas, scientific events and theories that led the field to its current state. Viewpoint representation and reasoning can be used constructively to motivate learners to engage in a critical thinking activity in order to choose or compare landmark achievements and historical results that led to the outbreak of the current level of technology in the programming domain. Traditionally, reference to different theses developed within particular scientific areas which were supported by theories, had been mainly recorded as subjects of historical significance and learning. However, comparing and contrasting the applicability of theses within different contexts, and engaging into a reasoning about their relevance, order of appearance, problems they tackle, can lead to the creation of (possibly conflicting) viewpoints that provide scientific insight. For example, the learners may be asked to decide which programming languages should be used to solve a particular problem. In this way they are motivated to justify their own point of view.

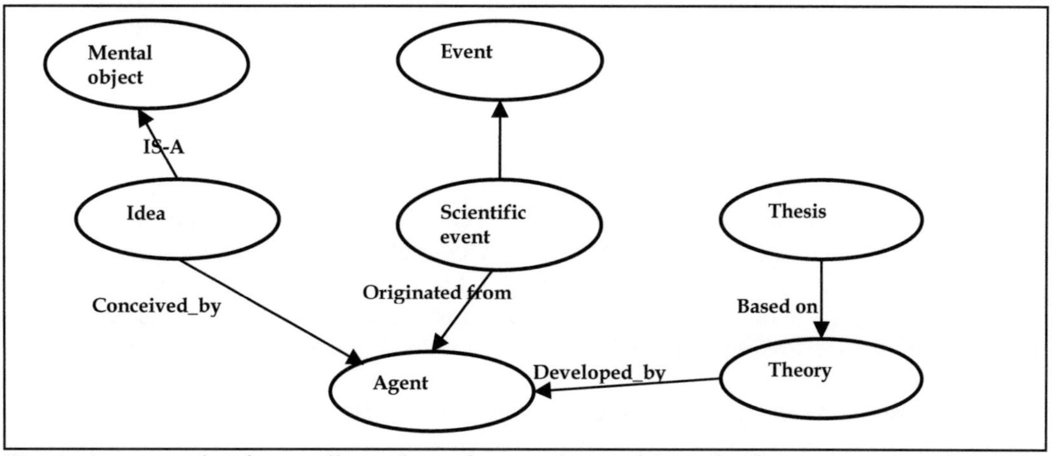

Fig. 1. An example of a small ontology that can be useful in clarifying concepts relevant to viewpoints.

The small ontology above is aimed to discuss the utility of a proper ontological approach to the definition of concepts associated to viewpoints for the purpose of reasoning. Of course the granularity at which the ontology will be represented is important and influences the representation of subtle differences in notions which are used similarly in natural language, as well as the range of inferences that can be drawn from them. Concepts such as *thesis, theory, idea,* and *mental object* are linked together: a theory had been initiated by an idea induced by a particular agent. The outcome of a theory is a thesis supported by scientific evidence, postulates, assumptions, justifications, and judgments. A *judgment* is the outcome of an evaluation, which is a higher level cognitive process. A *position* is supported by arguments driven from a theory or judgment(s). Unlike a thesis, a position is typically associated to the set of beliefs and attitudes (such as intentions and desires) of an agent. An agent is typically positioned about a topic if she is aware that it is a debatable issue. Each one of the above concepts is linked to the derivation and representation of viewpoints and their support via argumentation.

Linked to the recognition of viewpoints are also higher level cognitive processes, such as comparison, choice, etc, which are part of the critical thinking activity. Critical thinking is a higher level cognitive process (Wang et al., 2006) evoking, among others, the sub-processes of comparison and choice among alternatives via the process of argumentation, externalization of personal beliefs, and reflection. For example, a qualitative assessment stating that one programming language is better than another for a particular scenario can be interpreted as a 'reason for' a choice. The same applies when different theories are compared. The notion of theory is a multifaceted one. However, in all types of theories one expects to find a coherent (not self conflicting) set of principles, judgments and assumptions. Under this general definition of a theory, it follows that theories are prone to comparisons of theories of judgments, assumptions, principles, etc. A *judgment* is described in (ref. wikipedia) as a statement which is usually the evaluation of alternatives. According to the same resource, 'the existence of corroborating evidence for a judgment is necessary; it must corroborate and be corroborated by a system of statements which are accepted as true' (ref. wikipedia); Further, 'the corroborating evidence for a judgment must out-weight any contradicting evidence', as stated in (ref. wikipedia). From this definition of judgment, it follows that it is an output of a higher level cognitive process (evaluation) (Wang et al., 2008) rather than a simple assertion and that it is supported by some sort of factual evidence. The cognitive process of evaluation is part of comparison, another higher level cognitive process. So, the relationship between a comparison and a judgment seem to be that judgment is the outcome of comparison.

The notions of: judjement, position, thesis, reason, justification, and standpoint are closely associated and are related to the recognition and construction of viewpoints. The diagram below is not intended to provide a precise or even 'correct' model of the concepts mentioned above, at this stage. A thorough discussion of these concepts and their associations is a subject of a further philosophical exploration and my future research[1] which is beyond the scope of this chapter. Rather, it presents a possible model of the association of these concepts that can be used in the derivation of viewpoints. A possible model of some of the associations of these concepts (for illustration purposes) is shown below.

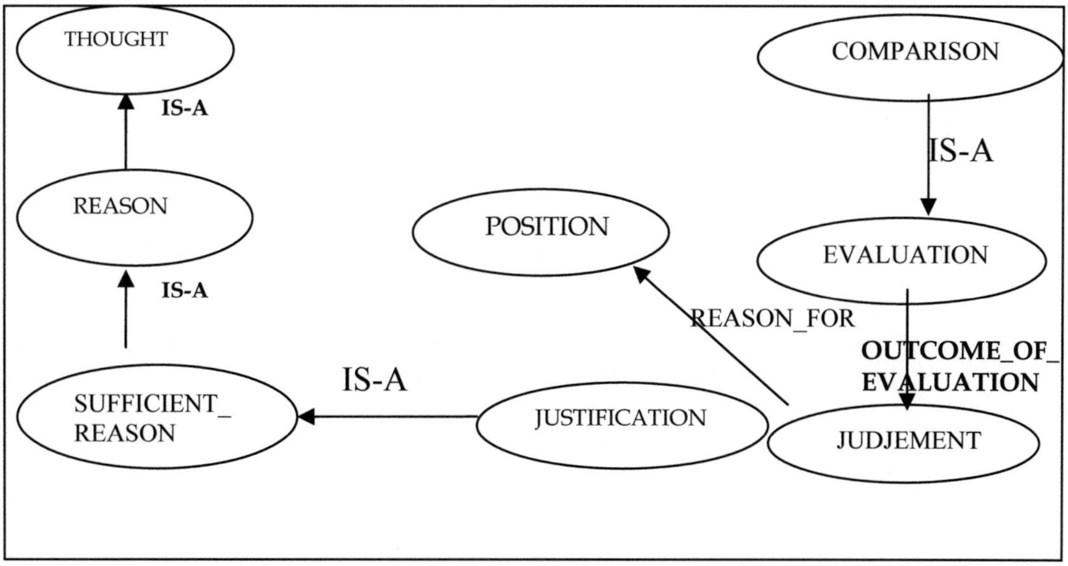

Fig. 2. An initial design of ontological associations between concepts relevant to the identification of viewpoints

Sufficiency conditions, causality and the classification problem. A *reason* is an explanatory or justificatory factor (wikipedia). In the context of explanation, the word "(a) reason" can be a synonym for "(a) cause" (wikipedia). In this paragraph we focus on sufficiency conditions which can be used as reasons for claims.

Although a domain representation explicitly in terms of viewpoints may be inflexible, the design of the domain representation can facilitate the extraction of viewpoints implicit in other tasks. Another example worth considering is the definition of concepts and the classification problem. An individual belongs to a particular class if it satisfies a particular set of properties. Differences or inconsistencises in the definition of concepts may be recognised via a comparison between the set of properties that sufficiently define concepts. If the definition of objects identifies sufficient and necessary concepts the task of raising refutals to claims of particular individuals' classifications (i.e. misclassifications) becomes easier. So, in order to reason with viewpoints, it is necessary to design systems so as to facilitate viewpoint representation, extraction and reasoning. This involves thinking about the design of systems at several levels: domain representation, upper ontology linking critical thinking tasks to reasons (meta-level), interactive level, and reasoning level.

5. Conclusion and Future Work

This chapter was concerned mainly with the representation of viewpoints from learning resources which are

represented as ontologies. We focused on the representation of domain knowledge via DLs and considered how reasons and arguments can be derived from these logics. The logic may be equally applicable to theories, or other languages provided that for each particular language we establish the set of rules which translate formulas to reasons or to domain rules where the latter is meant to represent statements of the form 'if...then...'. Although the content of each individual resource was assumed to be consistent, different resources may be inconsistent with each other. The software agent should be able to combine information from compatible resources in order to construct viewpoints. It should also be able to extract viewpoints from individual resources. Although in this chapter, reasons were derived from axioms of ontologies, this does not have to be the case. The reason schemata should be equally applicable to any relation expressing the fact that one (set of) premise(s) is a sufficient reason to deduce another. In the application issue section we outlined areas in the learning domain that could benefit from the use of viewpoints. It has been argued that apart from the merits of an explicit representation of viewpoints, viewpoints can also be extracted from other cognitive activities. It has also been stated that in order to make a better use of the notion of viewpoint, the relevant concepts of judgement, opinion, thesis, etc, which relate to the identification of implicitly stated viewpoints, need to be clarified and the domain ontology need to take into consideration these concepts. The same applies in case where differences in viewpoints exist about the definition of concepts: if the representation of concepts refers to its necessary and sufficient conditions then differences in viewpoints can be traced. Future research will help clarify further these issues. This chapter gave an initial account of certain concepts that relate to the derivation of viewpoints. For example, the notions of judgement, theory, idea, thesis, etc were not thoroughly discussed[1]. Viewpoints were also defined at an abstract level. Future work will focus on establishing a firm theory related to the notions that can be used to produce viewpoints as well as the viewpoints themselves.

[1] Research on this issue is not part of my PhD research at the University Of Leeds.

6. References

Bouquet, P. ; Giunchiglia, F. ; van Harmelen, F. ; Serafini, L. & Stuckenschmidt, H. (2004). Contextualizing Ontologies. Tech. Report, #DIT-04-013.

Blackburn, P. ; Rijke, J. & Venema, Y. (2001). *Modal Logic,* Cambridge University Press, ISBN 0-521-80200-8.

Borgida, A. & Serafini, L. (2002). Distributed Description Logics : Directed Domain Correspondences in Federated Information sources. Tech. Report #0209-07.

Donini, F.; Lenzerini, M. ; Nardi, D. & Schaerf, A. (1997). Reasoning in Description Logics, In : *CSLI Publications*, U. Gnowho and U. Gnowho-Else, (Ed.).

Divers, J. (2002). *Possible Worlds,* Routledge Taylor & Francis group, ISBN 0-415-15556-8, 2Park Square< Milton Park, Abingdon, Oxon, OX14 4RN

Dung, P.M. (1995). On the acceptability of arguments an dits fundamental role in nonmonotonic reasoning, logic programming and n-person games, *Journal of Artificial Intelligence,* Vol. 77. (321-357).

Ghidini, C. ; Serafini, L. & Tessaris, S. (2007). On Relating Heterogeneous Elements from Different Ontologies, *Context 2007, LNAI 4635,* (234-247).

Giunchiglia, F. & Serafini, L. (1994). Multilanguage hierarchical logics (or : how we can do without modal Logics). *Journal of Artificial Intelligence,* Vol. 65. (29-70).

Guha, R. V., (1991). *Contexts : A Formalization and Some Applications,* Stanford PhD Thesis.

Panayiotou, C. & Dimitrova, V. (2007). Dialectic Approach for Using Viewpoint Discrepancies in Learning, *Proceedings of the 2007 workshop on Representation models and techniques for improving e-learning (ReTIeL'07).*

Panayiotou, C. & Bennett, B. (2008). Semantic Web Reasoning Tutoring Agent, *Intelligent Tutoring Systems,* LNCS, Vol. 5091, Springer Berlin/Heidelberg.

Panayiotou, C. & Bennett, B. (2009). Critical Thinking Attitudes for reasoning with Points of View, *Proceedings of the 8th IEEE International Conference on Cognitive Informatics* (in press).

Patel-Schneider, P. (1990). A Decidable First-Order Logic for Knowledge Representation. *Journal of Automated Reasoning,* 6. (361-388)

Konolige, K. (1983). A Deductive Model of Belief, *International Joint Conference in Artificial Intelligence,(1298-1302).*

McCarthy, J. (1994). Notes on Formalising Context (Expanded Notes), Tech. Report CS-TN-94-13, Stanford University, Stanford, CA, USA.

Serafini, L. & Giunchiglia, F. (2000). ML systems : A Proof Theory for Contexts,

Toulmin, S.E. (2005). *The uses of Argument (Updated Edition),* Cambridge University Press, ISBN-10 0-521-53483-3, NY, USA.

Walton, D. (2006). *Fundamentals of Critical Argumentation,* Cambridge University Press, ISBN 0-521-53020-2, NY, USA.

Wang, Y. ; Wang, W. ; Patel, S. & Patel, D. (). A Layered Reference Model of the Brain (LRMB), *IEEE Trans. On Systems, Man, and Cybernetics,* Vol. 36., No.2.

Wooldridge, M. (2001). *An Introduction to MultiAgent Systems,* John Wiley & Sons, ltd, ISBN 0-471-49691.

11

Semantic Web technologies for managing EHR-related clinical knowledge

Catalina Martínez-Costa[1], Marcos Menárguez-Tortosa[1], José Alberto Maldonado[2], Jesualdo Tomás Fernández-Breis[1]
[1]Universidad de Murcia, [2]Universidad Politécnica de Valencia
Spain

1. Introduction

The Semantic Web (Berners-Lee et al, 2001) is a vision of the future Web in which information is given explicit meaning, making it easier for machines to automatically process and integrate information available on the Web. Semantic Web technologies promise to be capable of facilitating the management of knowledge and promote semantic interoperability between systems. There are different basic technologies for the success of the Semantic Web, amongst which the cornerstone technology is the ontology. In literature, multiple definitions for ontology can be found (see for instance (Gruber, 1993; van Heijst et al, 1997)). An ontology represents a common, shareable and reusable view of a particular application domain, and they give meaning to information structures that are exchanged by information systems (Brewster et al, 2004).
Semantic Web technologies and, in particular, ontologies have been identified in the final report of the Semantic Health project (SemanticHealth Report, 2009) as one of the basic technologies for the consecution of semantic interoperability of healthcare information systems. In healthcare, interoperability refers to the ability of different systems and organizations to exchange information and to use the information that has been exchanged.
On the other hand, the medical field is continually changing, and new findings about diseases and clinical treatments are continually made. Huge amounts of heterogeneous medical information and clinical terms are generated. However, the standardization of clinical information and knowledge has not been researched until the 90s. Recently, different architectures for exchanging clinical information and knowledge have been proposed, and the dual model-based one seems to be the most promising. This standard architecture introduces a separation between knowledge and information where knowledge reflects the possible changes. This separation is carried out by means of a double model (Beale, 2001), the reference model and the archetype model. The reference model reflects the generic and stable properties of the electronic healthcare record, whereas the archetype model represents the knowledge level, and consists of clinical concepts, called archetypes, that are based into entities of the corresponding reference model.
Hence, the methodology for the development of health information systems is changing and the dual model approach proposes a semantic layer defined by the archetypes. The

semantics in archetypes have a double nature: structural and terminological. By structural, we mean that the proper structure of the archetype provides some semantics. In addition to this, an archetype can be seen as a set of interrelated conceptual clinical entities. Each entity has a set of terminological bindings associated, which are specified by means of links to terms of specific medical terminologies, such as SNOMED-CT (SNOMED-CT).

Many medical terminologies have been recently or are in the process of being represented in the Web Ontology Language (OWL), because its formal nature allows for a better management of clinical knowledge. Furthermore, the common representation of archetypes and terminologies in OWL would allow a uniform management of clinical knowledge, which would also facilitate the consecution of semantic interoperability.

Hence, in this chapter we describe how Semantic Web technologies can be used to manage such clinical knowledge, and has two main streams:

- Representation of clinical archetypes: Clinical archetypes can be represented as OWL ontologies. We will describe an approach that combines Semantic Web technologies and Model-driven Engineering (Douglas et al., 2006) to achieve the goal. This approach can be applied to any dual-model based EHR standard.
- Management of clinical archetypes: The management of clinical archetypes will be illustrated by describing an EHR-independent Semantic Web system for managing archetypes. This system allows for annotating archetypes with external resources, performing searches and classification tasks.

2. Electronic Healthcare Records

Health information systems from hospitals and primary care organizations are expected to be capable of communicating to support the continuous medical process of the patient at local, regional, national and international level.

The Electronic Healthcare Record (EHR), defined as a repository of information regarding the health of a subject of care, in computer processable form (ISO/TC 215 TR, 2008), constitutes the cornerstone technology for the achievement of that goal. Its primary purpose is to provide a documented record of care that supports present and future care by the same or other clinicians. Among other benefits, the replacement of the traditional paper-based patient records with EHRs will increase the quality and efficiency of the patient medical care and will cut back on costs.

Nowadays there are different advanced approaches as standards or specifications for representing and communicating EHRs such as HL7 (HL7), OpenEHR (OpenEHR), and EN 13606 (UNE-EN 13606).

HL7 stands for Health Level Seven, and was founded in 1987 to provide healthcare standards for the exchange, management and integration of clinical information. There are several HL7 implementations. It is worth pointing out HL7 v2.X, that is focused on the exchange of messages and which have been widely used in America and Europe by the industry. More recently HL7 v3 was proposed, introducing the Reference Information Model (RIM) and the Clinical Document Architecture (CDA). This last standard version has (ISO).

On the other hand, the European Health Record (GEHR) project (1991-95) contributed to develop the OpenEHR specification. Following GEHR several projects extended and refined

its results. All these ones influenced the creation of the OpenEHR specification by the non-profit organization OpenEHR Foundation (OpenEHR).
Finally, the EN 13606 standard was influenced by OpenEHR. EN 13606 has been drawn on the practical experience of its predecessor ENV 13606. In fact, it is considered a subset of the full OpenEHR specification oriented to the exchange of EHR extracts.
Both the OpenEHR specification and the EN 13606 standard share the same modelling architecture. This architecture is named dual model-based architecture and has influenced the HL7 v3 standard. It is explained in next section in detail since our work will be focused on the semantic management of dual model-based standards.

2.1 Dual model architecture

The main feature offered by this modelling architecture is the separation between information and knowledge. On the one hand, information is modelled by means of a reference model (RM) and on the other hand, knowledge is modelled using an archetype model (AOM). The first one is specific to the healthcare domain but still very generic. It defines the set of classes that forms the generic building blocks of the EHR and it is stable over time. *Person or clinical session* would be classes of this reference model. The second one represents healthcare and application specific concepts such as the *measurement of cholesterol, the blood pressure* and so on by using archetypes.
An archetype describes configuration of data instances whose classes are described in the reference model. They are defined using the Archetype Definition Language (ADL). This language provides a concrete syntax for expressing them as text documents. Figure 1 illustrates the relationships of archetypes with data. Archetypes are instances of an archetype model which is a common formalism for expressing all archetypes. The archetype object model (right side) is formally related to the reference model, such that its semantics are those of constraint on instances of classes defined in the reference model (left side). If data are created and modified using archetypes, archetypes constrain the configuration of data instances to be valid according to the archetype.

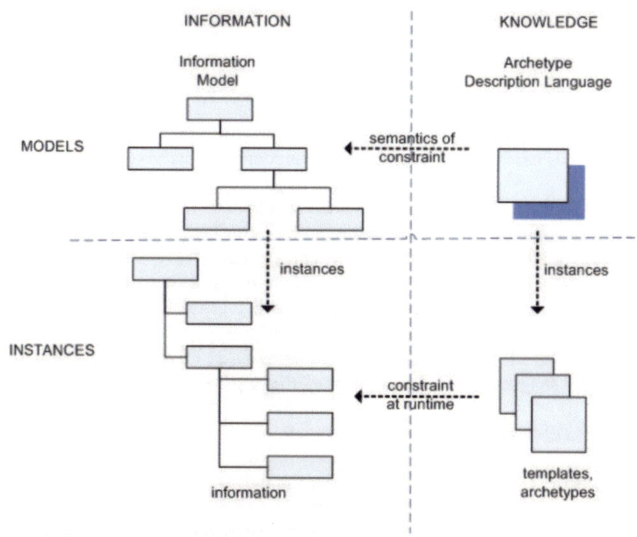

Fig. 1. Archetype Model Meta-architecture (Meta-Architecture)

Both OpenEHR and EN 13606 are based on the dual model architecture. However, they differ in how they structure the EHR domain, that is, they define different reference models. Thus, archetypes will be defined as constraints on these reference model classes for each standard and will be written in ADL.

Figure 2 shows an extract of an ADL archetype for the visual acuity recording for the EN 13606 standard. In the figure, the different ADL sections of the archetype can be observed: header, description, definition and ontology. The header includes the name of the archetype, specialization information and so on. In the Figure the header includes the name of the archetype *(CEN-EN13606-ENTRY.visual_acuity.v1)*, the language it is written in *(ISO_639-1::en)* and the archetype concept code *(at0000)*. The description section includes audit information, such as original author, purpose or lifecycle status. The definition section contains the structure and restrictions associated to the clinical concept defined by the archetype. Here, this section says that visual acuity is recorded by means of a table, whose row head is "Left", "Right", "Both eyes" and whose columns are the following values ("5/6" ,"6/6", "6/7.5", "6/9", "6/12", "6/18", "6/36", "6/60", "Count fingers", "Perceive light", "Blind"). That is, it expresses the acuity value of each eye separately and of both of them together. Finally, the ontology section includes the terminological definition and bindings. In this last section the linguistic expressions associated to the terms from the definition part are provided, as well as their possible bindings in other terminologies. For instance, the link to the SNOMED-CT term says how visual acuity is defined in the SNOMED-CT terminology.

Archetypes combine to form templates. They usually correspond to screen forms, printed reports, and in general, complete application-level information to be captured or sent. They are generally developed and used locally, recording the specific needs of the user or institution, while archetypes are usually widely used.

In fact, archetypes may constitute a clinical guide for clinicians and its importance can be noticed in some acts as the adoption of the European EHR EN 13606 standard by Sweden for their national EHR developments (Swedish-decision).

```
archetype (adl_version=1.4) CEN-EN13606-ENTRY.visual_acuity.v1
concept    [at0000]
language   original_language = <[ISO_639-1::en]>
description  ...
definition
  ENTRY[at0000] occurrences matches {1..1} matches { -- Visual acuity
    items existence matches {0..1} cardinality matches {1..1; unordered} matches {
          ...
            CLUSTER[at0003] occurrences matches {1..1} matches { -- Table
              parts existence matches {0..1} cardinality matches {0..1; unordered} matches {
                CLUSTER[at0004] occurrences matches {0..1} matches { -- row
                  parts existence matches {0..1} cardinality matches {2..2; ordered} matches {
                    ELEMENT[at0005] occurrences matches {0..1} matches { -- row head
                      value matches {
                        SIMPLE_TEXT occurrences matches {1..1} matches {
                          originalText matches {"Left","Right","Both eyes"}
                        }}}
                    ELEMENT[at0006] occurrences matches {1..1} matches { -- Visual acuity
                      value matches {
                        ORD occurrences matches {1..1} matches {
                          symbol matches {
                            CODED_TEXT occurrences matches {1..1} matches {
                              codedValue matches {
```

```
                                        CD occurrences matches {1..1} matches {
                                           displayName matches {
                                             "5/6","6/6","6/7.5","6/9","6/12","6/18","6/36",
                                             "6/60","Count fingers","Perceive light","Blind"
                                        }}}}}
                              value matches {5,6,7,9,12,18,36,60,100,200,300}
                           }}}}}}}...
ontology
  terminologies_available = <"SNOMED-CT", ...>
  term_definitions = <
    ["en"] = <
      items = <
        ["at0000"] = <
          text = <"Visual acuity">
          description = <"The functional acuity of vision, aided and unaided">
        >...
  term_binding = <
    ["SNOMED-CT"] = <
      items = <
        ["at0000"] = <[SNOMED-CT::363983007]>
      >>>...
```

Fig. 2. Extract of the visual acuity EN 13606 ADL archetype

2.2 ADL Limitations

Despite ADL is the language adopted for the archetypes description, it has some limitations. The parsing of an ADL archetype will return objects according to the Archetype Object Model (AOM). This model is common to all dual model-based standards, that is, it will have no information about the particular reference model for which the archetype has been built. Thus, the obtained objects cannot be used to perform any semantic activity, such as comparison, selection, or classification. Also, it does not provide any component that guarantees the consistency of the clinical knowledge but only at archetype level, that is, the conformance to ADL/AOM principles. Therefore, to process ADL content, two elements are needed: an ADL parser to get the AOM objects and the validator for the particular reference model to guarantee the clinical correctness of the ADL content. Figure 3 depicts a fragment of the AOM representation of the visual acuity archetype from Figure 2. As it can be observed, there are no explicit, semantic links between the objects obtained with the ADL parser. This last one will return a set of generic objects whose semantics is embedded mainly in string fields. In the figure example, for instance, the kind of a *C_COMPLEX_OBJECT* is shown by means of the *rmTypeName* attribute. It will point out if the object refers to an *ENTRY, CLUSTER, ELEMENT,* or any reference model class.

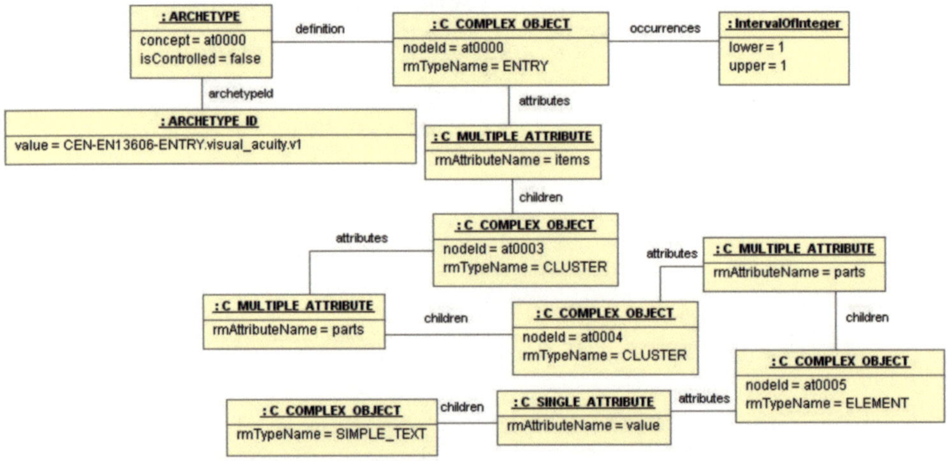

Fig. 3. Extract of the Archetype Object Model of the Visual Acuity archetype.

Thus, the possibilities of reasoning over ADL are currently very limited, as well as the availability of tools to use and manage ADL content is reduced. It does not allow performing any semantic activity on them. However, a semantic language would allow.

3. Semantic representation of EHR clinical knowledge

The main purpose of the Semantic Web (Berners-Lee et al., 2001) is to provide a framework in which data can be shared between applications. In order to do this, many technologies have emerged around it with the aim of giving explicit meaning to information, making it easier for machines to automatically process and integrate information. Clinical knowledge, as above stated, is represented by means of archetypes. They are defined using the Archetype Definition Language (ADL). However, this language has some limitations (see section 2.2) that can be solved using a semantic language. Thus, the representation of clinical knowledge, archetypes, as ontologies will be one of our goals and how to carry it out will be explained in this section.

3.1 The need for a semantic representation

The use of ontologies for representing clinical archetypes offers some benefits against the use of ADL. Ontologies allow performing the management of archetypes in an easier and more efficient way. Activities such as comparison, selection, classification and consistency checking can be performed over ontologies in a more generic, easier and efficient way.

In this work we use the Web Ontology Language (OWL), which is the recommendation of the W3C for the exchange of semantic content on the web, for this purpose. In particular, OWL-DL (where DL stands for "Description Logics") is used, because of its decidability and computability nature, offering enough expressiveness and the possibility of reasoning over the information that it describes.

OWL allows making annotations on classes or properties and semantic similarity functions are also available in the Semantic Web community. Thus, these resources help performing all these management related tasks. For instance, the selection of the set of archetypes to be

used in a clinical information system may be supported by semantic similarity functions and by semantic search filters based on the annotations of the archetypes.
Also, another benefit from the use of OWL is related to terminologies. They are very important in the medical field and some of them such as SNOMED-CT (SNOMED-CT) are currently in the process of adapting their representation to Semantic Web environments, so that OWL models for them are under development. Having the representation of both clinical and terminological information in the same formalism would facilitate better clinical knowledge management and would enrich archetypes by adding more information to them. Moreover, an archetype described in OWL might guarantee the consistency of the knowledge which cannot be granted by ADL (see section 2.2). To grant it, there is the need of implementing additional mechanisms. In addition to this, the access to clinical information described in OWL can be also done in a more natural way. OWL modelling brings all the information concerning a particular term together (code, definition, bindings, translations ...).
Among its benefits, the representation of archetypes in OWL makes the use of tools developed by the Semantic Web community possible. This community has been working for years in methodologies and tools for comparing different ontologies, merging them, identifying inconsistencies and so on. Also, OWL is continually being improved and there is currently a draft version of OWL 2.0 (OWL 2.0). Moreover, different technologies and languages for querying, defining rules and exploiting OWL content are in progress.

3.2 Development of an ontological representation for EHR clinical knowledge

The EN 13606 clinical standard and the OpenEHR specification are based on the dual model-based architecture. So, a first stage in our work was to do a semantic interpretation of clinical archetypes, analyzing their reference and archetype models. Figure 4 illustrates some of the main classes of the ontological representation for the EN 13606 standard case. As it can be observed, concepts from the reference and archetype models are put together expressing the archetype structure in a more comprehensible way. For instance, concepts such as *archetype, archetype description, archetype description item, occurrences, cardinality* or *archetype term* exist in the archetype model, but other ones, which are underlined in the Figure, such as *folder, composition, section, entry, element* or *clinical datatype* belong to the reference model. Thus, this modelling decision captures the common features of both standards, these are the mentioned archetype model concepts, and allows including the specific concepts that exist in each one. In fact, the OpenEHR ontological representation will be similar to the shown in Figure 4 for EN 13606 except for the concepts as *folder, composition, section...*, that is, those which belong to the respective reference model.

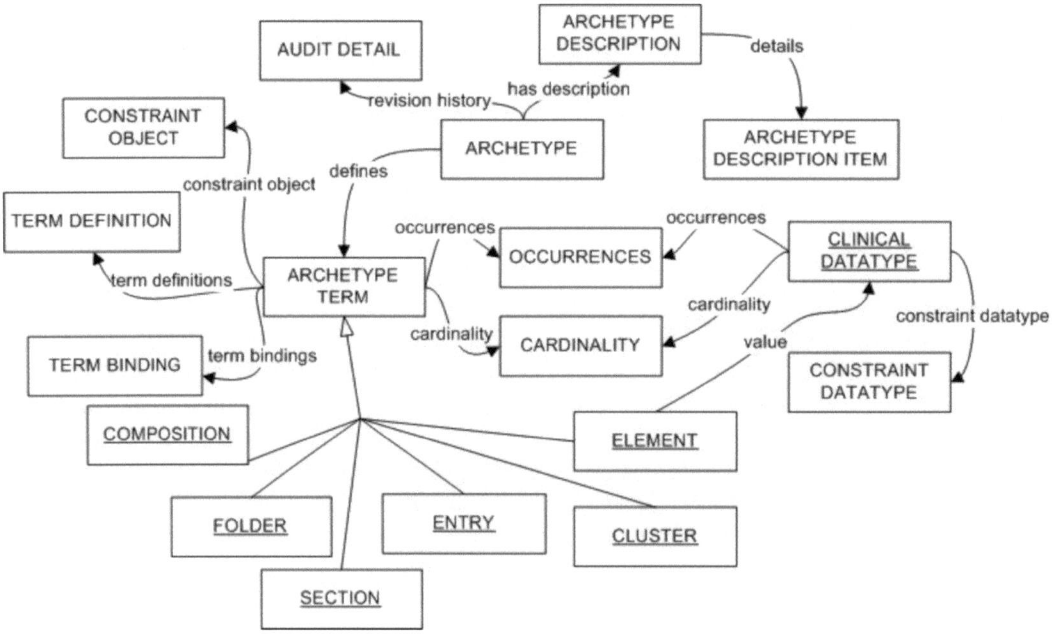

Fig. 4. Fragment of the archetype ontological representation for EN 13606

As a result of the semantic interpretation process (Fernandez-Breis et al., 2006) made for both standards, two main ontologies were built for each one (see Table 2 for details).

- EN13606-SP and OpenEHR-SP: They represent the clinical data structures and data types defined in the reference model of each standard.
- EN13606-AR and OpenEHR-AR: They are the archetype model ontologies; they include some classes of the archetype model, those common to both standards, and import the EN13606-SP and OpenEHR-SP ontologies.

Table 2 gives numeric details of these ontologies in terms of the classes, properties and restrictions. These ontologies allow representing archetypes in a more natural way than ADL does, and all the information regarding to the same clinical term can be accessed together. Moreover, an OWL-based archetype construction approach might guarantee the consistency of the knowledge, which cannot be granted by ADL.

Ontology	Classes	DP	OP	Restrictions
EN13606-SP	68	16	92	227
EN13606-AR	122	76	142	462
OpenEHR-SP	87	14	156	302
OpenEHR-AR	144	75	210	524

Table 2. Details of the OWL ontologies, in terms of classes, data properties (DP), object properties (OP) and restrictions.

3.3 The methodology for obtaining semantic archetypes

This methodology (Martinez-Costa et al., 2009) has been applied to OpenEHR specification and EN 13606 standard and it has been developed using Model Driven Engineering (MDE) techniques. The use of MDE in the development of the methodology allows to take advantage of the tools and experience of the MDE community and to communicate different technical spaces (TS) (Kurtev et al., 2003). The architecture of the solution is depicted in Figure 5, which involves four different technical spaces: Grammar, XML, MDE and Semantic Web. The transformation process is divided in three phases:

i) Representation of syntactic archetypes in MDE from the corresponding representation of archetypes in ADL.
ii) Transformation of models of syntactic archetypes into semantic ones in MDE.
iii) Obtention of OWL semantic archetypes.

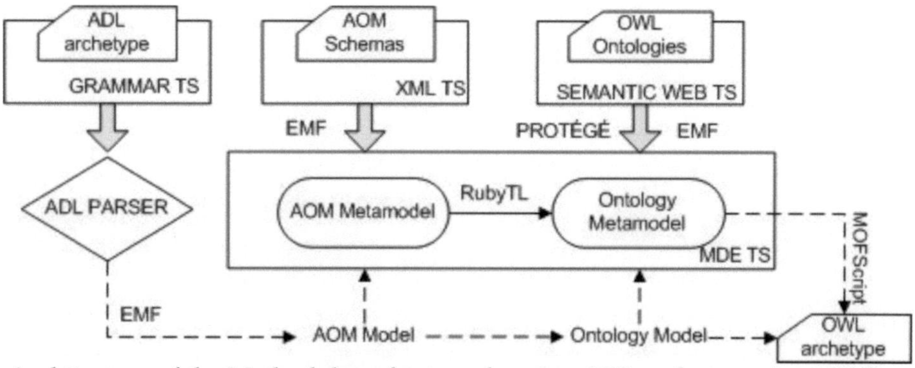

Fig. 5. Architecture of the Methodology for transforming ADL archetypes into OWL

This transformation process has been implemented in a tool which allows for transforming ADL archetypes into OWL for both EN 13606 and OpenEHR standard. This tool is available online (ADL2OWL) and has also been included in the LinkEHR editor (LinkEHR). Next, a more detailed description of the proposed methodology is given and its phases are explained in depth and illustrated through the running example for EN 13606 presented in Figure 2.

3.3.1 Phase I: Representation of syntactic archetypes in MDE

The input to the process is an archetype written according to the ADL Grammar (Grammar TS). This archetype has to be transformed into a generic model according to AOM. This model is generic because its representation is the same for every dual model-based standard. This transformation is carried out by using:

- An ADL parser (ADL-Parser): This is a syntactic parser for ADL, which returns the archetype as a tree of AOM objects.
- An XML serializer (XML-Serializer): This takes an AOM object tree as input and serializes it in XML according to the AOM XML Schema (AOM-Schemas).
- The Eclipse Modelling Framework (EMF): It obtains a metamodel from the AOM XML Schema and allows for serializing the previously obtained XML archetype as a model. Hence, the syntactic representation of archetypes is expressed in MDE.

At the end of this first phase a change of technical space has been produced, from Grammar TS to MDE. Figure 6 shows a fragment of the resulting AOM model for the Visual Acuity archetype example of Figure 2. It will be explained more detailed later in this section.

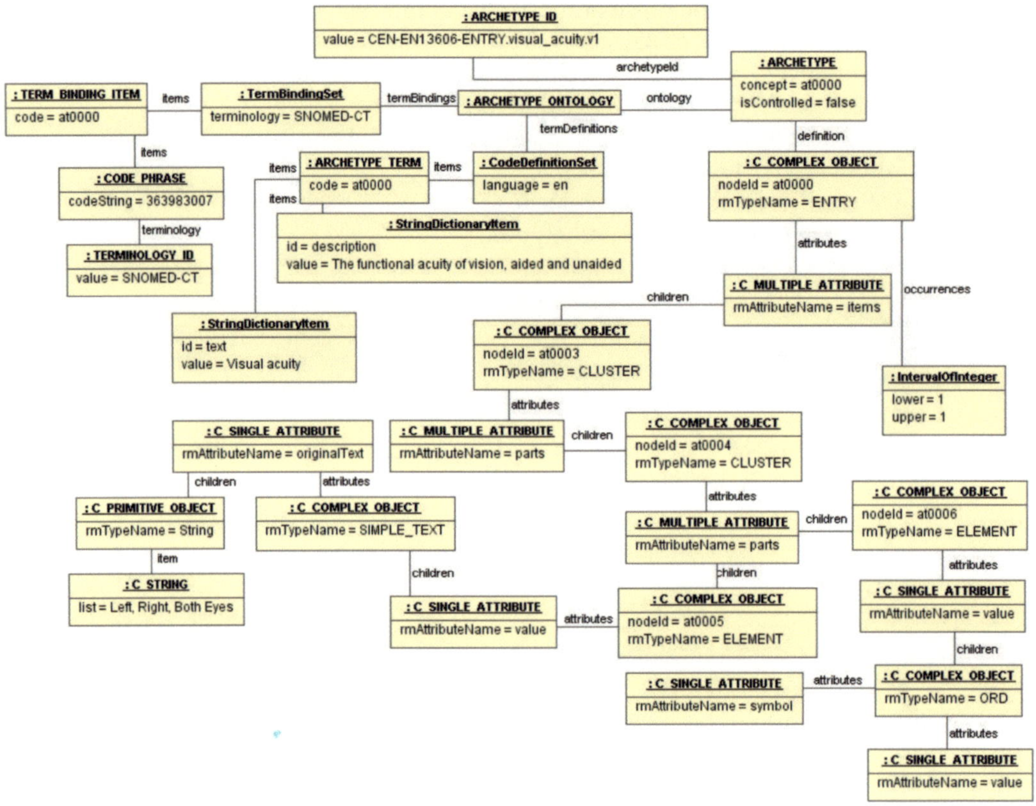

Fig. 6. The AOM model of the archetype obtained in phase I

3.3.2 Phase II: Transformation of models of syntactic archetypes into semantic ones in MDE

The second phase is carried out in the MDE space, and will make use the MDE representation of the archetype models used in both the Grammar and the Semantic Web TS to facilitate the transformation of archetypes from Grammar to Semantic Web. This requires the execution of two tasks:

- MDE representation of the semantic models for the EHR standards. In order to make the transformation, we need to obtain the metamodels for the semantic interpretation of the EHR standards. In this work, metamodels for the CEN-AR and OpenEHR-AR ontologies are obtained as a result of this task. The ODM standard (ODM) defines the representation of OWL ontologies in MDE TS. Protégé (Protege) implements the transformation from OWL to MDE TS and this was the technical solution used to get the metamodels from those ontologies.

- Definition of the transformations between the syntactic and the semantic representation in MDE. This task defines how to obtain a semantic archetype from a syntactic one. A model transformation language, RubyTL (Sanchez-Cuadrado et al., 2006), has been used to define the corresponding set of transformation rules to get semantic archetype models from AOM models.

Figure 7 depicts the corresponding semantic model obtained after performing the previous tasks over the AOM representation of the Visual Acuity archetype. Let us briefly describe some of the correspondences between both metamodels (the AOM metamodel and the semantic one) for the EN 13606 standard. According to the AOM, objects are represented as *C_COMPLEX_OBJECT* and attributes as *C_ATTRIBUTE (C_SINGLE_ATTRIBUTE/C_MULTIPLE_ATTRIBUTE)*. If the definitional part of the visual acuity archetype is analyzed the AOM model will be composed of:

- Nine *C_COMPLEX_OBJECT* having the following values for the pair (*rmTypeName, nodeId*): (1)("ENTRY","at0000"); (2)("CLUSTER", "at0003"); (3)("CLUSTER","at0004"); (4)("ELEMENT", "at0005"); (5)("SIMPLE_TEXT",""); (6)("ELEMENT","at00006"); (7)("ORD","").; (8)("CODED_TEXT",""); (9)("CD","").

- Ten *C_ATTRIBUTES* objects having the value for (*rmAttributeName)*: (1)("items"); (2)("parts"); (3)("parts"); (4)("value"); (5)("originalText"); (6)("value"); (7)("symbol"); (8)("value"); (9)("codedValue"); (10)("displayName").

The generic nature of AOM makes it impossible to make the semantics of these objects explicit, and it is embedded into the string attributes *rmTypeName* and *rmAttributeName*. By analyzing the value of these properties, the following mappings to the corresponding EN 13606 ontology model can be defined:

- Nine *C_COMPLEX_OBJECT* are converted into the following specific elements from EN 13606 reference model: (1)(ENTRY); (2)(CLUSTER); (3)(CLUSTER); (4)(ELEMENT); (5)(SIMPLE_TEXT); (6)(ELEMENT); (7)(ORD); (8)(CODED_TEXT); (9)(CD).

- Ten C_ATTRIBUTE are converted into specific attributes of the previous mentioned types from the reference model: (1)(items); (2)(parts); (3)(parts); (4)(value); (5)(originalText); (6)(value); (7)(symbol); (8)(value); (9)(codedValue); (10)(displayName).

-

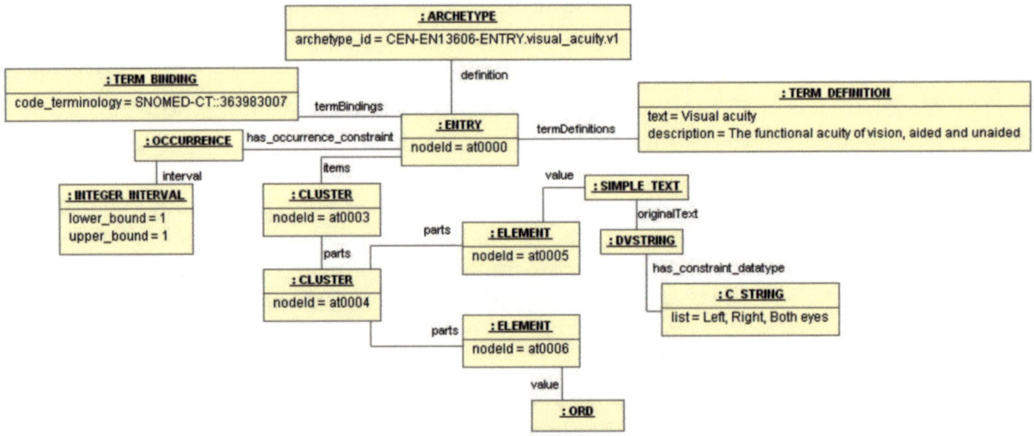

Fig. 7. Ontology model of the archetype obtained in phase II

3.3.3 Phase III: Obtention of OWL semantic archetypes

Finally, archetypes have to be expressed in OWL. In particular, an archetype will be represented as an individual of the class *ARCHETYPE* of the ontology of the particular standard. This transformation implies another technical space change: from MDE TS to Semantic Web TS. For this purpose, the process has to be formalized by specifying the transformation rules that would produce OWL archetypes from the semantic ones. These rules have been written using the model to text transformation language MOFScript (MOFScript). The result of this phase will be the OWL representation of the archetype which fragment is shown in figure 8.

Figure 8 depicts a fragment of the OWL representation of the ADL archetype introduced in Section 2. As it can be observed, an *entry*, which is a subtype of *archetype term*, has several properties as its *code*, *definition*, *occurrences* or *binding* to the SNOMED-CT terminology among others. In contrast, in the ADL archetype representation this information has to be found by string matching of some object attributes. For instance, the definition of this entry in the example should be found by looking up the definition term which code matches with the entry code *(at0000)*. The same situation occurs with its bindings or possible translations.

```
<?xml version = "1.0" encoding="ISO-8859-1"?>
  <rdf:RDF
    xmlns:cen-archetype="http://klt.inf.um.es/~cati/ontologies/CEN-AR-v2.0.owl#"
    ...
   <owl:Ontology rdf:about=""> .. </owl:Ontology>
   ...
   <cen:ENTRY rdf:ID="cen_ENTRY_749d135a-fbc5-4bf5-b761-46ac70728e09">
       <cen:cen_archetype_id rdf:datatype="http://www.w3.org/2001/XMLSchema#string">
         at0000
       </cen:cen_archetype_id>
       <cen-archetype:has_occurrence_constraint> ... </cen_archetype:has_occurrence_constraint>
        <cen-archetype:TERM_DEFINITIONrdf:ID="TERM_DEFINITION_b5476f5a">
                    <cen-archetype:text rdf:datatype="http://www.w3.org/2001/XMLSchema#string">
              Visual acuity
```

```
            </cen-archetype:text>
            <cen-archetype:description rdf:datatype="http://www.w3.org/2001/XMLSchema#string">
                The functional acuity of vision, aided and unaided
            </cen-archetype:description>
        </cen-archetype:TERM_DEFINITION>
        <cen-archetype:TERM_BINDING rdf:ID="TERM_BINDING_08b2e630">
           <cen-archetype:code_terminology rdf:datatype="
http://www.w3.org/2001/XMLSchema#string">
                363983007
          </cen-archetype:code_terminology>
         </cen-archetype:TERM_BINDING>
        <cen:cen_items>
           ...
        </cen:cen_items>
   ...
</rdf:RDF>
```

Fig. 8. Extract of the OWL representation of the visual acuity EN 13606 archetype

4. EHR clinical knowledge management

In the previous section, the methodology for obtaining OWL archetypes has been described. The motivation for this was also introduced in that section. There, it was stated that semantic activities could not be efficiently done with ADL but with OWL. Hence, once archetypes are expressed as semantic archetypes in OWL, they can benefit from the Semantic Web technologies. In this section, how such semantic activities can be performed on archetypes is described.

The Archetype Management System (ArchMS) (Fernandez-Breis et al., 2008) has been developed by our research group as the technological solution of the semantic management of archetypes. The objective of this system is to support the execution of clinical, semantics activities over archetypes. ArchMS is built on the idea of a virtual archetype repository for dual-model based EHR standards, whose basic unit is the archetype. In this way, it is capable of working with any dual model-based EHR standard. Given its virtual nature, archetypes are not physically stored in the system but their corresponding URI. Hence, batch processing for ensuring the validity of the links are required.

The current implementation of the system allows for working with both EN13606 and OpenEHR archetypes. It also allows performing two main types of activities with archetypes, namely, classification and search, which are described in the next subsections. Both ADL and OWL archetypes can be input to the system, although the semantic activities are launched on the OWL ones, so the ADL2OWL transformation described in the previous section would be executed for those supplied in ADL. The transformed archetypes are stored in the system. Furthermore, the semantic activities are currently performed over the base of archetypes of the same EHR standard, since the semantic interoperability of EN13606 and OpenEHR archetypes has not been achieved yet.

4.1 Classification of Archetypes

As it has already been mentioned in this chapter, clinical archetypes are specifications of clinical concepts that guide clinical practice and can be considered a template for data acquisition. Hence, the organization of archetypes is a critical issue for optimizing their use, and facilitating their sharing and reuse. Indeed, this would promote the homogeneous clinical practice and facilitate the exchange of clinical information across healthcare institutions.

In this work, the organization of the archetypes is provided by means of annotations, which can be defined in ArchMS with different granularity. The purpose of the annotation is not to facilitate the navigation of the archetype repository for humans but to add semantic metadata to the archetypes, so those can be used to support semantic activities. Hence, semantic annotations are provided. For this purpose, ArchMS makes use of an ontology of annotations, which model how annotations are associated to archetypes. This semantic metadata can be associated to a complete archetype or a term of it. In order to complete the definition process of the annotation, a classification resource is needed. The annotations of the (parts of the) archetype have to be done with respect to an OWL classification resource. Any type of domain ontology can be then used for annotation purposes. In this way, different types of annotations can be done, depending on the type of classification resource. On the one hand, governance ontologies might be used. This would allow for annotating the archetype according to their potential usage and application to particular patients, medical areas, etc. On the other hand, terminological annotations could be used, providing the clinical meaning of the terms of the archetype.

Figure 9 shows how annotations are created. In this example, the running visual acuity example of Figure 2 is associated to the eye concept defined in MESH (MESH), whose code is MESH_A.01.456.505.420, which the code for the eye. This annotation represents that such archetype is related to the eye. The selected archetype is shown on the left, whereas the classifier resource appears on the right. Since both are OWL content, they can be visually represented and browsed as trees, whose root nodes are, respectively, the archetype and the classifier resource. As a result of this annotation, new semantic metadata are added into the system for further exploitation, since the definition included in the archetype is enriched by the semantics associated from the MESH ontology.

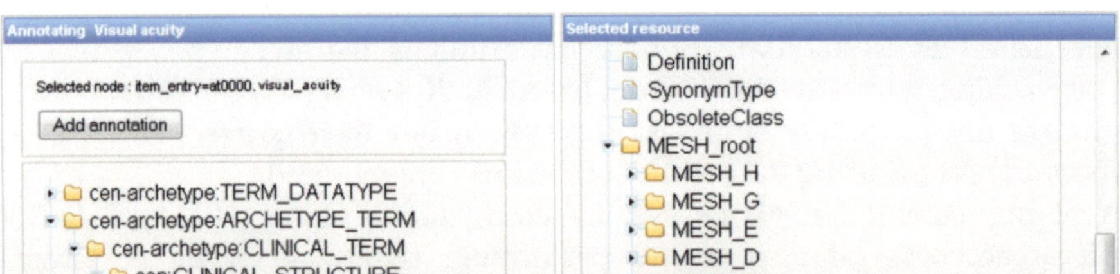

Fig. 9. Annotating the visual acuity archetype in ArchMS

4.2 Search

Semantic annotations are used in ArchMS for facilitating the organization of the archetypes in the repository and for supporting semantic search processes. ArchMS allows for the execution of different types of searches on the virtual base of archetypes, thus exploiting the repository in different dimensions. In general, two main searches can be performed: for similar archetypes, and for archetypes holding some properties, which are described next.

On the one hand, similar archetypes to a given one can be found by doing semantic comparisons in the context of the archetype ontology available for the particular standard. Archetypes are instances of that ontology, so that instances comparison mechanisms can be applied. These mechanisms would take into account the following categories:

- Conceptual proximity: It calculates the ontological distance between the classes in the ontology. For instance, in the context of OpenEHR, two Observation archetypes would be closer and, therefore, more similar than an Observation and a Folder.
- Annotations similarity: The annotations similarity compares the annotations associated to the archetypes. For this purpose, the annotations done with ArchMS are used.
- Property similarity: It compares the sets of properties defined for each archetype, that is, attributes and relations, including the annotations for each property.
- Linguistic proximity: It takes into account external resources to determine semantic distance between the medical concepts defined in the archetype. For this purpose, two external resources are used: Wordnet (Wordnet) and the UMLS metathesaurus (UMLS). Wordnet is more general, whereas UMLS is more exhaustive for medical domains. In order to calculate the similarity, hiperonymy and holonymy are the relations used.

The previous function returns a value between 0 and 1 for every pair of archetypes. Hence, the result of this search is a list of archetypes which is sorted by decreasing similarity. The most similar archetypes will then appear first.

This type of search is the base for suggesting annotations for new archetypes. In this way, the properties of the most similar archetypes can be displayed to the user, which may decide to add such annotations to the new archetype.

On the other hand, users can search for the archetypes that hold some properties. These can be either definitional or annotations properties:

- Definitional properties: They are defined in the proper structure of the archetype, mainly associated to the clinical data types and structures. For instance, we might be looking for archetypes written in a particular language, including an element measured in a certain unit, and so on.
- Annotation properties: They are the annotations associated to the archetype within the ArchMS system. For instance, we might be looking for archetypes related to a particular anatomic part, to a particular disease, for particular types of patients, and so on.

The queries can be mixed, that is, they can include both definitional and annotation properties. The result of this query is the set of archetypes that hold at least one of the requested properties. This set of archetypes is shown sorted by decreasing number of properties held. The archetypes holding more properties will then appear first.

5. Conclusions

In this chapter we have presented an approach for managing EHR-related clinical knowledge from a Semantic Web perspective. This effort constitutes an initial step in the context of the challenging task of achieving semantic interoperability between EHR systems. This would allow health care professionals to manage the complete EHR of patients, independently from which institution generated each clinical session. Semantic interoperability is then an essential factor for improving the quality and safety of patient care, public health, clinical research, and health service management.

To our opinion, the dual model-based architecture that distinguishes two modelling levels, information and knowledge, is the most suitable candidate for that purpose. In this architecture, archetypes represent the knowledge level and are an essential a tool for building clinical consensus in a consistent way and are considered basic to deliver fully interoperable EHRs (Kalra et al., 2008). Archetypes are defined by clinical domain experts using ADL, which is a generic language that does not support the execution of semantic activities. A significant fact of the importance of the dual model architecture and archetypes is the adoption of the European EHR EN 13606 standard by Sweden for their national EHR developments. Its usefulness is also strongly emphasized and its usage recommended by the final report of the Semantic Health project (SemanticHealth Report, 2009).

Hence, in this chapter a representation of archetypes using OWL has been proposed. This required the construction of OWL ontologies for EHR standards such as EN 13606 and OpenEHR standards. For this, the standards were semantically interpreted. A method for transforming ADL archetypes into OWL has also been presented in this chapter, because this allows performing semantic activities such as comparison, selection, classification and consistency checking in a more generic, easier and more efficient way. The OWL technology supports archetype management-related tasks, such as the selection of archetypes to be used in a health information system, the enrichment of archetypes based on the semantics of related-ones, and so on, which are some of the archetype management facilities offered by ArchMS, which has also been presented in this chapter. This system allows for annotating archetypes and performs different types of semantic searches on virtual archetypes repositories.

As further work, we will develop Semantic Web-based mechanisms for transforming OpenEHR archetypes into EN 13606 and vice versa, with the aim of achieving the semantic interoperability between these two dual model standards. The semantic integration of terminologies such as SNOMED-CT and our results should also be researched to enhance the execution of the semantic processes. Finally, we are also developing tools based on the semantic representation of archetypes for supporting the collaborative construction of archetypes and the automatic generation of web data forms.

6. Acknowledgements

This work has been possible thanks to the Spanish Ministry of Science and Innovation through project TSI2007-66575-C02 and to the Spanish Ministry of Industry, Tourism and Commerce through project TSI-020100-2008-577.

7. References

ADL-Parser. http://www.openehr.org/svn/ref_impl_java/trunk/adlparser/

ADL2OWL. http://klt.inf.um.es/~cati/Adl2Owl.htm

AOM-Shemas. http://www.openehr.org/releases/1.0.2/its/XML-schema/index.html

Beale, T. (2001). Archetypes, Constraint-based Domain Models for Future-proof Information Systems. http://www.deepthought.com.au/it/ archetypes/archetypes.pdf

Berners-Lee, T.; Hendler, J. & Lassila, O. (2001). The semantic web, Scientific American, May 2001 pp. 29-37

Brewster, C., O'Hara, K., Fuller, S., Wilks, Y., Franconi, E., Musen, M.A., Ellman, J., Buckinham Shum, S. (2004) Knowledge Representation with Ontologies: The Present and Future. IEEE Intelligent Systems vol 19(1): 72-81

Douglas C. Schmidt. (2006) Guest Editor's Introduction: Model-Driven Engineering, Computer, vol. 39, no. 2, pp. 25-31, Feb. 2006

EMF. http://www.eclipse.org/emf/

Fernandez-Breis, J.; Vivancos-Vicente, P.; Menarguez-Tortosa, M.; Moner, D.; Maldonado, J.; Valencia-Garcia, R. & Miranda-Mena, T. (2006). Using semantic technologies to promote interoperability between electronic healthcare records' information models. *Proceedings of 28th Annual International Conference of the IEEE Engineering in Medicine and Biology Society EMBS '06*, Aug. 2006 ,pp. 2614-2617, New York, United States

Fernandez-Breis, J.T.; Menarguez-Tortosa, M.; Martinez-Costa, C., Fernandez-Breis, E.; Herrero-Sempere, J.; Moner, D.; Sanchez, J.; Valencia-Garcia, R. & Robles, M. (2008). A semantic web-based system for managing clinical archetypes. *Proceedings of IEEE Eng Med Biol Soc 2008*, pp. 1482-1485, Vancouver, Canada

GEHR. http://www.chime.ucl.ac.uk/work-areas/ehrs/GEHR/index.htm

Gruber, T. R. (1993). A translation approach to portable ontology specifications. Knowledge Acquisition Vol. 5, pp.199-220.

HL7. Health Level Seven - http://www.hl7.org

ISO/TC 215 TR. (2008) Technical report about the EHR, its scope and context http://www.iso.org/iso/iso_catalogue/catalogue_tc/catalogue_detail.htm?csnumber=33397

Kalra, D. & Tapuria, A. (2008). EHR and Clinical Archetypes: time for Clinical Engagement. eHealth Planning and Management Symposium. Copenhagen, Denmark, November 2008

Kurtev, I.; Bezivin, J. & Aksit, M. (2003). Technological spaces: an initial appraisal. *Proceedings of CoopIS, DOA'2002 Federated Conferences, Industrial track*

LinkEHR. http://www.linkehr.com/

Martinez-Costa, C.; Menarguez-Tortosa, M.; Fernandez-Breis, J. & Maldonado, J. (2009) A model-driven approach for representing clinical archetypes for semantic web environments. *Journal of Biomedical Informatics* February 2009, Vol. 42, No. 1, pp. 150-164

Meta-Architecture. http://www.openehr.org/releases/1.0.2/

MESH. http://www.nlm.nih.gov/mesh/

MOFScript. http://www.eclipse.org/gmt/mofscript/

ODM. Ontology metamodel definition specification. http://www.omg.org/cgibin/ doc?ad/2006-05-01.pdf (2006)

OpenEHR. http://www.openehr.org

OWL. http://www.w3.org/tr/owl-ref/

OWL 2.0. http://www.w3.org/2007/OWL/wiki/OWL_Working_Group

Protege. http://protege.stanford.edu/

Sanchez-Cuadrado, J.; Garcia-Molina, J. & Menarguez-Tortosa, M. (2006). Rubytl: A practical, extensible transformation language. *Proceedings of ECMDA-FA 2006*. pp. 158-172

SemanticHealth Report. (2009) *Semantic Interoperability for Better Health and Safer Healthcare*, 2009, Deployment and Research Roadmap for Europe. ISBN-13 : 978-92-79-11139-6

Swedish-decision. A national decision in Sweden on healthcare information standard. http://www.e-recordcompany.eu/attachments/019_Info_about_Swedish_decision.pdf

SNOMED-CT. http://www.snomed.org/

UMLS. http://www.nlm.nih.gov/research/umls

UNE-EN13606. http://www.centc251.org

Van Heijst, G., A. T. Schreiber, & B. J. Wielinga (1997) 'Using explicit ontologies in KBS development'. International Journal of Human-Computer Studies, 45, 183-292.

Wordnet. http://wordnet.princeton.edu/

XML-Serializer. http://www.openehr.org/svn/ref_impl_java/TRUNK/xml-serializer/

12

Use Case Semantics for Business Process Validation

Michael Wolters and German Nemirovskij
Albstadt-Sigmaringen University
Germany

1. Introduction

During the last decade the technologies which emerged in the context of Semantic Web research are developed to meet the challenges that are arising in the rapidly growing e-business domain. The main intention of such approaches is to relieve humans of decision making tasks requiring analysis and comparison of significant volumes of information (that is often heterogeneous or badly structured).

This chapter introduces an approach to quality management of business process models. It is focusing on the analysis of correspondences between process models and use cases that as we believe should be considered as operational expression of requirements to the business processes being modeled. The correspondences figured out in this procedure allow for assumptions to be made about the process models quality which is defined with respect to the requirement on business processes.

To facilitate the search for such correspondences an ontology describing both domains of interest, the one of process models and one of use case descriptions, was developed. The ontology when used as a common vocabulary facilitates homogeneous representation and efficient comparison of process models and use cases originally represented in different notations. This ontology together with the methodologies for converting process models and use case descriptions into the ontology based notation form the focal point of this chapter.

The quality aspects of business processes such as compatibility of collaborating sub processes or detection and avoiding of dead-locks in the process flow are addressed by modern tools for process modeling and management as well as by modern technologies such as Semantic Web Services. Yet the main question in the context of quality management remains the assessment of process validity.

The validity of a business process is basically its ability to tackle the use cases that are typically specified in the beginning of the business process development. At the same time we believe that the validation of business processes should be carried out with respect to their "life cycle" starting with the requirement definition, followed by business processes design and proceeding further with selection, development and orchestration of (web) services and finally ending with processing and testing. The earlier in the life cycle the validation takes place, the easier it is to change the process being developed, and the more

efficient is the development procedure. Therefore we think of the comparison of use cases and business process models as key approach to the validation of business processes.
On this purpose use cases and process models should at first be specified using the same notation. After this step their specifications must be mapped onto each other and compared semantically, e. g. with respect to the meaning of terms expressed by relations between them. Finally the inconsistencies or conflicts among them should be identified and assessed.
To carry out these three steps a framework dedicated to this task is required. Such a framework includes the following components:
- An ontology defining the common vocabulary and relations between terms that occur in use case descriptions and in process models. Though there isn't any formal standard for use case descriptions they usually fulfill a kind of latent standard and hence use similar vocabulary and structures. The vocabulary of process models on the other hand is restricted by the notation used for modeling, e. g. BPMN.
- An information-extraction mechanism for informally described and tabular structured use cases, whereby the information extraction is currently implemented using the semantic annotation approach. The result of this process is a machine-readable data structure referring to the common ontology mentioned above.
- A mechanism for transforming formally specified process models (e. g. with WS-BPEL) into a machine-readable data structure again referring to the same ontology.
- A tool for mapping and comparing this kind of data structures, detection of inconsistencies and conflicts and finally the graphic visualization of the comparison results.
In order not to go beyond the scope of this chapter we will concentrate on the first of the above mentioned components. The other will be part of our further research.

2. Business process specification

2.1 Models for business processes

Non- or semi-formally a business process is often described as a set of activities or tasks carried out by machines or humans and sequenced by a set of executive rules and constraints. However such a description does not make any difference between activities carried out in reality within very certain terms of time, e.g. *from 12:00 to 12:15 on 19.04.2009*, by concrete actors, e.g. by a clerk *Mr. Smith* or by an application *AXF#675* hosted on a computer with *IP 192.168.1.1*, and those activities that are specified in the form of tasks, directives or assignments for execution and used as a reference by concrete actors at a specific time.
Yet, in a formal view on business processes such a distinction is taken into account: The term *Business Process Model* is defined basically as a set of sequenced activity models or tasks. A *Business Process Instance* consists basically of activity or task instances (in this paper we use these terms as synonyms) and represents an application of a business process model by specific actors and under concrete circumstances and terms of time.
Following the formal definition, every business process model consists of nodes and directed edges. The latter expresses the relationship respectively the control flow between the different nodes within process models, whereas every edge has a conjunction with exactly two nodes and each node has at least one associated edge. According to (Weske, 2007 pp. 89) a node may describe an activity model, an event model or a gateway model.

Activity models represent the work units that have to be performed to fulfill the goal of the business process. They have always exactly one incoming and one outgoing edge.
Event Models stand for the occurrence of states relevant for the business process.
The control flow of activities, including sequences, split or join nodes, is expressed by *Gateway Models*.
Business process models can be specified using different notations. One of them is Event-driven Process Chains (EPC) (Tsai et al., 2006). EPC models are semi-formal and if used as specifications for automated execution often need additional explanations. Petri Net is an alternative notation that is more formal than EPC (Desel & Juhás, 2001). However Petri Net notation may be less expressive for human actors, especially if a large business process is specified. This special concept is described in greater detail in section 3.3.
In the last years however a comparatively new (developed 2002) Business Process Modeling Notation BPMN (Allweyer, 2008) became highly popular. The reason for this is that BPMN assembles a number of advantageous concepts known from preceding notations. One of the main advantages of BPMN is that it provides of a good comprehensibility for both business analysts who create processes and for technical developers who have to implement them.

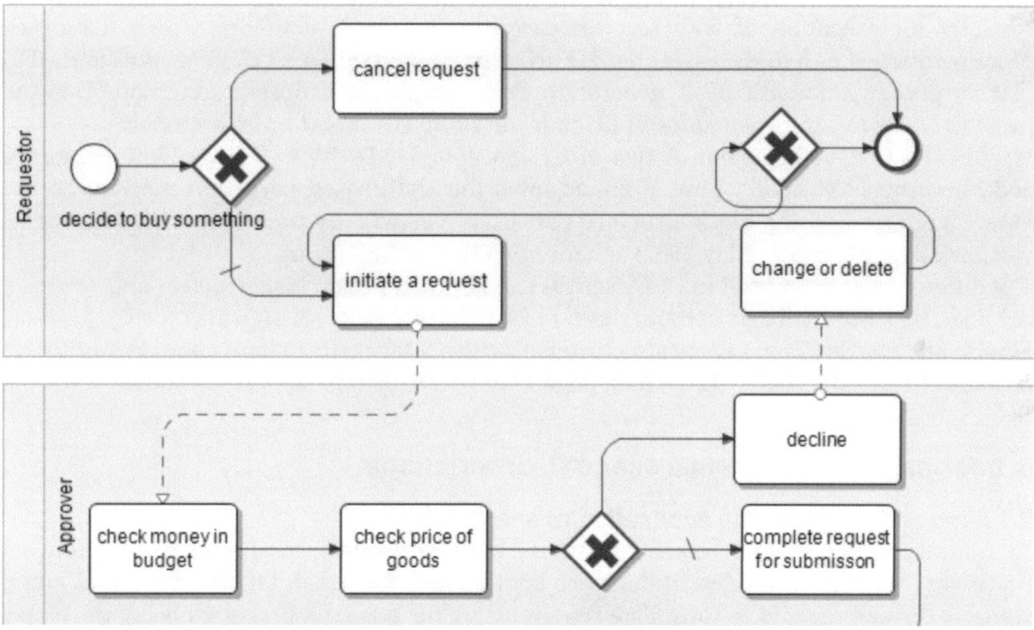

Fig. 1. Detail of a business process diagram created with Intalio Designer[1]

A sample business process model shown in figure 1[2] is specified by means of BPMN. It contains each of the three different node types mentioned above as well as the edges

---

[1] Intalio-Designer was one of the first implementations of BPMN, see http://www.intalio.com/products/designer/ for details.
[2] The business process model displayed in figure 1 is a simplified implementation of a use case developed by (Cockburn, 2001) using the BPMN. This specific use case example is described in greater detail in the chapter "Use cases".

represented by directed lines between the nodes. The two circles in the upper part of the picture specify event model nodes, whereas the left circle represents an initial event and the right (bold) circle represents a final event. Gateway models are displayed by diamonds, in this case used as XOR-splits, denoting the begin and the end of alternatively executed activity sequences. Finally the rectangles with rounded edges represent activity models. Another concept of BPMN are swimlanes modeling organizational aspects of a business process. Swimlanes can contain one pool (representing whole organizations) and two or more lanes (representing business entities like departments or single people). A pool can be seen in the upper part of figure 1 displayed as a grey colored rectangle labeled with "Requestor" at the left side of it. Lanes can split a pool in different parts by adding a horizontal line. The upper part of a lane called "Approver" is shown in figure 1 as well.

2.2 WS-BPEL

To enable automation of complex tasks such as processing, comparison or evaluation of business process models (the latter is strongly related to the approach described in this chapter) a formal executable specification of such models is needed. In this context Web Services Business Process Execution Language (WS-BPEL or short BPEL) developed basically for execution of web services carrying out single activities within a business process emerged as a de-facto standard. Furthermore there are a lot of BPM-tools and -IDEs that support an automatic BPEL generation. For example the Eclipse-based Intalio Designer (used to create figure 1) generates BPEL code out of BPMN based process models.
WS-BPEL was developed out of two other concepts: IBM's "Web Service Flow Language" and Microsoft's "XLANG". Thus BPEL adopted the XML based part from the Web Service Flow Language and the block structure part from XLANG. By now WS-BPEL has reached version 2.0 (published in May 2007) enhanced by the OASIS[3] group.
The different elements used in BPEL scripts can be divided into *basic activities* and *structured activities*. Some of the basic activities are: *Invoke, Receive, Reply, Assign* and *Empty*. *Sequence, Flow, While* and *Switch* are some structured activities. More information about WS-BPEL can be found in (OASIS, 2007). Figure 6 on page 9 shows an example of a BPEL code.

3. Informal and semi-formal scenario descriptions

3.1 Aims and goals for the application of scenarios

In contrast to the formal representation of process models aiming at their automated processing the scenarios' descriptions are kept usually informal. Often the general aim of scenario development is to formulate requirements for business processes being developed or to achieve a more thorough understanding of business processes by human actors. In the projects for establishing of new and reengineering of existing business process scenarios are usually described in the beginning phase, before specification of business process models.
(Beringer, 1997) defines scenarios as "… a sequence of interaction instances and/or state changes of objects. Interaction and state changes are also called actions." She writes furthermore of triggering scenarios with "trigger events" and defines the latter as an

---

[3] OASIS = Organization for the Advancement of Structured Information Standards

interaction or another event. In our approach we also use the term *trigger* to stress the causal or invoking role of events for actions or action sequences (see below).
In relation to business process models, scenarios represent one possible flow of activities or *operations* carried out by interacting actors. So all alternative flows are composed in different single scenarios. However usually scenarios reflect only the surface of interaction, and hence contain only the actions *seen* by interacting actors. Therefore some actions that take place in the *background* of interaction process may stay out of scenario, even though they are parts of a corresponding business process model.
For the business process model shown in figure 1, a quiet simple and short scenario can be specified as follows. Starting with the initial event (respectively *trigger)* labelled "decide to buy something" this scenario would continue with the *operation* "cancel request" and end after this step. An alternative more complex scenario for the same business process model would be: "initiate a request", "check money in budget", "check price of goods" and "complete request for submission".
In the following sections we briefly describe most popular notations for the specification of business scenarios.

3.2 Use Cases

Use Cases were developed for requirements engineering within the software development process. First mentioned by Ivar Jacobsen (Jacobson et al., 1994), Use Cases became quite popular especially in object-oriented Software Engineering. By using this concept an interaction with a (computer) system is defined from a user's point of view. Different steps of activities have to be processed to reach a certain goal which was originally specified by this user.

Use Case #	Use Case 5: Buy Something	
Primary Actor	Requestor	
Goal in Context	Requestor buys something through a system, gets it. Does not include paying for it.	
Preconditions	none	
Postconditions	*Minimal Guarantees*	Every order sent out has been approved by a valid authorizer. Order was tracked so that company can be billed only for valid goods received
	Success Guarantee	Requestor has goods, correct budget ready to be debited.
Trigger	Requestor decides to buy something	
Main Success Scenario	*Step*	*Action*
	1	Requestor: initate a request
	2	Approver: check money in budget, check price of goods, complete request for submission
	3	Buyer: ceck contents of storage, find the best vendor for goods
	4	Authorizer: validate Approver's signature
	5	Buyer: complete request for ordering, initiate PO with Vendor
	...	...
Extensions	*Step*	*Branching Action*
	...	...
	1b	At any time prior of receiving goods, Requestor can cancel request
	...	...
	2c	Approver decines: Send back to Requestor for change or deletion
	...	...
Secondary Actor	Vendor	

Fig. 2. Example of a use case description in tabular format

So the functional requirements of a system's behaviour can be specified in an objective and simple way without any loss of semantics. A more specific formalism about how Use Cases should be written and developed was given later by Alistair Cockburn (Cockburn, 2001). He differentiates between so called "casual" and "fully dressed" use cases. In the latter all possible requirements of a user-system-interaction are documented in detail. An example of a typical fully dressed use case description (this one is a simplified version of a use case originally created by (Cockburn, 2001)) is shown in extracts in figure 2.
Meanwhile the Object Management Group (OMG) has integrated the concept of Use Cases as a standard notation by developing a special UML diagram for their graphical modeling (see at e. g. OMG's http://www.uml.org). Although this diagram doesn't have the same detailed expressiveness as a fully dressed use case, UML can compensate this by an additional use of activity diagrams.
Text-based use case descriptions (usually documented in a tabular format) still lack such a widely approved formalism. However an analysis of text based use cases shows that such descriptions usually follow very few patterns determining a common vocabulary and structural principles. The set of such patterns can be generalized as a semi-formal *latent standard*.
This fact is acknowledged by a number of approaches for transformation of graphical and text based use case notation into each other (e. g. Pilarski & Knauss, 2008). In the approach described in this chapter we also utilize this fact for structure analysis and semantic annotation of text based use cases. Due to space limitation in this chapter we restrict the definition of use case description to text-based ones. Nevertheless the mapping of use cases and process models illustrated below can be applied as well for graphical use cases specified with UML.

3.3 Other Concepts for scenario description

Within this section we want to give a brief introduction to other notations for informal or semi-formal scenario descriptions. Even though these concepts differ from use cases in some aspects of representation they might be used for the validation of business process models in the way shown below.

Task Script

Ian Graham (Graham, 1995) created the concept of task scripts for modeling scenarios. A task script describes the interaction between actors and external entities with the objective of fulfilling the specified system's goal. In contrast to use cases, task scripts are implemented as objects so they can be organized into composition, classification, and usage structures. Among others Graham defines the following terms as parts of task scripts: Task Name, Task Body, Supertasks, Component Tasks, Task Attributes, Exceptions, Rules, etc. Task scripts are mainly used in the Financial Object-Oriented Rapid Analysis Method (FORAM) (Beringer, 1997).

Sequence diagram

The sequence diagram is part of the UML notation and a specialization of an interaction diagram. Sometimes sequence diagrams are called event-trace diagrams and are closely related to Message Sequence Charts (http://www.itu.int/rec/T-REC-Z.120). By using this kind of scenario description an interaction and an interchange of messages is graphically defined. Each partner participating in an interaction is denoted by a vertical line called lifeline. Messages are illustrated by horizontal arrows in the order in which they occur. (Rupp et al., 2007)

Event diagram

Mathias Weske introduced in (Weske, 2007) a concept, called event diagram, which can be used for scenario description. In these event diagrams the time flow is shown in arrows going left to right whereas events are displayed by single bullets. Directed arcs represent the relationship of these events. For example of this scenario describing concept is shown in figure 3. Event diagrams may be used for representation of scenarios as well as process instances.

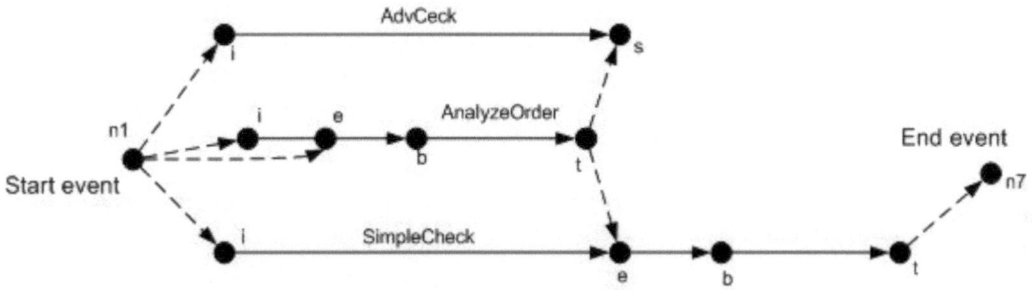

Fig. 3. Event Diagram example (see Weske, 2007, p. 95)

Petri net

Petri nets mentioned above can be used for specification of business process models as well as for representation of scenarios. The latter is especially realized by token concept, an approach for scenario-based modeling using Petri nets is introduced in (Fahland, 2008) for example.

Petri nets are represented as bipartite graphs and are composed of transitions, places and directed arcs which connect the places and transitions. Places can contain one or more token which can change their position when a transition *fires*. The current state of the petri net (thus the system or the process respectively that is modeled by this petri net) is represented by the position of its token(s).

In figure 4 an example of a simple Petri net is shown before (left side) and after (right side) a transition. While the token is at place p1 the transition t1 is enabled and may fire. After the transition the token was removed from p1 and added to p2.

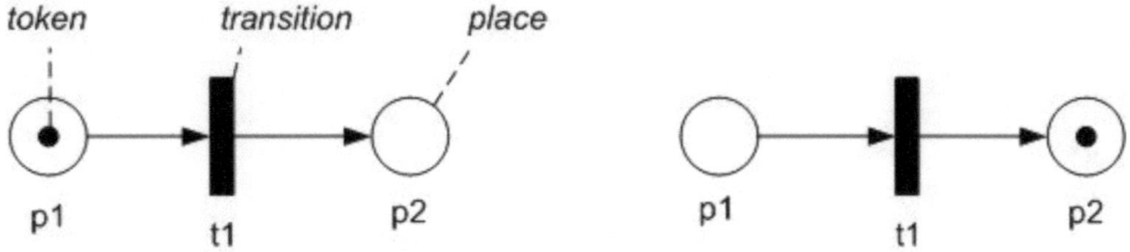

Fig. 4. Petri net example (Kashyap et al., 2008)

4. Validation of business process models using use case descriptions

As stated in the introduction the primary goal of the approach described in this paper is the validation of business process models. The validity of a business process model is assessed by searching for correspondences to the requirements for business processes and hence to the business scenarios, e. g. use case description, expressing these requirements.
Which correspondences are being searched for? When is a BPM valid? The formal definition of validity will be given in section 6. For now we define it informally.

Definition: A business process is valid with respect to a use case if the following rules are fulfilled:

1.) *Steps described in the use case correspond to particular activity model(s) of a considered business process*
2.) *The process flow connects these activity models to sub-processes corresponding to the Main Success Scenario and its Extensions specified in the use case*
3.) *In the business process model the connection of sub-processes corresponding to the Main Success Scenario and its Extensions is realized by means of gateway model(s) or event models*
4.) *The actor(s) is(are) involved in the use case correspond to the actor(s) involved in the business process being modeled*

As the space in this chapter is limited we restrict the definition to the four points introduced above. A definition of validity regarding other concepts that should be considered, for example trigger, is left out of our theory's demonstration but could be adopted analogous to our concept.
We will illustrate this definition by means of two examples. As we described in section 2 quite a few different notations can be used for specification of business process models. Figure 5 shows a sample of the mapping approach while BPMN is in use.

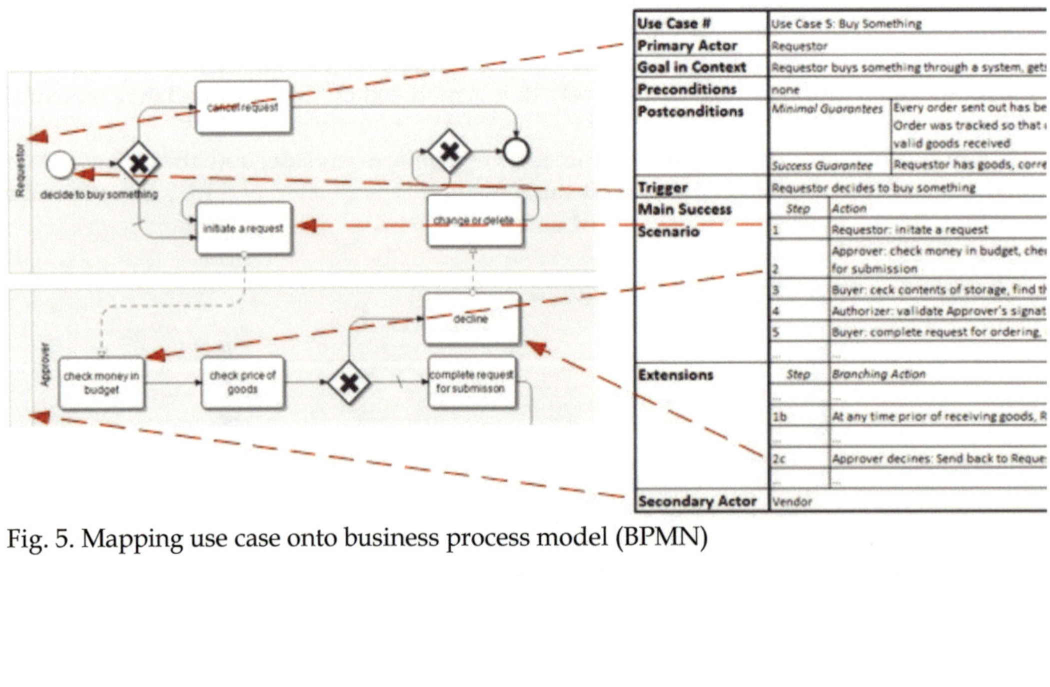

Fig. 5. Mapping use case onto business process model (BPMN)

1) As stated in the first rule of the definition above, all steps specified in the use case description (right part of the figure) are realized as activity models (rectangle with rounded edges). However, due to improvement of readability not all correspondences are shown in figure 5.
2) The starting point (*trigger*) of the use case equates to the start event model shown in the upper left part of figure 5 as a circle. The steps of the main success scenario (which are displayed in the use case specification *Scenario*) correspond to the activity models occurring in the process flow in the same sequence. This is true also for the steps of the *Extension-scenario*.
3) The steps specified in the use case as *Extension-scenario* correspond to the activity models of the sub-process started by a XOR-gateway (displayed as diamond).
4) The *primary* and *secondary actors* specified in the use case are mapped onto the pools of the business process model: The primary author *Requestor* is realized by the single pool in the upper part of the diagram and the secondary actor *Vendor* by another pool beneath it.

Figure 6 shows another mapping sample. However, a business process model is specified here using BPEL. Therefore the parts of the use case description have to be mapped to the BPEL components, e.g. the connection of *Main Success Scenario* and an *Extension* concept is realized by *<bpel:if>*- and *<bpel:else>*-constructs, while use case steps are represented by *<bpel:empty>*-, *<bpel:receive>*- or *<bpel:assign>*-tags.

Fig. 6. Mapping use case onto business process model (BPEL)

The examples shown above demonstrate that the mapping of business process models onto use cases can be applied to the effective validation of the former. People who have advanced knowledge in the field of process modeling can carry out this, doubtless complex and tedious work, in intuitive manner, even though business process models are often specified in different notations.

At the same time automation of this procedure promises to save significant resources while solving quality management tasks. Yet for machines searching for correspondences between use cases and business process models appears to be a big challenge. There are two reasons for that. First of all the comparison of artifacts specified in different notations (e.g. tabular use cases and graphical business process models) is difficult to formalize. Secondly use case specifications are informal per se.
However if searching for exact correspondences is replaced by searching for similarities, the automation of the mapping process becomes practicable. This idea is the foundation of the approach described in this paper.

5. Ontologies for Representation of Knowledge Semantics

5.1 Semantic Interoperability and Ontologies

For the automated search for correspondences between specifications of complex artifacts, e.g. between process models and use cases, a high level of semantic interoperability of these specifications is substantial.
In colloquial language semantic interoperability may be interpreted as a requirement, that terms or expressions occurring in different specification documents in equal form must have equal meaning. From the formal point of view the semantic interoperability of specifications facilitates avoiding of structural and semantic conflicts while interpreting. (Wache, 2003; Wache & Stuckenschmidt, 2001) describe basically three *structural* and two *semantic* conflicts.
To the category of *structural* conflicts belong:

- Bilateral conflicts, when in different description systems different identifiers, names or standard types (integer, float, string) for specification of the same world objects or artifacts are in use
- Multilateral Conflicts, when information represented in one source a single element can only partially be found in as a single element in another source.
- Meta-Level-Conflicts, when in different sources different modeling approaches are applied for representation of the same kind of information, e.g. a web site can be defined as a resource, as an entity or as an information unit

Semantic conflicts are:

- Data Conflicts, that appear when different metric systems or scales are used in different sources; however the single values located in these sources may look equal, in fact they should be distinguished with respect to the metric system currently in use, e.g. temperature according to Celsius or Fahrenheit scale.
- Domain Conflicts are situations when relations between classes specified in different classifications are not evident, e.g. overlapping: if a class of business tasks and a class of activity models specified in two classifications have a shared set of objects, however at the same time there are objects that belong to one class and do not belong to another.

To achieve the semantic interoperability of specifications, e. g. to avoid the conflicts listed above, the specifications' components, attributes and structure should be described using the same syntax and vocabulary. It is also necessary that within the domain of interest an agreement for the interpretation of expressions composed using the vocabulary is met. This

means that each term of the vocabulary should represent a group or a class of domain related objects sharing a well defined set of properties, whereby each of these properties is associated with a well defined set or space of values.
Such classes of objects are called concepts while the process of concept definition is called conceptualization. The explication of vocabulary shared by a group of specifications coming along with conceptualization of specific domain knowledge is commonly known as a Domain Ontology (compare to (Uschold & Gruninger 1996)). The descriptions of world objects or artifacts which are based on a domain ontology will be "understood" by actors (machines or humans) using the same ontology for the interpretation of the domain related expressions and specifications.

5.2 Foundation Ontologies

The development and usage of independent domain ontologies however reveals a number of drawbacks:

- Even within one specific domain the intention of ontology development is often a solution of a single specific task. From perspectives of different tasks however different conceptualization of the domain of interest may result. Therefore semantic interoperability of expressions and specifications based on different ontologies of the same domain is not guaranteed.
- Due to incompatibilities, e.g. conflicts described above, the knowledge exposed in different domain ontologies can't be shared easily and hence can't be taken into account for the solution of specific tasks. A good illustration for that are two ontologies developed in two strongly related projects aiming at the development of frameworks for semantic Business Process Management: *SemBiz* (http://www.sembiz.org) and *SUPER* (http://www.ip-super.org)[4]. Although the need for synergetic use of ontologies is stated on the SemBiz's web site, the lack of semantic interoperability between ontologies prevents the developers from achieving this goal.
- Extensions of domain ontologies to solve interdomain (mostly interdisciplinary) tasks may need a significant revision of given conceptualization. The reason for that is often the influence of the "other" domain, where the given conceptualization might be incorrect.
- If overlapping of different domains occurs the work for conceptualization of the overlapping parts may be carried out redundantly.

To address the problems listed above foundation ontologies (also known as upper-ontologies or top-level-ontologies) are developed. "Foundational ontologies are conceptualizations that contain specifications of domain independent concepts and relations based on formal principles derived from linguistics, philosophy, and mathematics." (Mika et al., 2004). In other words, development of a foundation ontology is an attempt to state a rough and abstract conceptualization of the world.
Domain ontologies usually use foundation ontologies as the "upper-level". Domain ontologies carry on the conceptualization started in a foundation ontology. Formally this

[4] Both ontologies are called BPMO (=Business Process Modeling Ontology)

means that in a domain ontology classes of objects or artifacts are defined as sub-classes of those specified in a foundation ontology.
For example the class "Business Process" in an ontology for the e-business domain can be specified as a sub-class of the class "Process" defined in a foundation ontology.
In spite of the fact that currently a number of foundation ontologies are known - e. g. *Cyc* one of the oldest ontology being developed since 1985 (http://www.cyc.com), *Basic Formal Ontology* that remarkably incorporates three-dimensional and four-dimensional (adding the time dimension) perspectives on reality (http://www.ifomis.org/bfo), or *Word Net* which exposes a set of psycholinguistic principles (http://wordnet.princeton.edu) - there is still no common standard or *the* foundation ontology that would be used as a base for all domain ontologies developed world wide. The question, if such an ontology will ever be developed is difficult to answer. There is a spectacular debate about feasibility and applicability of such common standard foundation ontology. The argumentation against such an ontology is based on the idea that ontologies developed by humans always expose the cultural, historical, linguistic and geographic context the developers live in. Hence the objective view on the world that could be reflected by a common standard foundation ontology cannot be stated by human beings. And vice versa: the feasibility of such an ontology comes close to the question if God exists.
Having in mind the conceptualization of Business Process Modeling domain on the one hand and use cases (UC) domain on the other hand we selected the Descriptive Ontology for Linguistic and Cognitive Engineering DOLCE (http://www.loa-cnr.it/DOLCE.html) as basis for our approach. DOLCE consists of different modules that can be used separately, e.g. *Plans, SpatialRelations, TemporalRelations, DOLCE-Lite* and *ExtendedDnS.* The latter module developed by Aldo Gangemi (Mika et al., 2004) is the *Description and Situation* ontology with an extended vocabulary for social reification. *DOLCE-Lite* which contains the most fundamental part of DOLCE and ExtendedDnS serve as base for all other modules.
DOLCE is one of the most popular foundation ontologies especially in the domain of e-Business that is related to Business Process Modeling and use cases as a super-domain to sub-domains. One of the basic ideas propagated in DOLCE is the distinction between perdurant and endurant objects. Perdurant objects such as *processes, events* or *activities live* in time whereas endurant objects are specifications related to perdurant objects separated from the time flow. *Workflows, plans, situations* or *people* belong to the endurant concepts (Magro & Goy, 2008).

5.3 ScIOn: Scenario and Business Process Model - Ontology

This paradigm of DOLCE corresponds well to the idea of business process specification. On the one hand business processes should be qualified as perdurant objects, e. g. artifacts *living* in time, artifacts that can be qualified by states achieved at certain moments described by certain temporal values. On the other hand the specification of such states related to the terms of time (that is a scenario) is endurant. The workflow specification (also known as a process model) is also endurant.
The description of relations between scenarios and process models as well as between their parts is the most important aim of the *ScIOn* (=*ScenarIo Ontology*) ontology developed by the authors of this paper to facilitate semantic interoperability of use cases (that is a particular form of scenario) and process model specifications.

The ScIOn that uses DOLCE as the upper-level ontology is shown in figure 7. All blue coloured oval forms show concepts of the DOLCE2.1-Lite-Plus. The fact that these concepts are specified in different sub-modules of DOLCE can be concluded from the name prefixes, e.g. concepts labelled with "edns:..." belong to the *ExtendedDnS* module. 13 concepts without prefixes belong to the core part of ScIOn. They all inherit properties of DOLCE concepts. The inheritance is represented by edges ending with triangle arrows. For example the core concept of ScIOn, *Scenario* is derived from the DOLCE concept *edns:path* that according to its description is "a concept used to sequence perdurant phenomena as components of some description". In turn the concept *Process Model* inherits the concept *sys:workflow* of the DOLCE module *Systems*.

ScIOn specifies a *Process Model*, according to definition from the section 2 as an aggregation (specified by diamond-ending arrows) of flow links (edges), gateways models, activity models (in ScIOn called *Operations*) and events models (ScIOn: *Triggers*). The process model elements are linked to each other using the DOLCE properties *edns:successor* and *edns:predecessor* and to the *Process Model* itself by the ScIOn property *elementOf*. At the same time *Operation* and *Trigger* are elements of the concept *Scenario*. In this case the relation is also implemented by the property *elementOf*.

By this means ScIOn facilitates direct mapping of process models (e. g. Business Process Models) onto *Scenarios*, and hence onto use cases. The concept Use Case, in turn, is specified as an aggregation of a set of scenarios, pre- and post-condition. By means of the DOLCE property *pla:main-goal* that was inherited from its super class *edns:plan* use case is associated with a certain goal, that should be reached after the use case is completed.

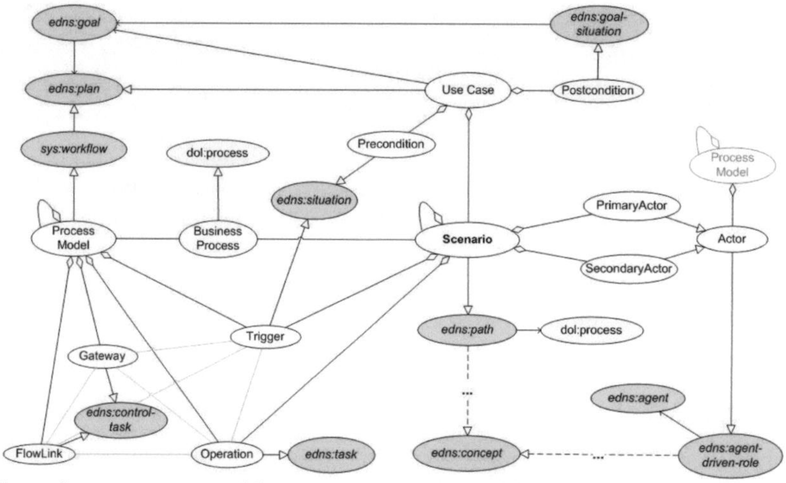

Fig. 7. Ontology for scenarios and business process models[5]

If one (perdurant) business process is on the one hand described by a process model and if there exists a set of scenarios federated in a use case, whose goal specifies one of the possible process results, we assume that the four rules of business process validity formulated in section 4 will be fulfilled.

[5] The grey colored concept "Process Model" above the concept "Actor" is the same as in the left part of figure 7 and was only added to not derange its clarity.

To demonstrate the contribution of ScIOn to semantic interoperability of use case and process model specifications we show a mapping of the use case and process model onto each other intermediated by ScIOn (compare to figure 5, showing the same mapping however without the ScIOn intermediation). For the simplification in figure 8 we show only 14 concepts: the 13 ScIOn core concepts and *edns:goal,* that is involved directly in the mapping. In this example we use a business process model specified with BPMN. As direct translation of BPMN to BPEL is proven to be feasible and even implemented in a number of tools such as *Intalio Designer* we skip the example showing the same process model specified in BPEL.

As shown in the example above ScIOn provides a common vocabulary for homogeneous representation of both artifacts being mapped onto each other. Furthermore, if expressed with ScIOn vocabulary the relations between artifacts' components and their semantics become explicitly and formally specified. The most important achievement of such representation is the prospect/opportunity for automation of correspondences identification, i. e. automation of validation process.

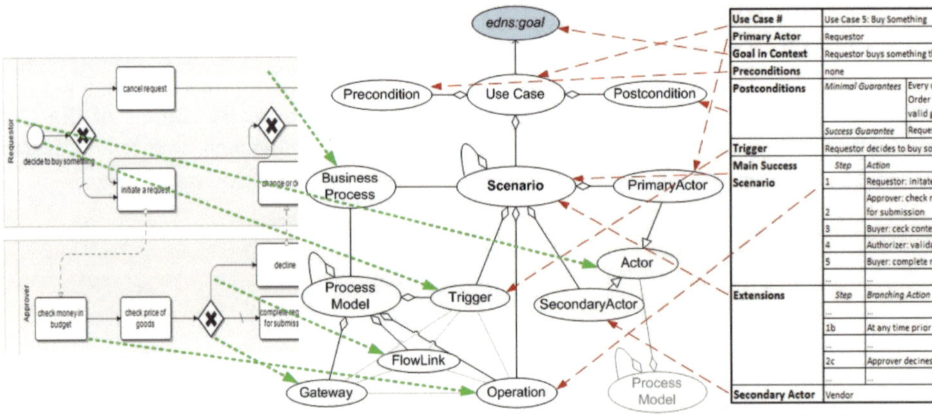

Fig. 8. Mapping use case to business process model (BPMN) intermediated by ScIOn

On the basis of ScIOn, business process models as well as use case descriptions can be semantically annotated or, in other terms, translated into *ScIOn language.* In this case their single parts, e. g. triggers and operations, are represented as instances of corresponding ScIOn concepts. Thus, machines or software programs respectively are now able to not only *understand* the meaning of these parts and of entire specifications but also to compare them effectively.

6. Automated validation of business processes using use case descriptions

6.1 Formal definition of business process model validity

To automate the validation of business process models the four validity rules defined in section 4 should be formulated in a manner that is understandable for machines, i.e. formally.

We will now formulate the four rules of business process models validity formally and with respect to the concepts definition given by ScIOn ontology:

An instance of the concept Process Model, *pm:ProcessModel* is valid with respect to an instance of the concept Use Case *uc:UseCase*,

$$pm \dashrightarrow uc$$

iff

1.) Each operation and trigger related to any scenario (that is related to the use case *uc* by the property *scenarioOf*) by the *elementOf* property, is related to the process model *pm* by the property *elementOf*.

$$(Trigger \sqcup Operation) \sqcap \exists elementOf.(Scenario \sqcap \exists scenarioOf.uc) \sqsubseteq \exists elementOf.pm \quad (1)$$

2.) The operations or triggers of scenarios participating in the use case *uc* keep their transitive *successor /predecessor* relations in the process model *pm*.

$$successor^{+} \sqsubseteq successor$$
$$predecessor^{+} \sqsubseteq predecessor$$

$$e: (Trigger \sqcup Operation) \sqcap \exists elementOf.(Scenario \sqcap \exists scenarioOf.uc)$$

$$\exists successor^{+}.e \sqcap \exists elementOf.(Scenario \sqcap \exists scenarioOf.uc) \sqsubseteq \exists successor^{+}.e \sqcap (Operation \sqcup Trigger \sqcup Gateway) \sqcap \exists elementOf.pm \quad (2)$$

$$\exists predecessor^{+}.e \sqcap \exists elementOf.(Scenario \sqcap \exists scenarioOf.uc) \sqsubseteq \exists predecessor^{+}.e \sqcap (Operation \sqcup Trigger \sqcup Gateway) \sqcap \exists elementOf.pm$$

3.) In the process model *pm* the connection of sub-processes corresponding to the *Scenarios* combined by the use case *uc* is realized by means of gateway model(s) or by event models. This means that the operations starting a scenario are preceded by a gateway or by a trigger in the process model *pm*.

$$Operation \sqcap \exists elementOf.(Scenario \sqcap \exists ScenarioOf.uc) \sqcap \nexists predecessor.(\exists elementOf.(Scenario \sqcap \exists ScenarioOf.uc)) \sqcap \exists predecessor(\exists elementOf.pm) \sqsubseteq (Trigger \sqcup Gateway) \quad (3)$$

4.) The actor(s) is(are) involved in the use case must be the actor(s) involved in the business process being modeled.

$$(Actor \sqcap \exists actorOf.(Scenario \sqcap \exists scenarioOf.uc)) \sqsubseteq (Actor \sqcap \exists actorOf.pm) \quad (4)$$

To sum the four rules described above form a base for the successful automated validation of business process models. These rules can be used as tasks for a semantic reasoner, a software that infers logical consequences from given knowledge, a set of facts or rules, that can carry out such validation, or be applied as axioms for specification of new process models.

6.2 Similarity and distance calculation

Yet, even if the analyzed instances don't match entirely they may have sufficient similarity to positively validate the business process under consideration. For example business processes can sometimes contain other business processes as intermediary but still fulfill the same function. Such a situation is illustrated by figure 9, where the middle activity of one process model is represented as sub-process in the other one. But both, the replaced activity and the more granular sub-process, realize the same task and thus both models are valid.
If the process model is changed as shown, a direct comparison with a use case could now result in a less than 100% correspondence. However such variation in composition of business processes needn't lead to negative validation results.

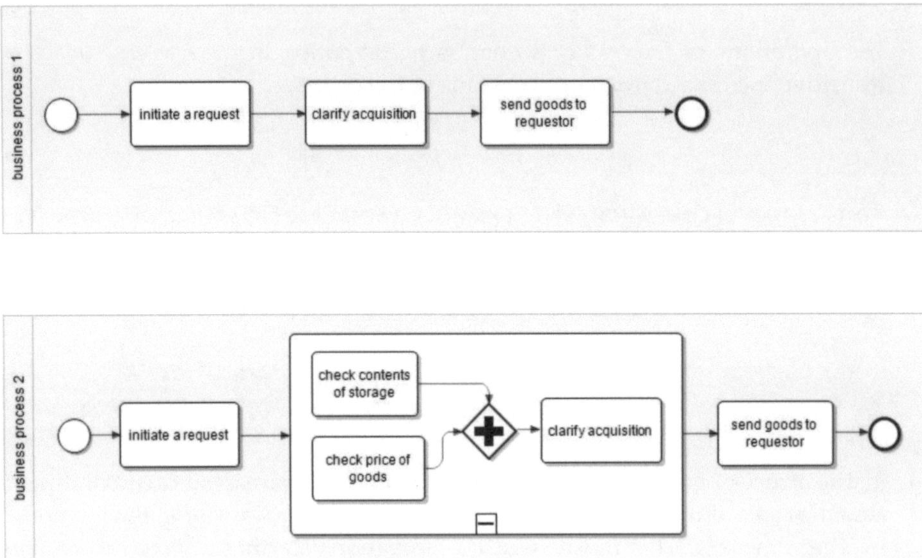

Fig. 9. Business process with sub-process

Consequently the new task arising in this context is to enrich the validation of process models by taking into account similarities between process models and uses cases.
Comparing two ontology individuals (instances or objects respectively) to analyze their similarity can be realized by a calculation of distance between this pair. An approach of such a distance calculation is introduced in (Maedche & Zacharias, 2002). According to this approach there are three dimensions of ontology-based similarity between objects: *taxonomy similarity (TS)*, *relation similarity (RS)* and *attribute similarity (AS)*.
One possible approach[6] to calculate similarity within TS is mentioned in (Lula & Paliwoda-Pękosz, 2008). There, similarity measures are based on path distance between concepts in the hierarchical tree of the ontology as applied in the following equation:

[6] There exist a couple of other approaches but describing all of them is out of the scope of this chapter.

$$sim_{WL}(C_1, C_2) = \frac{2 \times H}{N_1 + N_2 + 2 \times H} \tag{5}$$

N_1 and N_2 are the quantity of edges counted from the concepts C_1 and C_2 to the most specific common category C. H is the number of edges from this concept C to the root of the considered ontology.
We effectively use taxonomy similarity when comparing an individual of the ScIOn concept *Actor* with an individual of *PrimaryActor*. Although we deal with objects of two different classes a calculation of their taxonomy similarity gives us a measure for comparison of such objects.
In order to calculate similarity, the relation similarity RS dimension reflects the alikeness in relation to other objects. So when two compared instances are supposed to be similar to each other they should have relationships with concepts that are similar as well. For example if two compared *Operation* individuals have the same successors represented with the corresponding DOLCE property, they are considered to be similar Finally, using the *attribute similarity* dimension AS for comparison of instances of the same concept enables us for example to argue about similarity of operations by calculating distance between values of their *labels*. If labels of two operations are equal e.g. "initiate a request" on the figure above, there is high probability that we are dealing with two equal operations.
(Maedche & Zacharias, 2002) introduce the following formula for a calculation of similarity combining all three dimensions:

$$sim(I_i, I_j) = \frac{t \times TS(I_i, I_j) + r \times RS(I_i, I_j) + a \times AS(I_i, I_j)}{t + r + a} \tag{6}$$

In this formula *t, r,* and *a* stand for weights that can be specified separately to represent the potentially different importance of the similarity dimensions. I_i and I_j are the two instances or objects being compared.

7. Related Work

Quite a number of approaches deal with ontological representation of business process models. One of the most important of them is the EU funded research project called SUPER[7] (http://www.ip-super.org). It was aiming at the development of a framework for Semantic Business Process Management. The Web Service Modeling Ontology WSMO is another example. WSMO is used for *ontologization* of the BPM life cycle as well as concepts for semantic annotation of BPEL (called "sBPEL") and BPMN (called "sBPMN") are introduced (see for example in (Abramowicz, 2007)).
As mentioned in section 5.2 the Business Process Modeling Ontology (BPMO) was created as one of the deliverables of the SUPER project, to fulfill the specific requirements in this domain. Similar to the SUPER project a Business Process Modeling Ontology was developed

[7] SUPER = Semantics Utilised for Process Management within and between Enterprises

in the SemBiz workgroup. The intention of this project is the combination of the business level perspective and the technical implementation level in Business Process Management (BPM) using semantic descriptions of business processes.
To show parallels between the ScIOn approach and other projects in the related field on the one hand and to demonstrate the principle of ontology construction using upper-level ontologies on the other hand, we demonstrate two other options for ScIOn construction. The first of them (figure 10) exploits the *Business Process Modeling Ontology (BPMO)* developed in the SemBiz project.

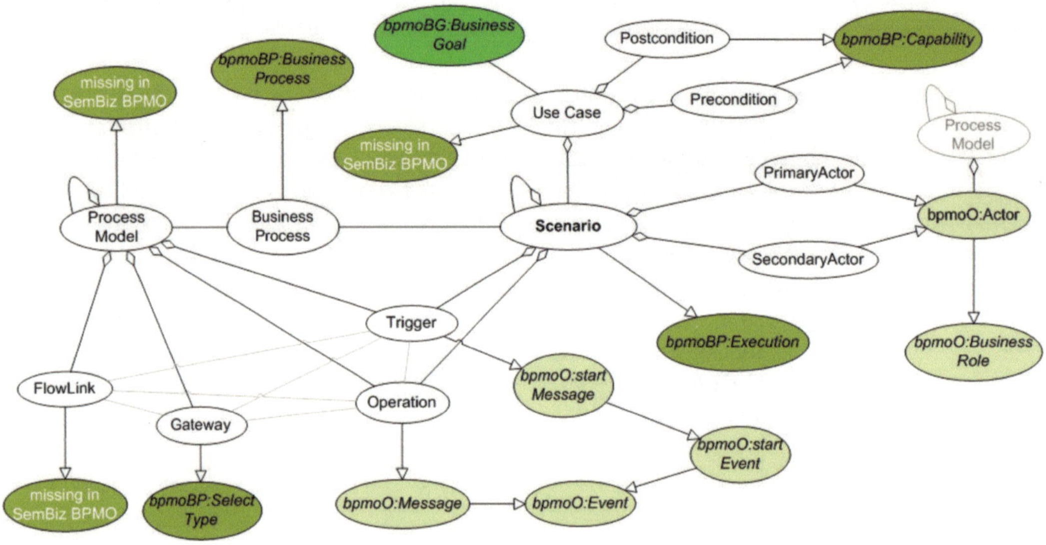

Fig. 10. Mapping to SemBiz BPMO

The second option demonstrates the use of SUPER BPMO in the role of an upper-level ontology of ScIOn:
Although these two ontologies were developed especially for business process modeling, we weren't able to find all required super-concepts for each of the 13 concepts of ScIOn. Furthermore the super-concepts we could identify aren't as suitable concerning semantical precision as the corresponding DOLCE counterparts. This fact demonstrates again the semantic expressiveness and role of foundation ontologies.
Therefore you can find some similarities between our approach and the one presented in (Mahl et al., 2007). The latter describes a bidirectional transformation between a DOLCE based reference ontology and BPEL. However, the approach is restricted to the support of cross-domain engineering in an e-business environment whereas the collaboration between different enterprises is improved by a common understanding supported by a specific ontology. The ontology-based approach enables a transformation of services and processes (developed in BPEL) into a standard representation so a cross-enterprise cooperation is possible. Another example of research aiming at semantic description of business processes is the one carried out at the Theory of Programming department8 of the Humboldt University in Berlin .

---

[8] See http://www2.informatik.hu-berlin.de/top/index.php?language=EN

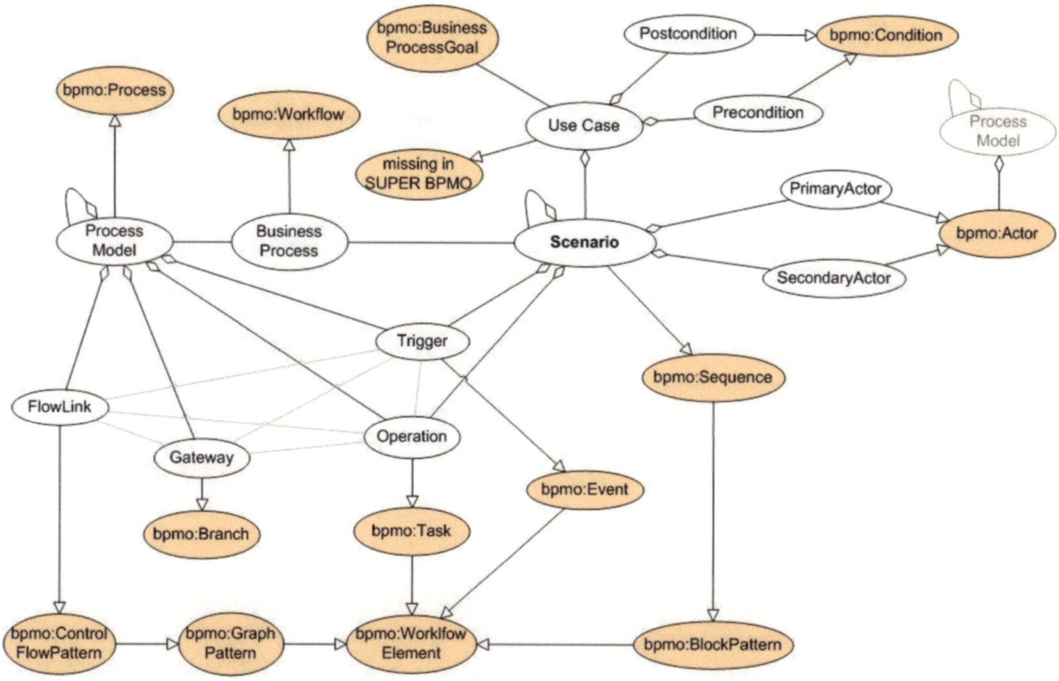

Fig. 11. Mapping to SUPER BPMO

It basically deals with problems of controllability in business process collaborations. One of the most interesting approaches generated in this context is introduced in (Lohmann et al., 2008). It focuses on using Petri nets semantics to describe business processes with the objective of transforming a BPEL into a Petri net model.

8. Conclusion and Future Work

This chapter described an approach addressing an important task in the context of quality management for business processes modelling. The approach is aiming at validating business process models with respect to the requirements on these models reflected in corresponding scenarios, e.g. use case descriptions. The approach focuses on homogeneous semantic-rich description of both issues (use cases and process models) followed by a comparison of the resulting specification documents.

Such a homogenisation is achieved by specification of elements (tasks, actions and events) used in the composition of business process models and use cases as individuals of concepts combined in one single ontology. In other words business process models specified using BPEL or BPMN and use cases basically written in text form are expressed using a common vocabulary. Therefore their direct comparison becomes a feasible task.

The ScIOn ontology described in this chapter is dedicated to this task. It gains high expressiveness from the DOLCE foundation ontology integrated by ScIOn as an upper level ontology. Application of ScIOn facilitates two methods of validity assessment for business process models. On the one hand a business process model is declared as completely valid with respect to a use case if both fulfil a set of axioms defined in ScIOn. On the other hand

ScIOn-based specification enables calculation of similarity between use cases and business process models and hence the relative validation of the business process models with respect to one particular use case.
Due to the lack of space this chapter does not cover the technology for automated translation of use case and process model specifications into the ScIOn vocabulary. Such technology is essential because the manual translation is highly complex and prone to errors. In this context the authors are currently working in two directions: 1) ScIOn based annotation of BPEL scripts and 2) ScIOn based information extraction from the tabular structured use case descriptions.
As stated in section 2 of this chapter there is a number of notations for specification of business process models. However during the last years the most popular notation became Business Process Model Notation (BPMN). A huge number of business process models developed recently was composed in BPMN. At the same time automated conversion of BPMN diagrams into executable WS-BPEL scripts containing commands for Web Service invocation is not a challenging task any more. It is widely applied and supported by a number of modelling tools such as Intalio Designer, Eclipse SOA Tools, Process Modeller for NS Visio, IBM Business Process Management (BPM) Suite, etc. Therefore, if technology for translation of BPEL scripts into ScIOn vocabulary was available, it would be sufficient for translation of a high number of business process models being developed in the close future.
Quite a different development can be observed concerning the notations for specification of use cases. Currently a number of various notations are in use: UML use case notation, tabular formatted text, activity diagrams, and some other notations (see section 3). To facilitate highly efficient validation of business process models a number of converting technologies should be developed: one for each existing notation. However tabular formatted text appears to be the simplest and hence the most popular form for the use cases' composition. Therefore the processing of use cases specified in this notation will be a future task of the ScIOn project.
Text structure analysis research is an important field in the information extraction technology. To the central works in this area belong among others (Tengli et al., 2004), (Tijerino et al., 2005) and (Gatterbauer et al., 2007). The technology dedicated to the special problem of structure analysis for use case specifications will incorporate some techniques described in these works. However, in contrast to the domain independent approaches presented in the papers mentioned above, structure analysis for use case specifications should be rather classified as a domain dependent one. Therefore it may rely on some document features, e. g. particular structural elements, typical for the domain of interest. This consideration let us suppose that the task to be solved is significantly simpler than a generic approach.

9. References

Abramowicz, W.; Filipowska, A.; Kaczmarek, M. & Kaczmarek, T. (2007). Semantically enhanced Business Process Modelling Notation, *Proceedings of the Workshop SBPM 2007*, ISSN 1613-0073, Innsbruck, April 2007, CEUR-WS, Aachen

Allweyer, T. (2008). *BPMN - Business Process Modeling Notation - Einführung in den Standard für die Geschäftsprozessmodellierung*, Books on Demand, ISBN 978-3-8370-7004-0, Norderstedt

Beringer, D. (1997). *Modelling global behaviour with scenarios in object-oriented analysis*, Ph. D. Thesis, Ecole Polytechnique Fédérale de Lausanne (EPFL), School of Computer and Communication Sciences, Lausanne, URL: http://library.epfl.ch/theses/?nr=1655, accessed 02/22/09

Cockburn, A. (2001). *Writing effective use cases*, Addison-Wesley, ISBN 0-201-70225-8, Boston

Desel, J. & Juhás, G. (2001). What Is a Petri Net? Informal Answers for the Informed Reader. *Lecture Notes in Computer Science*, Vol. 2128, January 2001, pp. 1-25, ISSN 0302-9743

Fahland, D. (2008). Oclets -- Scenario-Based Modeling with Petri Nets, *Proceedings of the 15th German Workshop on Algorithms and Tools for Petri Nets, AWPN 2008*, pp. 1-6, ISSN 1613-0073, Rostock, September 2008, CEUR-WS, Aachen

Graham, I. (1995). *Migrating to Object Technology*, Addison-Wesley, ISBN 0-201-59389-0, Reading

Gatterbauer, W. et al. (2007). Towards domain-independent information extraction from web tables, *Proceedings of the 16th international conference on World Wide Web*, pp. 71-80, ISBN 978-1-59593-654-7, Banff, May 2007, ACM, New York

Jacobson, I. et al. (1994). *Object-Oriented Software Engineering - A Use Case Driven Approach*, Addison-Wesley, ISBN 0-201-54435-0, Wokingham

Kashyap V.; Bussler, C. & Moran, M. (2008). *The Semantic Web - Semantics for Data and Services on the Web*, Springer, ISBN 978-3-540-76451-9, Berlin & Heidelberg

Lula, P. & Paliwoda-Pękosz G. (2008). An ontology-based cluster analysis framework, *Proceedings of the First International Workshop on Ontology-supported Business Intelligence, OBI 2008*, pp. 33-38, ISBN 978-1-60558-219-1, Karlsruhe, October 2008, ACM Press, New York

Lohmann, N.; Verbeek, E.; Ouyang, C. & Stahl, C. (2008). Comparing and Evaluating Petri Net Semantics for BPEL. *International Journal of Business Process Integration and Management (IJBPIM)*, (Accepted for publication), ISSN 1741-8763, URL: http://www2.informatik.hu-berlin.de/top/download/publications/Lohmann VOS2008_ ijbpim.pdf, accessed 04/20/09

Maedche, A. & Zacharias, V. (2002). Clustering Ontology-Based Metadata in the Semantic Web. *Lecture Notes in Computer Science*, Vol. 2431, January 2002, pp. 383-408, ISSN 0302-9743

Magro, D. & Goy, A. (2008). The Business Knowledge for Customer Relationship Management: an Ontological Perspective, *Proceedings of the First International Workshop on Ontology-supported Business Intelligence, OBI 2008*, pp. 33-38, ISBN 978-1-60558-219-1, Karlsruhe, October 2008, ACM Press, New York

Mahl, A.; Semenenko, A. & Ovtcharova (2007). Virtual organisation in cross domain engineering. *IFIP International Federation for Information Processing*, Vol. 243, September 2007, pp. 601-608, ISSN 1571-5736

Mika, P.; Sabou, M.; Gangemi, A. & Oberle, D. (2004). Foundations for OWL-S: Aligning OWL-S to DOLCE. *2004 AAAI Spring Symposium - Semantic Web Services*, No. SS-04-06, pp. 52-60, ISBN 1-57735-198-3

OASIS (2007). *Web Services Business Process Execution Language Version 2.0 - Primer*, OASIS, URL: http://docs.oasis-open.org/wsbpel/2.0/Primer/wsbpel-v2.0-Primer.pdf, accessed 04/13/09

OMG (2009). *Business Process Modeling Notation (BPMN) - Version 1.2*, Object Management Group, URL: http://www.omg.org/spec/BPMN/1.2/, accessed 02/23/09

Pilarski, J. & Knauss, E. (2008). Transformationen zwischen UML-Use-Case-Diagrammen und tabellarischen Darstellungen, *Proceedings of the Workshop on Domain-Specific Modeling Languages (DSML-2008)*, pp. 45-58, ISSN 1613-0073, Berlin, March 2008, CEUR-WS, Aachen

Rupp, C.; Queins, S. & Zengler. B. (2007). *UML 2 glasklar*, Hanser, ISBN 978-3-446-41118-0, München & Wien

Tengli, A. et al. (2004). Learning table extraction from examples, *Proceedings of the 20th international conference on Computational Linguistics*, pp. 987-993, Geneva, August 2004, ACM, New York

Tijerino, Y.A. et al. (2005). Towards Ontology Generation from Tables. *World Wide Web Journal*, Vol. 8, No. 3, September 2005, pp.261-285, ISSN:1386-145X

Tsai, A. et al. (2006). EPC Workflow Model to WIFA Model Conversion, *Proceedings of 2006 IEEE International Conference on Systems, Man, and Cybernetics*, pp. 2758-2763, ISBN 1-4244-0099-6, Taipei, October 2006, IEEE Xplore

Uschold, M. & Gruninger, M (1996). Ontologies: Principles, Methods and applications. *Knowledge Engineering Review*, Vol. 11, No. 2, 1996, pp. 93-155, ISSN 0269-8889

Wache, H. & Stuckenschmidt, H. (2001). Practical Context Transformation for Information System Interoperability. *Lecture Notes in Computer Science*, Vol. 2116, January 2001, pp. 367-380, ISSN 0302-9743

Wache, H. (2003). *Semantische Mediation für heterogene Informationsquellen* (Semantic mediation for heterogeneous information sources), Ph.D. Dissertation, Akademische Verlagsgesellschaft, ISBN 978-3-89838-261-8, Berlin

Weske, M. (2007). *Business Process Management - Concepts, Languages, Architectures*, Springer, ISBN 978-3-540-73521-2, Berlin & Heidelberg

13

Semantic-based eService Delivery for eGovernment Domain

Luis Alvarez Sabucedo and Luis Anido Rifon
University of Vigo, Spain
Flavio Corradini, Alberto Polzonetti and Barbara Re
University of Camerino Italy

1. Introduction

The introduction of Information and Communication Technology (here after ICT) support for services within the domain of Public Administrations (PA) is a one-way path. The more ICTs are used in the frame of public service, the more it will have to be used in years to come. This is due to clear and quick return of the investment in terms of cost and quality of services. In the opinion of the authors, in years to come a soaring of TIC-based solutions for eGovernment will be witnessed that will improve the service from administrations.

Therefore, it is of the utmost importance to provide with a interoperable support for operations among different Public Administrations. The final goal is boosting the cooperation among PAs. Thus, the cost of operations, the time-to-market and the quality of final services will be largely improved. At this point, it is clear that the proper care has to be put on the interoperability of provided solutions.

Interoperability must be considered from different points of view [Pollock and Hodgson, 2004]. Usually, it is generally understood to mean the ability of disparate IT to exchange and use data and information in order to work together in a networked environment. Nevertheless, it can be applied to different features of the system. In the domain of eGovernment, the Commission of European Community has underlined the importance of this topic [Commission of the European Communities, 2003a], and actually different levels for interoperability have been addressed: technical level, semantic level and organizational level. Therefore, we can state that interoperability is not just a technical feature but a fundamental semantic and organizational aspect.

As PAs evolves its support for eGovernment solutions, multi-layered solutions are introduced to support front and back-office interoperability (both intra and inter administrations). Nevertheless, an indeep review of these systems unveil different problems to deal with. In order to deal with this problems, a new tool is brought into scene: semantics. Nowadays, among the scientific community, semantics is usually considered the enabler technology to develop this sort of solutions where interoperability is of the first importance. As shown on the paper, our proposed solution introduces a semantic representation of reality to support computer-based reasoning and to specify in a formal manner tasks. Therefore, a fitting process about business process, PAs knowledge, and software

applications is developed. A proper knowledge management is needed to promote innovation in Public Administrations and to guarantee the adoption of appropriate solutions. In this way, it is easier for machines to automatically process and integrate available information.
A semantic description, i.e., an ontological model of the reality, can be considered as solid frame for developing knowledge in Public Administrations and, at the same time, it can be seen as a common ground used to build up a highly interoperable solution.
This paper intends to show the implementation of a solution offering customer-oriented services in a Web portal developed by Marche Region, the Tecut portal (www.tecut.it). Representing and processing semantic information regarding individual documents is desirable but not enough. To improve the efficiency and reusability of users' work with Web-based information management systems, it is essential to handle a shared document collections. A semantic-based approach on the so-called "Life Events", LEs here after, is followed to drive proposed features. Our proposal allows several advantages such as automatic services composition, advanced searching mechanisms, new functionalities as well as a better usability from the point of view of end users. Summing up, our approach provides a more friendly users support for eGovernment services. Finally, from our experience, we conclude that the introduction of semantic based LE portal based on intelligent documents facilitates the support of eGovernment solutions in a holistic manner.
The rest of the paper is organized as follows. Firstly, we present the current eGovernment state of the art and a brief introduction to the semantic technology. Secondly, we introduce Life Events, as an artifact to model citizen needs and Intelligent documents as a new and more powerful manner to store and deal with citizen data. Later on, a use case, the Tecut portal, where the proposed ideas are implemented is presented. Finally, conclusions are yielded.

2. Review on eGovernment

Since 2001 eGovernment represents one of the most dynamic application domain for Information and Communication Technologies. Moreover, it represents a test bed, not just in Europe and the United States but worldwide for challenges and opportunities in a cross-disciplinary area.
In literature we can find several definitions for eGovernment. Some of them are focused on the role of service, others take care of the point of view of citizens and other are centered in internal processes of the administration. We can outline some them.

- eGovernment is defined as "the use of ICT in Public Administrations combined with organizational changes and new skills in order to improve public services and democratic processes and strengthen support to public policies" [Commission of the European Communities, 2003b].

- According to the UN, eGovernment is defined as "the use of Information and Communication Technology and its application by the government for the provision of information and basic public services to the people" [UN, 2007].

- The World Bank states that eGovernment refers to "the use by government agencies of information technologies (such as Wide Area Networks, the Internet, and mobile computing) that have the ability to transform relations with citizens, businesses, and other arms of government" [The world bank, 2007].

Additionally, dealing with eGovernment requires the identification of the particular area according to which costumers we are dealing with. These may include individuals, organizations, technical systems, social relations and value systems [Traunmuller, 2003].

Government-to-Citizen (G2C) Services in this category deal with the relationships between government and citizens. They allow citizens to access government information and services instantly, conveniently, from everywhere, and, even, using multi-channels solutions.
We can also consider the case of Government-to-Employee (G2E). This area tackles the support for the civil servants themselves with services to manage their carrier, productivity and so on.

Government-to-Business (G2B) It drives eTransactions initiatives between government and the private sector such as eProcurement. It also support specific tools for paying online taxes. The opportunity to conduct on-line transactions with government reduces red tape and simplifies regulatory processes. It, therefore, helps businesses to become more competitive.
Close to this area, we can also refer to Government-to-Nonprofit (G2N). This area deals with the special needs of Non Government Organizations such access to specific support their initiatives, information about funding and related issues, etc.

Government-to-Government (G2G) This kind of services provides government departments or agencies cooperation and communication and internal exchange of information and commodities. As matter of fact, governments depend on other levels of government to effectively deliver services and allocate responsibilities. The introduction of full interpretability, inside Public Administrations, facilitate the sharing of data, resource and capabilities, enhancing the efficiency, and effectiveness of processes.

As already mentioned, eGovernment is currently a research field where a lot of effort is being placed. As a result, a large number of efforts and initiatives have arisen. In the literature, we can also find some interesting initiatives that make use, at different levels, of semantics applied to LE-based concepts in some manner: the Finnish Web site Suomi.fi (www.museosuomi.fi/suomifi), the EIP.AT project (eip.at), the SemanticGov project (www.semantic-gov.org), the Access-eGov project (www.accessegov.org) just to cite a few.
The promotion of eGovernment introduces a lot of advantages related to effectiveness, efficiency, service quality, transparency and accountability of government. It upgrades of government staff skills and facilitates ICT awareness. At the same time, it reduces the cost and improves the access and the delivery of government information and services to the public, other agencies, and other entities. In this context, the promotion of social agreement

allows the satisfaction of the stakeholders and the diffusion of ICT enabling eGovernment and simplifying integral government services.

3. Semantic Technology

The "semantic", as an IT researching field, was born in the earlier 2000's. In May, 2001, Sir Tim Berners-Lee published the foundational article presenting the semantic to the world [Berners-Lee et al., 2001].

> "The Semantic Web will bring structure to the meaningful content of Web pages, creating an environment where software agents roaming from page to page can readily carry out sophisticated tasks for users" [Berners-Lee et al., 2001].

The *ethos* of this idea is to make machines capable of understanding the information within the web. This feature will allow them to make more complex interactions with no need of human support. To accomplish this ambitious goal a long evolution on the technological side has been undertaken during these last years. Currently, the support for these features has been based on the use of OWL [W3C, 2004], a standard from the World Wide Web Consortium. This one allows the IT people to define knowledge about a concrete domain in a formal manner, i.e., to provide an ontology according to the Gruber's definition [Gruber, 1993].

The use of semantic support in IT-based solutions allows the introduction of "intelligence" in software based systems. Thus, it is possible to perform operations no possible in "*raw-data based solutions*". Taking advantage of this semantic support processes automatization is enabled.

We introduce semantic solution in service modeling for a number of reasons. It supports us in making implicit information explicit, which is needed for interoperability and reasoning. It, also, introduces support to describe service in such manner that it allows software agents to search and to obtain services on behalf of the users.

To make this knowledge available for machines, a formal, shared representation of the service must be provided. This knowledge is expressed by means of ontologies. And, in order to express an ontology in a formal manner, different languages [Gomez-Perez et al., 2003] are at our disposal. Ontology Web Language (OWL) [W3C, 2004] is the W3C Recommendation that covers most of DAML+OIL and it is intended to provide a fully functional way to express ontologies. To make possible different levels of complexity, OWL provides different sublanguages with increasing expressivity: OWL Lite, OWL DL and OWL Full. By using OWL, we are addressing a standard, solid and interoperable platform for the provision of this solution.

These ones are expressed, of course, in a particular language. Nowadays, the scientific community has reached an agreement around the use of OWL [W3C, 2004], a W3C [W3C, 2005] language to express semantic information.

4. Modeling services: Life Events

From the review of current fashion front-office for eGovernment service, some shortcomings and limitation become clear. These limitations are related to the following constraints.

- **Locating services is not a simple task.** When looking for a particular service in the web site of a PA, it is not a trivial task to find the proper place where the service is held. This is due to wide variety of classification for services, mechanisms for its invocations, visual interfaces and even problem to know before hand if the administration is the responsible for the wished service.

- **Very few administrations provide information about the evolution of services.** Once the operation is requested no more information or tracking is possible. So, in the case of services that take a lot of time, citizens may not feel involved in the process.

- **Web accessibility is not always a highlight in most Web portals.** Official web sites are often WAI-AA or WAI-AAA compliant [W3C, 2007] but this is not the general rule. Besides, the classification of the information itself and the interaction mechanisms are not always as simple and easy as we would wish.

- **Little information about the service, execution conditions, or its evolution is provided.** It is not common to find information about the level of security of invoked operation, the maximum life span for services allowed, laws that support and regulate that services, etc.

- **Several administrations can be concerned by the same topic.** In some operation there may be several administrations concerned (i.e., moving to a new home) and that may drive citizens to confusion.

- **Different mechanisms for identification are required in different administration for the same citizen.**
  No single and horizontal mechanism to access services is available on most official web sites. Usually, a citizen must authenticate himself using different mechanisms in different administrations: a pair user/password, a digital certification, a smart card,...

- **Usually it is not possible to customize the access to services.** It is not possible for citizens, once they are logged in, to access the most likely services to be invoked according to their profiles, their customized interfaces, and, even in most cases, no profiles are stored. We observe lacks on citizen profile managing.

This leads us to propose a new paradigm to model and characterize services in this domain. The use of LEs is proposed. At the same time, we discuss on a proper methodology useful in order to transform common service into a LE expressed under the terms of the provided ontology.

4.1 LE Definition and Characterization

LEs can be considered as an artifact to model those situations where a citizen needs support or license from a Public Administration to tackle a situation from his own point of view.

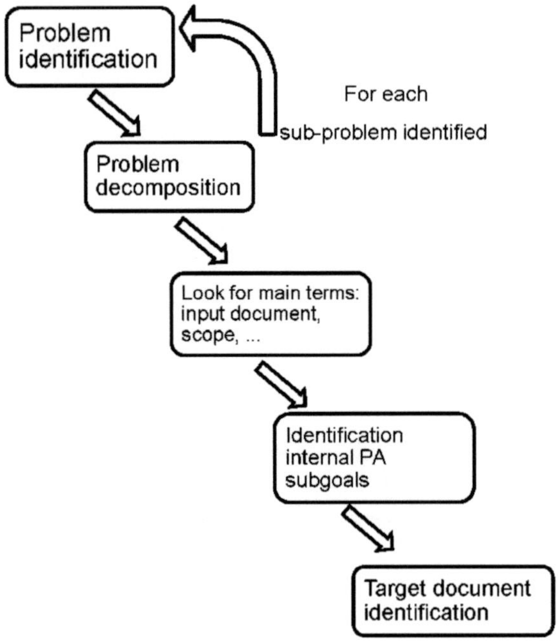

Fig. 1. Schema for the defintion of LE.

This would be case of LE such as moving, losing the wallet or requesting a grant; on contrary situation such as getting a form or a certification or submitting a piece of information to a Public Administration cannot be considerer in the same way. LE can be describing under the following topics.

- **Task.** Title for the considered operation. Folksonomies plays an interesting role as they provide support for semi-automatic enhancements of discovering services.
- **Description.** High level description of the desired operation expressed in natural terms from the point of view of the citizen.
- **Input Documents.** As previously stated, all operations carried out by the administration require some input documents. Citizen is requested to provide a signed form in order to invoke the operation. This element plays a role similar to *preconditions* in some environments. In the considered case, we can identify as inputs documents, the current certification.
- **Output Document.** Of course, as a result of any performed operation, the PA in charge must provide an output expressed in terms of the ontology. This information will be put together into one or several documents. This output will vary its content from the expected document (i.e., a certification, a license, . . .) to information about the failure to get the expected document.
- **Scope.** We must identify the scope of the operation (local, national, international, . . .) where we want the operation to be recognized.

- **Security Conditions.** This is intended to express the conditions for the security mechanism involved during the whole process. This includes the identification of both parties, citizen and PAs, and also the way is stored by any agent involved that could be able to use it.
- **Cost.** This will express the amount you have to pay for the requested operation and/or also the time it will take for the completion of the operation.
- **Steps.** A LE can go through different stages until its fulfilling. A description of them must be provided to be at the disposal of citizen willing to make use it.

4.2 Methodology

In order to transform common services into a LE expressed in the proposed terms, we must follow a simple methodology. For the sake of clarity, we are going to show the former by means of an example: the situation in which a citizen has to move to a new residence. This operation may require the collaboration of several different PAs and several processes the citizen does not have to be aware of. Thus, we propose the following schema (see Fig. 1).

1. Identify the problem and dealing features as PAs involved.

   Applied to our practical case, the task we are dealing with is the change of address for a citizen. The involved PAs are the cities council, of course, they should involve several offices or divisions but that should be transparent for the citizen.

2. Decompose the problem into several different problems that may be solved in a single step, i.e., each step must produce as output a document meaningful for the citizen.

   The considered operation in the example may involve one single operation and no subprocesses are relevant to the citizen.

3. For each identified subprocess, look for the input documents, scope and cost. These ones must be ex-
   pressed in terms of the LE ontology.

   The input document required in our case is the certification of the current citizen address, the document to prove the new address and the signed request for the change. The scope for the operation is national. No cost is put on the citizen and no limitations are related to it.

4. Identify internal partial aims for citizens and PAs. These steps usually involve internal documents. They
   can be meaningless for the citizen but relevant for the administration.

   In our example, several steps can be identified: check for the correctness about the former address data, look for pending payments, update internal data, notify related PAs, and, finally, generate the certification for the new address.

5. Identify possible documents as possible final steps of the operation.

   In our case, the target document is the certification for the new address. Nevertheless, if problems arise, mainly related to some internal step, documents to notify those errors may be generated. Those documents will inform about problems due to pending payments, problems with legal constrains, . . . These documents must be included in the ontology.

6. Update all services and agents that may be aware of the new service.

4.3 Applying semantics

So far, no technological binding has been established. This approach can be used in different frameworks or using several technologies. Nevertheless, in our work we take advantage of semantic support to unleash all possibilities within this technology.

The proposed approach benefits from the power of OWL to express the information relevant for the system. Nevertheless, we must keep in mind that OWL is just a tool to express knowledge with all its potential and limitations. Some limitations on the possibilities of OWL to express knowledge have been faced. In particular, OWL does not support relations that involve properties whose range is a class itself. Only an individual from a particular class is a possible range for properties. This leads us into shortcomings in the definition of some relations (for example, we would like to establish a relation between an individual from the class LE and a subclass of "document", not an individual from that class). This situation was overcome using a higher level of abstraction implicit in a single individual (the use of individual documents belonging to the class document as a generic one with no information by itself).

Additionally and for the sake of consistency of current and future information in the system, some rules has been defined (see Fig 2): all LEs generate some Document (Rule 1), all LEs are supported by some PA (Rule 2), all Documents are issued by some PA (Rule 3), etc.

Of course, lower level details about the conformance to local or national laws regarding document and legal procedures are not considered at this point. Therefore, further implementations of the system must take into account their own legal framework and stick to their own constrains.

5. Tecut: implementing concepts

Web portals are playing an important role in the provision of digital services for citizens and PAs. The evolution from the old-fashion Web sites to the current Web portals has allowed the development of new ways of doing business, learning, accessing services, ... They are referenced, in the modern information society, as eTechnologies. At the same time, PAs noticed the emerging of Web portals as significant tools enabling eGov-ernment and they are introduced as gateways to interact with citizens. The use of Web portals makes possible the reduction of time and cost for both Public Administration and citizens, enables 24/7 services, and provides a better quality of service for citizens.

A number of eGovernment portals have been already developed even though, in several cases, shortcomings related to interoperability and usability limit their usage and potentiality. Due to the unavoidable need for service integration, interoperability concerns must be solved. This issue involves concerns at administrative, operational, technical, semantical, legal and cultural level [Bekkers, 2005]. Thus, PAs must perform a long-term study to evaluate how to deploy their solutions. Theses ones must provide the highest possible level of satisfaction to really increase the level of interaction with citizens.

In this context, the introduction of LEs and intelligent documents bring us a new sort of eGovernment platforms. Full integration among documents and the LEs is provided. Thus, a system capable of presenting a standard representation for eGovernment documents and model citizen needs is developed.

5.1 Motivation

Several Italian Regions were suggested to develop eGovernment solutions aimed at increasing interactions between Public Administrations and citizen by means of ICTs infrastructures. In order to accomplish this high level goal, several issues related to key aspects in the eGovernment domain have to be taken into account, such as authentication and authorization, service publishing and discovery as well as composition. As results of these considerations and according to a study about skills for the case [Corradini et al., 2006a], it was developed the Tecut portal (see Figure 3), a fully integrated eGovernment portal for shared and standardized services. Tecut is developed in collaboration with one of the Italian local administration, the Marche Region. Taking into account the former considerations, LifeEvent and intelligent document based approach was used to deliver service in a more suitable way for users.

Rule	Definition
Rule 1 $R_1 = \{\forall LE \exists Doc,$ $generates(LE) = Doc\}$	<owl:Class rdf:about="#LifeEvent"> <rdfs:subClassOf> <owl:Restriction> <owl:onProperty> <owl:FunctionalProperty rdf:ID="generates"/> </owl:onProperty> <owl:someValuesFrom> <owl:Class rdf:about="#Document"/> </owl:someValuesFrom> </owl:Restriction>
Rule 2 $R_2 = \{\forall LE \exists PA,$ $isSupportedBy(LE) = PA\}$	<owl:Class rdf:about="#LifeEvent"> <rdfs:subClassOf> <owl:Restriction> <owl:someValuesFrom rdf:resource="#PA"/> <owl:onProperty> <owl:InverseFunctionalProperty rdf:ID="isSupportedBy"/> </owl:onProperty> </owl:Restriction> </rdfs:subClassOf>
Rule 3 $R_3 = \{\forall Doc \exists PA,$ $isGeneratedBy(Doc) = PA\}$	<owl:Class rdf:about="#Document"> <rdfs:subClassOf> <owl:Restriction> <owl:someValuesFrom rdf:resource="#PA"/> <owl:onProperty> <owl:InverseFunctionalProperty rdf:ID="isGeneratedBy"/> </owl:onProperty> </owl:Restriction> </rdfs:subClassOf>

Fig. 2. Rules defined in the system

5.2 Features

The portal implements the proposed transformation of final services as they are requested by citizens into new LEs expressed in terms of the semantic definition (as previously mentioned). This approach is suitable for eGovernment field, or at least more suitable than in other environments, due to several reasons: all operations require some input document, the most common output in the service is a new document, there is no need (opportunity) for bargaining about services, there are limits and conditions very explicit about the data managing in terms of trustability and security (non-repudiation, privacy, integrity and confidentiality) and operations does not have real time constrains.

A global vision of the Marche Region, the scenario of this successful use case, involves financial entities, big enterprises, SMEs and a large and highly distributed population. This environment is quite convenient in order to test the system.

Even a lot of issues deserve a special attention, we would like to outline some of them of special relevance at this point. In the next subsection we focus on the authentication, document management and discovery and composition.

Fig. 3. Tecut Portal Home-Page.

5.2.1 Authentication

The authentication process plays a main role in Tecut. It represents the instant when the system determines the association between the digital identity and the user. The recent proliferation of digital services has raised concerns about a lot of authentication mechanisms.

Marche Region supports the realization of a central authentication solution through Cohesion [Corradini et al., 2005]. It is an infrastructure that provides solutions for complex technical problems and a set of common standard services predisposed to realize applicative cooperation as the Italian eGovernment plan states. Authentication services for centralized management access in private areas are provided by Single Sign On (SSO) [Clercq, 2002] and Profiling system.

- The SSO's tasks are predisposed for the transfer of credentials between authenticated users and access portal. In particular, the authentication on the framework is possible with different levels: via weak registration using username and password and via strong registration using services regional cards "Raffaello". Furthermore, SSO allows a transparent access to the portal's reserved areas without further authentications and it allows that authentication credentials and user profiling are made available to different application domains. Indeed, the user authentication check is delegated to the service. It uses a regional services register to validate the profile in respect to the access roles.

- The profiling system is dedicated to the coordinated management of credentials information, logically divided in a static subsystem and in a dynamic one, containing a series of attributes capable to indicate the user's preferences when accessing the services. A part of user base profile will be requested during the registration phase, and another part is communicated after explicit request, when a service is used. The goodness of this approach is a semantic based representation of the profile to guarantee a proper users management.

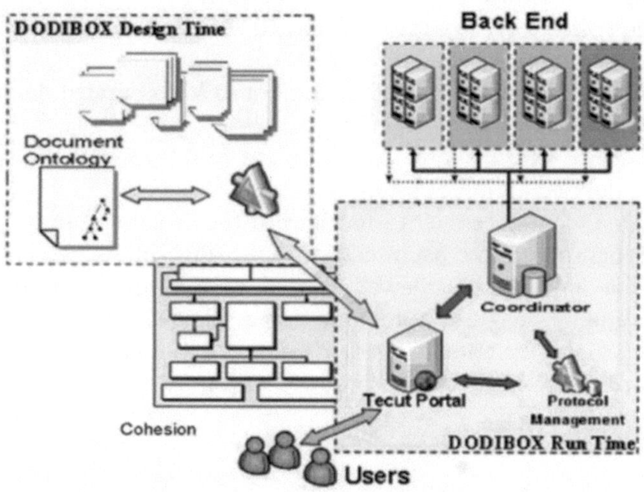

Fig. 4. Document Management System.

In users profiles we have reused former already defined data representation. For example, for the definition of the citizen, one main class in the system, FOAF (www.foaf-project.org) has been reused, and, to mark documents in the system, metadata in [CEN, 2004] has been taken into consideration. This is part of a general philosophy leading toward the maximum possible agreement and reusability both of ontologies and software derived from the former.

5.2.2 Intelligent Document Management

Tecut document management is based on Dodibox [Corradini et al., 2006b] (see Fig. 4 for a general overview). The framework presents two different subsystems considering the design time and run time functionalities. The first one, design time subsystem manages document repository through document ontology. On the other hand, the run time subsystem propose a component base approach. A **front-end component** manages the users filling in form fields (using a tracing system), and processes the digital signature. A **coordination component** processes the submitted forms and the forms storage. At the same time, it also forwards the forms to reach the right back-end capable of managing the documents. An **extra component** supports the system during the protocol and updating step. The point of collaboration between the two subsystems is a Web Service that can convert the submitted form into compiler instance for the runtime system.

The core of Dodibox system is based on the coordination, it represents an unique applicative gateway dedicate to intelligent documents. The gateway can manage an intelligent routing verso back-end systems strongly heterogeneity. We underline the role of the semantic of document header, it plays a fundamental role during the coordination. Beside header component previously mentioned, it transports the application gateway type with the aim to active the proper standard adapter (one for each applicative gateway type). At this time the expected gateway are:

- HTTP Post - to forward the document via HTTP;
- FTP - to forward the document via FTP;
- EMAIL - to forward the document via e-mail;
- Certified Electronic Mail - to forward the document via certified electronic mail managing the go back receipt;
- PROTOCOL - to forward the document to Web Service dedicate for the documents protocol;
- Web Service - to forward the document to a back-end Web Service on the base on WSDL defined at orchestration time;
- Message Queuing Services - to forward the document in a message queue allowing the asynchronous and asymmetric interaction with related back-end systems.

More than one application gateway related to a single document can be activated. A coordination engine provides autonomously a re-synchronization of parallel process. The engine manages also exceptions rising during the interaction with system outdoors. After the document is stored, the engine produces a log message allowing users feedback about document process.

5.2.3 Discovery and Composition

Processes related to discovery and composition of services were specially taken into account. The conditions to execute a particular LE can be checked in a automatic manner by a semantic engine. As LE are expressed in terms of OWL expressions, a semantic software was developed to discover if a certain LE can or can not be invoked. These conditions for the execution of a LE are based on the profile of the citizen and the document he/she is in possession at the time of invoking the LE.

Accordantly, the output of the operation is also defined also in terms of the same ontology and, in this case, involves also the documents addressed in the LE. Thus, it is quite simple to

make compositions using a semantic reasoner as it only will have to link outputs and inputs expressed in the same terms from the same ontology.
As a result of these design decisions, advanced ways for the composition and the discovery of services are possible within the project Tecut.

5.3 Discussion

This new approach brings several advantages in the design and planning of a semantic based solutions for government web portal focusing on the eGovernment portal main functionalities. Our approach supports the cooperation in an environment as Marche Region characterized by a lot of small municipalities. At the same time, this study case is aimed at supporting activities of small and medium enterprises. The introduction of LE and intelligent document promotes stakeholders cooperation reducing administrations cost and promoting the maturity of eGovernment taking into account diverse organizations of the administrations.
The provision of this sort of solutions requires the engagement of PAs in a long term bet. It is compulsory that PAs make up their mind and give a step ahead in the adoption of semantic in their applicatin. Even outcomes are clear, as this project shows, and almost mandatory in current state of the art, some PAs currently are not getting involved as it would be desirable. So, for the sake of future solutions, it is important to illustrate the scene of eGovernment with success use cases as the presented one.

6. Conclusion

Currently, PAs are or will be experiencing a large and deep transformation and this transformation has already begun and it is mainly focussed in improving the interface used by citizens. Nevertheless, it is expected to compel also transformations inside PAs themselves in order to achieve better internal procedures that facilitates the managing of back-office mechanism. That is in aim of the presented proposal that suggests the introduction of LifeEvents to support services with an homogeneous schema along all PAs involved.
This evolution in the provision of service is based on providing a semantic layer of service where PAs can build up their own services in a quite straight forward manner. Therefore, they can focus on the service itself and not of how this service can possible be delivered. By taking advantage of the proposed schema, PAs will be in position to provide a better service to their citizens and also to improve their own internal dynamics.
The *ethos* of the proposal lays in supporting in a holistic manner the concept of one-stop service when ever it is possible. As stated in [Commission of the European Communities, 2003a], the goal is that *the customer need not be aware of the various public administration bodies that co-operate in seamlessly delivering the service.*
In this approach, the use of Life Event and intelligent documents plays a main role to prove the status of performed operations and guarantee the conditions achieved in previous operations. Under this approach, it is possible to orchestrate services in a automatic manner.
The provision of a solution aimed to support operations in the scope of Public Administrations requires the collaboration of those last ones. Mechanisms and business logic involved in the frame of public service highly differs from other related environments such eBusiness. Methodologies and options available on one field are no possible on the

other and conversely. Thus, developers in the area must keep in mind a number of cautions that may increase the time-to-market in the eGovernment context.
These concepts presented along the paper are actually tested on the Tecut Platform, as shown in the article. This project provides with an empirical validation of suggested ideas. Making the best of available technologies, not very mature in the field of semantics, it was possible to develop a holistic software support that provides citizen with advanced services. With in this project, it is tested a solid and reliable method to support back-office procedures and tackle the proper use of documents in the context of the Public Administration.

7. Acknowledgment

This work has been funded by the Ministerio de Educacion y Ciencia through the project "Servicios adap-tativos para e-learning basados en estandares" (TIN2007-68125-C02-02) and Xunta de Galicia, Consellerla de Innovacion e Industria "SEGREL: Semantica para un eGov Reutilizable en Entornos Locais" (08SIN006322PR). We also thank "Regione Marche" Local Public Administration; and "Halley Informatica".

8. References

[FOAF, 2005] (2005).the foaf project. Web available [acc, 2006] (2006). Access-eGov. Web available. http://www.accessegov.org/.

[eip, 2006] (2006). EIP.AT. Web available. http://eip.at.

[sem, 2006] (2006). The SemanticGov Project. Web available. http://www.semantic-gov.org. [suo, 2007] (2007). SW-Suomi.fi. Web available.

[Tec, 2007] (2007). Tecut. Web available. http://www.tecut.it.

[Bekkers, 2005] Bekkers, V. (2005). The governance of back office integration in e-government: Some dutch experiences. In Wimmer, M., Traunmiiller, R., Gronlund, A., and Andersen, K. V., editors, *EGOV*, volume 3591 of *Lecture Notes in Computer Science*, pages 12-25. Springer.

[Berners-Lee et al., 2001] Berners-Lee, T., Hendler, J., and Lassila, O. (2001). The semantic web. *Scientific American*, 284(5):35-43.

Essay about the possibilities of the semantic web.

[CEN, 2004] CEN (2004). Dublin Core eGovernment Application Profiles. Web available. http://www.cenorm.be/cenorm/businessdomains/businessdomains/isss/cwa /cwa1486 0.asp.

[Clercq, 2002] Clercq, J. D. (2002). Single sign-on architectures. In *Proceedings of the International Conference on Infrastructure Security*, pages 40 - 58.

[Commission of the European Communities, 2003a] Commission of the European Communities (2003a). Linking up europe: the importace of interoperability for e-government service. *Commission StaffWorking Paper SEC.*

[Commission of the European Communities, 2003b] Commission of the European Communities (2003b). The Role of e-Government for Europe's Future. *Communication from the commission to the council the European parliament the European economic and social committee and the committee ofthe regions.*

[Corradini et al., 2006a] Corradini, F., Angelis, F. D., Ercoli, C., Polzonetti, A., and Re, B. (2006a). Consideration to improve e-government infrastructure. In *Proceedings of the International Conference on e-Society.*

[Corradini et al., 2006b] Corradini, F., Forastieri, L., Polzonetti, A., Pruno, R., Re, B., and Sergiacomi, A. (2006b). An integrate framework for document management: the role of semantic and administrative cooperation. In *IADIS 06, Murcia (Spain), October 2006.*

[Corradini et al., 2005] Corradini, F., Forastieri, L., Polzonetti, A., Riganelli, O., and Sergiacomi, A. (2005). Shared services center for e-government policy. pages 140-151.

[Gomez-Perez et al., 2003] Gomez-Perez, A., Fernandez-Lopez, M., and Corcho, O. (2003). *Ontological Engineering.* Springer.

[Gruber, 1993] Gruber, T. (1993). A translation approach to portable ontology specifications. *Knowledge Acquisition,* pages 199-220.

[Pollock and Hodgson, 2004] Pollock, J. T. and Hodgson, R. (2004). *Adaptive Information - impoving business through semantic interoperability, Grid Computing, and enterprise integration.* Wiley.

[Regione Marche, 2003] Regione Marche (2003).

[The world bank, 2007] The world bank (2007). About e-Governemtn. Web available. www.worldbank.com/ egov.

[Traunmuller, 2003] Traunmuller, R., editor (2003). *Electronic Government, Second International Conference, EGOV 2003, Prague, Czech Republic, September 1-5, 2003, Proceedings,* volume 2739 of *Lecture Notes in Computer Science.* Springer.

[UN, 2007] UN (2007). Global e-Government readiness report 2004. Towards access for opportunity. Web available. http://unpan1.un.org/intradoc/groups/public /documents/UN/UNPAN019207. pdf.

[W3C,2004] W3C (2004). Web ontology language. Web available. http://www.w3.org/ 2004/OWL/. [W3C,2005] W3C (2005). W3C. Web available. http://www.w3c.org/.

[W3C,2007] W3C (2007). Web Accessibility Initiative. Web available.

14

Context-aware Service Composition and Change-over Using BPEL Engine and Semantic Web

Yoji Yamato, Yuusuke Nakano and Hiroshi Sunaga
NTT Network Service Systems Laboratories, NTT Corporation
Japan

1. Introduction

With the advancement of IT technology, ubiquitous computing environments (Weiser, 1991) are rapidly becoming a reality where PCs and various other devices are connected to networks. Ubiquitous computing environments are expected to offer context-aware services (Schilit et al., 1994) and customization services. Users' needs change dynamically according to the user context such as location or time. The idea of dynamically composing appropriate service components in the network on the basis of the user context is a promising approach (e.g. (Minami et al., 2001) (Gribble et al., 2001)) to the conventional method of providing services, where service providers prepare services completely in advance.
Our study is on one of the service-composition technologies, and our approach uses dynamic interface resolution using semantic web techniques. We have already examined the methods through prototype implementation (Yamato et al., 2006) (Yamato & Sunaga, 2007). In this paper, we propose a new framework of context-aware service composition and change-over that consists of featured functions of our prototype service composition technology and commercial BPEL (Web Services Business Process Execution Language) (Jordan et al., 2007) engines to achieve a service composition system having commercial level quality at a low cost. We also consider service change-over, which is a problem in using the BPEL engine. We report the implementation of the proposed method, evaluation of its feasibility, multi-vendor compatibility, and processing performance.
This paper is comprised of the following sections. In section 2, we explain BPEL technology and our previous study of service composition technology. Section 3 shows the idea of applying the BPEL product for our service composition execution. In section 4, we implemented the proposed idea and evaluate the effectiveness. Section 5 shows some sample application and section 6 introduces related works. Section 7 concludes this paper.

2. BPEL and our service composition technology

BPEL, an existing service coordinating technology in the B-to-B area, is attracting attention. However, BPEL coordinates multiple web services for the purpose of semipermanent system integration. Therefore, BPEL is not suitable for binding unknown web services according to the user context. BPEL requires a rigid interface description such as the port type names and operation names of web services, so it can only be applied to pre-known web services whose port types and operations exactly match. In other words, BPEL is not flexible in terms of context awareness or user customization.

To solve the problems of BPEL, we use a service template (ST) that describes required service elements (SE) abstractly using semantic metadata, instead of a service flow that describes the rigid interface of individual web services. That makes finding multiple SEs with different interfaces but semantically equivalent functions possible, and the system can select an appropriate SE from candidate SEs according to the user context.

Here, SE is a service component where semantic metadata is assigned to web services or UPnP using OWL-S (Web Ontology Language for Services) (Martin et al., 2004) which is a description of semantic web service technology (e.g., (Paolucci & Sycara., 2004) (Sycara et al., 2003)). OWL-S consists of three parts: Profile, Process model, and Grounding. The Profile has information about properties that describe what capability the service provides. The Process model describes service behavior such as atomic process and its inputs, outputs, preconditions, and effects. The Grounding describes the mapping between abstract processes of OWL-S and actual operations such as WSDL or UPnP docs.

ST is a service scenario described by XML, and the ST grammar is similar to that of BPEL. The control tags of ST are the same as the ones defined by BPEL (e.g., invoke and while, for example). The difference between ST and BPEL is that in ST, SE is specified abstractly using semantic metadata. More precisely, the port type of BPEL is described using a category (a unit of categorization for equivalent SE function), and the operation of BPEL is described using an atomic process of OWL-S.

The flow of service composition is as follows. A user inputs the ST of the desired service into a service composition engine and the engine searches for candidate SEs from the SE-DB using semantic metadata described in the ST. Next, an SE appropriate for the user context is selected from candidate SEs. For appropriate SE selection, a score is marked for each SE by matching 3 elements: a user policy that designates which SE should take precedence, a user context that indicates the user situation, and an SE profile that designates the property of SE. The SE with high scores is automatically selected. Once the SE to be used is selected, the service composition engine converts semantic metadata to the actual interface of SE (WSDL or UPnP) and invokes SE (see, Fig. 1) using the OWL-S Grounding of the selected SE. Please refer to papers (Yamato et al., 2006) (Yamato & Sunaga, 2007) for details.

The following are three key features of our service composition technology:

(1) Interface resolution function

Using the semantic description of ST and OWL relationship, many SEs with a different interface but an equivalent function can be used (e.g., the print function of a printer and a fax machine can be used by the same ST).

(2) Context-aware service selection function

Matching user context, user policy, and OWL-S Profile, a score is assigned to each candidate SE, and using this score, an appropriate SE can be selected automatically (e.g., a printer that is nearest to a user is selected automatically).

(3) Service change-over function

During service execution, when an appropriate SE is found after a change in the user context, the service can be reconstructed by changing to the new appropriate SE while maintaining the service state (e.g., when a user moves, the monitor is automatically changed to the nearest one).

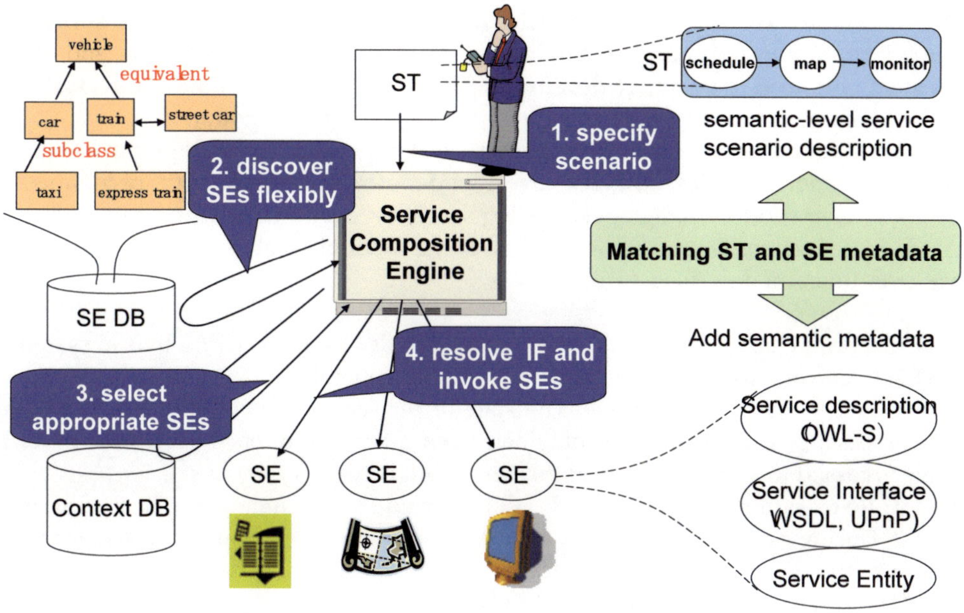

Fig. 1. Outline of our service composition technology

3. Applying commercial BPEL engine for service composition execution unit

We have already implemented a prototype service composition system with the functions mentioned above (Yamato et al., 2006) (Yamato & Sunaga, 2007). However, to develop this prototype system to commercial-use-level quality, many adjustments such as adding security functions, accommodating web service standard specifications, and tuning of middleware (Java VM, Tomcat, Axis, and RDF parser, for example) are required. These adjustments are ongoing and require a high maintenance cost. Meanwhile, in the market, with the spread of web service technology, there are many market products for the interpretation and execution of the BPEL language (BPEL engine). Therefore, in this study, we evaluate a method for achieving a commercial-level quality of the service composition engine at a low cost by combining featured functions of our prototype system and BPEL engines in the market.

When BPEL and WSDL are deployed, a BPEL engine interprets the BPEL description and executes activities such as the invoking of a web service. Therefore, we propose hybrid

methods where searching for SEs based on ST and selecting an appropriate SE are performed by U-ske (Ubiquitous Service Kernel Emulator) as a preprocess, and execution of an SE including SOAP messaging, for example, is performed by a BPEL engine. Here, BPEL is used, so the target component is limited to web services.
The flow of service composition is as follows. U-ske searches for available SE candidates based on the semantic description of an ST and selects the most appropriate SE using the OWL-S Profile of those candidate SEs and the user context. Next, a BPEL description is dynamically generated using control tags described in ST and WSDL of the selected SE. By deploying the generated BPEL and WSDL on a BPEL engine, the BPEL engine executes the composed service. Here, search and selection units can be reused from a previously developed prototype composition engine while a BPEL generation unit and a BPEL deployment unit need to be newly developed. The BPEL generation unit is universal but the BPEL deployment unit is dependent on the BPEL engine of each vendor.
In this way, featured functions (1)(2) of our service composition technology can be achieved. However, commercial BPEL engines are intended for composition of predefined web services and web service change-over during service execution according to the change of context is out of scope. Therefore, we discuss some methods that correspond to the service change-over function described in (3).

Method 1: Service change-over is out of the scope of this U-ske and BPEL hybrid system.
Method 2: According to the change of context, U-ske generates a new BPEL description and has it re-executed by a BPEL engine. The state of service (parameter value or the advance state of process) of the old BPEL is obtained from interfaces of each vendor BPEL engine. The state is copied to a new BPEL, and the new BPEL is restarted by U-ske.
Method 3: Re-execution of a new BPEL is performed in the same manner as described in Method 2. During execution, the BPEL engine writes the process state to U-ske periodically according to the description of BPEL, and when the SE change-over occurs, a new BPEL is executed by copying the state maintained in U-ske.
Method 4: SE changing is performed by a representative SE, and the BPEL engine invokes a fixed representative SE. The representative SE selects, changes, and invokes an appropriate SE according to the change in user context.

	Method 0 (full development of composition engine)	Market BPEL engine + U-ske			
		Method 1	Method 2	Method 3	Method 4
feasibility	Good	Good	Bad	Fair	Good
feature function sufficiency level	Good	Bad	Good	Good	Good
commercial function sufficiency level	Bad	Good	Good	Good	Good
development cost	Bad	Good	Fair	Fair	Fair
maintenance cost	Bad	Fair	Fair	Fair	Fair
low vendor dependency	Good	Fair	Bad	Fair	Fair
memory usage	Fair	Good	Good	Fair	Fair
process performance	Good	Good	Fair	Bad	Fair

Fig. 2. Evaluation table of five methods obtained through case study

In Method 2, the method of obtaining the execution state is vendor dependent, and that method is difficult in terms of feasibility. Method 3 leads to a lot of wasted processes because the execution state needs to be written in U-ske periodically. Method 4 has some difficulty to describe because the representative SE needs to be described in ST, but Method 4 is easy to implement. These Methods together with Method 0 (previous work -fully developed service composition engine by ourselves) are compared in terms of the following evaluation criteria: feasibility, feature function sufficiency level, commercial function sufficiency level, development cost, maintenance cost, low vendor dependency, resource usage, and process performance. As a result of case studies, Method 4 seems acceptable in terms of feasibility and feature function sufficiency level (see Fig. 2). On the basis of these case studies, we adopt Method 4 to achieve a service change-over function.

4. Implementation and evaluation of proposed method

So far, we have studied a context-aware service composition using a BPEL engine and U-ske. We adopted Method 4, which uses a representative SE to achieve service change-over. This method has the following features.
Using the BPEL engine as an execution unit, service composition and change-over can be performed according to the user context.
U-ske generates the standard BPEL1.1 language, so many BPEL engines that are compatible with BPEL 1.1 can be used (multi-vendor compatibility).
SE search, selection, BPEL generation, and deployment are performed before BPEL execution, so the overhead is large compared to the fixed BPEL execution.

Consequently, these features were evaluated through the implementation. Evaluation points were as follows.

1) Verification of feasibility of context-aware function: The feasibility of whether SE can be selected and composed according to user context needs to be confirmed and whether SE can be changed-over according to the change of user context during execution.
2) Implementation cost of vendor-dependent unit: From the viewpoint of multiple vendor compatibility, the cost of implementation of a vendor-dependent unit needs to be low.
3) Total performance of the system: Total performance of the system needs to be evaluated, SE search, SE select, BPEL generation, BPEL deploy, and BPEL execution.

4.1 Verification of feasibility of context-aware function

Outline of operation of Method 4 is shown in Fig. 3. First, the ST of the desired service is input into a SE search/selection unit. According to the method [5][6], the SE search/selection unit searches for and selects an SE appropriate for the user context and transfers information of the ST and selected SEs to the BPEL generation unit. The BPEL generation unit generates a BPEL description using this information. Then, the generated BPEL is deployed on a BPEL engine through a BPEL deployment unit. The BPEL engine executes the generated BPEL service.
During service execution, a representative SE is used for the SE change-over. The representative SE is generated as an inner resource of U-ske at the same time that the BPEL is generated from the ST. The grammatical difference between ST and BPEL is that in the ST, the invoked web service is specified abstractly, and there is an original control tag "search" that searches for an SE during execution. Other control tags are the same as those of BPEL. Therefore, the mapping from ST to BPEL is performed in the manner shown in Fig. 4. The "search" tag is mapped to the representative SE in the BPEL. The BPEL invokes a representative SE, which is inner resource of U-ske, and the representative SE changes and invokes an appropriate SE using the SE search/selection unit. The representative SE can be automatically generated from OWL-S Process model.
According to this design, the proposed method was implemented by Java language using an open source BPEL engine, Active BPEL2.0. Using this implemented system, the sample ST (Fig. 3), which shows the hotel map on the nearest monitor, is examined. We confirmed that an appropriate BPEL description could be generated for each user, and changing the SE to the nearest monitor SE according to the change in the user position during execution was performed. In this way, our system demonstrates the feasibility of context-aware composition and changing, which was impossible using the ordinary BPEL engine.

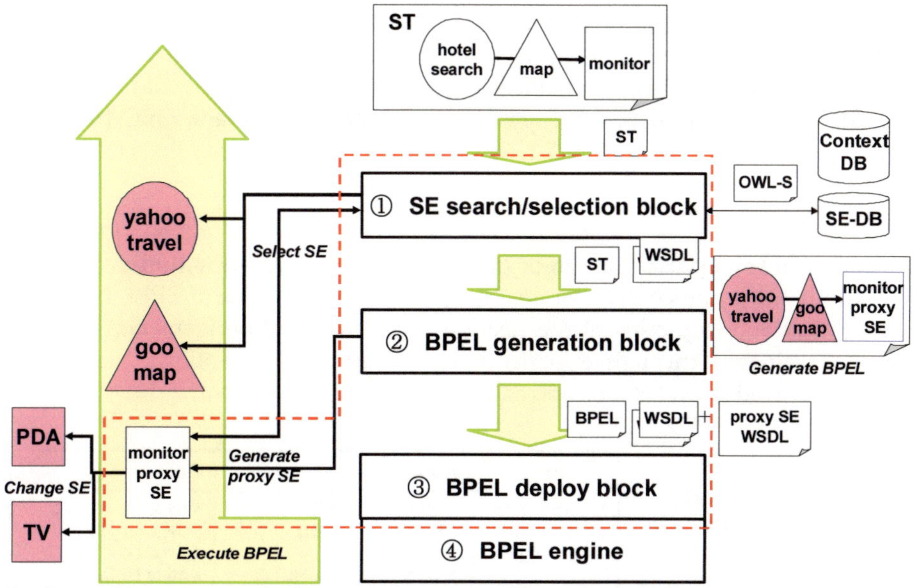

Fig. 3. Outline of service composition system using U-ske and BPEL engine. (U-ske function is inside dotted line)

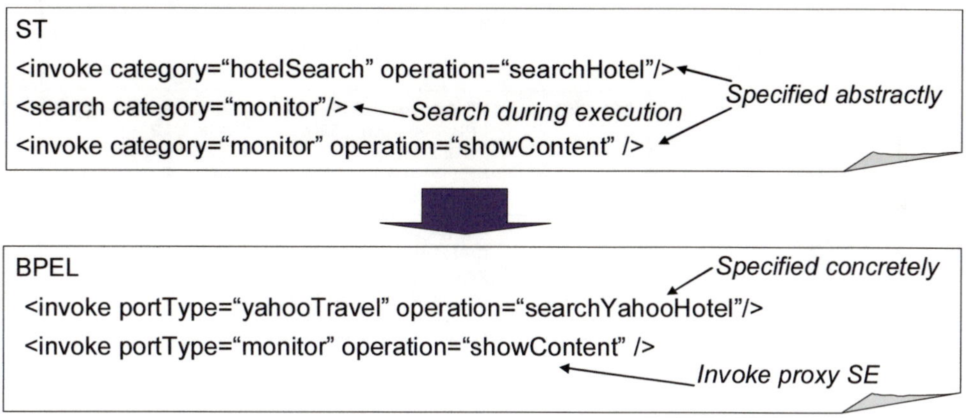

Fig. 4. Transforming example from ST to BPEL

4.2 Implementation cost of vendor dependent unit

There are many BPEL engines in the market, so an appropriate product needs to be selected according to the user policy (e.g., users wishing to use SAML for authentication can select a BPEL engine on which a WS-Security SAML token profile is implemented). In this method, a BPEL description is generated from an ST through a BPEL generation unit and then deployed and executed on a BPEL engine. Therefore, the only vendor-dependent unit is a BPEL deployment/un-deployment unit to deploy/un-deploy a BPEL description on a BPEL engine.

When this function was implemented on Active BPEL, the number of program code lines was approximately 800. In addition, we confirmed that the function could be implemented on the BPEL Process Manager of Oracle at approximately the same size. This indicates that in the proposed method, the interface is based on standard technologies such as BPEL and WSDL, so the service composition featured function can be implemented on various BPEL engines with the development of a small-scale vendor-dependent unit. Here, the BPEL generation function generates BPEL1.1, so this method cannot use the vendor-dependent BPEL extension.

4.3 Evaluation of total performance of proposed service composition system

In this method, performance deteriorates compared to normal use of BPEL because steps of BPEL generation and deployment are needed. Therefore, the performance of this method needs to be evaluated through a performance measurement. Follows are measurement conditions, and Fig. 5 shows the performance measurement environment.

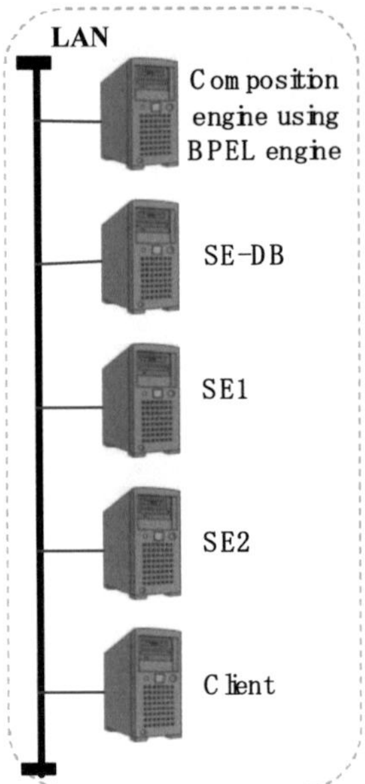

	Hardware	Software
Composition engine using BPEL engine	Dell Precision650 CPU: Xeon 3.2 GHz RAM: 3.0 GB NIC: Broadcom Gigabit ethernet	Windows XP SP2 JDK 1.4.2_13 Tomcat 4.1.31 Active BPEL2.0 U-ske program
SE-DB	HP Proliant ML310 CPU: Pentium4 2.53GHz RAM: 2.25GB NIC: Realtek RTL8139 Family PCI Fast Ethernet	Windows XP SP2 JDK 1.4.2_13 PostgreSQL 8.0
SE1, SE2	HP Proliant ML310 CPU: Pentium4 2.53GHz RAM: 2.25GB NIC: Realtek RTL8139 Family PCI Fast Ethernet	Windows XP SP2 JDK 1.4.2_13 Tomcat 4.1.31 Axis 1.2 sample Web service
Client (JMeter)	IBM Netvista CPU: Pentium4 2.53GHz RAM: 512MB NIC: Intel(R) PRO/100 VE NetworkConnection	Windows XP SP2 JDK 1.4.2_13 JMeter 2.0.1

Fig. 5. Performance measurement environment

<u>Measured items:</u>

· Throughput (CPU utilization and memory usage as the number of ST processes per hour is changed)

· The number of concurrent ST executions (CPU utilization and processing time of each processing section as the number of concurrent ST executions is changed)

<u>Measurement setting:</u>

· Candidate SEs matching OWL-S Process model are found from one SE-DB.

· SE is automatically selected according to its marked score (In this measurement, the physically nearest SE gains a high score and is selected automatically).

· Five sections are measured: SE search, SE select, BPEL generation, BPEL deployment, and BPEL execution.

<u>Measurement conditions:</u>

・An ST consists of five categories and there are ten candidate SEs for each category.
・An ST invokes each SE once and copies one parameter to the next SE (The process of copying a string variable of the former SE return value to the next SE argument is repeated five times).
・Response time of SE is fixed at 0.1 s.

As a result of the measurements, throughput of service execution by the above-mentioned ST was 3600 ST executions/hour with CPU utilization of 50% (Fig. 6 (a)). When the throughput exceeded 3600 ST executions/hour, BPEL deployment failed frequently while there was some extra capacity of CPU resources. This was due to Active BPEL. Therefore, the limit of throughput is about 1 ST per second. The measurement during concurrent ST executions demonstrates that BPEL deployment and BPEL execution require much processing time (Fig. 7). BPEL deployment in particular required a heavy CPU load because a grammatical validity check needed to be performed. To check the influence of BPEL deployment, the throughput was measured when the BPEL was generated from the ST for the first time, and the generated BPEL was executed repeatedly for each user. In this case, when CPU utilization was 50%, throughput was 44,000 BPEL executions/hour, and the throughput maximum was 52,000 BPEL executions/hour (Fig. 6 (b)). That is more than ten times the number of executions in the case of deploying BPEL every time. This value is nearly equivalent to the throughput value of a normal usage of the BPEL engine with the same environment. For the memory usage, the value increased to the heap size of JVM, and after that, the value became steady. Meanwhile, the variation of CPU utilization was large as shown in Fig. 6 due to the influence of garbage collection.

In the concurrent ST executions, CPU utilization was 100% when 50 STs were executed. Therefore, assuming commercial operation, the load needs to be distributed to multiple engines using a load balancer so that no more than 20 processes of BPEL generation and deployment occur concurrently. When a generated BPEL description is used repeatedly, the maximum number of concurrent ST is higher than 50, of course.

According to the performance measurement result, we found that concurrent processes with frequent BPEL deployment is a difficult task in terms of CPU processing load. However, we also found that sufficient performance is obtained by customizing, generating, and deploying BPEL descriptions according to the user for the first time only, using the generated BPEL descriptions repeatedly and changing SE, which is frequently changed by the representative SE.

In the areas where customization and context-awareness are required, our method can compose the service for each user. In these areas, there are several possible selections. For example, when the service is reconstructed frequently according to the user context, load distribution is needed, so the composition engine is implemented on each home gateway. In addition, when the service, once customized by a user, is used repeatedly, the composition engine is implemented on a network server to provide a service for many public users.

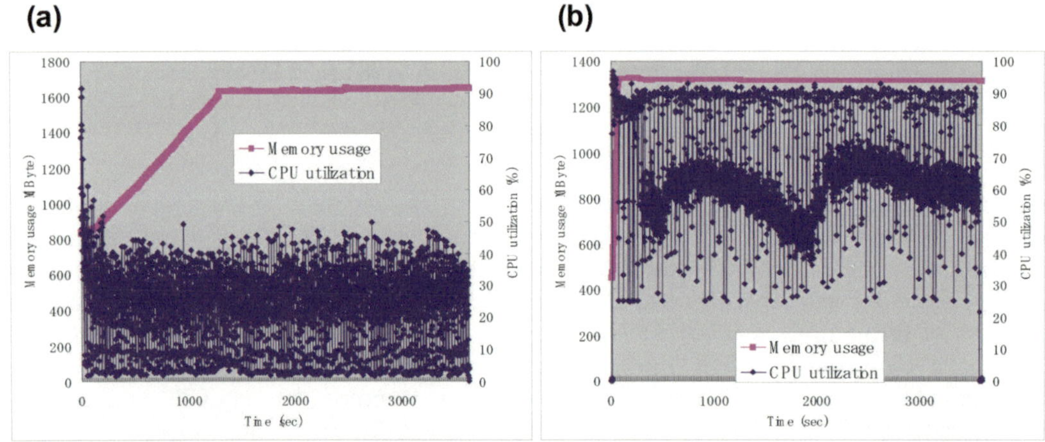

Fig. 6. (a) Memory usage and CPU utilization when the ST is used 3600 times per hour (when BPEL generation occurs every time).
(b) Memory usage and CPU utilization when the ST is used 52,000 times per hour (when the generated BPEL is used repeatedly).

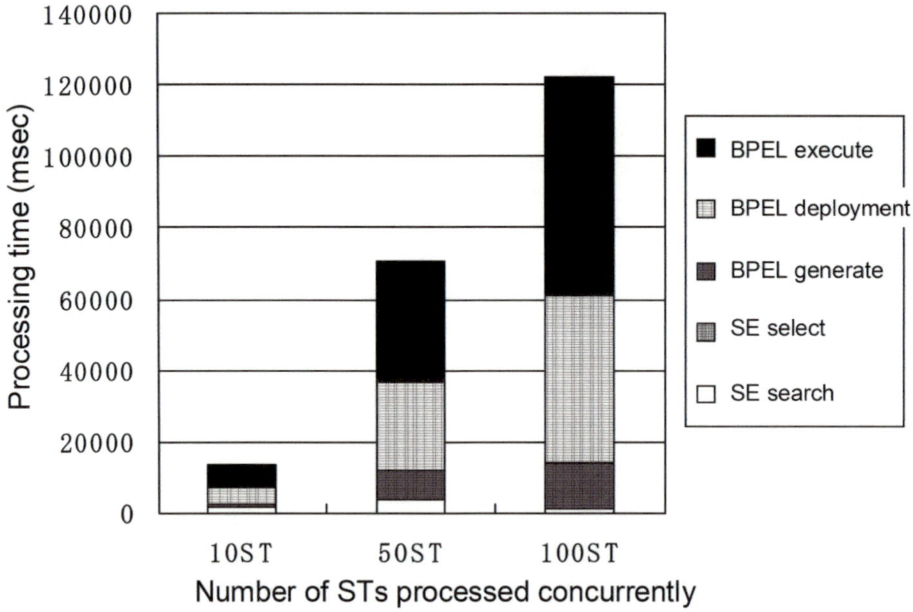

Fig. 7. The processing time sections during concurrent ST execution

5. Sample Application

An example application using the service composition technology, "business trip supporter" (see Fig. 8), was achieved. This service reduces routine work when a user makes a business trip. Wherever the user is, when the time to leave comes, a device containing an alarm function nearby reminds the user of the departure time (according to the event in a PDA scheduler), and trip information (maps, train timetable, weather, for example) is provided to the nearest printer or monitor.

The main features of this service are context-awareness and customization. The former means that an appropriate device is selected automatically according to the user's location without paying attention to differences in device interfaces due to the ST and SE change-over functions. In the office, a speaker may be invoked, while a pet robot with a sound device may be invoked at home because there is no other sound device at home. In the metadata DB, the pet robot is related to the sound device by the OWL subClassOf property, so the engine discovers the pet robot as a substitute for an alarm using metadata links. The customization allows a user to change an ST easily because the user can describe the ST without knowing rigid interface definitions of SEs. For example, a user can easily add weather information using the GUI ST editor.

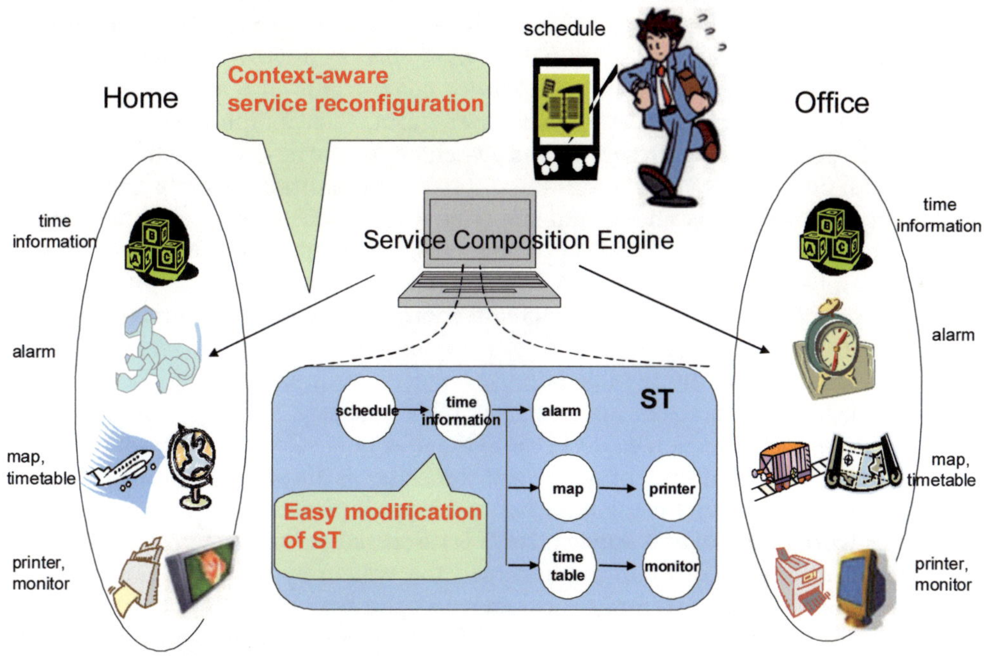

Fig. 8. Sample application of business trip supporter

6. Related works

In various related studies, multiple service components are composed on a network and composite services are provided. In particular, BPEL (Jordan et al., 2007), STONE (Minami et al., 2001) and Ninja (Gribble et al., 2001) have similar targets as this study. Those technologies compose service components based on service flow descriptions such as BPEL document, service graph, or Path, just as our ST does. BPEL is strongly dependent on WSDL, so changing WS is difficult. STONE names each component's input and output using an original naming system and binds components where the output of one component matches the input of another component. However, such original naming makes the system less extensible. The flexible composition techniques of our technology make it superior to other technologies. Standard semantic metadata is assigned to an SE, and SEs are searched with metadata using OWL links. Then, the SE is invoked after being converted to an actual interface using a grounding description.

Similar to our study, TaskComputing (Masuoka et al., 2003) and Ubiquitous Service Finder (Kawamura et al., 2005) also try to compose service components using Semantic Web technology. TaskComputing converts all devices and objects into services and describes their properties using OWL-S. In TaskComputing, a thing corresponding to our "SE" is called a "service," and possible combinations of services, in which service outputs match inputs of the next service, are proposed from all services that are available in the user area. Then, a user selects a desired combination manually to invoke a composite service. Ubiquitous Service Finder also composes service components in a sequence by invoking WSs in which one's output matches the next one's input. TaskComputing targets a bottom-up approach by focusing on each service and searching for the next service that matches. On the other hand, our study targets a top-down service composition where a user specifies a desired composite service as an ST, and the system finds and composes appropriate SEs. Therefore, our study and TaskComputing are complementary studies. However, TaskComputing has two problems. 1) A user's manual selection might be difficult because the number of candidate combinations increase enormously when the number of available services in the user area increases, and 2) complex combinations of services including branches and loops are hardly feasible because services are linked one-by-one in sequence. As a user's desired components are specified by a category in the ST description, our technology makes such selection easier because the user only selects appropriate SEs in each category. Available control tags of an ST are the same as those of BPEL, and of course, execution of a complex service using branches and loops is possible.

Our previous work (Yamato and Sunaga, 2007) is discussed service composition technology using semantic web techniqus and implemented the system by ourselves. This work uses commercial BPEL engine, therefore users can select the best BPEL engine based on their usage. U-ske unit of this work enables ordinal BPEL engines to user customizable service composition systems with small cost.

7. Conclusion

We presented a context-aware service-composition system using U-ske (Ubiquitous Service Kernel Emulator) and the BPEL engine to achieve commercial-level quality at a low cost. U-ske searches for and selects appropriate service components according to the user context, generates a BPEL description, and deploys that description in the BPEL engine. The BPEL engine invokes each web service based on the deployed BPEL description. We also presented a method for service change-over, which was a problem of using the BPEL engine. We have implemented the method and evaluated its feasibility, multi-vendor compatibility, and processing performance. The evaluation results demonstrate the effectiveness of our method. For the future, we will conduct a detailed evaluation of practical applications of customized and context-aware services.

8. References

Weiser, M. (1991) .The Computer for the 21st Century, *Scientific America*, Vol.265, No.3, (Sep. 1991) pp.99-104

Schilit, B.; Adams, N. & Want, R. (1994). Context-Aware Computing Applications, *Proceedings of IEEE Workshop on Mobile Computing Systems and Applications*, pp.85-90, Dec. 1994.

Minami, M.; Morikawa, H. & Aoyama, T. (2001). The Design of Service Synthesizer on the Net Workshop on Highly Distributed System, *Invited Presentation of IEEE Symposium on Applications and the Internet (SAINT2001)*, Jan. 2001.

Gribble, S.; Welsh, M.; Behren, R.; Brewer, E.; Culler, D.; Borisov, N.; Czerwinski, S.; Gummadi, R.; Hill, J.; Joseph, A.; Katz, R.; Mao, Z.; Ross, S. & Zhao, B. (2001). The Ninja Architecture for Robust Internet-Scale Systems and Services, *IEEE Computer Networks Special Issue on Pervasive Computing*, Vol.35, No.4 (Mar. 2001) pp.473-497.

Yamato, Y.; Tanaka, Y. & Sunaga, H. (2006). Context-aware Ubiquitous Service Composition Technology, *Proceedings of IFIP International Conference on Research and Practical Issues of Enterprise Information Systems (CONFENIS2006)*, pp.51-61, Apr. 2006.

Yamato, Y & Sunaga, H. (2007). Context-Aware Service Composition and Component Change-over using Semantic Web Techniques, *Proceedings of IEEE 2007 International Conference on Web Services (ICWS 2007)*, pp.687-694, July 2007.

Jordan, D.; Evdemon, J. et al. (2007). Web Services Business Process Execution Language Version 2.0, *OASIS Standard*, http://docs.oasis-open.org/wsbpel/2.0/OS/wsbpel-v2.0-OS.html, Apr. 2007.

Martin, D. et al. (2004). OWL-S: Semantic Markup for Web Services, *W3C Member Submission* , http://www.w3.org/Submission/OWL-S/, Nov. 2004.

Paolucci, M., & Sycara, K. (2003). Autonomous Semantic Web Services, *IEEE Internet Computing*, Vol.7, No.5, (Sep. 2003), pp34-41.

Sycara, K.; Paolucci, M.; Anolekar, A. & Srinivasan, N. (2003). Automated discovery, interaction and composition of semantic web services, *Web Semantics: Science, Services and Agents on the World Wide Web*, Vol.1, No.1, (Dec. 2003), pp.27-46.

Masuoka, R.; Parsia, B.; Labrou, Y. & Sirin, E. (2003). Ontology-Enabled Pervasive Computing Applications, *IEEE Inteligent Systems*, Vol.18, No.5, (Sep. 2003) pp.68-72.

Kawamura, T.; Ueno, K.; Nagano, S.; Hasegawa, T. & Ohsuga, A. (2005). Ubiquitous Service Finder - Discovery of Services semantically derived from metadata in Ubiquitous Computing, *Proceedings of 4th International Semantic Web Conference (ISWC 2005)*, pp.902-915, Nov. 2005.

15

Metaphor and the Semantic Web

Jonathan Biguenet[1], Bogdan D. Czejdo[2] and John Biguenet[3]
[1] *Tulane University,* [2] *Fayetteville State University,* [3] *Loyola University*
USA

1. Overview

Metaphor, a comparison of two entities, is a fundamental expression of human intelligence, offering a simple formulation of the assertion of a relationship. Though simple in form, the metaphor demands a complex interpretation of the relationship, revealing subtle correspondences between the two entities compared. Such an interpretation hinges on general background information and specific context. The metaphor's purpose is to shed new light on the two entities through their comparison.

While a simile, employing *like* or *as* in the comparison, makes clear that the two entities are only approximations of each other, a metaphor seems to suggest shared identity. However, to say a camera is an eye is not to say they are the same thing. So we cannot formally represent the relationship as an equality. Metaphor obviously requires a very complex cognitive operation to grasp its meaning. Similarly, an intelligent agent, such as a computer, faces a complicated problem in processing the data conveyed by a metaphor.

We will present a model for processing the relationship expressed in a metaphor. Examining the objects specified in the metaphor together with their properties exposes the layers of relationships implicit in the comparison. This examination is extended to other objects related by general background knowledge or specific context to the original paired entities. Through selection, rejection, and emphasis of the properties of all these objects, we establish a new complex relationship representing the metaphor. Ideally, this complex relationship contains all necessary information for the computer to understand the metaphor.

Human interpreters of a metaphor draw from their knowledge and the text itself; in our model, a computer would process a metaphor using knowledge databases expressed as Semantic Markups on the Web. If the Semantic Web is to support metaphor processing, these markups should define objects as well as their properties and relationships. Such a development would facilitate better use of the knowledge contained on the Web.

2. Introduction

Beginning with modern automatons and especially since Karel Čapek introduced the word *robot* in *R.U.R.*, his 1921 play, such mechanical creatures usually have been modeled on human beings, often in terms of form as well as function. "A robot is a human being" remains an influential, though debatable, metaphor.

Metaphor, a common device for the classification of objects and the assertion of newly recognized relationships, poses an array of challenges for natural language processing. A close analysis of the statement "a robot is a human being" quickly reveals the difficulties posed in the processing of the metaphor by a software agent.

The Semantic Web (Berners-Lee et al., 2001) offers the possibility of solutions to these challenges through its capacity for annotation. In this paper, we present the analysis of a common metaphor and its modeling, which can be a basis for annotating metaphorical statements.

Previous research (Booch et al., 1999; Czejdo et al., 2003; Czejdo et al., 2006; Delteil and Faron, 2002; Dori et al., 2003; Lehrnan, 1999; Sowa, 1984) demonstrates the need for appropriate models for the interpretation of complex statements such as metaphor. Here, we use the notation of Universal Modeling Language (UML) (Booch et al., 1999; Rumbaugh et al., 1999) for metaphor modeling. Such modeling has been employed to depict object-relationship systems (Rumbaugh, 1993). Concise graphical notation, availability of simple tools, and the possibility to use informal specifications if necessary make UML modeling very useful for defining ontologies. Therefore, UML diagrams can still play an important role even though new notations such as OWL (Smith et al., 2002) and new tools such as Protégé (Gennari et al., 2002) and SWOOP (Kalyanpur et al., 2005) allow for manipulation of ontologies.

In this paper, we first discuss the complexities of interpreting metaphor. We then examine the modeling of a specific metaphor as an example of this process. Continuing with an analysis of the inverse of the exemplary metaphor, we argue that metaphors are not commutative and thus illuminate one aspect of their complexity. The paper concludes that in order for the Semantic Web to interpret metaphors accurately, it must accommodate complex annotations.

3. Metaphor and Its Complexities

A metaphor is a direct comparison between two objects or states. A simile, another form of comparison, uses *like* or *as*. So "a robot is like a human being" is a simile and, perhaps, easier to interpret than the metaphoric form of the comparison. In the simile, the robot is merely an approximation of a human, sharing a limited number of attributes. In a metaphor, differences are either de-emphasized or masked by the superimposition of one of the two components of the metaphor upon the other. In a simile, such differences are acknowledged. As we have argued elsewhere (Czejdo et al., 2006; Biguenet et al., 2005), "*like* signals simply a congruence between the two entities compared; its use eliminates the possible confusion of the metaphor: that the two entities share identity. But the metaphor, while demanding a similar cognitive operation, declines to limit explicitly the relationship between the two entities compared to mere approximation. Instead, the metaphor hints at shared identity. In mathematical terms, we are tempted to express the metaphor as A equals B. The difficulty the computer faces in decoding such a statement's intended meaning is obvious." This potential for confusion becomes clear when the inverse of the metaphor is stated: "A robot is a human being" is not equivalent to "A human being is a robot."

The two elements of the metaphor's construction usually share only specific characteristics. In reducing the scope of the comparison to only those elements that are shared, the metaphor can efficiently express an essential relationship. But in doing so, it obscures difference. In fact, when applied to a human being, the adjective "robotic" is negative, suggesting the loss of intentionality and even freedom.

4. Extending UML Diagram to Capture Metaphoric Constructs

The UML diagrams, as previously mentioned, are well suited to the initial phase of knowledge extraction when all details are not yet clear. This feature is extremely important for systems of metaphor processing that require many phases of refinement.

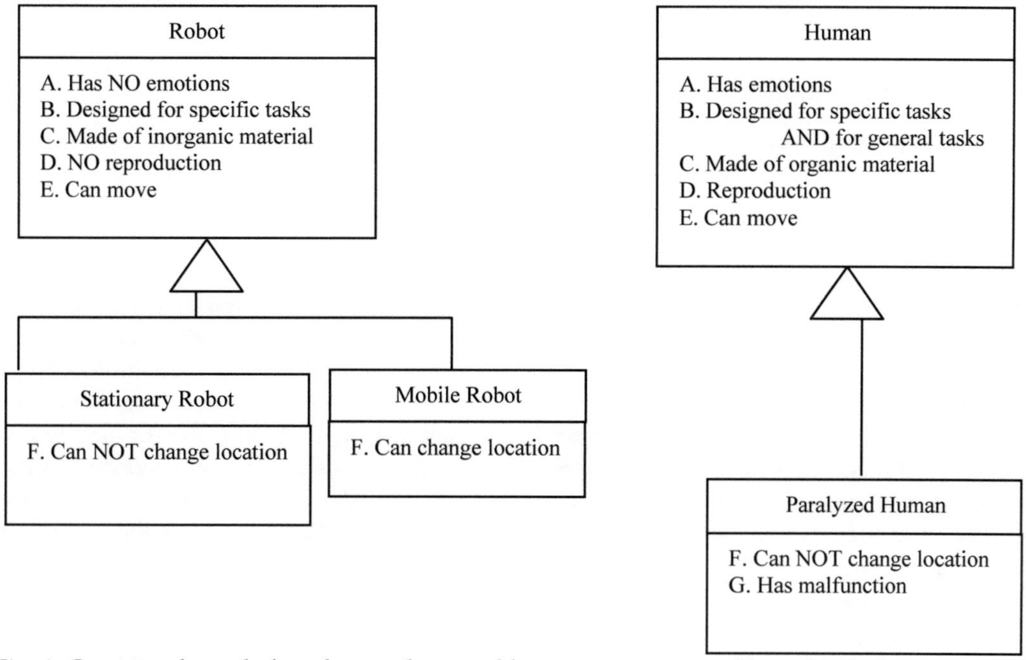

Fig. 1. Common knowledge about robots and humans represented by a UML class diagram

In the UML diagram used as an example in our paper describing a Robot and a Human as shown in Fig. 1, we define a Robot here (in a limited way) as an object that has no emotions, is designed for specific tasks, is made of inorganic material, cannot reproduce, can move, and can change location. We define Human here (in a limited way) as an object that has emotions, is designed for specific and general tasks, is made of organic material, can reproduce, can move, and can change location. Both Robot and Human are broken down into subclasses. For Robot, we have the two categories, Stationary Robots and Mobile Robots. A Stationary Robot we define as an object that cannot change its location. A Mobile Robot, on the other hand, can change its location. If a Mobile robot malfunctions, we call it a Malfunctioning Robot. A Malfunctioning Robot cannot change its location. A Paralyzed Human is one who cannot change location either.

The underlying UML diagram contains the knowledge about a specific subject or many subjects (e.g., about robots and humans). The database described by the UML diagram can therefore be used to answer both simple and complex queries in these subject areas. A simple query, similar to "Describe Robot," will include all properties and functions of the

class (object). Among various complex queries, the comparison queries are some of the most useful for this project, allowing for an extended comparison of classes. Such a comparison of classes requires the comparison of their properties and functions as well as of all relationships.
"Compare a robot with a human" is an example of a comparison query. The comparison would result in the identification of all common properties and functions. The common subclasses and relationships need to be identified as well. Some additional processing is necessary since the common relationship type is a super-class. Because all attributes from a super-class can be inherited, they are also indicated as common. Additionally, we have a common relationship indicated by "has."

5. Metaphor Modeling by UML Diagram

A natural-language metaphor can contain quite a complex meaning not only stressing the similarity between two classes (or objects) but also simultaneously emphasizing or de-emphasizing some properties, functions, and relationships of the pair. Modeling the metaphor described in section 2, "The robot is a human," by a UML diagram demonstrates these features of metaphor.
As previously mentioned, the metaphor hints at shared identity and symmetrical structure, but scrutiny of the inverted form of the metaphor shows that such symmetry does not exist. Obviously, the simplistic initial reading of the metaphor must yield to a more precise definition of metaphorical structure. The metaphor, in terms of UML modeling, is rather a non-symmetrical special subclass/superclass relationship that allows for modifying properties, functions, and relationships of one concept by another. We will call this special subclass/superclass relationship "is a metaphor" and indicate it by arrows on the diagram. Returning to our example, we can create a new relationship called "is a metaphor" between Robot and Human. The direction of the arrow from Robot to Human in Fig. 2 indicates that "Robot is a Human."
Determining the definition of a metaphor in the UML diagram is a complex process. It requires not only insertion of a new type of relationship called "is a metaphor" but also identification of the list of modified properties, functions, and relationships with respect to the given metaphor, as well as determination of the type of modification of each listed property, function, and relationship. The modification can include emphasis, de-emphasis, or superimposition. Superimposition does not erase the real values but only temporarily masks them with new values. We refer to such properties, functions, and relationships as "superimposed." In Fig. 2, we will mask the property "designed for specific tasks" by the superimposed property "designed for specific tasks AND for general tasks." The masking may serve various goals. One of these goals is to achieve an "amplification" of a property. In our case, the new property "designed for specific tasks AND for general tasks" is superimposed, replacing temporarily the previous property "designed for specific tasks."
We must also identify any component metaphors created on the basis of another metaphor using the process of "propagation." In our example, we have a component metaphor between "malfunctioning mobile robot" and "paralyzed human" derived from our initial metaphor by its propagation to the appropriate subclasses. Fig. 2 also reflects that specification. Once the derived metaphor is stated, all of the same steps discussed above must be taken to define it.

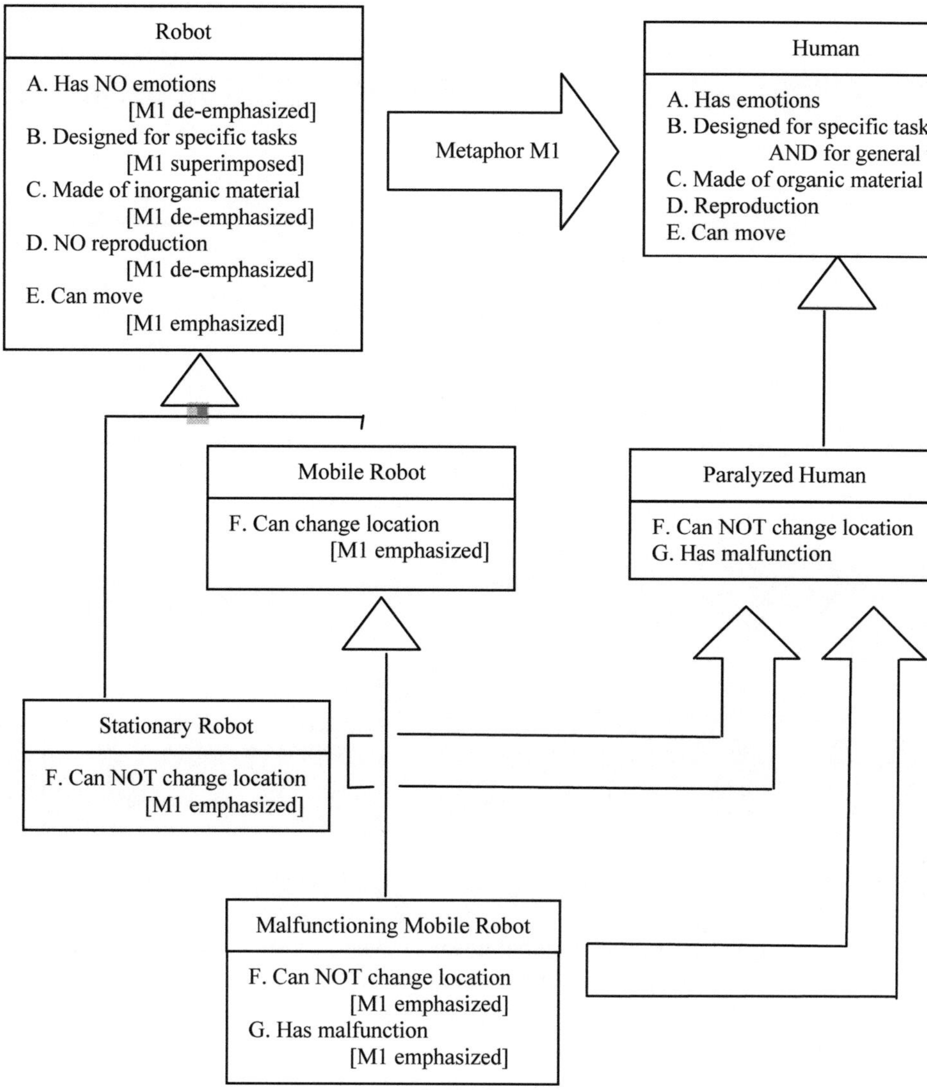

Fig. 2. Representation of a metaphor using UML diagrams

Let us expand our initial UML diagram to include components of robots and human beings, as shown in Fig. 3. A human has five senses. An eye is one of them. A robot has at least one sensor (e.g., camera). Included components of a robot are sensors, with a camera as a specific sensor type. Included components of a human are sense receptors, with an eye as a specific receptor. An eye captures an image and transmits an image to the human brain. A camera captures an image and records an image to digital memory.

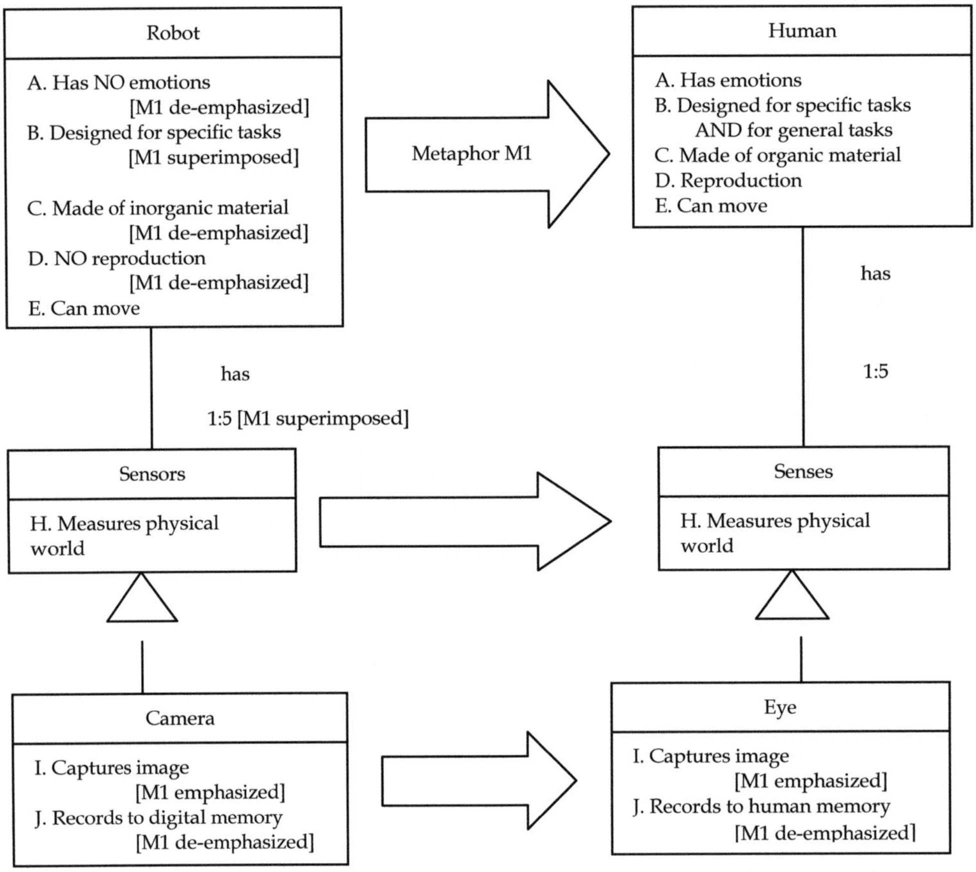

Fig. 3. Relationships between objects formed by extending our metaphor example

In Fig. 3, we have also another component metaphor between camera and eye derived from our initial metaphor by its propagation to the related ("has" relationship) classes. Fig. 3 reflects that specification.

6. Inverse Metaphor Modeling by UML Diagram

As we stated before, the metaphor is a non-symmetrical special subclass/superclass relationship that allows for modifying properties, functions, and relationships of one concept by another. The inverse metaphor might be similar to the initial (base) metaphor by stressing the compatibility of two classes (or objects), but it might be significantly different by emphasizing or de-emphasizing different properties, functions, and relationships. Let us model the inverse metaphor "The human is a robot" by a UML diagram. We can create a new relationship "is a metaphor" between Robot and Human in the direction from the Human to Robot as shown in Fig. 4.

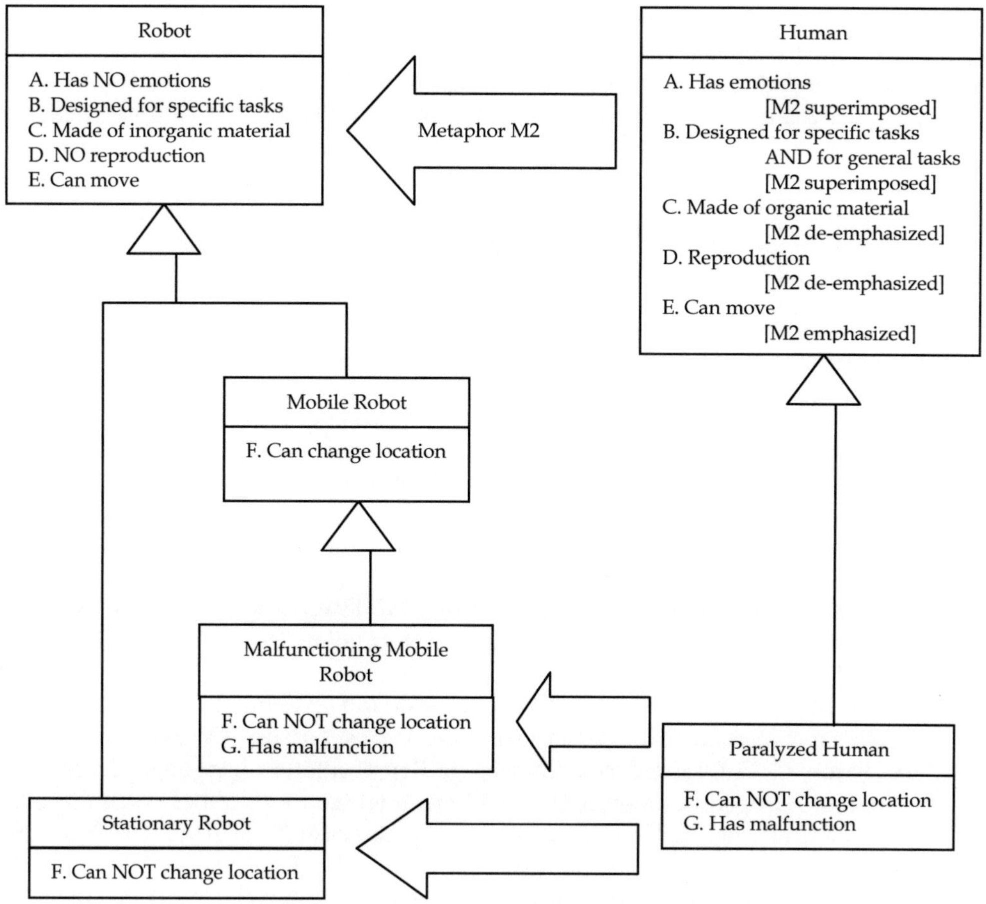

Fig. 4. Representation of a metaphor using UML diagrams

Let us look more closely at properties, functions, and relationships to be "superimposed." In our example in Fig. 4, we will identify the property "has emotions" to be "superimposed" by the new property "has no emotions" to indicate its new meaning for the metaphor. In this case, the masking served the goal of minimizing a property. If the property is positive, then decreasing its value may result in a negative metaphor. The propagation of this "negative" metaphor to the component classes ("has" relationship) could create a component metaphor "the eye is a camera," adding strength to the initial metaphor. It is interesting to note that propagation of the metaphor "A human is a robot" to the appropriate subclasses would make this metaphor negative, and perhaps even cruel, by suggesting that a paralyzed human is merely a malfunctioning mobile robot.

7. Summary

Metaphor obviously requires a very complex cognitive operation to grasp its meaning. Similarly, an intelligent agent, such as a computer, faces a complicated problem in processing the data conveyed by a metaphor. We have presented a model for processing the relationship expressed in a metaphor. Examining the objects specified in the metaphor together with their properties exposes the layers of relationships implicit in the comparison. Through selection, rejection, and emphasis of the properties of all these objects, we establish a new complex relationship representing the metaphor. Ideally, this complex relationship contains all necessary information for the computer to understand the metaphor. In our model, a computer would process a metaphor using knowledge databases expressed as Semantic Markups on the Web. If the Semantic Web is to support metaphor processing, these markups should define objects as well as their properties and relationships. Such a development would facilitate better use of the knowledge contained on the Web.

8. References

Berners-Lee T., Hendler, J., Lassila, 0.: The Semantic Web. Sci Am 284(5). (2001) 34-43

Biguenet, J., Czejdo, B, Biguenet, J.: "Creating Knowledge Databases from UML Diagrams", *Proceedings of Concurrent Engineering Research and Applications Conference,* Dallas (July 2005).

Booch, G., Rumbaugh, J., Jacobson, I.: The Unified Modeling Language User Guide. Addison Wesley, Reading, MA (1999)

Czejdo, B., Mappus, R., Messa, K.: The Impact of UML Diagrams on Knowledge Modeling, Discovery and Presentations. Journal of Information Technology Impact, Vol.3 (1). (2003) 25-38

Czejdo, B., Biguenet, J., Biguenet, J.: "Metaphor Modeling on Semantic Web", *Proceedings of Conceptual Modeling ER2006 Conference-Workshops,* Tucson (Oct 2006).

Delteil, A., Faron, C.: A Graph-Based Knowledge Representation Language. Proceedings of the 15th European Conference on Artificial Intelligence (ECAI), Lyon, France (2002)

Dori, D., Reinhartz-Berger, I., Sturm, A.: OPCAT—A Bimodal CASE Tool for Object-Process Based System Development. Proceedings of the IEEE/ACM 5th International Conference on Enterprise Information Systems (ICEIS 2003), Angers, France (2003) 286-291. www.ObjectProcess.org

Gennari, M. A. Musen, R. W. Fergerson, W. E. Grosso, M. Crubezy, H. Eriksson, N. F. Noy, S. W. Tu.: The Evolution of Protégé: An Environment for Knowledge-Based Systems Development. (2002)

Kalyanpur, A., Parsia, B., Sirin, E., Cuenca-Grau, B., Hendler, J.: Swoop - a web ontology editing browser, Journal of Web Semantics 4 (1). (2005)

Lehrnan, F. (ed): Semantic Networks in Artificial Intelligence. Pergamon, Oxford, UK (1999)

Rumbaugh, J.: Objects in the Constitution: Enterprise Modeling. Journal of Object Oriented Programming. (1993)

Rumbaugh, J., Jacobson, I., Booch, G.: The Unified Modeling Language Reference Manual. Addison-Wesley, Reading, MA (1999)

Smith, M.K., McGuinness, D., Volz, R., Welty, C.: Web Ontology Language (OWL) Guide Version 1.0. W3CWorking Draft (2002)

Sowa, J.F.: Conceptual Structures: Information Processing in Mind and Machine. Addison-Wesley, Reading, MA (1984)

16

Code Clone Detection Using String Based Tree Matching Technique

Ali Selamat and Norfaradilla Wahid
Universiti Teknologi Malaysia
Malaysia

1. Introduction

As the world of computers is rapidly evolving, there is a tremendous need of software development for different purposes. As we can see today, the complexity of the software being developed is different from one to another. Sometimes, developers take the easier way of implementation by copying some fragments of the existing programs and use the codes in their work. This kind of work is known as code cloning. Somehow the attitude of cloning can lead to the other issues of software development, for example plagiarism and software copyright infringement (Roy and Cordy, 2007). In most cases, in order to figure out the issues and help better software maintenance, we need to detect the codes that have been cloned (Baker, 1995). In the web applications development, the chances of cloning are bigger since there are too many open source software available on the Internet (Bailey and Burd, 2005). The applications are sometimes just a 'cosmetic' of another existing system. There are quite a number of researches in software code cloning detection, but not so particularly in the area of web based applications.

2. Background of the problem

Software maintenance has been widely accepted as the most costly phase of a software lifecycle, with figures as high as 80% of the total development cost being reported (Baker, 1995). As cloning is one of the contributors towards this cost, the software clone detection and resolution has got a considerable attention from the software engineering research community and many clone detection tools and techniques have been developed (Baker, 1995).

However, when it comes to commercialization of the software codes, most of the software house developers tend to claim that their works are 100% done in-house without using other codes copied from various sources. This has caused a difficulty to the intellectual property copyright entities such as SIRIM and patent searching offices in finding the genuine software source codes developed by the in-house companies. There is a need to identify the software source submitted for patent copyright application as a genuine source code without having any copyright infringements. Besides, cloning somehow brings up the issue of plagiarism. The simplest example can be seen in the academic field where students tend to copy their friends' works and submit the assignments with only slight modifications.

Generally, in software development process, there is a need for components reusability either in designing and coding. Reuse in object-oriented systems is made possible through different mechanisms such as inheritance, shared libraries, object composition, and so on. Still, programmers often need to reuse components which have not been designed for reuse. This may happen during the initial stage of systems development and also when the software systems go through the expansion phase and new requirements have to be satisfied. In these situations, the programmers usually follow the low cost copy-and-paste technique, instead of the costly redesigning-the-system approach, hence causing clones. This type of code cloning is the most basic and widely used approach towards software reuse. Several studies suggest that as much as 20% - 30% of large software systems consist of cloned codes (Krinke, 2001). The problem with code cloning is that errors in the original must be fixed in every copy. Other kinds of maintenance changes, for instance, extensions or adaptations, must be applied multiple times, too. Yet, it is usually not documented from where the codes were copied. In such cases, one needs to detect them. For large systems, detection is feasible only by automatic techniques. Consequently, several techniques have been proposed to detect clones automatically (Bellon et al., 2007).

There are quite a number of works that detect the similarities by representing the code in a tree or graph representation and also by using string-based detection, and semantic-based detection. Almost all of the clone detection techniques have the tendency of detecting syntactic similarities while only some detect the semantic part of the clones. Baxter in his work (Baxter et al., 1998) proposed a technique to extract cloned pairs of statements, declarations, or sequences of them from C source files. The tool parses source code to build an abstract syntax tree (AST) and compares its subtrees by characterization metrics (hash functions). The parser needs a "full-fledged" syntax analysis for C to build AST. Baxter's tool expands C macros (define, include, etc) to compare code portions written with macros. Its computation complexity is $O(n)$, where n is the number of the subtree of the source files. The hash function enables one to do parameterized matching, to detect gapped clones, and to identify clones of code portions in which some statements are reordered. In AST approaches, it is able to transform the source tree into a regular form as we do in the transformation rules. However, the AST based transformation is generally expensive since it requires full syntax analysis and transformation.

Another work (Jiang et al, 2007) presented an efficient algorithm for identifying similar subtrees and applied it to tree representations of source code. Their algorithm is based on a novel characterization of subtrees with numerical vectors in the Euclidean space R^n and an efficient algorithm to cluster these vectors with respected to the Euclidean distance metric. Subtrees with vectors in one cluster are considered similar. They have implemented the tree similarity algorithm as a clone detection tool called DECKARD and evaluated it on large code bases written in C and Java including the Linux kernel and JDK. The experiments show that DECKARD is both scalable and accurate. It is also language independent, applicable to any language with a formally specified grammar.

Krinke (Krinke, 2001) presented an approach to identify similar code in programs based on finding similar subgraphs in attributed directed graphs. This approach is used on program dependence graphs and therefore considers not only the syntactic structure of programs but also the data flow within (as an abstraction of the semantics). As a result, it is said that no trade-off between precision and recall - the approach is very good in both.

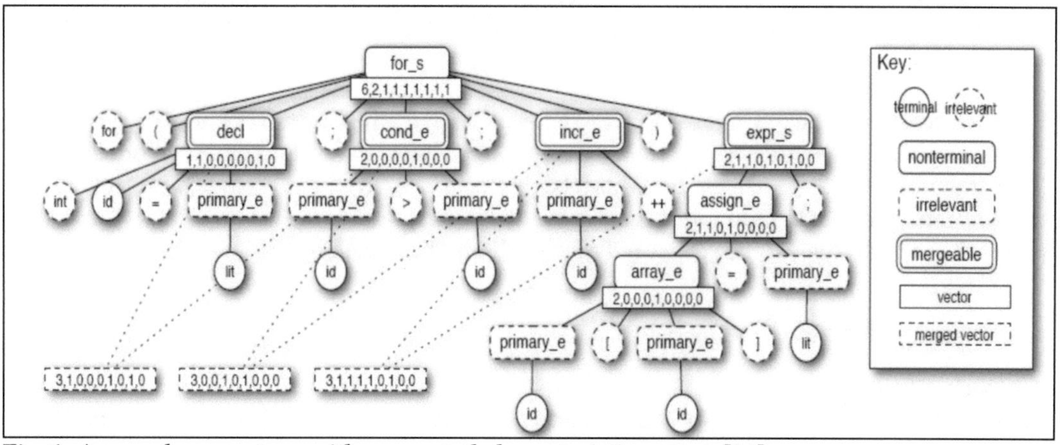

Fig. 1. A sample parse tree with generated characteristic vectors[14]

Kamiya in one of his works (Kamiya et al., 2002) suggested the use of suffix tree. In the paper they have used a suffix tree matching algorithm to compute token-by-token matching, in which the clone location information is represented as a tree with sharing nodes for leading identical subsequences and the clone detection is performed by searching the leading nodes on the tree. Their token-by-token matching is more expensive than line-by-line matching in terms of computational complexity since a single line is usually composed of several tokens. They proposed several optimization techniques specially designed for the token-by-token matching algorithm, which enable the algorithm to be practically useful for large software.

3. Problem Statement

As we can see from the previous works, some of the works are scalable, and are able to detect more than one type of clone. But some of them face the trade-off of the computational complexity. This could be due to the fact that most of the techniques apply expensive syntax analysis for transformation. From the literature that has been done, more than half of existing techniques used tree-based detection as it was more scalable. However, most of the techniques perform a single layer detection which means after the transformation into normalized data e.g. tree, graph, and etc, the process of finding the similarities of codes, i.e. code clones, were done directly by processing each node in the data. All possible clones need to be searched directly without some kind of filtering, which can increase the cost of computational process.

As ontology is being widely used nowadays, we cannot deny its importance in the current web technology. The major similarity of ontology and clone detection works is that both can be represented as tree. Besides that, many works have been done to do the mapping of different ontologies between each other, to find the similarities of the concepts among them. This activity is actually almost the same with what needs to be done in detecting clone codes.

Since there are some kinds of similarities in both problems, detecting clones in a source code can be done using the same way as mapping the ontologies. The research question of this thesis is to identify the possibility of using a technique of ontology mapping to detect clones in a web-based application. Obviously there will be no ontologies used in the experiments since we are dealing with source codes and not ontology. But we will use the technique of mapping to detect clones.
In order to achieve the objective, there are a few questions that need to be addressed:
(a) What are the attributes or criteria that might be possible to be cloned in web documents?
(b) What are the approaches that had been proposed in the previous research in the ontology mapping area than had been used in clone detection tool?
(c) What are the issues of the recovered approach and how to solve it?

4. Literature Review

4.1 Code Cloning

Code duplication or copying a code fragment for reuse by pasting with or without any modifications is known as code smell in software maintenance. This type of reuse approach of existing code is called code cloning and the pasted code fragment (with or without modifications) is called a clone of the original. Several studies show that duplicated code is basically the result of copying existing code fragments and using them by pasting with or without minor modifications. People always believe that the major cause of cloning is by the act of copying and pasting. Some say that it may happen accidentally. In some cases, a new developed system is actually a 'cosmetic' of another existing system. This type of case usually happens in the web based application. They tend to modify the appearance of the application or system by changing the background colour, images, etc.
Refactoring of the duplicated code is another prime issue in software maintenance although several studies claimed that refactoring of certain clones is not desirable and there is a risk of removing them. However, it is also widely agreed that clones should at least be detected. Several studies have shown that, the cost of maintenance is promisingly increasing wherever there are clones in the source code compared with the codes without any clones. Definition of code cloning had been mentioned in different researches and some of them used different terminologies to refer to the code cloning.
According to Koschke (Koschke, 2006), a clone is one that appears to be a copy of an original form. It is synonymous to 'duplicate'. Often in literature, there was a misconception of code clone and redundant code. Even though code clone usually leads to code redundancy, but not every redundant code is harmful, on the other hand cloned codes are usually harmful especially for the maintenance phase of software development life cycle. Baxter in his outstanding work (Baxter et al., 2008), stated that a clone is a program fragment that is identical to another fragment", Krinke (Krinke, 2001) used the term "similar code", Ducasse (Ducasse et al. 1999) used the term "duplicated code", Komondoor and Horwitz (Komondoor and Horwitz, 2001) also used the term "duplicated code" and used "clone" as an instance of duplicated code. Mayrand and Leblanc (Mayrand and Leblanc, 1996) used metrics to find "an exact copy or a mutant of another function in the system".
All these definitions of clones carry some kind of vagueness (e.g., "similar" and "identical") and this imperfect definition of clones makes the clone detection process much harder than the detection approach itself. Generally, it can be said that code clone pair is a fragment of

code that is syntactically or semantically identical or similar. From all arguments above, we could simplify the clones into four types:

(a) An exact copy without modifications (except for white spaces and comments) i.e. identical.

(b) A syntactically identical copy; only variable, type or function identifiers have been changed. i.e. nearly identical.

(c) A copy with further modifications; statements have been changed, added, or removed i.e. similar.

(d) A code portion that is partly similar to another code fragment. It may involve some deletion, modification and addition from the original code i.e. gapped clone.

According to our understanding from Ueda (Ueda et al., 2002), we may group the second and the third types as a single major type called renamed code clone. Renamed code clone still has similar structures between each other. So it is part of this report that the framework proposed should at least be capable to detect the identical clone and renamed code clone. Figure 2 shows an example of cloned code. Obviously the code in the example has the same code structure and the pair is considered similar.

```
int sum = 0 ;

void foo (Iterator iter){
        for(item = first (iter); has_more(iter); item = next(iter) ){
        sum = sum + value (item);
        }
}
```

```
int bar ( Iterator iter ){
int sum = 0 ;
        for(item = first (iter); has_more(iter); item = next(iter)) {
        sum = sum + value (item);
        }
}
```

Fig. 2. Example of a pair of cloned code in traditional program

4.2 Code Cloning in web applications

In this era, the computer has been a powerful tool to solve various kinds of problems in our everyday lives. The WWW has been the pit stop for people to find, share and exchange information all around the world. Today's web sites are not only a collections of static web sites that only display information but they also offer a lot more tasks and functions in more critical domains such as e-business, e-finance, e-government, e-learning, and so on that apply dynamic web pages with richer contents that are being retrieved from databases and such. These types of web applications require a lot more work efforts in their development life-cycles and thus require a lot more investments. People need to realize that web applications are not only meant for the Internet but if we can have at least a local area

network (LAN), we can still have web application and people within the network can still access the system.
Normally, web applications development needs shorter time of development processes and fuzzy initial requirement, thus brings to a lot of latent changes over the development life cycle (Jarzabek and Rajapakse, 2005). Since there is a need of shorter development time, there is a possibility of an increase in code cloning activities. Programmers are often forced to copy the code from existing works so that they can shorten the time to develop and make their jobs easier.
We can see there are quite a number of researches that have been carried out in the area of code cloning especially in traditional software (e.g. developed for stand alone application, using C, C++, etc) in the past decade. However, we can say that such researches are still in their infancy states for web-based application. The statement is due to the small number of researches that can be found available. Most of the researches revolve in the code clone detection whereby different strategies of detection are used. Callefato(2004) conducted an experiment of semi-automated approach of function cloned detection. Lucca et al. (2002) introduced the detection approach based on similarity metrics, to detect duplicated pages in Web sites and applications, implemented with HTML language and ASP technology. Meanwhile, Lanubile and Mallardo(2003) introduced a simple semi-automated approach that can be used to identify cloned functions within scripting code of web applications.
Some of the researches adopted the approaches that have been done in traditional software. The most frequently appeared in the researches is the use of CCFinder (Kamiya et al., 2002) as the clone detector which can detect exact clones and parameterized clones. While most of the researches are discussing about the strategies of clone detection, Jarzabek and Rajapakse(2005) conducted a systematic research to find out the extent of cloning in web domain in comparing with traditional software. They found out that cloning in web application has significantly exceeded the rate for traditional software. Jarzabek also introduced metrics that might be useful for similar studies.

4.3 Existing Work of Code Cloning Detection

Code cloning detection has been an active research for almost two decades. Within that period many tools and techniques have been invented either for commercial use or for academic purposes. At the same time, a number of issues have been raised along the researches in terms of number of clones detected, types of detected clones, the recall and precision, the scalability, and the coupling towards language i.e. language dependent/independent. Various researches have shown that their tools can detect almost up to 70% of clones within a particular source code.
According to Jiang (Jiang et al, 2007) the researches in this area can be classified into four main bases; string-based, token-based, tree-based and semantic-based. According to this classification, we found out that most of the clones that were detected could involve in two general ways which are syntactically and semantically. The first type of clones is usually found from the similarity of functions including scripting e.g. JavaScript, VBScript, the classes, the attributes, etc. On the other hand the semantic clones is related to the meaning of the content i.e. knowledge represented, sequence of declaration of statement (Baxter et al, 1998), etc.

Figure 3 shows the relationship of classification of detection and the type of clones detected. Most of the reports show that most of them tend to find clones syntactically rather than semantically. Syntactic clone detections cover from string-based to tree-based works. Some tree-based works also show the ability of finding clone semantically. Appendix B of this report presents some of previous works in clone detection area.

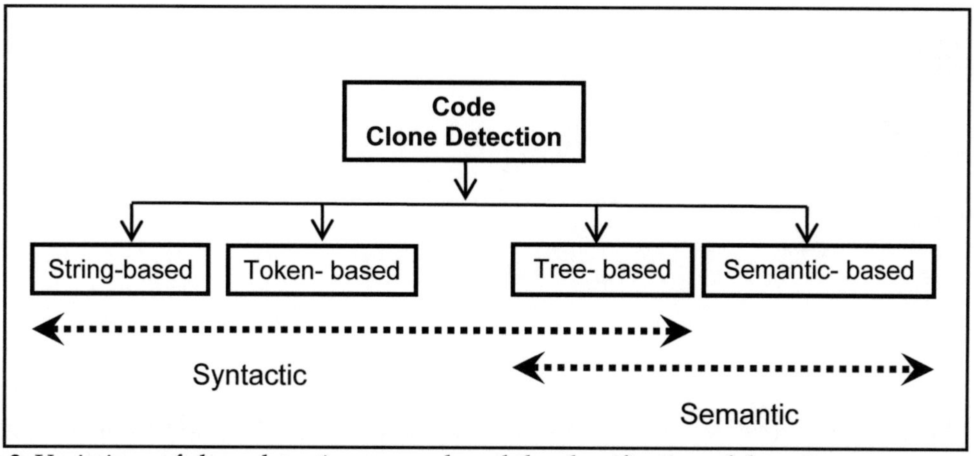

Fig. 3. Variations of clone detection research and the classification of detection

4.4 Semantic Web

It is obvious that the term 'ontology' has become a key word within the modern computer science world. It is becoming more important in fields such as knowledge management, information integration, cooperative information systems, information retrieval, and electronic commerce. One application area which has recently seen an explosion of interest is the so-called Semantic Web.

The Semantic Web is an evolving extension of the World Wide Web(WWW) in which the web content can be expressed not only in natural languages, but also in a format that can be read and used by automated tools, thus permitting people and machines to find, share and integrate information more easily. It was derived from W3C director Tim Berners-Lee's vision of the Web as a universal medium for data, information, and knowledge exchange.

In building one layer of the Semantic Web on top of another, there are some principles that should be followed; downward compatibility and upward partial understanding (Antoniou et al., 2003).

At the bottom we find XML, a language that lets one write structured Web documents with a user-defined vocabulary. XML is particularly suitable for sending documents across the Web. RDF is a basic data model, like the entity-relationship model, for writing simple statements about Web objects (resources). The RDF data model does not rely on XML, but RDF has an XML-based syntax. Therefore in Figure 4 it is located on top of the XML layer. RDF Schema provides modelling primitives for organizing Web objects into hierarchies. Key primitives are classes and properties, subclass and subproperty relationships, and domain and range restrictions. RDF Schema (RDF-S) is based on RDF. RDF Schema can be viewed as a primitive language for writing ontologies. But there is a need for more powerful ontology languages that expand RDF Schema and allow the representations of more complex relationships between Web objects.

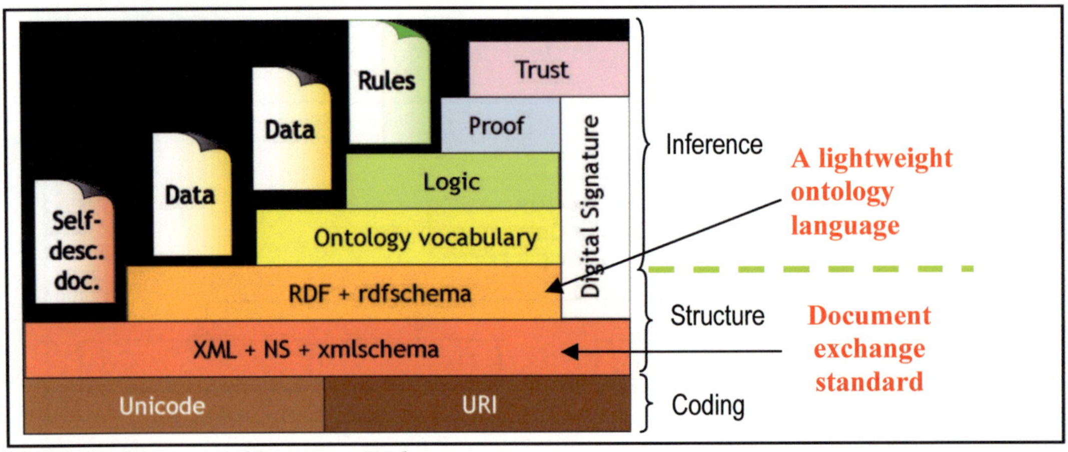

Fig. 4. Architecture of Semantic Web

The logic layer is used to enhance the ontology language further, and to allow writing application-specific declarative knowledge. The proof layer involves the actual deductive process, as well as the representation of proofs in Web languages (from lower levels) and proof validation. Finally trust will emerge through the use of digital signatures, and other kinds of knowledge, based on recommendations by agents we trust, or rating and certification agencies and consumer bodies. The Web will only achieve its full potential when users have trust in its operations (security) and the quality of information provided.

4.5 Clone Detection Evaluation

As we see in the previous researches, there are many clone detection techniques and their corresponding tools, and therefore, a comparison of these techniques/tools is worthy in order to pick the right technique for a particular purpose of interest. There are several parameters with which the tools can be compared. These parameters are also known as clone detection challenges. In the following we list some of the parameters we use for comparing the different tools/techniques:

(a) *Portability*: The tool should be portable in terms of multiple languages and dialects. Having thousands of programming languages in use with several dialects for many of them, a clone detection tool is expected to be portable and easily configured for different types of languages and dialects tackling the syntactic variations of those languages

(b) *Precision*: The tool should be sound enough so that it can detect less number of false positives i.e., the tool should find duplicated code with higher precision. Formula shown in (1)

(c) *Recall*: The tool should be capable of finding most (or even all) of the clones in a system of interest. Often, duplicated fragments are not textually similar. Although editing activities on the copied fragments may disguise the similarity with the original, a cloning relationship may exist between them. A good clone detection tool will be robust enough in identifying

such hidden cloning relationship so that it can detect most or even all the clones of the subject system. Formula shown in (2)
(d) *Scalability*: The tool should be capable of finding clones from large code bases as duplication is the most problematic in large and complex system. The tool should handle large and complex systems with efficient use of memory. In this thesis it can be concluded by analyzing computational time taken for different sizes of testing
(e) *Robustness*: A good tool should be robust in terms of the different editing activities that might be applied on the copied fragment so that it can detect different types of clones with higher precision and recall. In this thesis we apply the robustness by listing the type of clones the respective clone detector finds and their frequencies.

$$\text{Precision}\,,\text{p} = \frac{\text{number of correct found clone}}{\text{number of all found clone}} \qquad (1)$$

$$\text{Recall, r} = \frac{\text{number of correct found clone}}{\text{number of possible existing clone}} \qquad (2)$$

5. Proposed technique of code clone detection

We will start by defining the relation assumed by our model between ontologies and source code, on the one hand, and source code and instances on the other hand. A set of documents can serve as a base to extract ontological information (Stumme., and Maedche, 2001). In this model we represent the source codes using XML parse tree. Hence we assume that the ontological information in this case are all the tagging name in XML trees, i.e. known as concept in this thesis as stated in the following formal definition. The instances are all similar concepts that are actually populated in the source code. An instance will consist of the concept itself and the attributes and value of that concept.
In ontology mapping, given two schemas, A and B, one wants to find mapping μ from the concepts in A into the concepts of B in such a way that, if a = μ(b), then b and a have the same meaning. This clone detection basically uses the same concept as in ontology mapping work.
Definition 1: if a = μ (b), then b and a have the same meaning, hence derived code clones. Our strategy is to do a one-to-one mapping since using specific shared ontologies might request for a specific domain of knowledge for different applications that need to be compared. The idea is to derive mappings from candidate concept A to the concepts A′ with the same names as in the selected ontologies.
Definition 2: Ontology, $O' = \{C', R', CH', rel', OA'\}$ where (a) C is the set of concepts in each of the nodes in the tree, (b) $CH' \subseteq C' \times C'$ is concept hierarchy or taxonomy, where $CH'(C'_1, C'_2)$ indicates that C'_1 is a subconcept of C'_2, (c) $rel: R' \rightarrow C' \times C'$ is a function that relates the concepts non-taxonomically, R' is the set of relations where $R' = \emptyset$, (d) OA is a set of ontology axioms, where OA' is the properties of concepts, in practical the contents of tags, the attribute and the value.
Figure 5 shows the overall phases of clone detection. The key idea of the proposed technique is by combining detection by the structural information and the instance-based detection as both of the techniques have their own strengths and weaknesses (Todorov, 2008) and has

been discussed in the previous chapter. The output of the processes will be a set of similar fragments of code, i.e. under different types of clones between two different systems. In our framework we assume that the population phase had already taken place and there exists a set of source codes so that:

(a) It covers all concepts of the source code trees. "Covers" is understood as: Instances of every concept can be found in at least one of the trees in the collection of source code trees. Every tree contains instances of at least one concept,

(b) A tree node is considered to be assigned to a concept node if and only if it provides instances of that concept with a higher cardinality than a fixed threshold (Fig. 6).

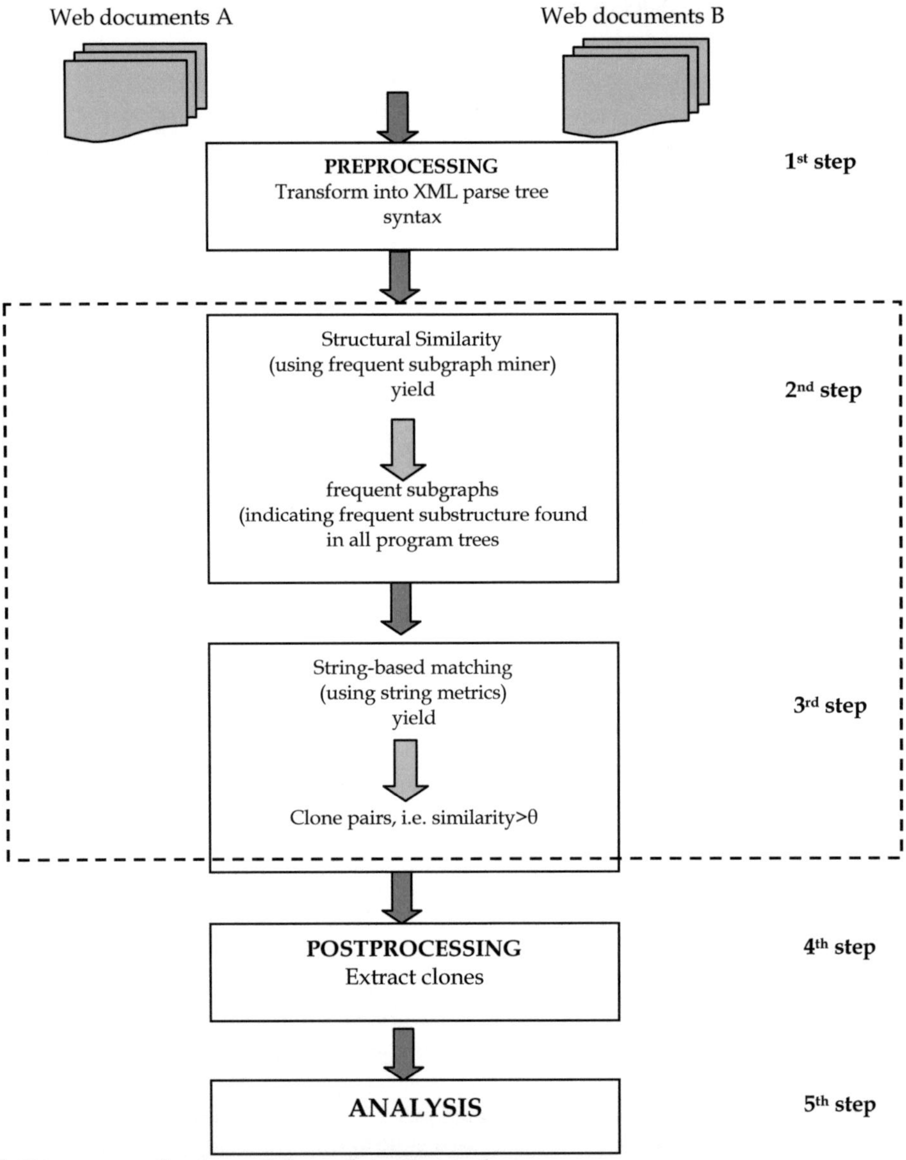

Fig. 5. Diagrammatic view of clone detection technique

In the sequel we will deal with hierarchical trees. We are concerned with studying their similarities on purely structural level, so let us assume that only the concept nodes are labeled but not for the relations. Under these assumptions we provide the following definition of a hierarchical source code tree.

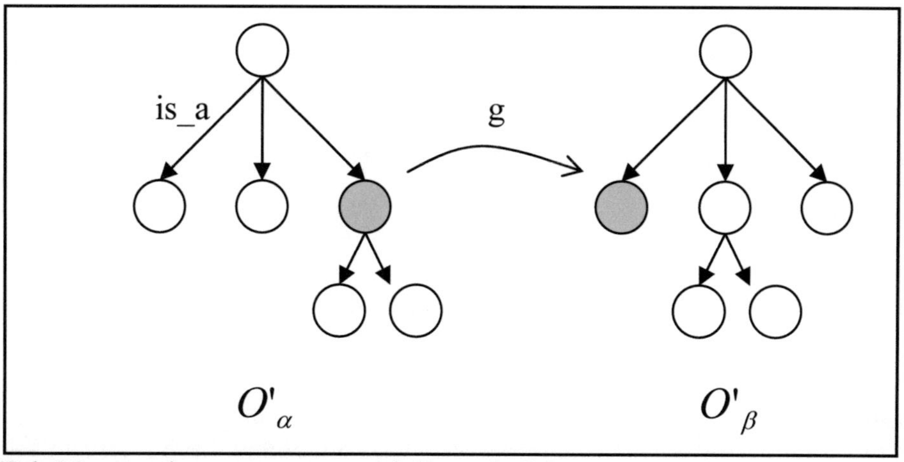

Fig. 6. Title Mapping between concepts of O'_α and O'_β

Definition 3: *A hierarchical tree is a couple* O':= (C, is_ a), *where* C is a *finite set whose elements are called concepts* and is_ a is a *partial order on* C. We proceed to formalize the association of tree of different source codes. Let α be a set of hierarchical source code trees of system 1 and β a set of hierarchical source trees of system 2 satisfying the assumption 1 and 2. Let $\gamma : \alpha \rightarrow \beta$ be an injection from the set of source code trees of system 1 to the set of source code trees of system 1. For every subtree of $O'_\alpha \in \alpha$ and subtree of $O'_\beta \in \beta$ that can be mapped so that there exists $\gamma(O'_\alpha) = O'\beta$, it exists an injection $g : C_{O'_\alpha} \rightarrow C_{O'_\beta}$ which map concepts in source code tree of system 1 to system 2. The following figure shows an illustration of the mapping between trees.

5.1 Structural Tree Similarity

As mentioned in the previous chapter, we are going to do two layers of tree comparing. The first layer is about the structural tree similarity. It eventually provides some kind of filtering to the model since it finds parts of the trees which is similar between each other before we do the real similarity comparison. As has been discussed in the literature review, XML tree is actually a directed rooted tree which can be represented formally using the definition of graph $G = (V, E)$. So a source code tree can formally be represented by the following definition:

Definition 4: Let O'_X be a source code tree. A source code tree corresponding to 0 is a directed rooted tree $G(V(G), E(G))$, so that (a) $V(G) = C$, (b) $E(G) \subseteq C \times C$ such that $\exists f$ where $\langle f(c_i, c_j) \rangle \in E_{O_X} \Leftrightarrow (ci, cj) \in is\_a$.

Todorov (Todorov, 2008), used Bunke's graph distance metric to calculate the distance of source code structure based on maximal common subgraph. We are not going to find the maximal subgraph since this technique is often an NP-complete problem and it has been used several times in the previous works of clone detection. So instead of using maximal common subgraph, we used the frequent subgraph miner available. Before that we start by giving a couple of definitions which are needed before introducing the distance ratio. The distance ratio is used to find out number of programs that could have high similarities of structures between each other. All definitions are given for general graphs and are also applicable for trees.

Definition 5: Graph Isomophism. A bijectie function $\mu : V_1 \rightarrow V_2$ is a graph isomorphism form graph $G_1(V_1, E_1)$ to a graph $G_2(V_2, E_2)$ if for any $v_1^1, v_2^1 \in V_1$ $\left\langle v_1^1, v_2^1 \right\rangle \in E_1 \Leftrightarrow \left\langle \mu(v_1^1), \mu(v_2^1) \right\rangle \in E_2$.

Definition 6: *Subgraph isomorphism*. An injective function $\mu : V_1 \rightarrow V_2$ is a subgraph isomorphism from G_1 to G_2 if it exist a subgraph $S \subseteq G_2$ so that μ is a graph isomorphism from G_1 to S.

Definition 7: Graph distance ratio: We simplify the distance of graph G1 and G2 by using the following ratio since we are using frequent subgraph mining. Let F_{G_1} (3) and F_{G_2} (4) as sets of frequent subgraphs which owned by G1 and G2.

$$F_{G_1} = \{ t_1, t_2, t_3, \ldots, t_m \} \quad (3)$$

$$F_{G_2} = \{ t_1, t_2, t_3, \ldots, t_n \} \quad (4)$$

Distance of G1 and G2 (5) can be calculated as follows:

$$d(G_1, G_2) = 1 - \frac{\#(t_{G_1} \cap t_{G_2})}{\max(\#t_{G_1}, \#t_{G_2})} \quad (5)$$

5.2 Preprocessing

The initial idea is by doing the detection with combination of tree detection and string detection. For this reason, the clone detection will start with the pre-processing where all documents will be standardized into XML documents in order to get the tags and contents of each node. We are going to test the model on HTML, ASP, PHP and JSP systems. Web page documents from system A and system B need to be compared to detect the cloning. Then the XML will be parsed into a tree. Fig. 7 shows the main process of pre-processing.

To minimize the code for each file, all XML codes will be cleaned to eliminate all useless lines of code so that we could maximize the code comparing without trying to compare the formatting information which is only used for the purpose of information appearance to the end user. For each and every XML source code, the tag names will be taken and inserted into a file called 'vocabulary' that will be used for XML node matching. Duplicate entries in the vocabulary will then be deleted from the list to minimize number of entries in the vocabulary.

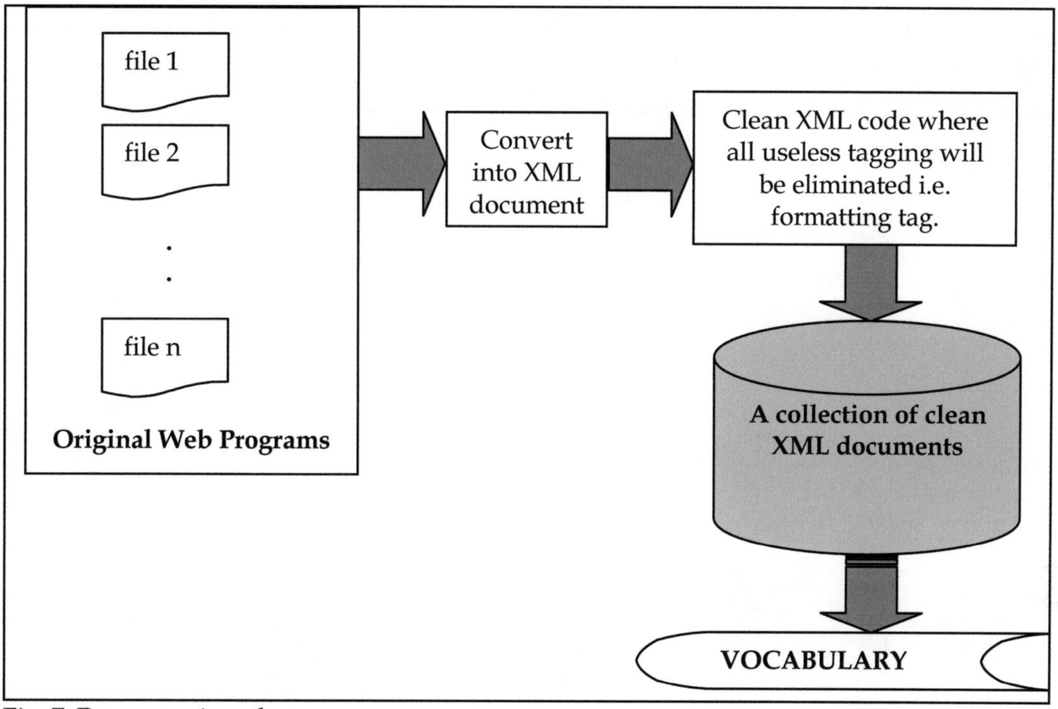

Fig. 7. Preprocessing phase

5.3 Frequent subgraph mining

The detection process will then start with the structural comparison of the tree. The comparison of nodes is done between O'_α and O'_β which represent two different systems.

After generating the frequent subgraphs, we store the shared subtree of different programs or source codes in a cross table. Table 1 shows the example of cross-table used to compare programs across two systems.

Program, *p*	p_1	p_1	...	...	...	...	p_n
p_1	t_1, t_2	-	-	t_1, t_3, t_4	-	-	-
p_1	-	t_1, t_2	-	-	-	-	-
...	-	-	-	-	-	-	-
...	-	-	t_1, t_3, t_4	-	t_1, t_3, t_4	-	-
p_m	-	-	-	-	-	-	t_1, t_3, t_5

Table 1. Example of cross table used to compare programs across two systems

For each subtree in the table that was generated by the frequent subgraph miner, we set the minimum size i.e. number of edges of subtree is 5 and the maximum is 6. The decision is made after an initial experiment where it showed the number of frequent subtree generated was not too large or too small in comparison with other value of parameter. Then the string-based matching will be done as described above. The example of a frequent subgraph between two trees is shown in Fig. 8.

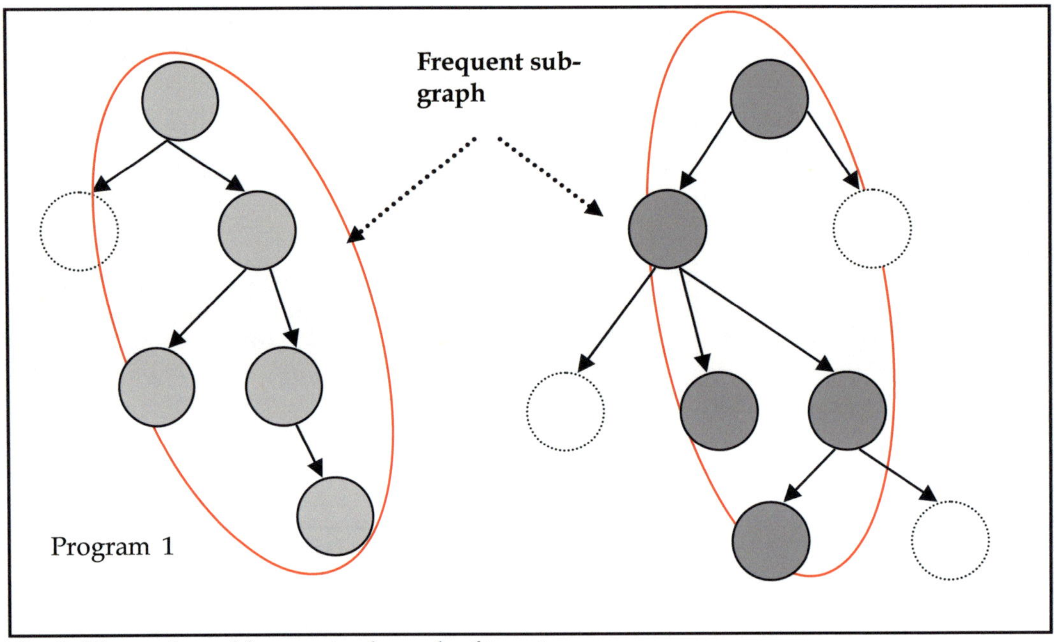

Fig. 8. Illustration of frequent subgraph of two trees

5.4 String based matching

In Fig. 9, an example of instance-based matching is presented. We found that depth of fragment 1 and fragment 2 are equal to three, so the comparison using string metric was done but in the original experiment we used five and six instead of depth equal to three. If the similarity is above the threshold, the string will be taken as a clone pair. Instead of using vocabulary as in our initial experiment, we compare the similar structure of subgraph found and it is recorded in the table above.

As mentioned before, we assumed that all elements of the subtree were treated as an instance i.e. including the node name, attribute and value, etc. We took all the elements as a string for simplicity in order to calculate the similarities of the set of instance in fragment 1 i.e. set A and the set of instance of fragment 2 i.e. set B. The last stage of the code clone detection would be the post-processing. At this stage, all clones will be extracted from the original code for further analysis.

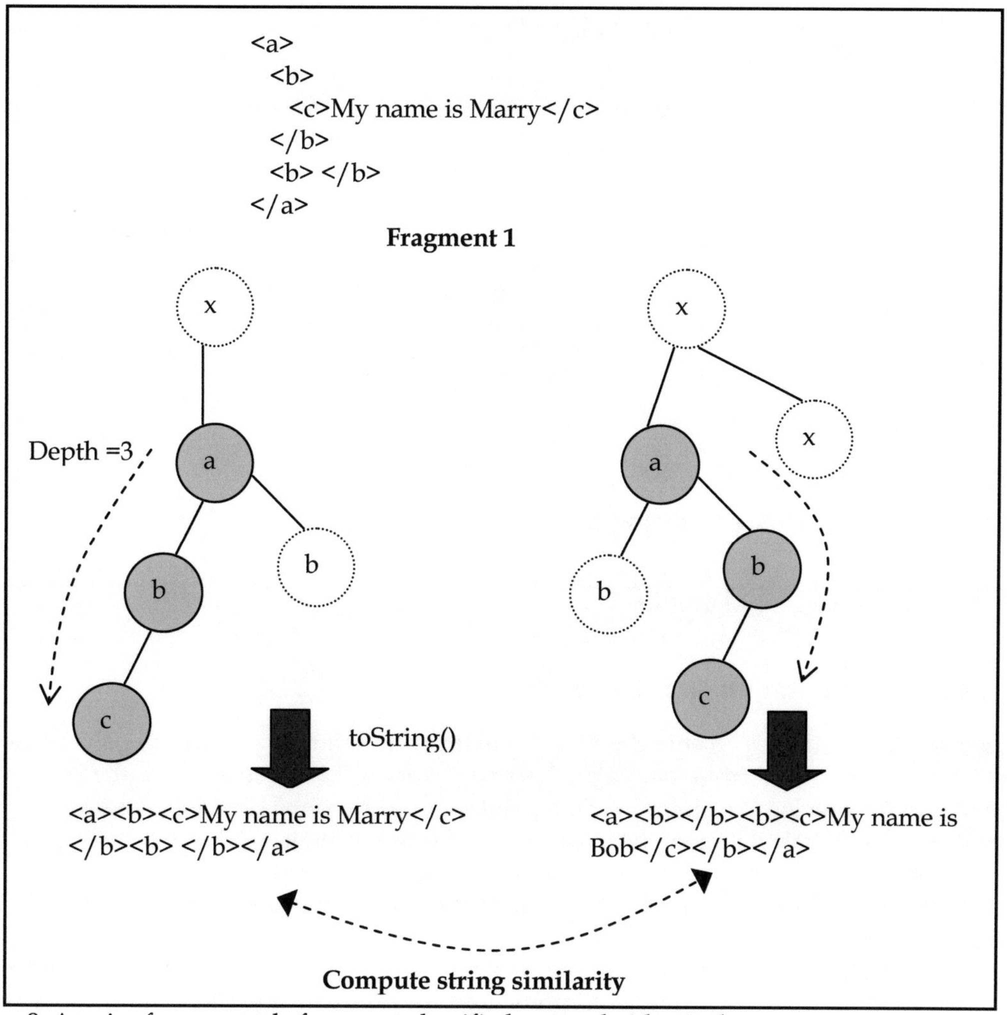

Fig. 9. A pair of source code fragment classified as nearly identical

5.5 Clone detection algorithm

The previous subtopics explained the process of the proposed clone detection. The process can be summarized into general algorithm in Fig. 10:

Variable:	*threshold, p, minNode.*
begin	
Step 1:	Define parameter *threshold, p, minNode.*
Step 2:	Convert all files of system A and system B into XML and clean files
Step 3:	Generate frequent subgrapghs and record in cross table, D.
Step 4:	For all subgraphs in D, begin-while

	Step 4.1:	For all XML code file in system A	
	begin-while		
		Step 4.1.1: For all XML code file in system B	
		begin-while	
		Step 4.1.1.1:	- read XML nodes as string - compute similarity using string metric.
		Step 4.1.1.2:	If *simm*> *threshold*, select string as clone.
		end-while	
	end-while		
	end-while		
Step 6:	Post-processing. Extract all clones.		
Step 7:	Determine program which highly in similarity.		
end			

Fig. 10. Clone Detection Algorithm

6. Experimental Result and Discussions

This chapter primarily presents the results obtained by searching for clone pairs using a methodology inspired from ontology mapping works. As mentioned in the previous chapter, in the ontology mapping work, the author used maximal common subgraph in the first layer and the calculating of the instances similarities using Jaccard coefficient. So in our methodology, instead of using maximal common subgraph, we are using frequent common subgraph miner as the maximal common subgraph technique is frequently reported as NP-complete problem.

Generally, methodology consists of four main stages, i.e. preprocessing stage, frequent subtree generation using frequent subgraph miner, subtree similarity computation, and extraction of clone pairs and analysis. The frequent subtree mining in this work is taken as the process of getting candidate cloned pairs which have similar subtree structure by only taking into account the node tags and omitting any other elements of the tree such as attributes, labels or values of the tree.

Before we discuss in depth about the result of code clone detection, we will discuss the experiment that has been carried out in this project. The following first two subchapters will discuss the pre-processing stage. In this stage, we do the preparation where the original source code is transformed into inexpensive standardized form and a representation of web source programs in order to induce the data into the frequent subgraph miner.

6.1 Data Representation

A few group of system files were used for testing purposes. We divided the data into three different sizes of data; i.e. small data size, medium size, and large size where all the programs were taken from open sources web applications. The original web program was in HTML, ASP and PHP format to test the portability of our system where our system is considered portable if it managed to process different types of web programming languages.

As mentioned before, all programs need to be transformed into a standard form of program. In our system, we transformed the programs into XML format where the transformations were inexpensive. This was because we needed to make sure that the entire program was in a valid form of tagging so that we could extract all the tagging names of each XML tree.

```
<?php
$conn=mysql_connect("localhost","","");
$db= mysql_select_db("inventory");

?>
```

(a) Original PHP code

```
<!DOCTYPE HTML PUBLIC "-//W3C//DTD HTML 4.0 Transitional//EN"
"http://www.w3.org/TR/REC-html40/loose.dtd">
<HTML>
<HEAD>
<!-- Converted by AscToTab 4.0 - fully registered version -->
  <TITLE>Converted from "C:\Documents and Settings\DiLLa
DiLLoT\Desktop\dbase.php"</TITLE>
  <META NAME="Generator" CONTENT="AscToHTM from www.jafsoft.com">
</HEAD>
<BODY BGCOLOR="white">

<!-- User-specified TABLE structure -->
<TABLE ID="table_1" BORDER=2 CELLSPACING=0 CELLPADDING=2>
<TR VALIGN="TOP">
<TD>&lt;?php<BR>
$conn=mysql_connect("localhost","","");<BR>
$db= mysql_select_db("inventory");<BR>
<BR>
?&gt;<BR>
</TD>
</TR>
</TABLE>
<!-- end of user-specified TABLE structure -->

<!-- Converted by AscToTab 4.0 - fully registered version -->
</BODY>
</HTML>
```

(b) Generated HTML code

Fig. 11. Transformation of original PHP code into HTML code

6.1.1 Original Source Programs into XML Format

The first step for data normalization is by converting all programs into the HTML format. This is to make sure that all XML documents generated are in a valid form of tagging. As for now, the process is done by using a freeware tool called AscToTab which can transform any form of text into HTML or RTF format. This stage needs to be done manually. After all the transformations are done, by using our system, the HTML programs will be converted into XML documents for further processes. For any program which is not an HTML program e.g. PHP and ASP, the programs are treated as text files. Transformation using the tool is done by applying formatting tags such as <br>, <p>, etc onto the text code. Fig. 11 shows an example of an original source code transformation into HTML. After transformation into HTML, the code is then converted into XML to ensure their validity. This process can be done automatically using our system where it provides a function to convert HTML into XML. Fig. 12 shows a result of converting HTML into XML.

```
<?xml version="1.0" encoding="iso-8859-1" ?>

<root>
    <doctype>HTML PUBLIC &quot;-//W3C//DTD HTML 4.0
Transitional//EN&quot;&quot;http://www.w3.org/TR/REC-html40/loose.dtd&quot;</doctype>
    <html>
        <head>
            <comment>Converted by AscToTab 4.0 - fully registered version</comment>
            <title>
                <text>Converted from &quot;C:\Documents and Settings\DiLLa
DiLLoT\Desktop\dbase.php&quot;</text>
            </title>
            <meta NAME="Generator" CONTENT="AscToHTM from www.jafsoft.com" />
        </head>
        <body BGCOLOR="white">
            <comment>User-specified TABLE structure</comment>
            <table ID="table_1" BORDER="2" CELLSPACING="0" CELLPADDING="2">
                <tr VALIGN="TOP">
                    <td>
                        <text>&lt;?php
$conn=mysql_connect(&quot;localhost&quot;,&quot;&quot;,&quot;&quot;);
$db= mysql_select_db(&quot;inventory&quot;); ?&gt;</text>
                    </td></tr>
            </table>
            <comment>end of user-specified TABLE structure</comment>
            <comment>Converted by AscToTab 4.0 - fully registered version</comment>
        </body>
    </html>
</root>
```
Fig. 12. XML form of the previous HTML code

6.1.2 Subtree Mining Data Representation

XML representation is not suitable to be fed directly into our frequent subgraph miner. So, as the solution we need to represent the tree structure into a simpler form of data. This is important so as to reduce the complexity of the mining process.

The simplest way is by representing the trees as a node and edge lists. Before generating the data, we extract all node names or tagging in XML code and treat them as a bag of concept or vocabulary, as had been used in Project I. The subgraph mining data is represented as a list of nodes and edges as in Figure 13 below. In the figure, t represents tree, v represents vertex and e represents edge. Label of node in figure below represents the node name or tagging of the XML. But instead of putting the node name in the list, we put the index of vocabulary as we had explained before.

```
t # <name of the graph>
v 0 <label of node 0>
v 1 <label of node 1>
...
e <node a> <node b> <edge label>
e <node x> <node y> <edge label>
...
```

Fig. 13. XML form of the previous HTML code

```
[0] text
[1] title
[2] a href
[3] p
[4] h1
[5] meta http-equiv
[6] head
```

(a) Vocabulary/ Bag of concepts

```
t # s1.XML_10.xml
v 0 1
v 1 6
v 2 0
v 3 3
...
e 0 1 1
e 0 2 1
e 2 3 1
...
```

(b) A tree represented as list of vertices and edges

Fig. 14. Example of tree as vertices and edges list

Fig. 14 shows the example of vocabulary generated and the tree representation following the format in Fig. 13. In example below, [v 0 1] means that node name for vertex0 is title and [e 0 1 1] means there is an edge between vertex0 and vertex1. The last digit 1 is the default labelling for all edges since we are working with trees instead of graphs, so we need to omit any labelling of all edges. Data in Fig. 14(b) will be fed in the frequent subgraph miner.

(a)	(b)
t # 24 v 0 11 v 1 10 v 2 3 v 3 0 v 4 12 e 0 1 1 e 1 2 1 e 1 3 1 e 3 4 1 => [2.0] [s2.XML_21.xml,s1.XML_10.xml] t # 26 v 0 11 v 1 10 v 2 3 v 3 0 v 4 9 e 0 1 1 e 1 2 1 e 1 3 1 e 3 4 1 => [2.0] [s2.XML_21.xml,s1.XML_10.xml] t # 28 v 0 11 v 1 10 v 2 3 v 3 0 v 4 2 e 0 1 1 e 1 2 1 e 1 3 1 e 3 4 1 => [2.0] [s2.XML_20.xml,s1.XML_11.xml] *(a) Example of frequent subtrees generated*	GSpan subgraph miner found 76 frequent fragments >>SIMILAR SUB TREE CROSS-TABLE ; x= for system 1, y= for system 2 BetweenFile[0][0]:77,72,70,68,66,64,38,36,34,32,30, BetweenFile[0][1]:176,171,169,155,153,151,149,147,145,143,141,139,137,132,130,128,116,114,112,110,108,106,104,102,100,93,91,89,87,85,77,72,70,68,66,64,56,54,52,50,48,46,44,42,40,38,36,34,32,30,26,24, BetweenFile[1][0]:192,184,164,162,160,120,118,95,77,72,70,68,66,64,62,60,58,38,36,34,32,30,28, BetweenFile[1][1]:77,72,70,68,66,64,38,36,34,32,30, *(b) Example of cross- table containing subtree id shared between different files*

Fig 15. Frequent subtrees generated by graph miner

6.2 Frequent Subtree Mining

As we mentioned before, we used four well-known frequent subgraph miners to get similar substructure of trees that existed between the files. We induced the data as in the previous example into the miner and the miner will generate all frequent subtrees or substructures that existed among the files. There are a few configurations that need to be set before doing the mining. The configurations are:

(a) *MinimumFrequencies* sets the minimum frequency (support) a subgraph must have to get reported. In the experiment, we set the value as low as 10% so that the miner will be capable to find all similar substructures even though the appearances in the codes are not so frequent,

(b) *MinimumFragmentSize* sets the minimum size (in edges) a frequent subtree must have in order to be reported,

(c) *MaximumFragmentSize* sets the maximum size (in edges) a frequent subtree can have in order to be reported.

In the experiment, we set the value of (b) and (c) with 5 edges in size. We selected this size after some preliminary experiments where this value is capable to generate the average number of subtrees. So instead of using minimal depth of a subtree, we used the minimum and maximum fragment size. After executing the graph miner, a list of frequent subtree will be generated from the system as well as the original tree that holds that particular subtree. So to summarize, we can generate a cross-table which contains all subtrees IDs that were shared among different files in different systems.

```
String s = <root><doctype>HTML PUBLIC &quot;-//W3C//DTD HTML 4.0
Transitional//EN&quot;&quot;http://www.w3.org/TR/REC-
html40/loose.dtd&quot;</doctype><html><head><title><text>Converted
from &quot;C:\Documents and Settings\DiLLaDiLLoT\Desktop\
dbase.php&quot;</text></head></root>
```

```
<root>
    <doctype>HTML PUBLIC &quot;-//W3C//DTD HTML 4.0
Transitional//EN&quot;&quot;http://www.w3.org/TR/REC-
html40/loose.dtd&quot; </doctype>
    <html>
        <head>
            <comment>Converted by AscToTab 4.0 - fully registered
version</comment>
            <title>
                <text>Converted from &quot;C:\Documents and
Settings\DiLLa DiLLoT\Desktop\dbase.php&quot;</text>
            </title>
            <meta NAME="Generator" CONTENT="AscToHTM from
www.jafsoft.com" />
        </head>
        ...
</root>
```

Fig. 16. Code fragment containing original frequent subtree

6.2.1 String Metric Computation

The most challenging part of the system is to extract the original subtree from the original XML documents according to the frequent subtree generated above. Once the original subtree is successfully extracted, it will be taken as a string so that we can compute the similarities of the subtree with another subtree from another file using a string metric. We realized that this technique is suitable in finding cloned pairs. Instead of using frequent subgraph miner, we used vocabulary element to find the subtree rooted with a node which has a similar name with the vocabulary element. As we discussed before, it was quite expensive to do it this way. So, for the similarity computation, we used all the string metric that were stated in section 4 before. In the following example, we will show how the subtree is represented as a string before we can compute the similarity. Consider if the bold italic lines match the frequent sub tree, the string equivalent would be as in Fig. 16.

6.3 Experimental Setup

The implementation process was done using Java language as the base language. To support the program, we used a Java library named Chilkat Java which can be found available on the Internet. This library offers a few features like XML parser and tree walker ability. All process of converting web pages into standard XML and generating the vocabulary for mapping purposes were done automatically in the program. All executions were done using an Intel® Core Duo 1.86GHz machine with 1.5 GB of RAM.

The following settings were meant for the Ontology-Winkler Similarity part. We set the most lenient values for all those parameter:

(a) The similarity threshold, θ is set to 0.7

(b) Define the similarity, *Sim* as $Sim(s_1,s_2) = Comm(s_1,s_2) - Diff(s_1,s_2) + winkler(s_1,s_2)$ where $Comm(s_1,s_2)$ is the commonality value between two strings and $Diff(s_1,s_2)$ is the difference between two strings

(c) Omit the $Winkler(s_1,s_2)$ calculation from the equation to simplify the programming. Value for *Winkler* is set to 0.1

(d) Value of parameter p is set to 0.6 as the original author of this technique reported that the result for their experiment works best with this value.

6.4 Experimental Results

This subsection is mainly to present the result of our code clone detection using all the metrics that have been discussed in the previous chapter. In this experiment, we will consider any valid candidate clone as a clone even though that code fragment is in fact an accidental clone.

Several experiments were conducted to investigate the performances of our clone detection program. The experiments were executed using the same parameters setting and data setups as in the previous subchapter. We conduct the experiment using two open source management systems as (a) Module 1.1 - 54.9Mb(size), >4000 files, (b) Tutor 1.55 - 49.7Mb(size), >3000 files.

For the test, we randomly selected the files from these two systems for comparison where the test is done on a different number of files. By using 1.5Gb RAM processor, the number of files that can be processed are quite limited and it only allowed a small size of detection which is less than 100 files. We split the testing in three groups of testings. Table 2 shows information of data being used for the testing process.

Number of testings	Number of files(NOF)	Line of codes(LOC)
Testing #1	10	259 lines
Testing #2	30	575 lines
Testing #3	50	1200 lines

Table 2. Data for program testing

As it is shown , our experiment is basically on a different subgraph miner and different string metric or similarity coefficients. The following figure shows an example of the realtime output of detection using our program which has been written in Java.

```
>>COMPARE FILES:

*Compare file between:
D:/Documents/MASTER/4thSEM/Project II/Code Clone
Detection/proc1/XML_10.xml
D:/Documents/MASTER/4th SEM/Project II/Code Clone
Detection/proc2/XML_20.xml
#1:
<head>Thisisatest<title>Thisisatest<text>ThisisatestThisisatestThis
isatest<meta><meta>
<head>Thisisatest<title>Thisisatest<text>ThisisatestThisisatestThis
isatest<meta><meta>
      = 1.0

*Compare file between:
D:/Documents/MASTER/4th SEM/Project II/Code Clone
Detection/proc1/XML_10.xml
D:/Documents/MASTER/4th SEM/Project II/Code Clone
Detection/proc2/XML_20.xml
#1:
<head>Thisisatest<title>Thisisatest<text>ThisisatestThisisatestThis
isatest<meta><meta>
<head>Thisisatest<title>Thisisatest<text>ThisisatestThisisatestThis
isatest<meta><meta>
```

Fig. 17. Realtime output from the clone detection system

We show the result of the experimental testing using our default subgraph miner which is GSpan miner. As mentioned before, the test is done on three different sizes of files as shown above. Table 3 shows some of the graphical output using Jaro Winkler and Levenshtein Distance as the string metric.

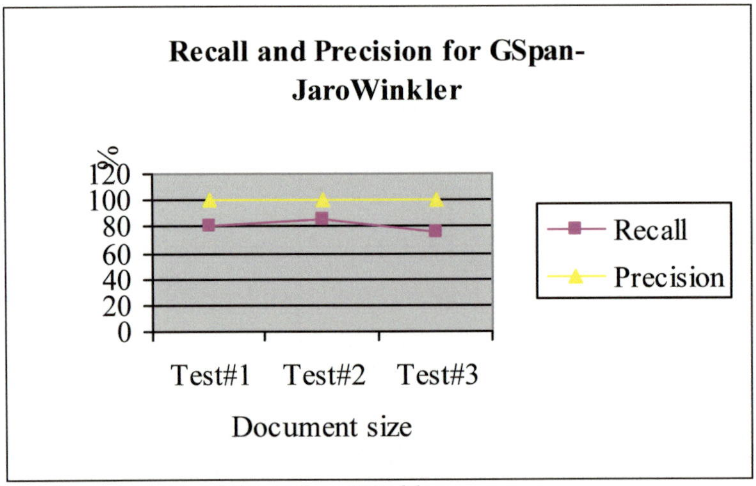

Fig. 18. Recall and precision for GSpan-Jaro Winkler

Fig. 18 to Fig. 23 show the result of using GSpan frequent subgraph miner. As we can see from the diagram, mining the similar structure using GSpan miner generated almost similar graph trends where the value generated is almost similar between these two string metrics.

As shown in the figure, all cloned pairs that were found by our code clone detection system were all positive clones. This situation yielded our precision to be 100% for small size or bigger data. But there was a trade-off for the recall. Our system only managed to find a small number of clones, where most of the clones found were identical clones, but we can say the limitation is on searching for similar clones.
Another big issue shown in the data above is the computational time taken was rapidly increasing as the number of documents increase. This is practically not feasible for detecting cloned pairs. However, we may need more testing done to find out whether the line will keep increasing towards the infinite as the number of document increased.

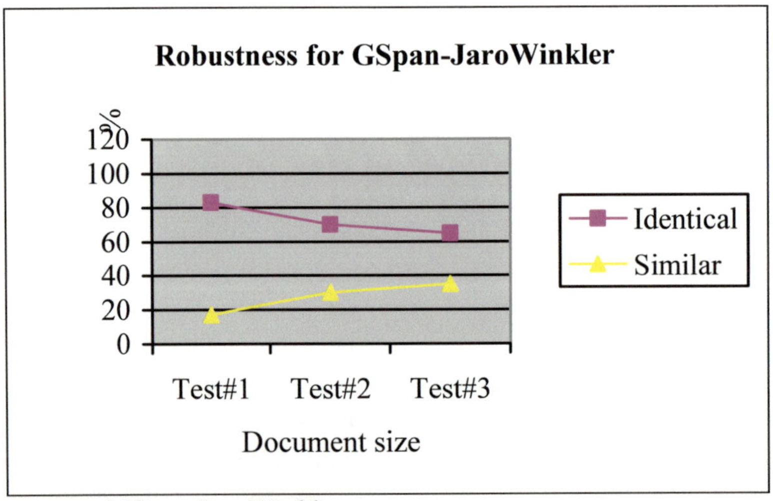

Fig. 19. Robustness of GSpan-Jaro Winkler

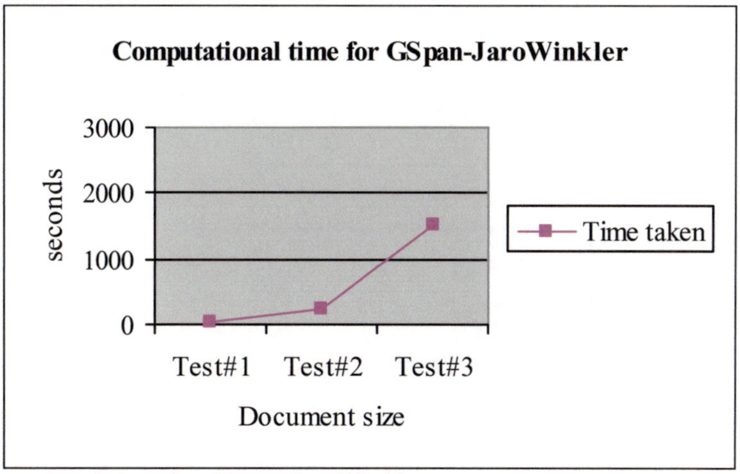

Fig. 20. Computational time for GSpan-JaroWinkler

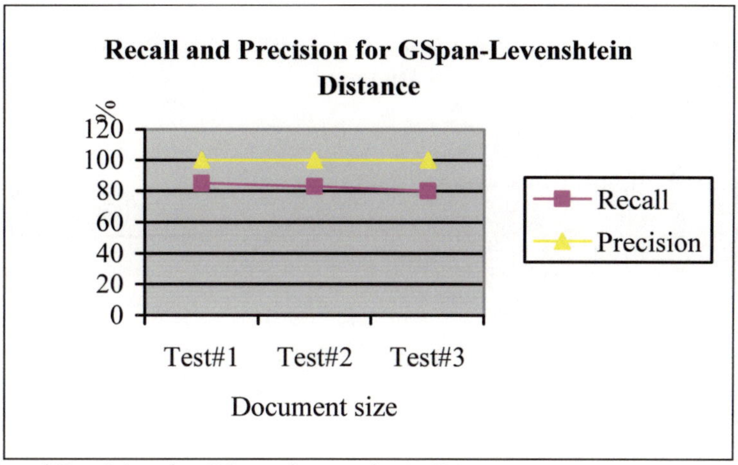

Fig. 21. Recall and Precision for GSpan-Levenshtein Distance

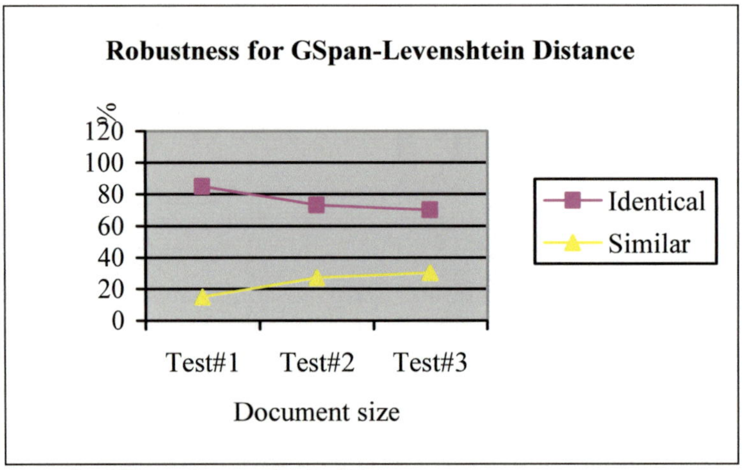

Fig. 22. Robustness for GSpan-Levenshtein Distance

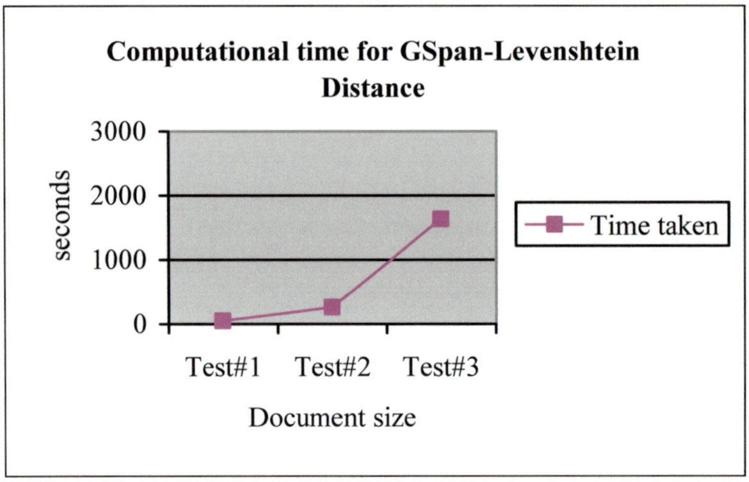

Fig. 23. Computational time for GSpan-Levenshtein Distance

Generally, there is not much difference in the trends of graphs using different frequent subgraph miner. The major difference is on the overall computational time of the detection as different frequent subgraph miner offers different performance in generating frequent subgraph. The result shows that Gaston offers the best computational time, followed by gSpan, FFSM and MoFa.

6.5 Limitation of the Code Clone Detection Program

As we can see, the overall result of our code clone detection program did not show the good result that we had expected. In general, we noticed that for each and every subgraph miner and string metric used, the computational time increased rapidly as the number of source codes increased. This is practically not healthy for code clone detection or for any experiments related to this area, e.g. plagiarism.

Another significant concern is the results showed a big trade-off between the recall and precision. From the precision view, the program managed to achieve very good results but not from the recall view, where only a part of all expected clones were found during the detection. For analysis purposes, we identified a few points that may affect the overall results. The points are:

(a) The computational time taken may be affected by the pre-processing time taken to convert the original code into the XML form.

(b) It may also be affected by processing taken by sub graph miner. The miner most probably will generate all subtrees from the code subtrees which sometimes reached thousands of subtree even for only a small number of source code being tested before it identifies which subtrees are the frequent ones.

(c) We need a higher specification of a machine to perform the test as the current machine is only capable to test less than 100 source files per time. We have initially tested more than 100 times, but the computational time had gone to infinite.

(d) The program is only capable to detect identical clones and near identical clones since our program is using the string-based detection. As we know the strength of string-based detection is it is able to detect more languages i.e. it is language independent, but the weakness is in terms of the robustness where it is only able to detect identical and near identical clones.

(e) The clones found were always the same size as the particular testing since we already predefined the fragment size of frequent subtree in the frequent subgraph miner. So, there might be similarities between the clones and the differences may only be a node in a subtree. Fig. 24 shows the illustration of the scenario. Assume that the shaded part of the tree is taken as a frequent subtree by the subgraph miner and detected as a clone in a source code. It shows there are nodes in both frequent subtrees that intersect and the subtrees actually can be taken as a single clone but our program was unable to do that.

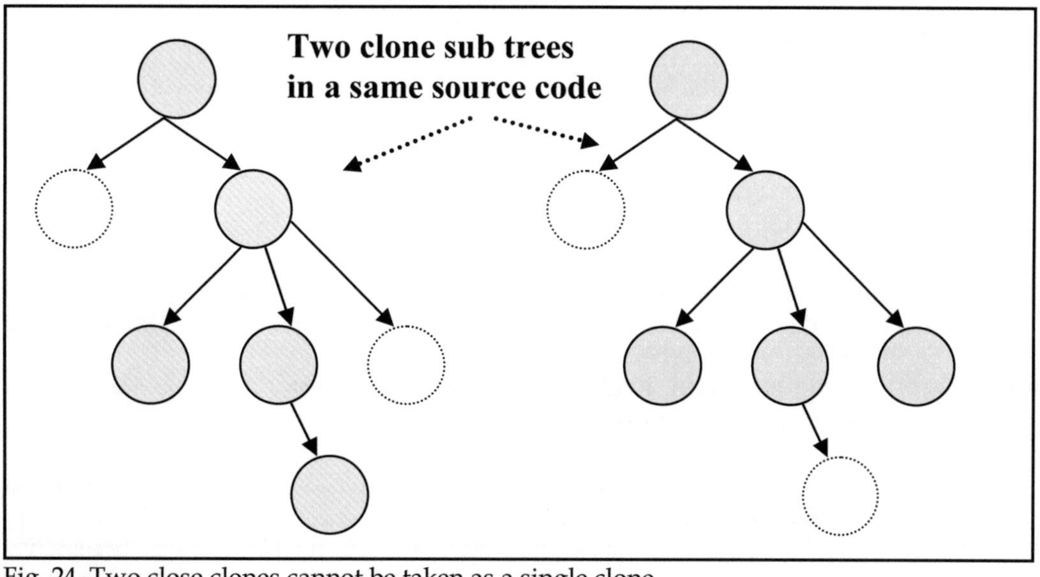

Fig. 24. Two close clones cannot be taken as a single clone

7. Conclusion

As the number of web pages extensively increases across the time, the number of possible clones among source codes may also increase. The programmer is always trying to find the easiest way to write the coding and that might result to cloning and would risk the maintenance of the system. As we know, the overall aim of this project is to be familiar with the ability of ontology mapping technique to solve the clone detection between files of different systems. There are already many researches that had done the code clone detection but none of them had used the ontology mapping as part of the detection.

From the findings that we get from the previous chapter, we know that there is a possibility of using a mapping technique to detect clones. Somehow the results shown are not so good and of course the next process should be to refine the proposed methodology in order to get a better result. Below are the strengths of our system:

(a) Capable in finding structural similarity among XML tree, i.e. structural clone,

(b) Capable in finding structural similarity among XML tree, i.e. structural clone.

In order for us to get a good result of clone detection, we need to do some refinements to the methodology. Below are a few things that can be considered as the project moves on in aiming for a better recall and precision such as:

(a) Refine the process of generating vocabulary

(b) Pre-processing phase where original codes were transformed into standard codes need to be refined to make sure all scripting and dynamic web pages lines of code e.g. PHP and ASP code clones can be detected as well

(c) In the process of mapping the tags using vocabulary, enhance the searching towards the end of every single page

(d) Manipulate the subgraph miner so that number subtree generated would be lenient without having any redundancy of subtrees, etc.

8. Acknowledgements

This work was supported by the Ministry of Science & Technology and Innovation (MOSTI), Malaysia, and the Research Management Center, Universiti Teknologi Malaysia (UTM), under Vot 79266.

9. References

Al-Ekram, R.; Kapser, C. & Godfrey, M. (2005). Cloning by Accident: An Empirical Study of Source Code Cloning Across Software Systems, *International Symposium on Empirical Software Engineering*

Antoniou, G. & Van Harmelen, F. (2003). *Web Ontology Language: OWL, In Handbook on Ontologies in Information Systems*, 67–92

Bailey, J. & Burd, E. (2002). Evaluating Clone Detection Tools for Use during Preventative Maintenance, *Proceeding Second IEEE International Workshop Source Code Analysis and Manipulation (SCAM '02)*, IEEE, 36-43

Bailey, J. & Burd, E. (2002). Evaluating Clone Detection Tools for Use during Preventative Maintenance, *Proceeding Second IEEE International Workshop Source Code Analysis and Manipulation (SCAM '02)*, IEEE, 36-43

Baker, B. S. (1995). On finding duplication and near- duplication in large software system, *In Proc. 2nd Working Conference on Reverse Engineering*, 1995, Toronto, Ont., Canada, IEEE, 86-95

Baxter, I.; Yahin, A.; Moura, L. & Anna, M. S. (1998). Clone detection using abstract syntax trees. In *Proc. Intl. Conference on Software Maintenance*. Bethesda, MD, USA, IEEE, 368-377

Baxter, I.D. & Churchett, D. (2002). Using Clone Detection to Manage a Product Line, *In ICSR7 Workshop*

Bellon, S.; Rainer, K. & Giuliano, A. (2007). Comparison and Evaluation of Clone Detection Tools, *In Transactions on Software Engineering*, 33(9), 577-591

Benassi, R.; Bergamaschi, S.; Fergnani, A. & Misell, D. (2004). Extending a Lexicon Ontology for Intelligent Information Integration, *European Conference on Artificial Intelligence (ECAI2004)*, Valencia, Spain, 278-282

Borgelt, B. & Berthold, M. R. (2002). Mining Molecular Fragments: Finding Relevant Substructures of Molecules, *IEEE International Conference on Data Mining (ICDM 2002, Maebashi, Japan)*, 51-58 IEEE Press, Piscataway, NJ, USA

Brank, J.; Grobelnik, M. & Mladenić, D. (2005). A survey of ontology evaluation techniques, *In SIKDD 2005 at Multiconference IS 2005*

Breitman, K. K.; Casanova, M. A. & Truszkowsk, W. (2006). *Semantic Web: concepts, technologies and applications*, Springer

Calasanz, R.T.; Iso, J.N.; Bejar, R.; Medrano, P.M. & Soria, F.Z. (2006). Semantic interoperability based on Dublin Core hierarchical one-to-one mappings, *International Journal of Metadata, Semantics and Ontologies*, 1(3), 183-188

Calefato, F.; Lanubile, F.; Mallardo, T. (2004). Function Clone Detection in Web Applications: A Semiautomated Approach, *Journal Web Engineering*, 3(1), 3-21

De Lucia, A.; Scanniello, G. & Tortora, G. (2004). Identifying Clones in Dynamic Web Sites Using Similarity Thresholds, *Proc. Intl. Conf. on Enterprise Information Systems (ICEIS'04)*, 391-396

Di Lucca, G. A.; Di Penta, M.; Fasilio, A. R. & Granato, P. (2001). Clone analysis in the web era: An approach to identify cloned web pages, *Seventh IEEE Workshop on Empirical Studies of Software Maintenance*, 107–113

Di Lucca, G. A.; Di Penta, M. & Fasolino, A. R. (2002). An Approach to Identify Duplicated Web Pages, *COMPSAC*, 481-486

Dou, D. & McDermott, D (2005). Ontology Translation on the Semantic Web, *Journal on Data Semantics (JoDS) II*, 35-57

Ducasse, S.; Rieger, M. & Demeyer, S. (1999). A Language Independent Approach for Detecting Duplicated Code, *Proceeding International Conference Software Maintenance (ICSM '99)*

Ehrig, M. (2006). *Ontology Alignment: Bridging the Semantic Gap*, New York, Springer

Ehrig, M. & Sure, Y. (2000). Ontology Mapping - An Integrated Approach, Lecture Notes in Computer Science, No. 3053. 76-91

Estival, D.; Nowak, C. & Zschorn, A. (2004). Towards Ontology-Based Natural Language Processing, *DF/RDFS and OWL in Language Technology: 4th Workshop on NLP and XML (NLPXML-2004), ACL 2004*, Barcelona, Spain

Fox, M. S.; Barbuceanu, M.; Gruninger, M. & Lin, J. (1998). An Organization Ontology for Enterprise Modeling, *In Simulating Organizations: Computational Models of*

Institutions and Groups, M. Prietula, K. Carley & L. Gasser (Eds), Menlo Park CA, AAAI/MIT Press, 131-152

Gašević, D. & Hatala, M. (2006). Ontology mappings to improve learning resource search, *British Journal of Educational Technology*, 37(3), 375-389

Gruber, T. R. (1993). A translation approach to portable ontologies, *Knowledge Acquisition*. 5(2), 199-220

Huan, J.; Wang, W. & Prins, J. (2003). Efficient Mining of Frequent Subgraph in the Presence of Isomorphism, in *Proceedings of the 3rd IEEE International Conference on Data Mining (ICDM)*, pp. 549-552

Ichise, R. (2008). Machine Learning Approach for Ontology Mapping Using Multiple Concept Similarity Measures, *Seventh IEEE/ACIS International Conference on Computer and Information Science (icis 2008)*, IEEE, 340-346

Visser, P. R. S. & Tamma, V. A. M. (1999). An experience with ontology-based agent clustering, *Proceedings of IJCAI-99 Workshop on Ontologies and Problem-Solving Methods (KRR5)*, Stockolm, Sweden, Morgan Kaufmann, 1-12

Jiang, L.; Misherghi, G.; Su, Z.; Glondu, S. (2007). DECKARD: Scalable and Accurate Tree-based Detection of Code Clones, *In Proc. 29th IEEE International Conference on Software Engineering (ICSE 2007)*, IEEE, 96-105

Jin, T.; Fu, Y.; Ling, X.; Liu, Q. & Cui, Z. (2007). A Method of Ontology Mapping Based on Sub tree Kernel, *IITA*, 70-73

Kamiya, T.; Kusumoto, S. & Inoue,K. (2002). CCFinder: a multilinguistic token-based code clone detection system for large scale source code, *IEEE Transactions on Software Engineering*, 28(7), 654-670

Kapser, C. & Godfrey, M. W. (2006). Clones considered harmful, *In Working Conference on Reverse Engineering*

Komondoor, R. & Horwitz, S. (2001). Using slicing to identify duplication in source code, In *Proceedings of the 8th International Symposium on Static Analysis*, July 16-18, 2001, Paris, France, In SAS. 40–56

Kontogiannis, K.; De Mori, R.; Merlo, E.; Galler, M. & Bernstein, M. (1996). Pattern matching for clone and concept detection, *Automated Soft. Eng.*, 3(1/2), 77–108

Krinke, J. (2001). Identifying Similar Code with Program Dependence Graphs, *Proceedings of the Eight Working Conference on Reverse Engineering*, October 2001, Stuttgart, Germany, IEEE, 301-309

Lanubile, F. & Mallardo, T. (2003). Finding Function Clones in Web Applications, *Proceeding Conference Software Maintenance and Reengineering*, 379- 386

Li, Z.; Lu, S.; Myagmar, S. & Zhou, Y. (2006). CP-Miner: finding copy-paste and related bugs in large-scale software code, IEEE Computer Society Transactions on Software Engineering, 32(3), 176–192

Maedche, A. & Staab, S. (2002). Measuring Similarity between Ontologies, Lecture Notes in Computer Science, 251

Mayrand, J. & Leblanc, C. (1996). Experiment on the Automatic Detection of Function Clones in a Software System Using Metrics, In *Proc. Conference on Software Maintenance*

McGuinness, D. L. (1999). Ontologies for Electronic Commerce, *Proceedings of the AAAI '99 Artificial Intelligence for Electronic Commerce Workshop*, Orlando, Florida

Nijssen, S. & Kok, J. N. (2004). A Quickstart in Frequent Structure Mining can make a Difference, *LIACS Technical Report*

Noy, N. F. (2004). Semantic Integration: A Survey Of Ontology-Based Approaches, *In ACM SIGMOD Record, Special Section on Semantic Integration*, 33(4), 65-70

Qian, P. & Zhang, S. (2006a). Ontology Mapping Approach Based on Concept Partial Relation, *In Proceedings of WCICA*

Qian, P. & Zhang, S. (2006b). Ontology Mapping Meta-model Based on Set and Relation Theory, *IMSCCS* (1), 503-509

Koschke, R. (2006). Survey of Research on Software Clones, *Dagstuhl Seminar Proceedings*

Rajapakse, D. C. & Jarzabek, S. (2005). An Investigation of Cloning in Web Applications, *5th Intl Conference on Web Engineering (ICWE'05)*, Washington, DC, IEEE, 252-262

Roy, C. K. & Cordy, J. R. (2007). A Survey on Software Clone Detection Research, *Technical Report 2007-541, School of Computing, Queen's University, Canada*

Sabou, M.; D'Aquin, M. & Motta, E. (2006). Using the semantic web as background knowledge for ontology mapping, *ISWC 2006 Workshop on Ontology Mapping*

Schleimer, S.; Wilkerson, D. S. & Aiken, A. (2003). Winnowing: Local Algorithms for Document Fingerprinting, *Proceeding SIGMOD International Conference Management of Data*, 76-85

Stevens, R. D.; Goble, C. A. & Bechhofer, S. (2000). Ontology-based knowledge representation for bioinformatics, *Brief Bioinform* 1(4), 398-416

Stoilos, G.; Stamou, G. & Kollias, S. (2005). A String Metric for Ontology Alignment, in *Proceedings of the ninth IEEE International Symposium on Wearable Computers*, Galway, 624- 237

Stumme, G. & Maedche, A. (2001). FCA-Merge: BottomUp Merging of Ontologies, *IlCAl*, 225-234

Stutt, A. (1997). Knowledge Engineering Ontologies, Constructivist Epistemology, Computer Rhetoric: A Trivium for the Knowledge Age, *Proceedings of Ed-Media '97*, Calgary, Canada

The World Wide Web Consortium Official Site at www.w3c.org

Todorov, K. (2008). Combining Structural and Instance-based Ontology Similarities for Mapping Web Directories, *The Third International Conference on Internet and Web Applications and Services*

Ueda, Y.; Kamiya, T.; Kusumoto, S. & Inoue, K. (2002). Gemini: Maintenance support environment based on code clone analysis, *In Proceedings of the 8th IEEE Symposium on Software Metrics (METRICS'02)*, Ottawa, Canada, 67-76

Ueda, Y.; Kamiya, T.; Kusumoto, S. & Inoue, K. (2002). On detection of gapped code clones using gap locations, *In Proceedings 9th Asia-Pacific Software Engineering Conference (APSEC'02), Gold Coast, Queensland, Australia, 327-336*

Vallet D.; M. Fernández & P. Castells (2005). An Ontology-Based Information Retrieval Model, *Proc. Second European Semantic Web Conf. (ESWC '05)*

Visser, P. R. S.; Jones, D. M.; Beer, M. D.; Bench-Capon, T. J. M., Diaz, B. M. & Shave, M. J. R. (1999). Resolving Ontological Heterogeneity in the KRAFT Project, *In Proceedings of Database and Expert Systems Applications 99*, Lecture Notes in Computer Science 1677, Berlin, Springer, 688-697

Winkler, W. E. (1999). The State of Record Linkage and Current Research Problems, *Statistical Society of Canada, Proceedings of the Section on Survey Methods*, 73-79

Yan, X. & Han, J. (2002). gSpan: Graph-Based Substructure Pattern Mining, *Proc. 2002 of Int. Conf. on Data Mining (ICDM'02)*, Expanded Version, UIUC Technical Report, UIUCDCS-R-2002-2296

Zhang, Z.; Xu, D. & Zhang, T. (2008). Ontology Mapping Based on Conditional Information Quantity, *IEEE International Conference on Networking, Sensing and Control, 2008, ICNSC 200*, Sonya, IEEE, 587-591